CULTURALLY RESPONSIVE
COGNITIVE BEHAVIOR THERAPY

CULTURALLY RESPONSIVE COGNITIVE BEHAVIOR THERAPY

Practice and Supervision

Edited by Gayle Y. Iwamasa and Pamela A. Hays

SECOND EDITION

AMERICAN PSYCHOLOGICAL ASSOCIATION
Washington, DC

The opinions and statements published are the responsibility of the authors, and such opinions and statements do not necessarily represent the policies of the American Psychological Association.

Published by
American Psychological Association
750 First Street, NE
Washington, DC 20002
www.apa.org

APA Order Department
P.O. Box 92984
Washington, DC 20090-2984
Phone: (800) 374-2721; Direct: (202) 336-5510
Fax: (202) 336-5502; TDD/TTY: (202) 336-6123
Online: http://www.apa.org/pubs/books
E-mail: order@apa.org

In the U.K., Europe, Africa, and the Middle East, copies may be ordered from
Eurospan Group
c/o Turpin Distribution
Pegasus Drive
Stratton Business Park
Biggleswade, Bedfordshire
SG18 8TQ United Kingdom
Phone: +44 (0) 1767 604972
Fax: +44 (0) 1767 601640
Online: https://www.eurospanbookstore.com/apa
E-mail: eurospan@turpin-distribution.com

Typeset in Goudy by Circle Graphics, Inc., Columbia, MD

Printer: Thomson-Shore, Dexter, MI
Cover Designer: Beth Schlenoff, Bethesda, MD

Library of Congress Cataloging-in-Publication Data
Names: Iwamasa, Gayle, editor. | Hays, Pamela A., editor.
Title: Culturally responsive cognitive behavior therapy : practice and
  supervision / edited by Gayle Y. Iwamasa and Pamela A. Hays.
Description: Second edition. | Washington, DC : American Psychological
  Association, [2019] | Includes bibliographical references and index.
Identifiers: LCCN 2018024228 (print) | LCCN 2018024413 (ebook) |
  ISBN 9781433830242 (eBook) | ISBN 1433830248 (eBook) | ISBN 9781433830167
  (pbk.) | ISBN 1433830167 (paperback)
Subjects: LCSH: Cognitive therapy. | Behavior therapy.
Classification: LCC RC489.C63 (ebook) | LCC RC489.C63 C85 2019 (print) |
  DDC 616.89/1425--dc23
LC record available at https://lccn.loc.gov/2018024228

British Library Cataloguing-in-Publication Data
A CIP record is available from the British Library.

Printed in the United States of America

http://dx.doi.org/10.1037/0000119-000

10 9 8 7 6 5 4 3 2 1

CONTENTS

CONTRIBUTORS

Nuha Abudabbeh, PhD, Department of Psychology, The George Washington University, Washington, DC, and Court Services and Offender Supervision Agency for the District of Columbia

Kimberly F. Balsam, PhD, Palo Alto University, Palo Alto, CA

Rebecca P. Cameron, PhD, Department of Psychology, California State University, Sacramento

Daniel Cukor, PhD, Department of Psychiatry and Behavioral Sciences, SUNY Downstate Medical Center, Brooklyn, NY

Steven Friedman, PhD, ABPP, Department of Psychiatry and Behavioral Sciences, SUNY Downstate Medical Center, Brooklyn, NY

John Gonzalez, PhD, Psychology Department, Bemidji State University, Bemidji, MN

Pamela A. Hays, PhD, Independent Practice, Soldotna, AK

H'Sien Hayward, PhD, Department of Psychiatry & Behavioral Sciences, Stanford University School of Medicine, Stanford, CA

Devon Hinton, MD, Psychiatry, Massachusetts General Hospital, Chelsea, and Harvard Medical School, Boston, MA

Curtis Hsia, PhD, Orange County Anxiety Center, Mission Viejo, CA

Gayle Y. Iwamasa, PhD, Department of Veterans Affairs, VHA Central Office, Lafayette, IN

Kyle P. Jones, MS, Palo Alto University, Palo Alto, CA

Shalonda Kelly, PhD, Graduate School of Applied and Professional Psychology, Rutgers University, Piscataway, NJ

Lisa M. Kinoshita, PhD, Psychology Service, VA Palo Alto Health Care System, Palo Alto, CA

Angela W. Lau, PhD, Mental Health Department, Tibor Rubin Medical Center, VA Long Beach Healthcare System, Long Beach, CA

Christopher R. Martell, PhD, Department of Psychological and Brain Sciences, University of Massachusetts Amherst

Justin Douglas McDonald, PhD, Psychology Department, University of North Dakota, Grand Forks

Linda R. Mona, PhD, Spinal Cord Injury/Disorder, VA Long Beach Healthcare System, Long Beach, CA

Kurt C. Organista, PhD, School of Social Welfare, University of California, Berkeley

Christine A. Padesky, PhD, Center for Cognitive Therapy, Huntington Beach, CA

Cheryl M. Paradis, PsyD, Department of Psychology, Marymount Manhattan College, New York, NY, and Department of Psychiatry and Behavioral Sciences, SUNY Downstate Medical Center, Brooklyn, NY

Shilpa P. Regan, PhD, Psychology Department, University of North Carolina at Pembroke

Steven A. Safren, PhD, Department of Psychology, University of Miami, Coral Gables, FL

Emily Sargent, MA, Department of Psychology, University of North Dakota, Grand Forks

Sheetal Shah, PhD, Student Health and Counseling Services, University of California, Davis

Kristen H. Sorocco, PhD, Department of Geriatric Medicine, University of Oklahoma Health Sciences Center, Oklahoma City, and Independent Practice, Oklahoma City Veterans Affairs Health Care System

Nita Tewari, PhD, Independent Scholar and Consultant, Newport Beach, CA

FOREWORD

CHRISTINE A. PADESKY

Over the past 40 years, I have had the privilege of teaching cognitive behavior therapy (CBT) in more than 20 countries on five different continents. There is a remarkably strong interest in CBT, and its ideas have been disseminated to nearly every country on the planet, from Aboriginal leaders in Australia to community clinics in Zimbabwe. CBT ideas resonate with people from many different cultures. Further, most of the fundamental ideas of CBT theory appear to apply cross-culturally: Thoughts, behaviors, emotions, physical reactions, and environments are interconnected whether one grows up in Africa, Asia, or the Americas. Negative thinking characterizes depression on every continent. Approach rather than avoidance reduces anxiety in every land. CBT is a therapy that can be practiced around the world.

At the same time, none of us should assume that CBT will be practiced around the world in ways that we always recognize. Thirty years ago Korean counselors brought me wooden masks they said they gave to their clients to hold in front of their faces when they needed to talk about uncomfortable emotions. The male mask had a moveable mouth, and the female mask's mouth did not move. The first time a Japanese psychiatrist came to one of our training courses in California, I asked him if he understood our teaching, given that English was not his first language. He said that he did. I asked whether he thought he would be able to use CBT in Japan. He thought awhile and then answered, "Yes. But first I will spend about 6 months thinking about how to do this therapy in a Japanese way." That is the essence of cross-cultural CBT. Most of the theory and practices of CBT have universal utility but only if practiced in ways that are good cultural fits for our clients.

A challenge for therapists around the world is that there is no longer one culture per location, so learning one cultural way to practice therapy is not enough. For example, people from hundreds of different cultures live in North America, greatly outnumbering the diverse indigenous peoples who once populated this continent. Further, there are layers of culture within each identifiable group. Males and females born into the same family often grow up in distinct cultures. There are wide generational culture gaps, religious and spiritual cultures, and even political ones. A person can belong to many cultures simultaneously. It would not be unusual for a client to identify as Irish, cisgender, lesbian, rural, Southern, and a digital native. Each of these identities might have some impact on understanding her therapy issues and choosing methods used during her course of CBT.

How can a therapist be prepared to be knowledgeable about all the cultures encountered during the day? No one can. What we can do is be aware that each person who sits with us has many different cultural experiences that may be important to understand, and some of these cultures will be different from our own. Best clinical practices include regularly and proactively inquiring about client cultures, even when clients appear as if they come from the same culture we do. At the same time, we can recognize that even if a client comes from quite different cultures than our own, we share many human experiences in common. Mutual understanding is possible if we are open, curious, and nonjudgmental and welcome feedback on what we are getting right and wrong.

Culturally Responsive Cognitive Behavior Therapy, Second Edition: Practice and Supervision edited by Gayle Y. Iwamasa and Pamela A. Hays offers an invaluable treasure trove of cultural insight. No chapter will help you perfectly understand any of your clients. But, taken as a whole, these chapters inform a richer appreciation of many cultures and some of the ways these can affect people's experiences. Read this book to learn creative ways others have learned to make CBT more culturally responsive. Better yet, take inspiration from this book and collaborate with your clients to develop cultural adaptations when they are needed so your clients get the most benefit possible from CBT. Learning more about other cultures and best practices for working with multicultural clientele is a sure path to improving your overall therapy practice. Like world travel, it will enrich your appreciation of the human experience as well. Enjoy traveling these pages!

ACKNOWLEDGMENTS

We would like to thank our editor Tyler Aune and the excellent staff at the American Psychological Association, and especially Susan Reynolds for her encouragement of this second edition. Gayle would like to thank Russell, William, Robert, and GraceAnn Koch for their patience, understanding, encouragement, and support. Pam would like to thank Marjorie and Hugh Hays and Bob McCard for their support and helpful feedback. We are both grateful to our professional mentors, colleagues, clients, and students for all they have taught and shared with us.

CULTURALLY RESPONSIVE
COGNITIVE BEHAVIOR THERAPY

INTRODUCTION

PAMELA A. HAYS

Shelby[1] is a 28-year-old, recently divorced woman who was referred for counseling by her physician who could find no medical reason for her frequent digestion problems and stomachaches. At your first meeting, Shelby tells you she is a nursing student and hospital health aide, and she lives with her parents, who babysit her 3-year-old daughter while she is at work or in school. She reports that she has always been a good student and likes her job, but the workload now feels overwhelming, and her supervisor is frequently upset with her for being late and for occasional mistakes she makes when tired. In addition, she says a couple of her coworkers have "turned against" her and report any little mistakes she makes to the supervisor, which makes matters worse. She has only 1 year left to obtain her nursing degree, but she is starting to wonder whether she can do it all. She says her parents criticize her parenting skills and were disappointed with her divorcing her husband, telling

---

[1]Case material in this chapter and throughout the book has been disguised to protect client confidentiality.

http://dx.doi.org/10.1037/0000119-001
Culturally Responsive Cognitive Behavior Therapy, Second Edition: Practice and Supervision, G. Y. Iwamasa and P. A. Hays (Editors)

her, "Marriage isn't always easy—that's just the way it is." She says that sometimes she feels so low about herself that she does not see the point in trying, although she quickly admits she would never kill herself because she cares about her family too much.

If you already use cognitive behavior therapy (CBT), you are probably thinking about Shelby's situation in terms of the five key components of CBT—namely, cognition, emotion, behavior, physical symptoms or sensations, and environmental influences (Greenberger & Padesky, 2015). You may also be looking for factors that contribute to Shelby's distress, including those that are external to Shelby (i.e., environmental) and internal, in the form of unhelpful beliefs and thoughts. You might consider interventions aimed at helping Shelby take specific actions to decrease the external stressors—for example, talking directly with her coworkers, proactively meeting with her supervisor, or practicing self-care activities. And you might consider cognitive restructuring as a way to help Shelby engage in more helpful self-talk and change beliefs that may contribute to her stress.

But what if I told you that Shelby is short for Shelbiya, and Shelby is Arab American? Would this information raise questions or additional hypotheses you had not previously considered regarding her distress? For example, could her supervisor's and coworkers' attitudes toward her be related to her ethnic identity or, if she is Muslim, to her religious identity? Did her parents immigrate to the United States, and if so, are there language, political, value, or other differences between Shelby and her parents that might contribute to their family conflicts? Given the dominant culture's fear of and hostility toward Arab people today, could Shelby's experience of stress be aggravated by sociopolitical events, as well as microaggressions and other forms of racism directed at her and her family? Could her self-doubts be aggravated by experiences of prejudice and discrimination?

Shelby's ethnicity was omitted initially to make the point that when cultural information is left out, the assumption is often made that the client is of European American heritage. This assumption can occur even when face to face with clients who appear to be White. As a result, important questions and hypotheses may not even be considered. When a therapist does not consider the possibility of minority or cultural identities, it is more likely that the therapist will use language and engage in behaviors that reflect this lack of consideration. Furthermore, this tendency holds true with regard to other minority identities too. For example, a therapist who does not consider the possibility that a client is gay or bisexual is more likely to use noninclusive pronouns when asking about partners and spouses, a therapist who does not consider nonvisible disability may make assumptions about the supportiveness of a client's environment and the challenges the client faces, and a therapist who does not consider the possibility that a client is biracial may overlook important influences and experiences relevant to the client's situation.

Unfortunately, the omission of ethnic and other cultural information is the rule rather than the exception in clinical and counseling research, including CBT. This neglect is due in part to the cultural homogeneity of the field. People of color currently comprise over one third of the U.S. population yet constitute only between 11.5% and 14% of health service providers (Hamp, Stamm, Lin, & Christidis, 2016). Psychology faculty who educate these providers are similarly nonrepresentative of the larger society: Only 15% are people of color (Kohout, Pate, & Maton, 2014) and few are people with disabilities, immigrants, transgender, or members of minority religions.

In many cases, therapists of dominant cultural identities may simply not perceive cultural influences because they do not have experience with minority cultures or with any culture that might provide a contrast to their own. However, the dominance of European American perspectives and assumptions in CBT is not due solely to the disproportionate number of European American faculty and providers. It is also related to the reinforcement of dominant cultural values and perspectives by the larger society, of which psychotherapy is a part. Consider, for example, the social and therapeutic emphasis placed on the European American values of assertiveness in social interactions (over subtlety), change (over acceptance, perseverance, and patience), personal independence (over interdependence), and open self-disclosure (over protection of the family's reputation; Kim, 1985; Pedersen, 1987; Wood & Mallinckrodt, 1990).

CBT research has historically focused almost exclusively on European Americans, with little to no attention given to cultural influences related to ethnicity, religion, sexual orientation, disability, or social class. In 1988, a review of the preceding 20 years found only three empirically based outcome studies of cognitive behavioral treatments of anxiety in people of racial or ethnic minority groups (two of which had samples of only two people; Casas, 1988). In 1996, a survey of three leading behavioral journals found that only 1.31% focused on ethnic minority groups in the United States (Iwamasa & Smith, 1996). And over the past 15 years, research on race, ethnicity, and diversity has made up less than 4% of the articles published in the *Journal of Consulting and Clinical Psychology*, *Developmental Psychology*, and the *Journal of Personality and Social Psychology* (Hall, Yip, & Zárate, 2016).

Upon publication of the first edition of *Culturally Responsive Cognitive–Behavioral Therapy* in 2006, we had hoped that research in this area would grow as rapidly as it has in the relatively separate fields of CBT and multicultural practice, but this has not been the case. The field of multicultural therapy or MCT[2] has expanded to include a greater number of minority cultures, aided in part by the gradually increasing numbers of psychologists of minority identities. There is now an enormous number of books on MCT, and MCT researchers are calling attention to the exclusion of minority groups from most evidence-based practice research. However, the bulk of the multicultural literature does not address the integration of multicultural perspectives into major theories in psychotherapy (i.e., behavior therapy, CBT, psychodynamic, interpersonal, dialectical behavior therapy, acceptance and commitment therapy, humanistic, existential, client-centered therapy).

At the same time, the field of CBT has also grown, facilitating and facilitated by at least two significant developments: the societal and clinical interest in mindfulness-based approaches (Davidson & Kaszniak, 2015) and the profession's emphasis on evidence-based practice research (more on this later). However, here again, the majority of these CBT studies do not integrate multicultural perspectives into the theory or practice.

The relatively slow integration of multicultural perspectives into CBT is surprising for several reasons. First, CBT and MCT share a number of basic premises. Both emphasize the need to tailor therapeutic interventions to the unique situation of the individual. Both emphasize the empowerment of clients—MCT through its affirmation of clients' cultural identities and CBT through recognition of each client's expertise regarding their own needs and situation. Both MCT and CBT also emphasize the therapeutic aspects of clients' strengths and supports. And the CBT field has a great deal to gain from multicultural considerations. Understanding how CBT works and does not work with minority populations offers a multitude of opportunities for CBT researchers to challenge, expand, and refine their theories. Such work could lead to creative approaches that help a much wider range of people.

But recognizing such possibilities also requires a consideration of the potential limitations of CBT with minority cultures. CBT is as value-laden as any other psychotherapy. Its emphasis on cognition, logic, verbal skills, and rational thinking strongly favors dominant cultural perspectives, including definitions of rationality (Kantrowitz & Ballou, 1992). This cognitive emphasis can easily lead to an undervaluing of the importance of spirituality. The focus on changing oneself may contribute to the neglect of important cultural influences, and if not balanced by a behavioral perspective that recognizes the power of environmental influences, may contribute to blaming the client for problems that are primarily environmentally based (e.g., racism,

---

[2]I use the term *multicultural therapy* (MCT) as shorthand for the field of clinical and counseling psychology that focuses on diversity. However, I do not consider MCT a therapy in the sense that CBT is a therapy; rather, I see it as an orientation to all therapeutic approaches.

heterocentrism, ableism). However, such limitations are not insurmountable, and figuring out ways to address them is part of the process of making CBT more responsive to people of diverse cultural identities.

EVIDENCE-BASED PRACTICE, COGNITIVE BEHAVIOR THERAPY, AND MULTICULTURAL THERAPY

In 2006, the American Psychological Association (APA) published a formal definition of evidence-based practice in psychology. Before this, the assumption was frequently made that evidence-based practice was synonymous with randomized, controlled, empirically supported treatments. This assumption excluded the case study, qualitative, and expert opinion research that makes up most of the multicultural literature. The APA definition corrected this assumption by clarifying that evidence-based practice consists of "the integration of the best available research with clinical expertise in the context of patient characteristics, culture, and preferences" (APA Presidential Task Force on Evidence-Based Practice, 2006, p. 273). This definition acknowledges that when there are relevant randomized, controlled, empirically supported treatments, the clinician certainly considers these approaches. However, this consideration must take into account the particular patient's characteristics, preferences, and culture. The MCT research is a wellspring of information regarding the latter.

Although the integration of CBT and MCT has not occurred as rapidly as we had hoped, there has been a slow but steady increase in the number of culturally adapted CBT studies, along with a broadening of the definition of diversity. For example, using the term *ethnic* to search from 2006 to 2016 in one of the primary CBT journals published by the Association of Behavioral and Cognitive Therapy, *Cognitive & Behavioral Practice*, I found 90 studies, several of which were grouped within special sections of the journal. These 90 studies addressed ethnic and racial influences and minority groups (e.g., Fuchs et al., 2016; and a special section on Latinx families, 2010, Volume 17, Issue 2) but also a number of related cultural influences and minority groups. Specifically, they included articles regarding multiethnic and international populations (Friedman, Braunstein, & Halpern, 2006; Hinton & Jalal, 2014), sexual minorities (special section, 2010, Volume 17, Issue 1), members of religious groups (special section, 2010, Volume 17, Issue 4), older adults (2012, Volume 19, Issue 1), gay youth (Lucassen, Merry, Hatcher, & Frampton, 2015), rural populations (Shealy, Davidson, Jones, Lopez, & de Arellano, 2015), refugees (Hinton, Pich, Hofmann, & Otto, 2013; and a special section, 2006, Volume 13, Issue 4), Deaf and hearing persons with language and learning challenges

(Glickman, 2009), and attention to the influence of socioeconomic status and gender (Neblett, Bernard, & Hudson Banks, 2016).

Moreover, there are now at least five books in addition to this one that focus on diversity and evidence-based interventions (which are often CBT or contain cognitive behavioral components): *Evidence-Based Psychological Practice With Ethnic Minorities* (Zane, Bernal, & Leong, 2016), *Cultural Adaptations: Tools for Evidence-Based Practice With Diverse Populations* (Bernal & Domenech Rodriguez, 2012), *Cognitive Behaviour Therapy in Non-Western Cultures* (Naeem & Kingdon, 2011), *Psychological Assessments and Interventions With Children of Color* (Graves & Blake, 2016), and *Treating Depression, Anxiety, and Stress in Ethnic and Racial Groups: Cognitive Behavioral Approaches* (Chang, Downey, Hirsch, & Yu, 2018). Of these, *Culturally Responsive Cognitive Behavior Therapy* is still the only one that uses a broad definition of culture, with attention to older adults, people with disabilities, religious and sexual minorities, and ethnic/racial minority cultures.

CULTURAL ADAPTATIONS OF COGNITIVE BEHAVIOR THERAPY

The results of three recent meta-analyses suggest that cultural adaptations to CBT are helpful, and the more specific the adaptation to the culture, the more effective therapy is with regard to psychotic, mood, and behavioral disorders (Benish, Quintana, & Wampold, 2011; Huey, Tilley, Jones, & Smith, 2014; Smith, Domenech Rodríguez, & Bernal, 2011). In a systematic review of 20 years of research, Chu and Leino (2017) looked at the specific types of changes being made in "evidence-based intervention" adaptation studies. Although the authors did not focus specifically on CBT, their findings are relevant because many adaptation studies integrate cognitive behavioral concepts and practices. The authors found that only about 11% of the studies involved changes to the actual core components of the therapy, although substantial changes were made in the form of additions, delivery, and contextualization. One of the exciting aspects of cultural adaptation research is the creativity of these changes. Here are just a few examples of studies that focus specifically on adapting CBT to diverse cultural groups:

- Fuchs et al. (2016) interviewed an ethnically diverse group of participants about their experience of acceptance-based behavioral therapy and found that most individuals reported positive experiences and many gave detailed descriptions that could be helpful with others. For example, one African American woman from a working-class background did not find a mindfulness exercise with imagery to be helpful, noting,

> So, when my sister is leaving her kids alone in a house for some unknown reason, and I'm trying to convince her . . . don't do that, it's irresponsible. I'm supposed to believe that my nieces are like floating on a leaf as the police get called? (Fuchs et al., 2016, p. 478)

However, the same woman found the mindfulness exercise of chewing a raisin slowly with nonjudgmental awareness to be helpful in slowing her tendency to make assumptions about what other people were thinking about her.

- *Taoist cognitive therapy* is a manualized adaptation of an indigenous Chinese psychotherapy that conceptualizes anxiety and worry as the result of rigid attachments to beliefs, goals, and desires that do not reflect the natural order of the universe. Emphasis is placed on the eight Taoist principles of collective benefit, noncompetition, moderation, acceptance, humility, flexibility, *wu wei*, and harmony with the laws of nature (p. 205). *Wu wei* is described as more than simply accepting the way things are but, rather, as consisting of "an attentive awareness and spontaneous responding to situations, opportunities, and changing events as they present themselves" (Chang et al., 2016, p. 214).
- Recognizing the social orientation of many Latinx people, La Roche, D'Angelo, Gualdron, and Leavell (2006) found that a visual imagery exercise worked better when therapists changed the instruction from "Imagine yourself alone in a beautiful place" to "Imagine sharing a moment with a person who makes you feel at peace" (p. 558).
- In their work with Maori New Zealanders, a group of psychologists, in cooperation with a Maori advisory group, used the concept of the *whare* (house) to explain how thoughts contribute to emotions and behaviors. The foundation of the house represents early childhood experiences; the first floor, core beliefs; the second floor, intermediate assumptions and rules for living; and the roof, coping strategies, which may or may not be protective. The psychologists also integrated prayer and Maori sayings that could be used as helpful self-talk (Bennett, Flett, & Babbage, 2014).
- Beau Washington, a psychologist and member of the Eastern band of Cherokee Indians, used the trickster coyote as a metaphor for how cognitive distortions can trick people and mislead

them. Noting that one coyote thought "isn't much of a problem," but "a pack of coyotes will take you down," he explained
cognitive restructuring as

> When we dwell on things, the coyotes start to gather, creating bigger
> and bigger problems. . . . Knowing the names of the coyotes brings
> them out of the dark into the light. Recognizing them is our best
> chance of ending the darkness and pain they bring. (Washington,
> 2012, para. 8)

- In their work teaching behavioral interventions to Mexican
  American parents, psychologists noted that given the high
  value placed on family relationships, when using rewards to
  reinforce children's good behavior, opportunities for family
  rewards were just as important as individual rewards (Barker,
  Cook, & Borrego, 2010).
- Also with regard to the use of reinforcement, therapists working
  with transgender clients created the idea of a "Trans-Affirmative
  Hope Box" filled with inspiring items the client chooses, such as
  photos of caring people, symbols of joy and safety such as a genderqueer rights button, a lesbian, gay, bisexual, transgender, and
  queer logo, favorite songs, and poems (Craig, McInroy, Alaggia,
  & McCready, 2014). A smartphone app has been developed that
  allows the client and therapist to cocreate a Virtual Hope Box
  (see http://www.t2health.dcoe.mil/apps/virtual-hope-box).
- Recognizing the challenges in using exposure therapy with
  ethnic groups that have experienced high levels of trauma,
  Hinton and Jalal (2014) used culturally specific metaphors with
  Iraqi clients to create positive expectancy. For example, they
  used the metaphor of the fear many women have of making
  bread on an open fire because over time and with repeated
  exposure to the task, the fear diminishes. In another example,
  they described learning the cognitive triangle as "a spoonful of
  treatment" because taking medications for ills was a common
  local expectation (Hinton & Jalal, 2014, p.141).
- With individuals who were less verbally oriented, Malchiodi
  and Rozum (2012) integrated CBT with art therapy. Examples
  of this integration included asking clients to "create an image"
  of their sadness, anxiety, depression, or anger. The words *art*
  and *draw* were avoided because many people are intimidated
  by both. Clients were then asked to create an image that would
  counter the painful one. In one case, a female client created a
  hurt-filled picture of her body, which she reported hating. Then

in response to the therapist's request to create a healing image, the client drew her husband's loving arms wrapped around her body. Art was also used as a stress reduction strategy—for example, as a sort of time out via the project of collecting magazine photos to create a visual journal.

COGNITIVE BEHAVIOR THERAPY: AN OVERVIEW

In the 1950s and early 1960s, the field known as behavior therapy called attention to how environments could be manipulated to elicit, shape, and reinforce desired behaviors. A number of behavioral researchers subsequently became interested in the influence of cognition on behavior, and it was out of this interest that the field of CBT developed.

CBT involves a consideration of five components to any problem: cognitions, emotions, physiological reactions (e.g., physical sensations and symptoms), behavior, and the environment (Greenberger & Padesky, 2015). CBT presumes that cognitions (which include perceptions, beliefs, images, and self-talk) mediate one's emotions, behavior, and physiological reactions in response to the environment (Beck, 2011). Dysfunctional cognitions are believed to contribute to maladjustment, whereas functional cognitions contribute to healthy adjustment (Dobson, 2001).

It is the role of the cognitive behavior therapist to help clients become aware of the relationships between these five areas. Clients learn to recognize how certain negative, unhelpful, or unrealistic thoughts can generate distress in the form of uncomfortable physical sensations, maladaptive behavior, and emotions that feel uncontrollable or out of proportion to the situation. Clients also learn that social and physical aspects of their environment can contribute to their distress. Once the client understands these connections, the therapist then helps the individual to recognize steps they can take to either change the problem or cope more effectively with it. Solutions may involve changing one's behavior or the environment (what I call *action steps*) or internal cognitive changes.

With regard to changing the environment or behavior, in my work with clients, I use an acronym that spells the word CLASS to summarize the types of action steps one can take:

- Change something in one's environment (or create a healthy environment);
- Learn a new skill or behavior;
- Assertiveness, conflict resolution, and other communication skills;

- Social support; and
- Self-care activities (emotional, physical, spiritual; Hays, 2014).

In addition, the internal cognitive changes, called *cognitive restructuring*, involve more than simply thinking positively. Rather, clients learn to recognize common cognitive errors, automatic dysfunctional thoughts, and cognitive tendencies related to the schema (a sort of cognitive template) by which human beings take in and organize their experience. By considering a broader range of possible interpretations of events and beliefs that one may never before have considered, clients learn to see themselves, the world, and the future more fully and realistically (Beck, 2011; Beck & Beck, 2011; Greenberger & Padesky, 2015; Wenzel, Dobson, & Hays, 2016).

Making Cognitive Behavior Therapy More Culturally Responsive

A *culturally responsive* approach to CBT begins long before the start of one's therapeutic work with clients. It begins with therapists' attention to those areas in which they may hold biases. Cognitive scientists recognize that, from birth, we humans are wired to create categories as a way of organizing and making sense of our experiences. We then make generalizations based on subsequent experiences using these categories (Tropp & Mallett, 2011). This process of categorizing and generalizing is normal and can even be helpful when it facilitates our relationships, but when the categories become too rigid and the generalizations too broad, there are problems. Bias can also develop in the absence of experience with specific groups because dominant cultural messages about minority groups (which are usually negative) exert a subtle yet powerful influence, often without the perceiver's awareness.

What is important to recognize (and which keeps us humble) is that we all have biases. The first step is to begin to look for them, while recognizing that some biases exert more power than others, resulting in systems of privilege and oppression. Once we understand how this works, we can then actively work to replace our inaccurate beliefs and assumptions with reality-based information. This type of work is personal, and it cannot be accomplished in one course or even in several cross-cultural encounters. Rather, it is an ongoing process that involves exploring the impact of cultural influences on one's beliefs (i.e., cognitions), behaviors, and identities.

One way to begin this process is with a cultural self-assessment. In the workshops I teach, I start with an exercise that uses the acronym ADDRESSING to call attention to nine key cultural influences and related minority and dominant cultural groups: Age and generational influences, Developmental or other Disability, Religion and spiritual orientation, Ethnic and racial identity, Socioeconomic status, Sexual orientation, Indigenous

TABLE 1
ADDRESSING Cultural Influences

Cultural influences	Dominant group	Nondominant/minority
Age and generational influences	Young or middle-aged adults	Children, older adults
Developmental or other Disability[a]	Nondisabled people	People with cognitive, intellectual, sensory, physical, and/or psychiatric disabilities
Religion and spirituality	Christian and secular	Muslims, Jews, Hindus, Buddhists, and other religions
Ethnic and racial identity	European Americans	Asian, South Asian, Latinx, Pacific Islander, African, Arab, African American, Middle Eastern, and multiracial people
Socioeconomic status	Upper and middle class	People of lower status by occupation, education, income, or inner city/rural habitat
Sexual orientation	Heterosexuals	People who identify as gay, lesbian, or bisexual
Indigenous heritage	European Americans	American Indians, Inuit, Alaska Natives, Métis, Native Hawaiians, New Zealand Maori, Aboriginal Australians
National origin	U.S.-born American citizens	Immigrants, refugees, and international students
Gender	Men	Women and transgender people

Note. Adapted from *Addressing Cultural Complexities in Practice: Assessment, Diagnosis, and Therapy* (3rd ed., p. 8), by P. A. Hays, 2016, Washington, DC: American Psychological Association. Copyright 2016 by the American Psychological Association.
[a]With the increased use of the term *intellectual disability*, the term *developmental disability* is being used less often, particularly within the Disability community; however, it is included in the *Diagnostic and Statistical Manual of Mental Disorders, Fifth Edition* and *International Classification of Diseases, Tenth Edition, Clinical Modification.*

heritage, National origin, and Gender (see Table 1; Hays, 2016). Of course, there are other cultural influences, but I focus primarily on these nine because they are the ones that have been noted by the APA (2017) and the American Counseling Association (Arredondo & Pérez, 2006) as requiring special attention because of their historical neglect.[3]

If you would like to begin this exercise right now, take a blank sheet of paper and write the ADDRESSING acronym vertically on the left side of the paper. Then take a few minutes to fill in the influences on you related to each of these categories. These influences might be related to a dominant cultural identity, a minority identity, or both. For example, regarding Age and

---

[3]See also the *Report of the APA Task Force on the Implementation of the Multicultural Guidelines*, which focuses primarily on implementation of the *Guidelines* with regard to ethnic and racial identity but notes the importance of these additional factors too (http://apa.org/about/policy/multicultural-report.pdf).

generational influences, do not just record your chronological age. Rather, think about your particular age cohort (e.g., Generation X, millennial, baby boomer) and the societal, cultural, and historical influences on people your age. Also, think about your generation-related roles. For example, are you an oldest child, adult child of aging parents, aunt, or uncle? With regard to Developmental or other Disability, write about your own experience or inexperience with disability because, with regard to the latter, a lack of experience with people of a particular identity also shapes your thoughts and behavior with others. (For more detailed questions to facilitate this self-assessment, see Hays, 2013, and Hays, 2016.)

Once you have a description of the ADDRESSING influences on yourself, put a star next to each category in which you hold a dominant cultural identity. For example, if you are a young or middle-aged adult (i.e., you are not a child or older adult), put a star next to Age and generational influences; if you do not have any disability, put a star next to Developmental or other Disability; if you are of Christian or secular heritage, put a star next to Religion and spiritual orientation; if you are of European American heritage, put a star next to Ethnic and racial identity; if you grew up middle class or are currently middle class, put a star next to Socioeconomic status; if you are heterosexual, put a star next to Sexual orientation; if you do not have any Indigenous heritage, put a star next to Indigenous heritage; if you are a U.S.-born American citizen, put a star next to National origin; and if you identify as male, put a star next to Gender. Now, look at your list. I call this starred list your *constellation of privileges*, and everyone's constellation is unique.

Identity is complex, and it can shift with context and over time (Ferguson, Nguyen, & Iturbide, 2017). For example, it is possible to hold both a minority and a dominant cultural identity simultaneously (e.g., if you have a White parent and an African American parent). There is no right or wrong identity with this exercise. The point is to recognize the influences on you and the privileges you hold in relation to your dominant-culture identities. This recognition can be extremely difficult because, as the saying goes, privilege is like oxygen; you don't notice it unless it's not there. The reason it is important to recognize privilege is that the areas in which we hold privilege are usually the areas in which our knowledge and experience regarding minority groups are most limited. And as therapists, the less we know about and understand our clients' experiences, the less effective we are.

There are a number of things you can do to stay engaged in the process of recognizing your cultural influences and privileges. These include obtaining cultural information from culture-specific sources (e.g., news published by ethnic and other minority communities), attending cultural celebrations and other public events, obtaining supervision from a person who belongs to and is knowledgeable about a minority culture, consulting with a culturally diverse professional group, reading from the wealth of multicultural counseling research now available, and developing relationships with people of diverse cultures. Clients should not be expected to educate you about the broader social and cultural meanings of their identities. However, you will have to obtain information from clients regarding their unique personal experience of their culture. Engagement with these forms of learning facilitates the development of the cognitive schema or template into which client-specific information can be considered and incorporated. The development of this cultural schema is the responsibility of you, the therapist.

Cognitive Behavioral Assessment

One of the first steps in a cognitive behavioral assessment involves conceptualization of the problem. CBT divides problems into two general categories. The first category consists of problems in the client's environment (e.g., a difficult task, a conflict, a stressful situation) that imply an environmental solution (e.g., changing the task, obtaining help, decreasing stressors in the situation). The second category consists of problems that are more internal—namely, those involving dysfunctional cognitions and undesirable overwhelming emotions. Difficulties in this second category are commonly referred to as *cognitive problems*. Many problems involve both environmental and cognitive elements, but distinguishing between the two is important in developing the most effective intervention.

Environmental Problems

One would think that cultural influences would be included in the definition of any environment, but this has not been the case with CBT. Cultural aspects of clients' environments have often been overlooked or framed in negative terms.

A *culturally responsive* assessment takes into account both positive and negative aspects of clients' cultural environments. Culturally related *stressors* can include acculturation; discrimination; living in an unsafe neighborhood, in inadequate housing, or extreme poverty; receiving insufficient welfare support; inadequate health care or social services; legal problems; and exposure to disasters or war (American Psychiatric Association, 2000).

Even if clients do not perceive cultural stressors such as racism and other forms of oppression, it is important that therapists be aware of them. In their work with transgender clients, Austin and Craig (2015) used an inverted pyramid (upside-down triangle) to illustrate the effects of societal oppression on mental health—an illustration that could be helpful with clients experiencing various forms of societal oppression. The top and widest level of the inverted pyramid represents oppressive dominant cultural beliefs and messages regarding the minority group; the second level down, institutional levels of discrimination such as laws, business practices, the media, and religions; the third level down, direct interpersonal interactions that are hurtful; and the bottom tip of the inverted pyramid represents the individual, including internalized beliefs and feelings. This illustration can be helpful in validating clients' struggles because it affirms the individual is "doing their best to cope with complex and often hostile environmental circumstances" (p. 24).

Positive aspects of a person's cultural environment have received much less attention. These positive aspects can be considered in two categories: environmental conditions and interpersonal supports (Hays, 2016). The first category, *environmental conditions*, may be natural or constructed. Examples of *natural conditions* include rivers, beaches, and land available for subsistence and recreational fishing, hunting, gardening, and farming. *Constructed environmental conditions* may be an altar in one's home or room to honor deceased family members, a space for prayer and meditation, availability of culturally preferred foods, the presence of culture-specific art and music, a place for animals, and communities that facilitate social interaction (e.g., villages in which homes are within walking distance of one another).

Interpersonal supports include extended families (blood related and non–blood related), religious communities, traditional celebrations and rituals, recreational activities, storytelling activities that pass on the history of a group, and involvement in political and social action groups. Having a child who is successful in school can also be an important source of pride and strength for parents and extended family.

The explicit consideration of these positive aspects of cultural environments is important for a number of reasons. For one, helping clients to recognize culturally related supports communicates respect for a client's cultural heritage. Respect is a central concept among many people of minority cultures, and as such, it is important for the purposes of establishing a good working relationship (Boyd-Franklin, 2003; El-Islam, 1982; Kim, 1985; Matheson, 1986; Morales, 1992; Swinomish Tribal Community, 1991).

In addition, cognitive behavioral research encourages the incorporation of strengths and supports in the development of effective therapeutic interventions. The use of naturally occurring supports works precisely because the supports are naturally occurring and thus easier to implement and maintain. The explicit consideration of culturally related environmental conditions and supports opens up an array of interventions that might otherwise be overlooked from a dominant cultural perspective.

When investigating cultural supports, it is important to consider the client's orientation to their culture of origin and the dominant culture. LaFromboise, Coleman, and Gerton (1993) proposed a model of *bicultural competence* that emphasizes the reciprocal relationship between the person and the environment or, in this case, two environments (the culture of origin and the second culture). They suggested that competence in each of these cultures can be observed in the individual's (a) knowledge of cultural beliefs and values, (b) positive attitudes toward both majority and minority groups, (c) bicultural efficacy, (d) communication ability, (e) role repertoire, and (f) sense of groundedness in a social support system.

This model may be helpful in one's exploration and choice of supports. For example, consider the situation of a middle-aged, urban American Indian woman. If the woman grew up in an American Indian family and cultural context, identifies strongly with her specific Native culture and functions well in the dominant cultural setting in which she works and lives, and currently is well grounded in a social support system that includes Native and non-Native people, the range and types of environmental supports that would be appropriate for her would be quite different from those of another middle-aged, urban American Indian woman who grew up in an adopted European American family with little connection to her cultural heritage. Whereas the first woman might be open to traditional rituals, supports, or healing practices in addition to some dominant cultural approaches, the second woman could interpret the suggestion of traditional rituals, supports, or healing practices as presumptive and thus involving racist assumptions.

Cognitive Problems

This brings us to the second category of problems—namely, those that can be thought of as internal to the client. These include overwhelming emotions, disturbing thoughts, frightening physical sensations, and maladaptive behavior. CBT refers to these problems as *cognitive* because the disturbance is seen as emanating from dysfunctional cognitions and cognitive processes. As noted earlier, CBT proposes that we can increase our control over disturbing physiological sensations, overwhelming emotions, and self-defeating behaviors if we recognize our unhelpful cognitions and change them to more helpful, realistic, and positive ones.

Attention to cultural influences within this second category of problems is important for several reasons. Culture plays a role in the creation, shaping, and maintenance of cognitions and cognitive processes (Dowd, 2003). Cultural influences can be seen in one's definitions of rationality and in one's view of what constitutes adaptive and maladaptive behavior. Cultural influences are interwoven with beliefs regarding acceptable coping behaviors and forms of emotional expression and with religious and social values that affect clients' perceived choices.

Because minority cultural influences are often framed as negative by the dominant culture, therapists will give deliberate attention to the positive aspects of cultural influences on internal processes. These can be conceptualized as *personal strengths* and include pride in one's culture and identity; a religious faith or spirituality; musical and artistic abilities; bilingual and multilingual skills; a sense of humor; culturally related knowledge and practical living skills regarding fishing, hunting, farming, cooking, and the use of medicinal plants; culture-specific beliefs that help one cope with prejudice and discrimination; and commitment to helping one's group—for example, through social action.

Here again, the client's connection to and competence in their culture of origin and the dominant culture are important. For example, consider the situation of a young Vietnamese man in his early 20s who lives in the United States with his parents and younger siblings and who presents with anxiety related to family and work conflicts. From a dominant cultural perspective, the therapist might conceptualize the client's problem as one of individuation and encourage him to question the authority of his parents and find his own place to live. Such an approach could involve challenging culturally based beliefs regarding interdependence of family members, responsibility to others, and respect for elders. If the client and his family are open to alternative cultural perspectives, considering these different views could be helpful. However, if they are not, such an approach would probably diminish the therapist's credibility and lead the young man to terminate therapy. More helpful approaches might involve teaching the client (and possibly the family) skills for problem solving, conflict resolution, and frustration tolerance that do not involve challenging core cultural beliefs.

Addressing the Complexity of Problems

Of course, environmental and cognitive aspects of problems often overlap. An ever-present danger with CBT lies in the inaccurate conceptualization of a client's problem (i.e., distress) as due to dysfunctional cognitions when it is a consequence of unacceptable environmental conditions (e.g., an abusive relationship, a racist workplace, physical and social barriers to a person who has a disability). As therapists, we do not want to be in the position of encouraging a client to adapt to an environment that is dangerous or harmful. Attempts to change a client's thinking about such conditions without trying to change the conditions may give the message that the conditions are acceptable and that the client is to blame for them.

Returning to the example of Shelby, let us say that her coworkers and supervisor resent her and that their feelings emanate from racial prejudice. In response to this environmentally based problem, the therapist would explore with Shelby the possibility of taking action aimed at changing her work environment (e.g., proactively talking with her supervisor to respond to the complaints, talking to someone above her supervisor, filing a complaint, looking for a new job, consulting an attorney). However, if Shelby's anxiety is so great that it prevents her from engaging in this type of problem solving, it may be necessary to take a more internal (cognitive) focus to managing the anxiety. This internal focus would involve helping Shelby change her self-defeating thoughts to more helpful ones that decrease her anxiety. Such cognitive restructuring might be conducted first or in combination with the problem solving aimed at changing Shelby's work environment.

Building on the existing literature in the domains of CBT and multicultural therapy, this book provides clinicians and counselors with practitioner-oriented suggestions, guidelines, and examples illustrating the use of CBT with people of diverse cultural identities. The book is intended for psychologists, counselors, family therapists, social workers, and psychiatrists who are interested in using cognitive behavioral approaches to assessment, therapy, and supervision with clients and students of diverse identities. It should appeal to those who already hold multicultural expertise and want to learn specific skills and interventions, as well as to cognitive behavior therapists who wish to expand their approaches to more diverse populations. An underlying premise of the book is that culture influences us all, and the consideration of culture is an essential component of assessment and therapy with everyone. By focusing on the application of CBT with people of minority identities, we hope to call attention to how cultural considerations can enhance and facilitate CBT with people of minority, dominant, bicultural, and multicultural identities.

OVERVIEW OF THE BOOK

This Introduction is followed by eight chapters focusing on the use of CBT with specific ethnic groups—namely, American Indian, Alaska Native, Latinx, African American, Asian American, South Asian, Arab, and Orthodox Jewish cultures—followed by chapters on CBT with people of nonethnic minority groups: older adults, people with disabilities, and sexual and gender minorities. Ethnic groups are included first because ethnicity and race were the initial focus and have continued to be the primary focus in the field of multicultural psychology. In this initial section on ethnic and racial minority groups, we place American Indian and Alaska Native people first because Indigenous people literally are the First Peoples. In keeping with the conceptualization of identity as complex and multidimensional, these chapters do not assume a European American norm but rather include people of multidimensional identities (e.g., people of color who are older, have a disability, or are gay, lesbian, bisexual, or transgender).

This second edition builds on the first with the following changes: All chapters have been updated to include relevant demographic information and studies since 2006, culture-specific assessment information is now embedded in each chapter rather than in one separate general chapter, and a chapter has been added regarding CBT with South Asian clients, particularly people of Asian Indian heritage.

Each of Chapters 1 through 11 offers an overview of the respective cultural group, including sociodemographics and information regarding within-group diversity, followed by a discussion of the advantages of using CBT with each group, potential limitations, and suggested adaptations for assessment and therapy. Case examples illustrate the practical application of these adaptations. Chapter 12 addresses cultural considerations in supervision and training.

One final note: Although we have done our best to include a diverse range of cultural influences and minority groups, there is still a long way to go. We recognize the need for more empirically based research involving minority cultures. In the meantime, we hope that the clinically based suggestions and modifications provided in this book will contribute to the search for and consideration of evidence-based practices. We look forward to future research involving an even greater number of cultural groups from a variety of countries.

REFERENCES

American Psychiatric Association. (2000). *Diagnostic and statistical manual of mental disorders* (4th ed., text rev.). Washington, DC: Author.

American Psychological Association. (2017). *Multicultural guidelines: An ecological approach to context, identity, and intersectionality.* Retrieved from http://www.apa.org/about/policy/multicultural-guidelines.pdf

American Psychological Association, Presidential Task Force on Evidence-Based Practice. (2006). Evidence-based practice in psychology. *American Psychologist, 61,* 271–285. http://dx.doi.org/10.1037/0003-066X.61.4.271

Arredondo, P., & Pérez, P. (2006). Historical perspectives on the Multicultural Guidelines and contemporary applications. *Professional Psychology: Research and Practice, 37,* 1–5. http://dx.doi.org/10.1037/0735-7028.37.1.1

Austin, A., & Craig, S. L. (2015). Transgender affirmative cognitive behavioral therapy: Clinical considerations and applications. *Professional Psychology: Research and Practice, 46,* 21–29. http://dx.doi.org/10.1037/a0038642

Barker, C. H., Cook, K. L., & Borrego, J., Jr. (2010). Addressing cultural variables in parent training programs with Latino families. *Cognitive and Behavioral Practice, 17,* 157–166. http://dx.doi.org/10.1016/j.cbpra.2010.01.002

Beck, J. S. (2011). *Cognitive therapy: Basics and beyond* (2nd ed.). New York, NY: Guilford Press.

Beck, J. S., & Beck, A. (2011). *Cognitive therapy for challenging problems: What to do when the basics don't work.* New York, NY: Guilford Press.

Benish, S. G., Quintana, S., & Wampold, B. E. (2011). Culturally adapted psychotherapy and the legitimacy of myth: A direct-comparison meta-analysis. *Journal of Counseling Psychology, 58,* 279–289. http://dx.doi.org/10.1037/a0023626

Bennett, S. T., Flett, R. A., & Babbage, D. R. (2014). Culturally adapted cognitive behaviour therapy for Maori with major depression. *The Cognitive Behaviour Therapist, 7,* 1–16. http://dx.doi.org/10.1017/S1754470X14000233

Bernal, G., & Domenech Rodriguez, M. M. (Eds.). (2012). *Cultural adaptations: Tools for evidence-based practice with diverse populations.* Washington, DC: American Psychological Association. http://dx.doi.org/10.1037/13752-000

Boyd-Franklin, N. (2003). *Black families in therapy.* New York, NY: Guilford Press.

Casas, J. M. (1988). Cognitive-behavioral approaches: A minority perspective. *The Counseling Psychologist, 16,* 106–110. http://dx.doi.org/10.1177/0011000088161009

Chang, D. F., Hung, T., Ng, N., Ling, A., Chen, T., Cao, Y., & Zhang, Y. (2016). Taoist cognitive therapy: Treatment of generalized anxiety disorder in a Chinese immigrant woman. *Asian American Journal of Psychology, 7,* 205–216.

Chang, E. C., Downey, C. A., Hirsch, J. K., & Yu, E. A. (Eds.). (2018). *Treating depression, anxiety, and stress in ethnic and racial groups: Cognitive behavioral approaches.* Washington, DC: American Psychological Association.

Chu, J., & Leino, A. (2017). Advancement in the maturing science of cultural adaptations of evidence-based interventions. *Journal of Consulting and Clinical Psychology, 85,* 45–57. http://dx.doi.org/10.1037/ccp0000145

Craig, S. L., McInroy, L. B., Alaggia, R., & McCready, L. T. (2014). Like picking up a seed, but you haven't planted it: Queer youth analyze the It Gets Better Project. *International Journal of Child, Youth & Family Studies, 5,* 204–219. http://dx.doi.org/10.18357/ijcyfs.craigsl.512014

Davidson, R. J., & Kaszniak, A. W. (2015). Conceptual and methodological issues in research on mindfulness and meditation. *American Psychologist, 70,* 581–592. http://dx.doi.org/10.1037/a0039512

Dobson, K. (Ed.). (2001). *Handbook of cognitive-behavioral therapies.* New York, NY: Guilford Press.

Dowd, E. T. (2003). Cultural differences in cognitive therapy. *The Behavior Therapist, 26,* 247–249.

El-Islam, F. (1982). Arabic cultural psychiatry. *Transcultural Psychiatric Research Review, 19,* 5–24. http://dx.doi.org/10.1177/136346158201900101

Ferguson, G. M., Nguyen, J., & Iturbide, M. I. (2017). Playing up and playing down cultural identity: Introducing cultural influence and cultural variability. *Cultural*

Diversity & Ethnic Minority Psychology, 23, 109–124. http://dx.doi.org/10.1037/cdp0000110

Friedman, S., Braunstein, J. W., & Halpern, B. (2006). Cognitive behavioral treatment of panic disorder and agoraphobia in a multiethnic urban outpatient clinic: Initial presentation and treatment outcome. *Cognitive and Behavioral Practice, 13,* 282–292. http://dx.doi.org/10.1016/j.cbpra.2006.04.009

Fuchs, C. H., West, L. M., Graham, J. R., Kalill, K. S., Morgan, L. P. K., Hayes-Skelton, S. A., . . . Roemer, L. (2016). Reactions to an acceptance-based behavior therapy for GAD: Giving voice to the experiences of clients from marginalized backgrounds. *Cognitive and Behavioral Practice, 23,* 473–484. http://dx.doi.org/10.1016/j.cbpra.2015.09.004

Glickman, N. S. (2009). Adapting best practices in CBT for deaf and hearing persons with language and learning challenges. *Journal of Psychotherapy Integration, 19,* 354–384. http://dx.doi.org/10.1037/a0017969

Graves, S. L., & Blake, J. J. (Eds.). (2016). *Psychoeducational assessment and intervention for ethnic minority children: Evidence-based approaches.* Washington, DC: American Psychological Association. http://dx.doi.org/10.1037/14855-000

Greenberger, D., & Padesky, C. (2015). *Mind over mood: Change how you feel by changing the way you think.* New York, NY: Guilford Press.

Hall, G. C. N., Yip, T., & Zárate, M. A. (2016). On becoming multicultural in a monocultural research world: A conceptual approach to studying ethnocultural diversity. *American Psychologist, 71,* 40–51. http://dx.doi.org/10.1037/a0039734

Hamp, A., Stamm, K., Lin, L., & Christidis, P. (2016). *2015 APA survey of psychology health service providers.* Retrieved from http://www.apa.org/workforce/publications/15-health-service-providers/index.aspx

Hays, P. A. (2013). *Connecting across cultures: The helper's toolkit.* Thousand Oaks, CA: Sage.

Hays, P. A. (2014). *Creating well-being: Four steps to a happier healthier life.* Washington, DC: American Psychological Association. http://dx.doi.org/10.1037/14317-000

Hays, P. A. (2016). *Addressing cultural complexities in practice: Assessment, diagnosis, and therapy* (3rd ed.). Washington, DC: American Psychological Association. http://dx.doi.org/10.1037/14801-000

Hinton, D. E., & Jalal, B. (2014). Parameters for creating culturally sensitive CBT: Implementing CBT in global settings. *Cognitive and Behavioral Practice, 21,* 139–144. http://dx.doi.org/10.1016/j.cbpra.2014.01.009

Hinton, D. E., Pich, V., Hofmann, S. G., & Otto, M. W. (2013). Acceptance and mindfulness techniques as applied to refugee and ethnic minority populations with PTSD: Examples from "culturally adapted CBT." *Cognitive and Behavioral Practice, 20,* 33–46. http://dx.doi.org/10.1016/j.cbpra.2011.09.001

Huey, S. J., Jr., Tilley, J. L., Jones, E. O., & Smith, C. A. (2014). The contribution of cultural competence to evidence-based care for ethnically diverse populations.

Annual Review of Clinical Psychology, 10, 305–338. http://dx.doi.org/10.1146/annurev-clinpsy-032813-153729

Iwamasa, G., & Smith, S. K. (1996). Ethnic diversity and behavioral psychology: A review of the literature. *Behavior Modification, 20,* 45–59. http://dx.doi.org/10.1177/01454455960201002

Kantrowitz, R. E., & Ballou, M. (1992). A feminist critique of cognitive-behavioral therapy. In L. S. Brown & M. Ballou (Eds.), *Personality and psychopathology: Feminist appraisals* (pp. 70–87). New York, NY: Guilford Press.

Kim, S. C. (1985). Family therapy for Asian Americans: A strategic-structural framework. *Psychotherapy: Theory, Research, Practice, Training, 22,* 342–348. http://dx.doi.org/10.1037/h0085513

Kohout, J. L., Pate, W. E., & Maton, K. I. (2014). An updated profile of ethnic minority psychology: A pipeline perspective. In F. T. L. Leong (Ed.), *APA handbook of multicultural psychology: Vol. 1. Theory and research* (pp. 19–42). Washington, DC: American Psychological Association. http://dx.doi.org/10.1037/14189-002

LaFromboise, T., Coleman, H. L. K., & Gerton, J. (1993). Psychological impact of biculturalism: Evidence and theory. *Psychological Bulletin, 114,* 395–412. http://dx.doi.org/10.1037/0033-2909.114.3.395

La Roche, M. J., D'Angelo, E., Gualdron, L., & Leavell, J. (2006). Culturally sensitive guided imagery for allocentric Latinos: A pilot study. *Psychotherapy: Theory, Research, Practice, Training, 43,* 555–560. http://dx.doi.org/10.1037/0033-3204.43.4.555

Lucassen, M. F. G., Merry, S. N., Hatcher, S., & Frampton, C. M. A. (2015). Rainbow SPARX: A novel approach to addressing depression in sexual minority youth. *Cognitive and Behavioral Practice, 22,* 203–216. http://dx.doi.org/10.1016/j.cbpra.2013.12.008

Malchiodi, C. A., & Rozum, A. L. (2012). Cognitive-behavioral and mind-body approaches. In C. Malchiodi (Ed.), *Handbook of art therapy* (2nd ed., pp. 89–102). New York, NY: Guilford Press.

Matheson, L. (1986). If you are not an Indian, how do you treat an Indian? In H. P. Lefley & P. Pedersen (Eds.), *Cross-cultural training for mental health professionals* (pp. 115–130). Springfield, IL: Charles C Thomas.

Morales, E. S. (1992). Counseling Latino gays and Latina lesbians. In S. H. Dworkin & F. J. Gutierrez (Eds.), *Counseling gay men and lesbians: Journey to the end of the rainbow* (pp. 125–140). Alexandria, VA: American Counseling Association.

Naeem, F., & Kingdon, D. (Eds.). (2011). *Cognitive behaviour therapy in non-Western cultures.* New York, NY: ANOVA Science.

Neblett, E. W., Jr., Bernard, D. L., & Hudson Banks, K. (2016). The moderating roles of gender and socioeconomic status in the association between racial discrimination and psychological adjustment. *Cognitive and Behavioral Practice, 23,* 385–397. http://dx.doi.org/10.1016/j.cbpra.2016.05.002

Pedersen, P. (1987). Ten frequent assumptions of cultural bias in counseling. *Journal of Multicultural Counseling and Development, 15*, 16–24. http://dx.doi.org/10.1002/j.2161-1912.1987.tb00374.x

Shealy, K. M., Davidson, T. M., Jones, A. M., Lopez, C. M., & de Arellano, M. A. (2015). Delivering an evidence-based mental health treatment to underserved populations using telemedicine. The case of a trauma-affected adolescent in a rural setting. *Cognitive and Behavioral Practice, 22*, 331–344. http://dx.doi.org/10.1016/j.cbpra.2014.04.007

Smith, T. B., Domenech Rodríguez, M., & Bernal, G. (2011). Culture. *Journal of Clinical Psychology, 67*, 166–175. http://dx.doi.org/10.1002/jclp.20757

Swinomish Tribal Community. (1991). *A gathering of wisdoms, tribal mental health: A cultural perspective.* La Conner, WA: Author.

Tropp, L. R., & Mallett, R. (Eds.). (2011). *Moving beyond prejudice reduction: Pathways to positive intergroup relations.* Washington, DC: American Psychological Association. http://dx.doi.org/10.1037/12319-000

Washington, B. (2012, May 31). Coyote thoughts: A Native explains mental health. *Indian Country Today.* Retrieved from https://newsmaven.io/indiancountrytoday/archive/coyote-thoughts-a-native-explains-mental-health-PMJLklx4xUGMPdkvNgBB6Q/

Wenzel, A., Dobson, K. S., & Hays, P. A. (2016). *Cognitive behavioral therapy techniques and strategies.* Washington, DC: American Psychological Association. http://dx.doi.org/10.1037/14936-000

Wood, P. S., & Mallinckrodt, B. (1990). Culturally sensitive assertiveness training for ethnic minority clients. *Professional Psychology: Research and Practice, 21*, 5–11. http://dx.doi.org/10.1037/0735-7028.21.1.5

Zane, N., Bernal, G., & Leong, F. T. L. (2016). *Evidence-based psychological practice with ethnic minorities.* Washington, DC: American Psychological Association.

I

ETHNIC MINORITY CULTURAL POPULATIONS

1

COGNITIVE BEHAVIOR THERAPY WITH AMERICAN INDIANS

JUSTIN DOUGLAS McDONALD, JOHN GONZALEZ,
AND EMILY SARGENT

As increasing numbers of American Indians receive doctorates in psychology (Benson, 2003), it logically follows that a new generation of culturally competent psychologists will fuel an interest in empirical clarity, and we should build and move in this direction. In this revised chapter, we have compiled and synthesized what information is available from the clinical literature with information from traditional American Indian oral history and contemporary practice. Although the two perspectives are reflexively considered oppositional, and indeed they often are, we suggest some intriguing parallels and even intersections.

In addition, we present a new section reflective of the events that transpired at the Sacred Stone Camp on the Standing Rock Reservation during the Dakota Access Pipeline (DAPL) protests in 2016. Two of the authors (McDonald and Sargent, among many others) ventured to the camp on multiple occasions, providing mental health services to the water protectors. We

http://dx.doi.org/10.1037/0000119-002

Culturally Responsive Cognitive Behavior Therapy, Second Edition: Practice and Supervision, G. Y. Iwamasa and P. A. Hays (Editors)

consider the complex and profound experiences of the protest within the context of aspects of American Indian perceptions of history, self, and future in regard to life as Natives in America in general and cognitive behavior therapy (CBT) in particular. We also provide the reader with a brief history of American Indian demographic and cultural issues relevant to psychology in general and CBT in particular, followed by a case example that integrates consideration of these issues with the clinical application of CBT.

From the beginning, we must note that although this chapter is authored by three American Indians representing several different tribes, our collective perspectives are inadequate to represent all Native nations on the North American continent. Although many tribes were decimated by military genocide or disease, numerous Native cultural entities remain (U.S. Census Bureau, 2012). Current estimates of the numbers of American Indians and Alaska Natives indicate that 2.9% of U.S. citizens identified themselves as exclusively Native and 5.2% as Native/combined with another race in the 2010 U.S. Census (U.S. Census Bureau, 2010). Many question the estimates of the data given the procedures used for self-reporting ethnicity and race (see Trimble & Thurman, 2002, for a discussion). Although there are certainly some areas of cultural overlap among all American Indian tribes (i.e., spirituality, collective orientation, reverence for elders and children), some groups are as ethnically diverse as the nations (tribes) of Europe (see Snipp, 1996).

HISTORICAL OVERVIEW

Many American Indian cultures have a creation story that indicates their people existed on the North American continent since the beginning of time. Anthropologists and archeologists have suggested that the earliest inhabitants of North America date back to about 28,000 years ago. Regardless of which timeline is fact, for Indigenous people, history does not begin with European contact (Page, 2003). The oral (and written) histories of American Indians provide accounts of intercultural (tribal) contacts, migrations, and cultural adaptations.

For the most part, early relations between Europeans and Natives were collaborative. Within the worldview of many Native tribes, a humanistic ideology existed that is still present today (Gonzalez & Bennett, 2000). This ideology views all people as being similar regardless of race or ethnicity. Therefore, most tribes were initially helpful and welcomed the Europeans with generosity and friendship. However, many Europeans typically had an agenda, whether it was colonization or finding inexistent water passages, cities of gold, or fountains of youth. When tribes began to realize they were being exploited, they began to withdraw their support. This resistance was met with swift and sometimes sweeping punishment. Entire bands and tribes were exterminated in the most atrocious, unspeakable manner (for more information, see Faragher, Buhle, Czitrom, & Armitage, 2000).

Manifest destiny provided the holy and legal rationale for the westward expansion. The choices for Eastern tribes were to (a) flee west into unknown and often inhospitable territory, (b) stay and fight, or (c) stay and submit to total domination. In reality, all these options carried the probability of cultural disintegration and physical annihilation. Those who fled were forced to give up their lands and lifestyles and were often wiped out by unfamiliar climates or disease. Being forced to leave territory that many groups had roamed for centuries was devastating. Those groups who "staked themselves out" ultimately lost either mostly or completely, and if any survived, they were relegated to reservations or chased off and not officially recognized. Treaties were made but were consistently broken by the drafters. By the time of the last major battle between the U.S. Army and a band of starving and freezing Brule Lakota (Sioux) at Wounded Knee, South Dakota, in 1891, most tribes had been slaughtered, scattered, or relocated to reservations. The Indian Relocation Act of 1830 marked the beginning of a series of laws and treaties aimed at controlling and quashing Indian resistance and assimilating them as quickly and quietly as possible. This act empowered the federal government to forcibly relocate "friendlies" and punish "hostiles" who resisted relocation.

Soon after forcing Natives onto reservations, the federal policy shifted to one of assimilation in an attempt to "civilize" the Native. This assimilation process included teaching and expecting Native Americans to become farmers rather than the hunters and gatherers many of them had been (Collier, 1947; Edwards & Smith, 1979). One of the first policies enacted to force assimilation was the Dawes Act or the Land Allotment Act of 1887, which provided for the allotment of plots of Native American land to "competent" Native Americans. The Dawes Act was disastrous for Native Americans. Because they were unable to farm their land properly and ended up selling it to Whites, the act resulted in the loss of three fifths of all Native American lands (LaDuke, 1999; Meyer, 1994). Life on the reservation became difficult as tribes were prohibited from using their languages, participating in cultural ceremonies, and fulfilling traditional roles (Collier, 1947). In addition, the transfer of the culture to the next generation was denied when the federal government established the boarding school system. The main objective of the off-reservation boarding school was to assimilate Native American children into "American" culture by teaching them in a closed environment and not allowing them to speak their languages or practice cultural traditions (Choney, Berryhill-Paapke, & Robbins, 1995). The effects of this policy on Native communities have lingered for generations.

Acculturation and Cultural Identification of American Indians

Although few empirical studies exist regarding acculturation and American Indians, some researchers have attempted to delineate a lexicon to describe the possible levels of acculturation of American Indian tribes and individuals. LaFromboise, Trimble, and Mohatt (1990) discussed four possible levels of acculturation or cultural identification: traditional, transitional, bicultural, and assimilated.

More recently, Garrett and Pichette (2000) formulated five types or levels of acculturation: traditional, marginal, bicultural, assimilated, and pantraditional. Although slightly different in definition, these are similar to those of LaFromboise et al. (1990). The main distinctions are the use of *marginal* instead of *transitional*, and the inclusion of the pantraditional category. According to Garrett and Pichette, the *marginal* individual may speak both languages but has lost touch with Native cultural ways and is not fully accepted or comfortable in the mainstream society. The *pantraditional* category of acculturation describes the American Indian who has only been exposed to or adopts some mainstream values but has made a conscious effort to return to the old ways.

Fleming (1992) described the efforts by some Native communities to teach positive Native traditions, such as singing, dancing, and Native languages, and at the same time encourage the skills needed to function in the majority culture. Many Native American researchers and practitioners have stressed the importance of forming and strengthening Native cultural identification to ensure positive outcomes in school achievement and coping strategies while protecting against undesirable outcomes such as depression and substance abuse (Dehyle, 1992; May & Moran, 1995). These efforts and programs suggest that an acculturation level or cultural identification that is bicultural is desirable for positive mental health in the American Indian community. Later in the chapter, we discuss the assessment of acculturation or cultural orientation of Native clients, but for now, we turn to the topic of mental health and care.

American Indian Mental Health and Care

Accurate determination of the incidence and prevalence of psychopathology among American Indians is difficult for several reasons. First, the cross-cultural equivalence of many psychological disorders is controversial and poorly understood (Matsumoto, 2000). Differences between Native tribes regarding symptomatology and the diagnostic validity of categories can complicate the most basic assessment efforts. Even for straightforwardly defined problems such as completed suicides, the rates between tribes can be drastically different, making any efforts to generalize misleading (Suicide Prevention Resource Center, 2011). Finally, health care delivery is significantly different for American Indians, particularly those on reservations. The Indian Health Service (IHS), a branch of the U.S. Public Health Service, is responsible for general health care delivery. The IHS is chronically underfunded and understaffed, and the majority of psychologists who work for the IHS are non-Native providers (McDonald, 1994, 1998).

These general issues aside, limited data exist on the prevalence and incidence of mental health problems and substance abuse in Native communities and populations. Some larger scale epidemiological reports have been published by the National Center for American Indian and Alaska Native Mental Health Research (see Beals, Manson, Mitchell, & Spicer, 2003; Beals, Spicer, Mitchell, Novins, & Manson, 2003; Mitchell, Beals, Novins, & Spicer, 2003, for summaries). These data lend support to what most Native American health providers and leaders attest to regarding the existence of serious behavior health problems in their communities. Furthermore, the historical context leading to the current social environment compounds the unique mental health problems in Native communities (Trimble & Thurman, 2002).

Recent Treatment Research

Although these challenges mostly remain, the treatment literature for American Indians, especially that involving cognitive behavior therapy, has grown considerably. This welcome evolution was stimulated by several important early calls from prominent American Indian researchers. In an article on the difficulties in mental health treatment in Native American communities, Gone (2004) recommended a more comprehensive assessment of therapeutic outcomes—a challenge because the bulk of the literature regarding Native Americans does not subscribe to a cognitive behavior approach, making it difficult to establish external validity. Trimble and Thurman (2002) noted a significant increase in the number of published articles related to counseling and psychotherapy with Native populations; however, most of these either educate the reader on Native history and general cultural considerations in treatment (e.g., Anderson & Ellis, 1995; Herring, 1999; Sue & Sue, 1999) or delineate a traditional Native American healing practice (e.g., Colmant & Merta, 1999; Heilbron & Guttman, 2000). In other words, they do not involve empirically based research.

An online search of the literature for the initial version of this chapter revealed only two articles that specifically mentioned CBT with Native clients. In the first, Renfrey (1992) suggested that CBT is congruent with Native American community mental health needs and made a strong argument for the cognitive behavior assessment of the client's cultural identification as a guide to the therapeutic process. Renfrey also called for a bicultural treatment plan that integrates Western practices with a Native worldview. In the second article, Trimble (1992) described a community based, cognitive behavior approach to the treatment of substance abuse in adolescents and called for the teaching of bicultural competence in communication skills and coping strategies. Trimble argued that by incorporating the Native American worldview of community and social environments, it is possible to apply cognitive behavior concepts from social learning theory to the needs of Native American individuals and communities.

COGNITIVE BEHAVIOR THEORY AND AMERICAN INDIAN PSYCHOLOGY

Although vastly different in practice, American Indian concepts of healing and the Western model of CBT are compellingly similar in some respects. The following sections highlight some issues relevant to understanding wellness and healing from a traditional American Indian perspective.

Worldview

As described by Triandis (1994), most cultural groups can be categorized as either individualistic or collectivistic. Matsumoto (2000) distinguished the two orientations by suggesting that "members of individualistic cultures see themselves as separate and autonomous individuals, whereas members of collectivistic cultures see themselves as fundamentally connected with others" (p. 41). It is essential for non-Indians to understand that the ontological perspective of traditional American Indians is collectivistic, in that both the well-being and the pathology of the group supersede and sometimes even determine that of the individual. An illustrative example of this point is apparent in the fact that some tribes (i.e., the female Northern Cheyenne dialect) do not have a word in their vocabulary for *I*.

Spirituality

Most American Indian belief systems are animistic in that all things are believed to possess a spirit, be it people, animals, trees, wind, or even inanimate, nonliving objects such as rocks. This animistic ontology presumes the existence of a spirit world, a plane of existence that is both distinct and coexistent with the physical world. People can see, hear, touch, or communicate with other spirits on particular, usually significant occasions (Jackson

& Turner, 2004). Whereas many non-Natives find it difficult to appreciate or conceive of two seemingly distinct realities existing in simultaneous harmony, traditional American Indians are quite comfortable with this reality.

The most salient aspect of American Indian spirituality for non-Natives to grasp is that *personhood* is not a unitary construct but a combination of components. Different tribes have subtly different conceptualizations regarding the composition of the person, but most include three facets: the mind, the physical body, and the spirit (Chavez Cameron & Turtle-Song, 2003). Some tribes distinguish the mind from feelings or the heart from the body, but for the most part, the mind, body, and spirit form the three aspects of individual existence.

Harmony and Wellness

Harmony or balance between mind, body, and spirit forms the foundation of the Native conceptualization of wellness (Choney et al., 1995; Cross, 2003; Swinomish Tribal Community, 1991). Conversely, disharmony or imbalance manifests itself in pathology. The challenge in understanding American Indian ideas of pathology lies in conceptually grasping the significance of disharmony. Playing "teeter-totter" is fun and works well if both players are similar in weight. If one is more or less heavy, then some compensation—either moving in or out on the board or one player working harder than the other—must be made. If one player is far too heavy or light, the game goes on but eventually becomes burdensome and frustrating to both for different reasons. Personal disharmony works much the same way in that if, for example, the body is ill, the spirit and mind must compensate for life (the game) to go on. The more significant the physical pathology, the more taxing the strain for mind and spirit to keep up, and disharmony and imbalance develop.

Given this scenario, American Indians may perceive such maladies as depression or anxiety as weakness of the mind and body, while the spirit— although intact and fully functional—is seen as being weakened from shouldering the burden of the other two. Eventually, the individual presents as ailing not only physically and mentally but also spiritually as well. An individual may also experience spiritual malaise as a result of mentally and physically caused problems. An example is a functional disruption resulting from engaging in behaviors that violate tribally accepted norms, encountering taboo animals or spirits, or having "bad medicine" or witchcraft performed on one (Swinomish Tribal Community, 1991). It is crucial to note that whether a non-Indian practitioner recognizes such possibilities as bad medicine or witchcraft is irrelevant. Working with American Indians, particularly with those who hold traditional beliefs, requires an appreciation of the fact that they believe in the existence of these phenomena and in their power to influence wellness.

It is at this point that we begin to realize the similarity between American Indian psychology and the cognitive behavior paradigm. Consider one of the most basic tenets of CBT: Thoughts that occur most frequently are the ones we tend to believe. The rationality, logic, or positive–negative relevance of the thought does not matter; frequency is the key. In this regard, a firm belief that one is "worthless" must be dealt with regardless of its origin. In the same vein, the belief that one is being spiritually punished for a behavior transgression must also be proactively addressed. The degree to which the first person truly is worthless or the second person is being punished by spirits is inconsequential. The key is that both believe these thoughts are true and real. Thus, the source of people's contributions to their own pathology is the same: their own schema, based on their own worldview. The following section provides several empirical applications of this notion occurring since the original publication of this chapter.

Application of Cognitive Behavior Therapy

Recent research has examined the application of CBT in different treatment settings among American Indian people. Haozous, Doorenbos, and Stoner (2016) explored the cultural appropriateness of cognitive behavior pain management (CBPM) treatment, a nonpharmacologic option, for American Indians. Via qualitative data collection, Native participants expressed their preferences for nonpharmacological pain management treatment approaches (i.e., CBPM). Most participants reported using traditional healing methods such as ceremonies and using herbal remedies for pain management. However, CBPM techniques such as guided imagery, deep breathing, distraction, and goal setting were considered as aligning with traditional cultural healing. However, results suggested more should be explored with culturally adapted CBPM among American Indians.

Another study examined evidence-based treatments (EBTs) such as CBT in American Indians struggling with substance abuse by evaluating clinical administrators' attitudes toward using CBT and other evidence-based interventions to assist in the treatment of substance use. Results demonstrated that CBT was thought of most highly, as reported by administrators' attitudes (82.2%); however, other EBTs (motivational interviewing and release prevention therapy) were reported as being the most culturally appropriate by the treatment programs that were using them (Novins, Croy, Moore, & Rieckmann, 2016). Overall, participants endorsed EBTs such as CBT to be low in cultural appropriateness, even though they are frequently used in substance use treatment. Novins et al. (2016) suggested future research should aim to make EBTs that are culturally adapted more available to American Indians in substance use treatment.

Listug-Lunde, Vogeltanz-Holm, and Collins (2013) examined American Indian middle school-aged students who had depressive symptoms in a culturally adapted Adolescent Coping With Depression course intervention. Results indicated a significant improvement in depressive symptoms as well as clinical improvement in anxiety symptoms. The treatment was culturally adapted by having students discuss the relevance of assertiveness, eye contact, constructive criticism, and self-disclosure to their culture. In addition, students responded overall that they were significantly satisfied with the culturally adapted treatment. However, the authors advised that the study should be replicated with a larger sample to improve the validity of the culturally sensitive treatment.

Trauma exposure among American Indians is extremely prevalent due to multiple factors such as historical trauma, genocide, adverse living conditions, depression and suicide, and violence (BigFoot & Schmidt, 2010; Kessler, Sonnega, Bromet, Hughes, & Nelson, 1995). A treatment called Honoring Children, Mending the Circle (HC-MC) is an adaptation of trauma-focused CBT to serve better American Indian children who experience traumatic symptoms (BigFoot & Schmidt, 2010). HC-MC defines an individual's well-being as having balance and harmony among a person's overall health functioning (spiritual, relational, physical, mental, emotional, and relational). This intervention combines American Indian traditional teachings with cognitive behavior techniques. For example, one step of trauma-focused CBT is to teach children deep breathing and muscle relaxation to cope with posttraumatic stress disorder (PTSD) symptoms. HC-MC adapts this component by having children focus on soothing traditional images (e.g., a woman's shawl during traditional dancing) while deep breathing. Another evidence-based practice, Cognitive Behavior Intervention for Trauma in Schools (CBITS), has been used in American Indian reservation schools. As a part of the process to make the treatment more culturally sensitive, elders were invited to give traditional cultural teachings and activities at the start and end of treatment. Results demonstrated a significant reduction in traumatic symptoms in students, and counselors reported the treatment as being accessible and stated they would use CBITS in the future (Morsette, van den Pol, Schuldberg, Swaney, & Stolle, 2012). These notable efforts provide tangible support for the argument espoused in our original chapter, most notably that the American Indian schema and worldview could successfully combine with best practice CBT efforts to produce effective treatment outcomes.

Oppression, Social Dominance, and Cognition

One of the more damaging aspects of racial and social oppression is the myriad and consistent cognitive assaults on the minority group by the dominant group. Although not dissimilar to the psychological assaults experienced by other minority groups, American Indians have the added sorrow of knowing they are not only the smallest ethnic minority group in the United States but also that they were once the dominant group. This distinction provides considerable content for self-deprecation at both the group and individual level. Generations of propaganda waged by the dominant culture often form the basis for negative cognitive, emotional, and behavior processes. "Indians are: lazy, stupid, worthless, drunks, heathens, animals, dirty." Such cognitive assaults have been so consistently reinforced by the dominant culture that Indian people no longer require majority culture members to tell them this; they tell themselves. And, as stated previously, the thoughts that occur most frequently are the thoughts we tend to believe and, unfortunately, behave in accordance with. Duran and Duran (1995) conceptualized this belief system, in part, as a result of historical and intergenerational trauma that contributes to suicide, alcoholism, domestic violence, child abuse, and other social problems in Native communities. Indeed, traumatic historical events can shape the mind-sets of entire cultures, as we witnessed last year during the DAPL protests.

The Sacred Stone Camp Resistance to the Dakota Access Pipeline

In early 2015, the United States Army Corps of Engineers initiated the permitting process for the 1,200-mile DAPL at the behest of Dakota Access, LLC, a subsidiary of the Texas-based Energy Transfers Partners. The proposed pipeline would transfer oil from the Bakken oil fields of northwestern North Dakota to refining facilities in southern Illinois. The route proposed originally was changed because of its proximity to municipal drinking water near the state capital of Bismarck. The new route would pass within several thousand yards of the Standing Rock Reservation and just upstream from the tribe's water source thereby, in the minds of many tribal members, threatening their fresh water source.

A year of controversial and mostly unproductive interactions between the tribe and the corps resulted in lawsuits and countersuits filed and, for the tribe, and an ever-alarming sense of an impending and unavoidable injustice reminiscent of generations of similar injustices at the hands of the federal government. Native and non-Native "water protectors" flocked to the hastily constructed Sacred Stone Camp, mounting a protest that would eventually draw thousands to the ruggedly beautiful Cannonball River in southwest North Dakota. At the height of the protest, corresponding with an early

November Veterans Day call for all veterans (particularly Native) to protect the protectors from the possibility of a large-scale military or law enforcement assault (which thankfully never occurred), an estimated 20,000 protectors lined the river, inadvertently creating the fifth largest population center in North Dakota. The DAPL protest effort was entirely regulated and maintained by the water protectors themselves with no support from federal, state, or local agencies. The protectors established and maintained their own security, even banishing one individual suspected of sexual assault. Health and wellness volunteers flocked in from around the world to offer support with several dozen babies delivered during the effort and medical and mental health support for protectors wounded in clashes with the military, National Guard, and even attack dogs allegedly used by the pipeline owners.

The combination of the onset of early winter blizzards and the announcement by the secretary of the interior indicating that President Obama denied the easement needed for the development of the pipeline brought an end to the protest. The Standing Rock tribe's relief was short-lived, as the newly inaugurated President Trump signed an executive order overturning the ruling and allowing for the DAPL's completion. For many Native Americans, Uncle Sam's indomitable hand had once again turned from a proffered handshake to a slap in the face for its Indigenous citizens. Although the conclusion of the protest's efforts may be intuitively suggestive of futility and defeat, for many, the opposite mind-set has emerged. Many protectors, including those who championed their efforts from afar, are proud of their efforts and engage a positive schema that suggests "we did our best," "we didn't just lay down," and "we fought the good fight."

Why do we tell the story? How is it relevant to providing cognitive behavior therapeutic services to American Indian clients? Not only is the story of the DAPL protest timely, but it also represents a microcosm of over 500 years of painful, stressful, and at times, even fatal relationships between the federal government and American Indians. Although all our non-Native brothers and sisters from oppressed groups have experienced persecution and mistreatment, once again the circumstances are unique and different for Native Americans because of the nation-to-nation protocol born of tribal recognition and sovereignty. To deliver services to American Indians with any degree or measure of competence, non-Native CBT practitioners must understand this history and how recent events such as the DAPL protest can rip the scabs off old wounds still shared via the oral tradition for many American Indians.

Assessment of Cultural Identity

Much of our research, writing, and teaching is based on the orthogonal cultural identification theory (OCIT) of biculturalism (Oetting & Beauvais,

1990–1991), which suggests that ethnic minority individuals with high levels of cultural competence in both their own traditional culture and the majority culture (i.e., described as bicultural) will demonstrate less psychopathology and higher levels of adaptive functioning in both cultural realms (Oetting & Beauvais, 1990–1991). Conversely, those individuals who have lower levels of cultural competence in traditional and majority cultures (described as marginal) present with more pathology and dysfunction. Those who have low levels of affiliation in their traditional culture but who affiliate highly with the majority culture are described as assimilated and appear more similar to their majority culture peers regarding diagnosis and treatment preferences.

As an example, consider the scenario described previously in which some traditional Native languages lack the word *I*. A mainstream manualized treatment that encourages the use of I-statements (e.g., assertiveness training) would be inappropriate for a traditional Native client but might be fully appropriate for a more bicultural or assimilated client. Assessment of a Native client's degree of cultural orientation and competence is therefore crucial in developing a valid diagnostic hypothesis and treatment plan. Unfortunately, few scales exist for assessing cultural orientation with American Indian populations. Most of the research on cultural identification (orientation) with American Indians has been with adolescent populations (Bates, Beauvais, & Trimble, 1997; Moran, Fleming, Somervell, & Manson, 1999).

For American Indian adults, we have used the Northern Plains Bicultural Inventory (NPBI; Allen & French, 1994, 1996) and the American Indian Bicultural Inventory (AIBI; McDonald, Ross, & Rose, 2016). These measures ask the client to indicate how much they engage or participate in American Indian and European American cultural activities, languages, and spiritual events, yielding an American Indian Cultural Identification (AICI) subscale score and a European American Cultural Identification (EACI) subscale score. For example, clients are asked to indicate on a 5-point Likert scale how often they attend Native spiritual events (sweat lodges, sundance, etc.) and how often they attend non-Native religious or spiritual events (church, communion, etc.). A median split procedure is then conducted that attempts to place the individual in one of the four possible cultural orientations defined by OCIT, described earlier. For the NPBI, reliability for the AICI subscale was excellent ($r = .82$), and reliability for the EACI subscale was good ($r = .70$).

However, as with any assessment measure, there are cautions to consider. The median-split procedure has its limitations in that true differences in cultural orientation may be hard to detect for individuals who score near the median. We have found it useful to supplement the NPBI or AICI data with information gathered from the clinical interview regarding the client's personal and family history, worldview, and current social environment, for example. Therefore, we suggest considerable cross-cultural competence is required for a non-Indian therapist to assess a Native client's biculturalism, particularly if the client is more traditional. Readers are referred to the American Psychological Association's (2017) guidelines for multicultural competence. Simply reading the document will not make a person competent to work with Indian clients. However, the document provides helpful suggestions regarding process and content and a wealth of suggested readings.

As a final note regarding bicultural competence, we suggest that non-Indian therapists be aware that cultural identification should not be judged by skin color. Therapists are advised to avoid jumping to conclusions regarding an Indian client's cultural competence on the basis of how light or dark the client's hair, skin, and eyes are. As a result of Indian removal and the inappropriate placement of Indian children with non-Indians before the Indian Child Welfare Act, many with high blood quanta grew up isolated from their Native culture. Conversely, other Native people with lower blood quanta may have grown up on a reservation or in an urban Indian community and be much more traditional than they "look."

Although traditional American Indian and mainstream psychological treatments may differ, they share a primary goal: changing the way the client thinks. If one's negative and dysfunctional thoughts can be changed, so too will one's feelings and behaviors change. In this way, harmony is restored between mind, body, and spirit. The following case highlights the degree to which traditional treatments and CBT may differ, but the two approaches can be complementary and their goals the same.

CASE EXAMPLE

Billy[1] was a 45-year-old American Indian from a Northern Plains tribe. He was divorced and unemployed despite being a qualified and bonded electrician. He was a combat veteran who had completed two tours in Vietnam, with the second being voluntary. At the time of this assessment, he was receiving veterans' benefits, having been deemed fully service-connected disabled and diagnosed with PTSD. Billy reported graduating from high school on his home reservation. He had been physically and verbally abused by a stepfather in high school and had been in trouble for truancy, alcohol violations, fighting, and vandalism, for which he served a total of 1 year in juvenile detention centers and local jails. He could identify no close relatives

---

[1]Case material in this chapter has been disguised to protect client confidentiality.

with psychiatric disorders and had always been healthy and fit. He had never received psychological or psychiatric services, and none had been offered or court ordered. A judge (as was not uncommon during this period) had given him the choice of an extended jail sentence or enlistment in the military during the Vietnam War.

Following Marine Corps basic training in San Diego in 1969, Billy was stationed with a unit responsible for providing reconnaissance and fire support for an Army contingent seeking to engage Viet Cong soldiers and identify collaborators. Billy had difficulty speaking about some of the encounters he had survived, and there were others he could not bring himself to articulate. It is unnecessary to describe Billy's accounts graphically. Suffice it to say they were often horrific, and over the course of the 8 weeks of treatment, his description of the depth and scope of what he had endured was astonishing.

Honorably discharged in 1972, Billy spent several years "drifting around" southern California working sporadically as a day laborer for area produce farmers. He reported difficulty sleeping because of intrusive images, racing thoughts, and combat-related nightmares. He began drinking heavily "just to knock myself out; to sleep so I could work more." He found himself becoming increasingly dependent on alcohol and began experiencing flashbacks during the day. The flashbacks involved vivid visual, auditory, tactile, olfactory, and even gustatory sensations connected to his combat experiences. He also began to experience overwhelming feelings of survivor guilt and anger at America's anti-Vietnam War sentiment. Those with long memories can remember how poorly Vietnam veterans were treated on their return home. In Billy's case, he felt ostracized and shunned whenever it became known that he had served in the war.

On his return to the reservation several years after his discharge, Billy fell even deeper into a pattern of alcohol and drug abuse, violence, and general antisocial behavior. He shunned the attention of elders and Native healers who attempted to advise him regarding healing ceremonies and rituals. He spent time solely with other veterans, many of whom were experiencing similar symptoms and thus were in similar situations. He was admitted to the psychiatric unit of the regional veterans hospital six times for suicidal ideation and two suicide attempts.

Finally, Billy's behavior tailspin landed him in the state penitentiary for 2 years for aggravated assault. While incarcerated, Billy was befriended by an older veteran who spoke of the "Red Road" approach to healing and living. He learned that walking (i.e., living in accordance with) the Red Road meant embracing his spirituality and traditional values. The Red Road is a "holistic approach to spiritual, mental, physical, and emotional wellness based upon Native American healing concepts and traditions" that uses prayer as the basis of all healing (Gene Thin Elk, 1994, as cited in Arbogast, 1995, p. 319).

On his release from prison, Billy completed an electrician's apprenticeship and worked for 2 years for a mining company in Montana. He reported this as the most productive and positive period of his life, yet he soon began experiencing again the flashbacks, nightmares, and subsequent emotional and social disruptions that had haunted him previously. Ultimately, his employer referred him for therapy through the company's employee assistance program at which point I (McDonald) met him.

Assessment

Following a diagnostic interview, it was determined that Billy was of sufficient bicultural orientation and competence to be administered standardized psychological measures. As suggested previously, we contend that determining an American Indian client's degree of cultural orientation and competence is crucial (McDonald, Morton, & Stewart, 1992). If it had been determined that Billy's cultural identity was traditional or marginal, the use of standardized psychological tests might have been deemed inappropriate.

Billy was administered the Beck Depression Inventory–II (BDI-II; Beck, Steer, & Brown, 1996), the State–Trait Anxiety Inventory (STAI; Spielberger, Gorsuch, & Lushene, 1970), and the AIBI. The AIBI, which we developed, yields subscale scores for American Indian and European American cultural orientations. A median-split technique allows for placement of the individual into one of the four cultural quadrants defined by the orthogonal theory of biculturalism. As might be expected, Billy's scores on the BDI-II and STAI were clinically elevated, and his AIBI scores suggested he was culturally competent in both his own Native and the majority culture. Some authors have suggested using measures of cultural orientation to moderate standardized testing scores (Dana, 2000). This suggestion is intriguing, but there is not currently sufficient research to demonstrate its efficacy. In our view, whether standardized test scores may be moderated by cultural competence or not, their use with traditionally or marginally oriented American Indians is highly questionable.

From the results of the testing and interview, it was determined that Billy was experiencing PTSD. It is at this point that we emphasize the importance of multicultural competence. In working with American Indians, therapists should become fully knowledgeable about the tribes in their area of practice and are encouraged to befriend tribal members in a sincere effort to learn more. This thoughtful and proactive approach to obtaining cross-cultural knowledge and experience for the good of one's practice is strongly encouraged. In this instance, it was known that Billy's worldview contained strong Native values, evident in his upbringing and his positive response to the Red Road approach. This information was as vital as his psychological testing scores.

Treatment

Billy's high degree of bicultural competence was a key determinant of his treatment plan. With his high degree of orientation toward and affiliation with the majority culture, he appeared to be a good candidate for CBT. However, his traditional competence suggested that therapy would also have to incorporate his Native values. Thus, the Takes Life ceremony was considered.

Most American Indian tribes with significant histories of battle and intertribal conflict practice some form of the Takes Life ceremony. (The name of the ceremony has been changed but is generally described later in terms of historical significance and process. This is in accordance with a declaration passed by Lakota spiritual leaders at the Lakota Summit V, aimed at protecting the privacy and preventing the exploitation of American Indian spiritual and ceremonial practices; Mesteth, Standing Elk, & Swift Hawk, 1993.) The intent of these ceremonies is to ease the adjustment of a warrior who has taken the life of an enemy in battle. As discussed previously, Hollywood and other popular media have painted a distorted picture of American Indians in many ways, perhaps most notably in terms of war. By and large, armed and lethal conflict was avoided, and ritualistic and symbolic confrontation was preferred. The practice of "counting coup" was considered more honorable and courageous than actually killing an enemy. When counting coup, a warrior would charge an enemy warrior and touch or strike him with a "coup stick" or their bow and escape unharmed. Only in the most extreme circumstances, such as competition for territory or other resources, were lives taken. The elders knew that although killing enhanced the reputation of the warrior, it also took a heavy psychological toll.

The Takes Life ceremony involves some manner of individual treatment from a spiritual healer, who uses a combination of herbal medicines, songs, prayers, and other sacred procedures. There is a purification process and, in some tribes, prayer for the spirit of the one killed and his family. These ceremonies often end by calling together the warrior's family and friends and having another veteran, such as the one who witnessed the taking of the life, recount the specifics of the fight and the bravery of the warrior. The "narrator" or "testifier" proclaims such points as "I know, I saw, I was there. Here is what I saw my brother do. He is brave—honor him." In the end, the crowd accepts this, and often there is an honor song and everyone dances in an ever-closing circle toward the warrior. At the conclusion of the song, he is embraced, and there are war cries from other veterans and ululations from the women. The Takes Life ceremony is a perfect example of how a collectivist society helps heal an individual.

On consultation with a spiritual advisor from Billy's tribe, a Takes Life ceremony was arranged during the upcoming Veterans Day *Wacipi* (powwow). Billy was introduced to the medicine man, who began a series of individual traditional treatments (which were private and therefore unknown to me). Billy also engaged in individual CBT for PTSD and chemical dependency counseling, and he started on an antidepressant medication following a psychiatric consultation.

The CBT consisted of 12 weekly sessions, primarily focused on cognitive restructuring as described by McMullin (1998). This approach is multifaceted and includes education, training, and practice. For the education component, Billy was given extensive reading and video materials describing PTSD and its treatment. The training phase included systematic identification and revision of Billy's typical negative thoughts combined with deep muscle relaxation and guided imagery. The goal of these sessions was to encourage Billy to cognitively experience some of the difficult memories and images he had encountered, while remaining deeply relaxed. As will be seen in the following section, a countering cognitive restructuring focus was used. Billy was asked to practice and log all homework exercises, which were gradually increased in frequency over the 12 weeks. He was also administered the BDI-II and STAI every 2 weeks to monitor symptom remission.

Cognitive Behavior Therapy Session 1

The first session is by far the most significant one for the therapist and the Indian client because it is during this session that the client decides whether to trust the therapist and engage in the treatment process. The competent therapist, regardless of cultural background, will ask (as the first author did with Billy) many questions about the client's family and family history. The therapist will focus as much on the ground as on the figure and make it clear he or she understands that this person's social context is key in understanding what the client perceives to be "wrong" (see McDonald et al., 1992). Because I am of the same tribal group as Billy, the therapeutic connection was more easily attained. Also, in this initial session, Billy's bicultural competence was clarified, and he was encouraged to reconnect with a traditional healer.

An initial goal of this first session of CBT was to explain the basic principles and process of cognitive restructuring. Kanfer's (1998) description of the components of CBT is helpful in this regard. The first of these is the idea that "the thoughts that occur most frequently are those we tend to believe." A corollary to this is "when a client argues against an irrational thought repeatedly, the irrational thought becomes progressively weaker" (McMullin,

1998, p. 3). The cognitive restructuring process can be drawn as a triangle with thoughts, feelings, and behaviors located at the three points. Examples of the client's negative schema are then elicited and applied to illustrate how the client's negative cognitions fuel his emotional distress and maladaptive behaviors. The process for changing this pattern, along with image-laden metaphors, such as "making the engine run smoother," gives the client an idea of what to expect. At this point, Billy was excused with a homework assignment to return the next week with a list of five of his most common negative self-statements and 10 sincere, rational positive attributes formed into statements.

Session 2

The first part of this session was used to review Billy's homework. Billy and the therapist then engaged in role playing, with the therapist reading the negative self-statements to Billy and Billy countering each with the entire list of positive attributes. Billy was asked to practice the list of positive attributes twice daily before the next session.

Billy was also introduced to relaxation therapy with guided imagery. Deep breathing was used for the induction, followed by the strategy of tensing and relaxing each muscle group. Once relaxed, Billy was asked to cognitively visit a calm scene from either his memory or his own creation. An audiotape of the session was made, and Billy was also assigned daily relaxation practice as homework.

At this point, it was also important to monitor the client's efforts toward spiritual healing. Therapists do not have to be fully knowledgeable about the traditional healing rituals and ceremonies being practiced. Instead, their role is to ensure they are occurring, to monitor their impact on the client, and to learn as much as possible in the process. In Billy's case that effort took the following form:

McDonald: So, how's it going with Ralph [the healer, different name]?

Billy: Oh, pretty good.

McDonald: How did you guys hook up?

Billy: I went out to his place the other night. He was working some horses [pauses].

McDonald: What did you do?

Billy: I offered him some tobacco [a traditional show of respect] and asked if I could talk to him. He asked me some questions first, then said "yes" and took the tobacco.

McDonald:	Great, so what's going to happen from here?
Billy:	He wants to have an *inipi* [sweat-lodge ceremony] tonight and on Tuesdays. He said when he finds out what's wrong he'll know better.

As this brief exchange indicates, cultural knowledge is important in understanding even the smallest amounts of information (e.g., that the offering of tobacco was a demonstration of respect). Cultural knowledge also helps the therapist to know what to ask (e.g., how the connection with the healer was going) and what not to ask (details about the healer's practice).

Sessions 3 Through 8

The focus of these sessions was on practicing and expanding the treatment elements and monitoring the traditional healing efforts and their effects. We began every session by reviewing the homework in terms of content and practice during the week. The role playing became more intensive because Billy had memorized the list of positive attributes by Week 3 and could counter negative statements more easily and with greater enthusiasm. His home practice of the list-recall task was increased by one session each week during this phase.

The relaxation sessions also increased in length and time spent in guided imagery. As clients become more skilled at self-induction, more effort can be spent guiding them through specific scenarios related to the traumatic incidents with which they struggle. In Billy's case, we revisited some of the scenes he had endured while in combat. As a form of systematic desensitization, Billy was gradually guided to reexperience some of the more distressing encounters he endured, while remaining relaxed and retreating to his calm scene when necessary. Each relaxation session was terminated after several minutes in the calm scene.

Billy also participated diligently in the traditional healing regimen. He signed a release allowing for communication between the therapist and the healer that facilitated the flow of communication regarding his case. This practice is strongly suggested both as a show of respect for traditional healers and as a means for less experienced non-Indian therapists to become more competent regarding traditional practices.

Sessions 9 Through 12

Most therapists would agree that the therapy termination process should be considerately and respectfully managed, and this is equally true with Native clients whatever their cultural orientation. Traditional Indian clients may offer a gift to the therapist if the treatment has been beneficial to them. We suggest you accept. To do otherwise is seen as disrespectful in many Native cultures.

By this point, Billy was accomplished at self-monitoring his negative thoughts and their subsequent effects on his affect and behavior. His "list of positives" began to occur more frequently in his mind than the negatives, and he expanded them to include positive self-statements aimed at building his confidence in coping with the troubling memories. He was able to relax more readily with each session and home practice and to induce a relaxation response when negative images or impulses occurred. Eventually the latter decreased in intensity and frequency. These improvements encouraged him to discuss his experiences with others, including other veterans and his family and friends, for which he received a great deal of support.

Billy completed the treatment plan within the 12-week time frame. The Takes Life ceremony took place during Week 10, which allowed several weeks of debriefing and processing before termination. Billy's final STAI and BDI-II scores were in the nonclinically elevated range, and although he admitted to "thinking about" his experiences in Vietnam, he described them as "only bad memories now, not nightmares." He continued his sessions with his medicine man and participated in traditional ceremonies on a regular basis for years afterward. On 6-month follow-up, Billy had experienced no recurrences of the flashbacks or nightmares that had plagued him. He was sober and still employed.

CONCLUSION

We hope this case study illustrates our firm contention that cultural orientation should always be considered when working with American Indian clients and research participants. Billy's successful treatment illustrates several important issues in this regard. First, therapists should become as cross-culturally competent as possible, particularly when they know they will be working with ethnic minorities or those different from themselves. Second, part of that competence should include the ability to measure the level of bicultural competence in a client and incorporate it into all aspects of diagnosis and treatment. Finally, CBT can be an effective treatment modality for American Indians, particularly if the client displays high degrees of bicultural or assimilated cultural competence. Those Indian clients who are more traditional or marginal may not respond as readily and may prefer more traditional treatments. We admit that case studies of one do not provide much in terms of external validity; however, they can provide guidance and help to clarify ideas for empirically based research.

We began this chapter speaking of differences and misunderstandings. We close with some straightforward and hopeful suggestions toward reconciliation and clarity. You do not have to "go Native" to help one! And that goes for psychology as a field. There are reasons why (despite the increases we documented previously) still too little empirical research exists on the effectiveness of CBT (or anything else) with American Indians. One of the biggest reasons is that training more ethnic minorities and more American Indians, in particular, has not been a high priority. Doing so would require departments and training programs to shift their academic worldviews. Many have been unwilling to make this shift, whereas some have shifted a little, and few have shifted significantly. The face of psychology is still White, and so are its values and priorities. As long as this situation remains, empirically based cross-cultural enlightenment will dance away outside our reach, for we know that to dance together we must first take each other's hands.

REFERENCES

Allen, J., & French, C. (1994). *Northern Plains Biculturalism Inventory: A preliminary manual*. Unpublished manuscript, University of South Dakota, Vermillion.

Allen, J., & French, C. (1996). *Northern Plains Bicultural Immersion Scale: Preliminary manual and scoring instructions* (Version 5). Vermillion: University of South Dakota.

American Psychological Association. (2017). *Multicultural guidelines: An ecological approach to context, identity, and intersectionality*. Retrieved from http://www.apa.org/about/policy/multicultural-guidelines.pdf

Anderson, M., & Ellis, R. (1995). On the reservation. In N. Vacc & S. DeVaney (Eds.), *Experiencing and counseling multicultural and diverse populations* (pp. 179–197). Muncie, IN: Accelerated Development.

Arbogast, D. (1995). *Wounded warriors: A time for healing*. Omaha, NE: Little Turtle Publications.

Bates, S. C., Beauvais, F., & Trimble, J. E. (1997). American Indian adolescent alcohol involvement and ethnic identification. *Substance Use & Misuse, 32*, 2013–2031. http://dx.doi.org/10.3109/10826089709035617

Beals, J., Manson, S. M., Mitchell, C. M., & Spicer, P. (2003). Cultural specificity and comparison in psychiatric epidemiology: Walking the tightrope in American Indian research. *Culture, Medicine and Psychiatry, 27*, 259–289. http://dx.doi.org/10.1023/A:1025347130953

Beals, J., Spicer, P., Mitchell, C. M., Novins, D. K., & Manson, S. M. (2003). Racial disparities in alcohol use: Comparison of 2 American Indian reservation populations with national data. *American Journal of Public Health, 93*, 1683–1685. http://dx.doi.org/10.2105/AJPH.93.10.1683

Beck, A. T., Steer, R. A., & Brown, G. K. (1996). *Manual for the Beck Depression Inventory–II.* San Antonio, TX: Psychological Corporation.

Benson, E. (2003, June). Psychology in Indian country. *Monitor on Psychology, 34,* 56–57.

BigFoot, D. S., & Schmidt, S. R. (2010). Honoring children, mending the circle: Cultural adaptation of trauma-focused cognitive-behavioral therapy for American Indian and Alaska Native children. *Journal of Clinical Psychology, 66,* 847–856. http://dx.doi.org/10.1002/jclp.20707

Chavez Cameron, S., & Turtle-Song, I. (2003). Native American mental health: An examination of resiliency in the face of overwhelming odds. In F. Harper & J. McFadden (Eds.), *Culture and counseling: New approaches* (pp. 66–80). Boston, MA: Allyn & Bacon/Pearson Education.

Choney, S. K., Berryhill-Paapke, E., & Robbins, R. R. (1995). The acculturation of American Indians. In J. G. Ponterotto, J. M. Casas, L. A. Suzuki, & C. M. Alexander (Eds.), *Handbook of multicultural counseling* (pp. 73–92). Thousand Oaks, CA: Sage.

Collier, J. (1947). *The Indians of the Americas.* New York, NY: Norton.

Colmant, S., & Merta, R. (1999). Using the sweat lodge ceremony as group therapy for Navajo youth. *Journal for Specialists in Group Work, 24,* 55–73. http://dx.doi.org/10.1080/01933929908411419

Cross, T. L. (2003). Culture as a resource for mental health. *Cultural Diversity and Ethnic Minority Psychology, 9,* 354–359. http://dx.doi.org/10.1037/1099-9809.9.4.354

Dana, R. H. (2000). *Handbook of cross-cultural and multicultural personality assessment.* Mahwah, NJ: Erlbaum.

Dehyle, D. (1992). Constructing failure and cultural identity: Navajo and Ute school leavers. *Journal of American Indian Education, 32,* 24–27.

Duran, E., & Duran, B. (1995). *Native American postcolonial psychology.* Albany: State University of New York Press.

Edwards, E. D., & Smith, L. L. (1979). A brief history of American Indian social policy. *Journal of Humanics, 7,* 52–64.

Faragher, J., Buhle, M., Czitrom, D., & Armitage, S. (2000). *Out of many: A history of the American people.* Englewood Cliffs, NJ: Prentice Hall.

Fleming, C. M. (1992). American Indians and Alaska Natives: Changing societies past and present. In M. A. Orlandi, R. Weston, & L. G. Epstein (Eds.), *Cultural competence for evaluators: A guide for alcohol and other drug abuse prevention practitioners working with ethnic/racial communities* (pp. 147–171). Rockville, MD: Office for Substance Abuse Prevention.

Garrett, M. T., & Pichette, E. F. (2000). Red as an apple: Native American acculturation and counseling with or without reservation. *Journal of Counseling & Development, 78,* 3–13. http://dx.doi.org/10.1002/j.1556-6676.2000.tb02554.x

Gone, J. (2004). Mental health services for Native Americans in the 21st century United States. *Professional Psychology: Research and Practice, 35*, 10–18. http://dx.doi.org/10.1037/0735-7028.35.1.10

Gonzalez, J., & Bennett, R. (2000, February). *Self-identity in the indigenous peoples of North America: Factor structure and correlates*. Poster presented at the annual meeting of the Society for Personality and Social Psychology, Nashville, TN.

Haozous, E. A., Doorenbos, A. Z., & Stoner, S. (2016). Pain management experiences and the acceptability of cognitive behavioral strategies among American Indians and Alaska Natives. *Journal of Transcultural Nursing, 27*, 233–240. http://dx.doi.org/10.1177/1043659614558454

Heilbron, C., & Guttman, M. (2000). Traditional healing methods with First Nations women in group counseling. *Canadian Journal of Counselling, 34*, 3–13.

Herring, R. D. (1999). *Counseling with Native American Indians and Alaska Natives: Strategies for helping professionals*. Thousand Oaks, CA: Sage.

Jackson, A. P., & Turner, S. (2004). Counseling and psychotherapy with Native American clients. In T. Smith (Ed.), *Practicing multiculturalism: Affirming diversity in counseling and psychology* (pp. 215–233). Boston, MA: Allyn & Bacon/ Pearson Education.

Kanfer, G. (1998). *Guiding the process of therapeutic change*. Champaign, IL: Research Press.

Kessler, R. C., Sonnega, A., Bromet, E., Hughes, M., & Nelson, C. B. (1995). Posttraumatic stress disorder in the National Comorbidity Survey. *Archives of General Psychiatry, 52*, 1048–1060. http://dx.doi.org/10.1001/ archpsyc.1995.03950240066012

LaDuke, W. (1999). *All our relations: Native struggles for land and life*. Cambridge, MA: South End Press.

LaFromboise, T., Trimble, J. E., & Mohatt, G. V. (1990). Counseling intervention and American Indian tradition: An integrative approach. *The Counseling Psychologist, 18*, 628–654. http://dx.doi.org/10.1177/0011000090184006

Listug-Lunde, L., Vogeltanz-Holm, N., & Collins, J. (2013). A cognitive-behavioral treatment for depression in rural American Indian middle school students. *American Indian and Alaska Native Mental Health Research, 20*(1), 16–34. http:// dx.doi.org/10.5820/aian.2001.2013.16

Matsumoto, D. (2000). *Culture and psychology: People around the world*. New York, NY: Wadsworth.

May, P. A., & Moran, J. R. (1995). Prevention of alcohol misuse: A review of health promotion efforts among American Indians. *American Journal of Health Promotion, 9*, 288–299. http://dx.doi.org/10.4278/0890-1171-9.4.288

McDonald, J. D. (1994). New frontiers in clinical training: The UND Indians into Psychology Doctoral Education (InPsyDE) Program. *American Indian and Alaska Native Mental Health Research, 5*(3), 52–56. http://dx.doi.org/10.5820/ aian.0503.1994.52

McDonald, J. D. (1998). Completing the circle: Indian health training. *Federal Practitioner, 4*, 22–38.

McDonald, J. D., Morton, R., & Stewart, C. (1992). Clinical issues with American Indian patients. *Innovations in Clinical Practice, 12*, 437–454.

McDonald, J. D., Ross, R., & Rose, W. (2016, August). *The American Indian Biculturalism Inventory—Northern Plains.* Poster session presented at the meeting of the American Psychological Association, Denver, CO.

McMullin, R. (1998). *Handbook of cognitive therapy techniques.* New York, NY: Norton.

Mesteth, W. S., Standing Elk, D., & Swift Hawk, P. (1993). *Lakota declare war against "shamans" & "plastics."* Retrieved from http://www.thepeoplespaths.net/articles/ladecwar.htm

Meyer, M. L. (1994). *The White Earth tragedy: Ethnicity and dispossession at a Minnesota Anishinaabe reservation.* Lincoln: University of Nebraska Press.

Mitchell, C. M., Beals, J., Novins, D. K., & Spicer, P. (2003). Drug use among two American Indian populations: Prevalence of lifetime use and DSM–IV substance use disorders. *Drug and Alcohol Dependence, 69*, 29–41. http://dx.doi.org/10.1016/S0376-8716(02)00253-3

Moran, J. R., Fleming, C. M., Somervell, P., & Manson, S. M. (1999). Measuring bicultural ethnic identity among American Indian adolescents: A factor analytic study. *Journal of Adolescent Research, 14*, 405–426. http://dx.doi.org/10.1177/0743558499144002

Morsette, A., van den Pol, R., Schuldberg, D., Swaney, G., & Stolle, D. (2012). Cognitive behavioral treatment for trauma symptoms in American Indian youth: Preliminary findings and issues in evidence-based practice and reservation culture. *Advances in School Mental Health Promotion, 5*, 51–62. http://dx.doi.org/10.1080/1754730X.2012.664865

Novins, D. K., Croy, C. D., Moore, L. A., & Rieckmann, T. (2016). Use of evidence-based treatments in substance abuse treatment programs serving American Indian and Alaska Native communities. *Drug and Alcohol Dependence, 161*, 214–221. http://dx.doi.org/10.1016/j.drugalcdep.2016.02.007

Oetting, E. R., & Beauvais, F. (1990–1991). Orthogonal cultural identification theory: The cultural identification of minority adolescents. *International Journal of the Addictions, 25*, 655–685. http://dx.doi.org/10.3109/10826089109077265

Page, J. (2003). *In the hands of the Great Spirit: The 20,000-year history of American Indians.* New York, NY: Free Press.

Renfrey, G. S. (1992). Cognitive behavior therapy and the Native American client. *Behavior Therapy, 23*, 321–340. http://dx.doi.org/10.1016/S0005-7894(05)80161-3

Snipp, C. M. (1996). The size and distribution of the American Indian population: Fertility, mortality, residence, and migration. In G. Sandefur, R. Rindfuss, & B. Cohen (Eds.), *Changing numbers, changing needs: American Indian demography and public health* (pp. 17–52). Washington, DC: National Academy Press.

Spielberger, C. D., Gorsuch, R. L., & Lushene, R. D. (1970). *Manual for the State–Trait Anxiety Inventory*. Palo Alto, CA: Consulting Psychologists Press.

Sue, D. W., & Sue, D. (1999). *Counseling the culturally different*. New York, NY: Wiley.

Suicide Prevention Resource Center. (2011). *Suicide among racial/ethnic populations in the U.S.: American Indians/Alaska Natives*. Newton, MA: Education Development Center, Inc. Retrieved from http://www.sprc.org/resources-programs/suicide-among-racialethnic-populations-us-american-indiansalaska-natives

Swinomish Tribal Community. (1991). *A gathering of wisdoms; Tribal mental health: A cultural perspective*. La Conner, WA: Author.

Triandis, H. C. (Ed.). (1994). *New directions in social psychology: Individualism and collectivism*. Boulder, CO: Westview Press.

Trimble, J. E. (1992). A cognitive behavior approach to drug abuse prevention and intervention with American Indian youth. In L. A. Vargas & J. D. Koss (Eds.), *Working with culture: Psychotherapeutic interventions with ethnic minority children and adolescents* (pp. 246–275). San Francisco, CA: Jossey-Bass.

Trimble, J. E., & Thurman, P. (2002). Ethnocultural considerations and strategies for providing counseling services for Native American Indians. In P. B. Pedersen, J. G. Draguns, W. J. Lonner, & J. E. Trimble (Eds.), *Counseling across cultures* (5th ed., pp. 53–91). Thousand Oaks, CA: Sage.

U.S. Census Bureau. (2010). *Census of the population: General population characteristics, American Indians and Alaska Natives areas, 2010*. Washington, DC: Government Printing Office.

U.S. Census Bureau. (2012). *The American Indian and Alaska Native Population: 2010*. Retrieved from https://www.census.gov/history/pdf/c2010br-10.pdf

2

COGNITIVE BEHAVIOR THERAPY WITH ALASKA NATIVE PEOPLE

PAMELA A. HAYS

Although American Indians and Alaska Natives comprise about 1% of the U.S. population, in Alaska (which has a total population of about 739,000), 15% of the state's population identifies as American Indian or Alaska Native alone. Another 7% identifies as belonging to one Alaska Native tribe or culture and another Native or non-Native race (U.S. Census Bureau, 2017). In my experience working in the community mental health system, tribal health system, and private practice for 18 years, it would be highly unusual for an Alaskan therapist to not work with Native people. In the smaller villages, Alaska Native people are the majority of the population, and even in the largest city, one in 13 Anchorage residents are Alaska Native (Dunham, 2016). Outside Alaska, therapists may also encounter Alaska Native clients, particularly in the Pacific Northwest.

The author is grateful to E. J. R. David for his feedback regarding this chapter.

http://dx.doi.org/10.1037/0000119-003
Culturally Responsive Cognitive Behavior Therapy, Second Edition: Practice and Supervision, G. Y. Iwamasa and P. A. Hays (Editors)

Empirically based psychological research regarding psychotherapy and Indigenous people, in general, is limited, and even more so regarding Alaska Native people. In a review of the empirical evidence for psychotherapeutic treatments with Indigenous Australians, Canadians, Pacific Islanders, New Zealand Maori, American Indians, and Alaska Natives, only 44 studies were found (Pomerville, Burrage, & Gone, 2016). Of these 44 studies, only two were with Alaska Native people: one on "therapeutic community retention" (Fisher, Lankford, & Galea, 1996) and one on Alaska Native college students' preferences for mental health treatment options (Stewart, Swift, Freitas-Murrell, & Whipple, 2013).

In my search, I found a few additional studies. These included articles on the benefits of discussing suicide with Alaska Native college students (DeCou, Skewes, López, & Skanis, 2013), the prediction of Alaska Natives' attitudes toward seeking professional psychological help (Freitas-Murrell & Swift, 2015), the Yup'ik understanding of stress in the context of rapid cultural change (Rivkin et al., 2017), the assessment of health using a wellness survey developed with and for Yup'ik people (Lardon, Wolsko, Trickett, Henry, & Hopkins, 2016), the influence of Alaska Native therapists' accent and reputation on perceived therapist credibility (Swift, Mayra, Justice, & Freitas-Murrell, 2015), and protective factors for alcohol abuse and suicide prevention among Alaska Native youth (Allen, Mohatt, Fok, Henry, & Burkett, 2014). In addition to these articles, two books have been written regarding psychotherapy with Alaska Native people: *Counseling the Iñupiat Eskimo* (Swan Reimer, 1999) and *With the Wind and the Waves* (Droby, 2000).

Other than this chapter, I know of no other published research regarding cognitive behavior therapy (CBT) with Alaska Natives. For this reason, I include information drawn from my own experiences and the experiences of other Native and non-Native therapists working with Alaska Native people. I also include references that are not specifically on CBT with Alaska Natives but are relevant to understanding such work. Because Alaska Native communities are so small, I describe only composite case studies that represent real situations but no real person.

OVERVIEW OF ALASKA NATIVE CULTURES

Native people in Alaska have many of the same experiences and values held by other Indigenous people—for example, historical and current colonization and domination by European and European American populations, an emphasis on the importance of family and spirituality, respect for the earth and all living beings, and connection to one's particular geographical origins.

However, the history and experience of Alaska Native people are also unique in many ways. The following section describes this unique history, including information regarding religion, political events, cultural identity, living conditions, and the impact of climate change.

Early History

As noted in the preceding chapter on American Indians, many Alaska Native people have creation stories that place their origins in the land now known as Alaska (e.g., see Kawagley, 2006). According to Langdon (2002), most archeologists believe that sometime between 50,000 and 15,000 years ago, humans began migrating from Siberia to western Alaska across vast Arctic grasslands that existed when sea levels were much lower. These archeologists also believe that the ancestors of Alaska Natives living today migrated to Alaska more recently, between 10,000 and 5,000 years ago, possibly in an initial wave of Indians and a later wave of Eskaleuts. These early ancestors followed a traditional way of life that is now called *subsistence*.

Although the term *subsistence* is currently used by the dominant culture as a synonym for hunting and fishing rights, Native people commonly define it more broadly to include the traditional worldview and lifestyle. In the Yup'ik language, the word for this worldview and lifestyle is *yuuyaraq* (Napoleon, 1996), which Kawagley (2006) defined as a complex way of life involving specific mandates that dictate correct behavior between human beings and correct ways of thinking and speaking about all living things. Cooperation and sharing are central, and respectful attitudes, speech, and behavior help to ensure harmony and balance within and between the human, natural, and spiritual realms (Fienup-Riordan, 2000b). The exceptional awareness of one's surroundings that is inherent in this worldview has enabled Native people to survive in and adapt to extremely harsh and continually changing environmental conditions (Fienup-Riordan, 1990, as cited in Kawagley, 2006).

Before Western contact, the Yup'iit believed that following the principles of *yuuyaraq* ensured their survival. However, the arrival of Russian and European explorers turned this belief on end when an influenza epidemic to which the people had no immunity killed an estimated 60% of the Alaska Native population (Napoleon, 1996). Subsequent famine, starvation, and epidemics of measles, chickenpox, polio, and tuberculosis overpowered the efforts of the shamans who had previously been considered the spiritual leaders and healers. In the confusion, shock, and despair that followed, the people abandoned their old beliefs and were more inclined to accept those of the Christian missionaries who promised salvation and deliverance (Napoleon, 1996).

Religion

Despite the colonialist roots of Christianity in Alaska, the current relationship between Alaska Natives and the Church is complex (Fienup-Riordan, 2000b, p. 137). In February 2017, the Presbyterian church issued an official apology to the Native people of the North Slope of Alaska (Townsend, 2017). In southwestern Alaska, using the example of the Catholic Church, Fienup-Riordan (2000b) observed that the incorporation of Yup'ik traditions and concepts into Catholicism benefits both the Church, which becomes more relevant to people's lives, and the Yup'ik people, through support of the revitalization of Yup'ik traditions (e.g., naming ceremonies in baptisms, dancing, drumming, purification rituals). Whatever therapists' personal beliefs, it is important to recognize that Christianity plays a powerful role in the lives of many Alaska Natives today. In rural areas, in particular, religion often provides emotional, social, and spiritual support and at times even financial help.

Political Events

In the last century, Alaska Native people experienced extraordinary sociocultural changes, including a number of political events that continue to affect their lives today. Boarding schools led to the devaluing of Native languages and traditions, including parenting practices, subsistence knowledge, and survival and coping skills. It was not until 1976 (much later than in the Lower 48) that a lawsuit brought by a Yup'ik student (*Hootch v. Alaska State-Operated School System*, 1975; commonly known as the Molly Hootch decree) forced the state to support the rights of students to be educated in their home villages.

Alaska Natives did not become U.S. citizens until 1924, despite the status of Alaska as a U.S. territory since 1867. "White only" signs were present in the state's capital as recently as the 1940s (McClanahan & Bissett, 2002). The development of the Alaska–Canadian highway during the war opened the way for thousands of non-Native people to move to the state and quickly outnumber Native people.

On obtaining statehood in 1958, the state was granted 104 million acres by the federal government and began filing claims to some of Alaska Natives' most important land. The discovery of oil in 1968 led to increased pressure from state legislators and oil developers to resolve the conflicting claims. The Alaska Federation of Natives was formed during this time to fight for Native claims. In 1971, the Alaska Native Claims Settlement Act (ANCSA) was passed. At the time, the losses from the Act seemed greater than the gains (Native people received only about one tenth of Alaska's 3.75 million acres and a capped sum of $1 billion for all lands given up, with several structural problems embedded in the Act). The subsequent financial successes of many of the Native corporations have, however, opened doors for many people (Haycox, 2002), but because not all of the corporations allow for enrollment of people born after 1971, a growing number of Alaska Native people do not receive shares or benefit from these successes.

Impact of Climate Change

Alaska has been called the "canary in the coal mine" regarding the global effects of climate change. In many parts of Alaska, the temperature is on average 4°F hotter, and because this is an average, it means that it is often much hotter. Even small changes in temperature, especially in the far north, contribute to catastrophic wildfires in summer, a decline in snow and ice in the winter, and destructively strong wind patterns. In addition, the following changes are taking place on an ongoing basis:

- disappearing sea ice, which threatens the survival of polar bears and other marine mammals;
- thawed permafrost, which makes the ground unstable, throwing off the foundation of homes and causing the "drunken forests," in which trees lean over because the ground does not hold them firmly in place;
- melting glaciers and eroding shorelines;
- warmer water, which affects the habitat and survival of fish populations; and
- the infestation of pests such as the spruce bark beetle as far south as the Kenai Peninsula (my home community), where it has killed 50% of the forested land on 1.2 million acres (Alaska Department of Natural Resources, Division of Forestry, 2016; Alaska Native Science Commission, n.d.).

The coastline of Alaska is greater than all the other lower 48 states' coastlines combined (Beaver, 2006), and because many Native villages are located on the Alaskan coast, they are affected directly by rising sea levels. Thawing permafrost and ice has led to the loss of clean water, saltwater intrusion, and sewage contamination. Rivers previously frozen in winter and used as roads are now too dangerous for travel. The northward expansion of diseases threatens Arctic animals and plants that Native people rely on for food, and shrinking sea ice makes hunting more dangerous and also affects the availability of animals and fish (U.S. Environmental Protection Agency, 2017).

One of the most widely reported examples of a community's threatened survival is the Iñupiaq village of Shishmaref, located on a sand island in northwest Alaska and accessible only by air and sea. In her book *Early*

Warming: Crisis and Response in the Climate-Changed North, Nancy Lord (2011) described the effects of warming on this village. Erosion is eating away at the airstrip, sea ice no longer blocks the severe winter storms, and thawing permafrost has made the land unstable. In 1997, a storm took 125 feet from the island's shoreline and dropped buildings into the sea. And Shishmaref is not the only village that is being destroyed by climate changes. According to a Government Accountability Office report, Shishmaref is one of six villages listed as requiring "immediate action," and another 184 villages are being affected by erosion and flooding (Lord, 2011, p. 142).

Over the ages, Alaska Native people have excelled in finding ways to adapt and survive in a harsh environment, and in response to climate change, they are continuing to do so. For example, the Alaska Native Tribal Health Consortium (2017) has a climate change program called the LEO (Local Environmental Observer) Network which connects local Native observers and topic experts to document and increase understanding of significant, unusual, or unprecedented environmental events in local communities. The network uses web-accessible maps containing descriptions, photos, expert consultations, and links to information resources and is available to the world (see https://toolkit.climate.gov/tool/local-environmental-observer-leo-network).

Similarly, the Inuit Circumpolar Council–Alaska (2016), part of the International Inuit Circumpolar Council, "seeks to connect the world with Alaska Inuit (Iñupiaq, Yup'ik, Cup'ik, and St. Lawrence Island Yup'ik)" people (para. 1), through work that prioritizes, among other things, using Indigenous knowledge and encouraging sustainable economic development in the Arctic. For more on how Alaska Native people are contributing to the world's knowledge base, also see the Alaska Native Knowledge Network website (http://www.ankn.uaf.edu; Lord, 2011; Wolforth, 2005; and the UAA Institute of Social and Economic Research, http://www.iser.uaa.alaska.edu/).

Cultural Identity

The term *Alaska Native* refers to a diversity of Native cultures located in Alaska. The organization of these cultures varies depending on whether one considers language, geography, or historical political influences to be primary. At the most general level, Alaska Native cultures can be divided into two language groups, those belonging to (a) the Eska-Aleutian language family, including "Eskimo" and Aleut, and (b) the Na-Dene languages of the Athabascans, Eyak, and probably Tlingit cultures (Langdon, 2002).

Eska-Aleutian Speakers

Included in the Eska-Aleutian language speakers are the two largest "Eskimo" cultures: the Iñupiat, who speak Iñupiaq, live in the far north, and are related to the Inuit of Canada and Greenland; and the Yup'iit, the majority of whom live in southwestern Alaska. (Note that the "-it" ending in this context signifies nouns referring to the people and culture, whereas "-q" and "-ik" endings signify adjectives and the languages.) Together, the Iñupiat and Yup'iit constitute a little over half of the total Alaska Native population (Alaska Conservation Foundation, 2003). Although some Iñupiaq and Yup'ik people self-identify as "Eskimo," many younger people are moving away from the use of this term. The term is considered pejorative because it was used by Whites during colonial times. In addition, it lumps together distinct cultures (i.e., the Iñupiat and the Yup'iit), while excluding other Alaska Native cultures. In 2016, President Obama signed federal legislation officially replacing the term with *Alaska Native* (Zak, 2016).

Also in the Eska-Aleutian language are the Unangan (Aleut) and the Sugpiat (Alutiit). The Alutiit were initially misnamed Aleut by the Russians, but in reality, their language is completely unrelated to that of the Aleut (Langdon, 2002).

Na-Dene Speakers

The second broad language grouping of the Na-Dene speakers includes people of Alaska Indian heritage who are genetically more closely related to Indian people in the Lower 48 (i.e., than to the Iñupiat or Yup'iit; Langdon, 2002). The largest of the Alaska Indian cultures are the Athabascans of the interior and southcentral Alaska. The Athabascans are divided into a number of cultures whose members speak 11 languages related to those of the Apaches and Navajo (Krauss, 1982). The remaining Alaska Indian cultures reside in southeast Alaska and are often grouped together: the Tsimshian, Tlingit, Haida, and Eyak. Although the Haida and Tlingit languages were once thought to be related, Haida is now considered unrelated to any Alaska language, and there is evidence that Tlingit diverged from the other Athabascan languages as early as 6,000 years ago (Langdon, 2002). The Tsimshian came to southeast Alaska from British Columbia in the late 1800s and established a community on Metlakatla, which is currently the only reservation in Alaska (McClanahan & Bissett, 2002). The Tlingit, Haida, and Tsimshian cultures were traditionally matrilineal (as were several other Alaska Native cultures traditionally), with marriage regulated according to social divisions known as *moieties*. Members of the Tlingit and Haida belonged to either the Eagle-Wolf or Raven moiety, whereas the Tsimshian belonged to the Wolf, Killer Whale or Bear, Eagle, or Raven moieties. Individuals were allowed to marry only those of the opposite moiety (Ketchikan Museum, n.d., cited in McClanahan & Bissett, 2002). The Eyaks were a relatively small group, and due in part to similarities in social structure with the Tlingit culture, intermarriages with the Tlingit became common.

In addition to the specific cultural identities described earlier, for many Alaska Natives, the geographical location of one's home village may be a primary form of self-identification (e.g., "I'm from Port Graham" rather than "I'm Alutiiq"). For others, self-identification as *Alaska Native* is primary (i.e., over a specific identity). This may reflect a positive connection with people of other Alaska Native cultures. However, in some cases, people do not know their specific cultural origin. High rates of migration and adoption, along with a dominant culture and mass media that lump Native people's cultures together, have contributed to this loss of knowledge and connection.

Many Alaska Native people hold bicultural or multicultural identities. According to the U.S. Census Bureau (2017), Alaska has the second highest proportion (7.3%) of self-identified biracial or bicultural persons in the United States (Hawaii has the first). As Alaska Natives make up the largest ethnic minority group in the state, this statistic suggests that many Alaska Natives are more likely to identify with both (or multiple) aspects of their cultural heritage. Given the range of possibilities regarding identity, for counseling purposes, it is preferable to allow clients to self-identify rather than assume an identity based on geographical origin, family name, or physical appearance.

It is important to remember that each individual's orientation to his or her culture and the dominant culture can involve a variety of unique adaptations. For example, the therapist may encounter a client who lives in a rural area and engages in traditional activities such as hunting and fishing but also uses the Internet at home to check e-mail, maintains a responsible position of paid employment in the community, frequently travels Outside,[1] and holds a worldview that includes a combination of traditional Native and mainstream European American beliefs. The therapist may also meet individuals who are more traditionally oriented in their behaviors, beliefs, and lifestyles but live in the cities of Anchorage or Fairbanks and have difficulty adjusting to the faster-paced, European American–dominated lifestyles there.

With some clients, particularly those who are more comfortable with the dominant culture, it may be appropriate and even helpful to ask specific questions about the person's connection to their cultural heritage. However, with other individuals, such questions may be perceived as irrelevant or intrusive, particularly coming from a non-Native therapist. In these latter situations, therapists will often be able to obtain information regarding cultural heritage and bicultural competence simply by listening for it—for example, in the clients' use of language, their place of origin and current residence, and in their responses to questions regarding experiences growing up and current

---

[1]Alaskans use the capitalized word *Outside* to signify anywhere outside the state, synonymous with *Lower 48.*

activities (Jackson & Turner, 2004). To maximize one's ability to make accurate hypotheses and inferences, therapists will have to do their own work in learning about each client's cultures and then use this cultural information as background for understanding the client's experiences.

Living Conditions

Although approximately 20,000 Alaska Natives reside in Anchorage, the majority live in rural areas, including 225 remote villages accessible only by boat or air (Haycox, 2002). These villages range from communities as small as 50 people to larger hub communities of a few thousand people, such as Bethel, Nome, Dillingham, and Utqiagvik (formerly called Barrow). In most of the villages, a health aide and a safety officer are available, with at least a telephonic connection to a doctor and state trooper office in a larger town (Haycox, 2002). Unemployment is high, and limited economic opportunities lead many Native people to migrate to Anchorage, Fairbanks, and other towns, where urban living presents many new challenges (Fienup-Riordan, 2000a). Over 3,300 rural Alaskan homes use *honey buckets*, the slang term for indoor portable toilets, because they do not have piped water or a septic system. Dozens of villages use water points where community members go to collect and then haul water home (D'Oro, 2015).

Alcohol and drug abuse, along with the related problems of suicide, domestic violence, and fetal alcohol spectrum disorder, are chronic problems in many villages (Langdon, 2002). Suicide is the fourth leading cause of death among Alaska Native people, with approximately 41 suicides per 100,000 (Alaska Native Tribal Health Consortium Epidemiology Center, 2017). Since the 1980s, a strong sobriety movement has developed, and many villages have asserted their power to take control of alcohol abuse by voting to prohibit the importation and/or sale of alcohol.

STRENGTHS AND LIMITATIONS OF COGNITIVE BEHAVIOR THERAPY WITH ALASKA NATIVE PEOPLE

Several elements of CBT make it especially suited for work with Alaska Native people. Consideration of the physical, cognitive, emotional, and environmental components of a problem fits well with the Yup'ik understanding of stress in terms of emotional, physical, and cognitive responses (Rivkin et al., 2017). The problem-solving focus fits well with the expectation of many clients that the therapist will provide practical solutions to problems, and the emphasis on empowerment and attention to clients' strengths facilitates clients' sense that they are being respected by the therapist (Hays, 2016). In addition, a careful consideration of the environmental components of the client's situation can include attention to the healing components (or lack thereof) in the person's environment (e.g., opportunities to spend time outdoors, breathe fresh air, watch wildlife, pick berries, hunt, fish, and observe the sky—all of which are important in Alaska Native cultures). Similarly, attention to the social aspects of environment reinforces the Native valuing of family and community. (As an illustration of how important family is, Kawagley noted that the Yup'ik word for *relative* is associated with the term for viscera; cited in Rivkin et al., 2017, p. 47.)

An additional advantage is that cognitive restructuring (i.e., the changing of unrealistic, unhelpful, and distressing thoughts to more realistic and helpful ones) has a parallel in the traditional subsistence worldview of being careful in one's thoughts and actions to avoid injuring another person's mind or offending the spirits (Kawagley, 2006). Positive, realistic thoughts and correct behavior are seen as contributing to one's ability to survive in harsh conditions (Kawagley, 2006).

At the same time, several aspects of CBT do not fit well with Alaska Native cultures. The emphasis on logic and rationality, particularly when the rationality of the belief or action is defined by the dominant culture, is problematic. In addition, if specific attention is not given to the role of spirituality in the client's life, the cognitive focus of CBT may seem too narrow or simplistic to the client. Finally, the verbal nature of CBT can be limiting with traditionally oriented clients who speak English less fluently, who prefer silence over talking, and who are more reserved. The following sections offer suggestions for avoiding or working around these limitations with regard to assessment and therapeutic interventions.

COGNITIVE BEHAVIORAL ASSESSMENT

During the assessment and throughout therapy, the more knowledge and experience a therapist has about a client's culture, the closer the therapist's hypotheses will be to the client's real situation. In my attempts to stay mindful of the diversity of cultural influences affecting Alaska Native clients, I keep in mind the ADDRESSING acronym (Hays, 2012, 2016), which calls attention to the following range of experiences and identities:

- Age and generational influences. These include generational cohort influences (e.g., generations born before and after ANCSA, boarding school experiences, intergenerational trauma) and generational roles that may be important to a person, such as being a father, an auntie, or an elder. Alaska Native people are proportionally younger than the general

U.S. population, but the number of Native people over 65 is growing and estimated to triple between 2000 and 2030 (Alaska Native Epidemiology Center, 2009).

- Developmental or other Disability. Statistics are unavailable regarding Alaska Natives with disability in general; however, approximately 27% of Alaska's total population over the age of 18 experience a disability (Behavioral Risk Factor Surveillance System, 2011, cited in Atkinson et al., 2014). Alaska has the highest injury rates in the United States, and the unintentional injury mortality rate for Alaska Natives is twice as high as the rate for all Alaskans (Alaska Department of Health and Social Services, Division of Public Health, 2001, pp. 22, 35), suggesting that Alaska Native people have disproportionately high rates of disability related to accidents. The harsh climate and lack of services in rural areas increase the risk of accident-related disability, as well as the obstacles that people with a wide range of disability face. Regarding developmental disability, Alaska overall has one of the highest rates of fetal alcohol spectrum disorder, with a prevalence rate for the state of 13.5 per 10,000 and for Alaska Native people, 32.4 per 10,000 (Schoellhorn, 2010).

- Religion or spiritual orientation. As noted earlier, religious beliefs and affiliations vary widely among Alaska Native people. In addition to Christian denominations, Alaska Native people commonly have a strong sense of spirituality connected to the natural world.

- Ethnicity. As previously noted, many Alaska Natives hold bicultural or multicultural identities and identify with both or multiple aspects of their cultural heritage.

- Socioeconomic status. There are enormous differences among Alaska Natives related to socioeconomic status, particularly between college-educated individuals living in Anchorage and those living in the smaller villages. The poverty rate for Alaska Native children is 22%, double the proportion of U.S. White children (Alaska Native Epidemiology Center, 2009).

- Sexual orientation. Alaska has a strong lesbian, gay, bisexual, transgender, queer, and questioning community centered primarily in Anchorage, and Native people are a part of that community. Regarding traditional attitudes toward people who are gay, Jenny Miller, a gay Iñupiaq photographer, noted that although not much is known about the Iñupiat traditionally regarding different gender identities before contact with the outside world, "the first British visitors found much more equality" among the Iñupiat than in Britain, with "fluid relationships built on respect and ability rather than strict social roles" (Wolforth, 2016, para. 12). The Alaska Native Tribal Health Consortium's website (http://www.iknowmine.org/for-youth/lgbtq) provides resources aimed at Alaska Native youth.

- Indigenous heritage. As noted earlier, there are many levels to an Alaska Native's Indigenous identity. For example, a person from the Kenai Peninsula may self-identify as Alaska Native and Athabascan and Dena'ina (one of the Athabascan languages and cultures) and Kenaitze (the Dena'ina people living in the Kenai area; although this is a Russian word, it is the identification used by the Kenaitze Tribe). Finally, some Alaska Natives identify with the global movement of Indigenous peoples.

- National origin. Most Alaska Natives were born and raised in Alaska and are thus Americans, but there are Alaska Natives who have lived outside the United States or been influenced by a parent or grandparent who is of another country.

- Gender. Traditionally, the roles and activities of Alaska Native cultures (e.g., the Yup'iit) were highly gender specific, although at the same time intricately interdependent. For example, only the men hunted and trapped, and only the women sewed clothes. This meant that whereas women were dependent on men's hunting success for meat, the hunter's success was dependent on the warmth of his clothing that kept him alive (Kawagley, 2006). The strictness of these roles has changed significantly during the last few decades, and as noted earlier with regard to sexual orientation, Native cultures tend to be more accepting than the dominant culture when it comes to diversity.

The influences included in the ADDRESSING acronym are not arbitrarily chosen. Rather, they are highlighted in multicultural and related guidelines published by the American Psychological Association (e.g., 2003, 2004; American Psychological Association, Div 44, Committee on Lesbian, Gay, and Bisexual Concerns Task Force, 2000) and the American Counseling Association (e.g., Roysircar, Arredondo, Fuertes, Ponterotto, & Toporek, 2003). The acronym can be helpful in generating hypotheses about a client's beliefs, values, emotional expression, strengths, and symptom presentation. For example, when therapists do not understand why a client is responding in a particular way, they might ask themselves, "Could this client's behavior be explained by age or generational influences, disability, spiritual orientation, ethnic culture, or other (ADDRESSING) factors that I may be overlooking, including the interaction of my identity with theirs?" In this way, cultural influences become central to the generation of hypotheses regarding the client.

Establishing a Relationship

One of the first steps in working with Alaska Native clients is the establishment of a respectful and friendly working relationship. The following information opens up a wide range of hypotheses for non-Native therapists to consider in their attempts to understand what facilitates therapeutic relationships with Alaska Native people.

In an initial meeting, introducing oneself with first as well as last name is often preferred. The use of titles and degrees is generally not emphasized (except with some elders), in keeping with the value placed on personal humility (De Coteau, Anderson, & Hope, 2006). It may be helpful to ask clients how they prefer to be addressed, but to show respect for elders, start with Mr., Mrs., or Ms., and use first names if requested to do so. It is also expected in an initial meeting that one will engage in some casual social conversation, a custom that Hornby (cited in Allen, 1998) called *common basing*. Such conversation may touch on events, activities, or people that the speakers have in common, with the shared understanding that "people and relationships are not viewed in isolation but instead as parts of an interconnected community" (Allen, 1998, p. 34).

The role of silence and communication among many Alaska Natives is also important to consider. In the dominant culture, silence is often interpreted as a sign of anger or a signal that the speaker is finished. Among many Alaska Native people, silence is a way to communicate respect for the speaker and what they have just said. It may also simply reflect the fact that the listener is thinking, formulating thoughts, or waiting for a sign to speak (Allen, 1998). Aleut instructor Sally Swetzof noted that one of the more offensive responses to silence or a pause occurs when the non-Native speaker "jumps in with another question or, worse yet, asks the question in another way, as if the Native person hadn't understood" (cited in Gerjevic, 2004, p. A-1). She advised simply "waiting a few beats" after asking a question.

Alaska Native psychologist Denise Dillard noted that "some elders have a narrative way of speaking and the intake questions are offensive" (personal communication, September 5, 2003). In such cases, Dillard may not follow the standard intake process but instead allow the elder to provide her with information that the elder deems important. Dillard added that this presents the dilemma that it may not be possible to obtain all the information desired in an initial session. However, if the client is offended, the accuracy of the information obtained will be questionable anyway, and it is unlikely the person will return.

In adapting manualized treatments for anxiety disorders with American Indians in the Lower 48, De Coteau and colleagues (2006) noted that elders and individuals raised traditionally may be less fluent in English and have difficulty reading and writing. They suggested that instead of using some of the less relevant manual components, therapists might ask clients to construct a drawing to show how they understand their anxiety and the interactions of its components. With regard to homework that often requires reading or writing, they also suggested considering more traditional forms of communication, including story, song, dance, and prayer. Clients may use one or more of these approaches to illustrate their experience of anxiety and as a form of therapeutic practice that facilitates healing. Along the same lines, although not specifically with Native people, the art therapists Malchiodi and Rozum (2012) described their use of art therapy with people who are less verbally oriented, with the advice to avoid the words "art" and "draw" because the terms may be intimidating and instead asking the client to "create an image." They too noted that clients could be asked to express their emotions in this way and create images as a form of nonverbal cognitive restructuring to counter hurtful thoughts and images.

A nonverbal response that can lead to misunderstanding is the raising of one's eyebrows or widening of one's eyes to mean "yes." This is an expression sometimes used by the Yup'iit and Iñupiat. European American Nick Jans (1993) described a humorous example of such a misunderstanding as he was working in a village store and a 4-year-old Iñupiaq girl came in with a handful of change that she silently placed on the counter. He asked whether she wanted candy and she looked at him with widened eyes. She then looked at the candy, and he asked, "Which one?" More silence. "This one?" Silence. "What about this one?" Exasperated, he picked out some candies and gave them to her, taking the right amount of change. Only later, he said, did he learn that via raised eyebrows and widened eyes she had been nonverbally shouting at him, "Yes, yes, yes!" (p. 25).

Clarification of the Problem, Strengths, and Supports

Once a respectful rapport has been established, the next step in a culturally responsive approach to CBT involves clarification of the client's problem, strengths, and supports. Consider the following example:

> Mark presented as a friendly, cheerful 25-year-old bicultural young man who came to his college's counseling center requesting career counseling. Specifically, he said that he wanted help in figuring out what jobs to apply for now that he was graduating with his A.A. degree in business.

The young European American counselor began the session by asking Mark about his upbringing and background. Mark explained that his mother was Athabascan and father Russian and European American. He lived with both parents in a small town on the road system (i.e., not a village) until they divorced, then he and his brother went back and forth between his father in Anchorage and mother in the rural area. When he was 18, his father died, and he decided to stay with his mother for a while before going to college. Two years later, his maternal grandparents died within the same year of one another. Mark became tearful when he talked about their deaths and changed the subject back to his reason for coming in—to obtain help with his career search. The counselor was familiar with the many losses experienced by Alaska Native people, and he told Mark that he could see that he had experienced many losses in his life and might need an opportunity to grieve more fully. He added that counseling could help with this. At his strong encouragement, Mark made another appointment. However, the next week at their scheduled time, Mark did not appear, and the counselor did not hear from him again.

Although well-intentioned, this counselor made a couple of mistakes. At the most basic level, he failed to listen to what the client wanted and instead focused on what he thought Mark needed. Although he did hold some knowledge about Alaska Native cultures, his knowledge focused mainly on the negative (i.e., cultural losses) without recognition of the positive (i.e., culturally related strengths and supports). For example, if he had asked, he would have learned that Mark had good friends and close relationships with his mother, brother, and aunt and that he was involved in a Native youth dance group that provided him with a positive connection to his Athabascan culture. He was also a positive role model for his brother and several younger cousins. With all these supports and strengths, he did not need to see a counselor for the grief he experienced at times. All he needed and wanted from counseling was what he requested—help in articulating his work interests and strengths and then in matching these with potential careers.

Attention to clients' strengths and supports is a core task in any cognitive behavioral assessment for at least two reasons. First, a problem can often be improved by enhancing, building on, or reinforcing strengths and supports that are already in place and thus easier to maintain. Second, by actively looking for strengths and supports in the client's culture, the therapist communicates recognition of the client's culture as a resource for healing, self-help, and mental health. (See also Allen et al., 2014, for an excellent example of the search for and description of culturally related factors that contribute to a sober and healthy lifestyle among Alaska Natives.)

Another core principle in cognitive behavioral assessment is the acceptance of the client's presentation of the problem (Wenzel, Dobson, & Hays,

2016). Once a respectful relationship is established, the therapist may offer an alternative perspective, but the therapist's role is generally that of a listener, facilitator, and teacher of coping skills. Ultimately, clients decide what is needed and what will work for them in their particular contexts (Wood & Mallinckrodt, 1990).

Explaining Cognitive Behavior Therapy

As part of my initial assessment, I always explain to clients what I do. I use the term *counseling* more often than *therapy* because the former seems to be less intimidating and more familiar to people. I rarely use the phrase *cognitive behavior therapy*, in part because it emphasizes the cognitive and behavioral aspects of therapy and does not include the words *emotional, spiritual,* or *social*. I do not want people to think that these latter areas are not important in counseling. My explanation goes something like the following:

> It can be helpful to think of problems in terms of two main categories. The first group includes problems you can do something about. For example, if your child gets into trouble at school, you could talk with your child, or you could call the teacher, or you could ask your mother for advice, and so on. Counseling can be helpful with these kinds of problems in figuring out what to do and then how to do it.
>
> But there are some problems that we can't do anything about, or we make a decision that we don't want to. This second group of problems includes, for example, a really stressful job that you have to stay in because you are only 6 months short of retirement or having to take care of a sick family member. [I try to use an example that the person has already provided.] With these kinds of situations, in which you can't change the problem itself, the one thing people can do is change the way they feel about the problem. And one of the ways we can do this is to change how we think about the problem. Counseling can be helpful in finding new ways to think about a problem, and this includes new ways of talking to ourselves about problems. [This often leads to the joke that I try to get people to start talking to themselves.]

This explanation can be adapted to the situation of each individual, couple, or family. For example, often with single mothers, I add a piece on self-nurturing activities under the first category of problems. I explain that part of building oneself up and making oneself stronger is good self-care. This includes good nutrition and exercise but also activities and rewards that help to lift one's mood. If the person looks perplexed, I say that this is person specific, but some examples I have heard include taking a hot bath, lighting favorite candles, beading, sewing, going to the women's AA group, going for a walk outside, or taking time to pray or meditate. Many of the people I see do not have much money, so I try to give examples that are free or inexpensive. To explain the concept of cognitive restructuring further, I often add the following:

> Have you ever had the experience where you start to get down on yourself and say things to yourself like, "I'm such a loser, that was so stupid of me, I'll never get that job, nobody cares . . ."—that kind of thing—and as you say those things to yourself, you just feel worse and worse? [Pause for a response.] That negative self-talk can really pull you down. But the good news is that we can change that negative self-talk into more positive self-talk to help us feel better. When we say things to ourselves like "Okay, I can do this, I can get through this, I know that I'll do better next time" and remind ourselves of our past successes and strengths, we build ourselves back up to be stronger.

To illustrate the use of cognitive behavioral interventions, let us consider a client who is different from the bicultural young man previously discussed.

CASE EXAMPLE

Clara,[2] a 48-year-old woman of a Yup'ik mother and a Norwegian American father, came to the counselor, Beth, a 50-year-old European American woman, with symptoms of crying easily, difficulty sleeping, and worrying "constantly." Clara told Beth she was worried about her daughter, June, who left high school before graduating and was now heavily into alcohol and drugs. In response to Beth's questions, Clara told Beth that she (Clara) was born in a Yup'ik village of about 100 people and lived there until she was 12 years old; her mother had died in an accident. Within the year, her father had killed himself, and she and her three younger siblings went to live with their paternal grandparents in Bethel (the largest Yup'ik village, with a population of about 6,000). Clara described her grandparents as good people who taught her traditional values. They rarely talked about her parents. Clara did well in school, obtained her high school diploma, began working as a secretary at the local school, and married at the age of 20. She and her husband wanted children, but she had three miscarriages and then never again became pregnant. However, one of Clara's sisters had chronic problems with alcoholism and was unable to take care of her daughter June. (At this point, Clara explained that June was her biological niece.) June's biological father was physically abusive to both June and her mother and no longer had any contact with either of them. June was initially placed in the

---

[2]Case material in this chapter has been disguised to protect client confidentiality.

custody of child protective services, but when June was 8 years old, Clara and her husband were able to adopt her.

Clara said that "things went good" until June was about 12, and then she began drinking and hanging out with boys. She stopped going to school in her junior year and came and went from the house. At the age of 18, she agreed to go to treatment with the understanding that if she did not, she would not be able to live with Clara and her husband any longer. June completed a 30-day inpatient treatment program and was "clean and sober" for 2 months before she began using again. This had been about 6 months earlier, and now Clara only heard from June when the latter called her needing money or a place to stay. Clara said that after talking with her pastor many times about June, he suggested that she see a counselor. She then went to her doctor, who prescribed medication for her high blood pressure, advised her to lose weight, and also told her to see a counselor. Clara acknowledged her weight problem (about 70 pounds over) but was clearly more concerned about June.

Regarding social supports in her life, Clara described herself as a Christian and said that she attended church regularly and had two good women friends with whom she talked daily. She described her faith as strong, adding "If I didn't have God in my life, I don't know what I'd do." Her 60-year-old husband, Ronald, would not go to church with her, but she described their relationship by saying "we get along good most times." She said he had his own health problems, including emphysema from years of smoking. Clara stated that she had never become "a drinker," and although her husband drank heavily at an earlier point in his life, he had been sober for over 20 years.

One of the most striking aspects of Clara's situation is its complexity. Among Alaska Natives who present to mental health and substance abuse clinics, this complexity intertwined with a history of exceptional loss and trauma is not uncommon (Napoleon, 1996). Therapists have to be especially aware of the possibility of posttraumatic stress disorder (PTSD) in clients who have experienced such an accumulation of loss and trauma. Moreover, the experience of trauma is not limited to individuals but has often been passed down through generations. In such complicated situations, the therapist is faced with the question "In the midst of such an overwhelming number of stressors, both present and past, where does one begin?"

By the end of this assessment session, the therapist, Beth, had learned enough about Clara to determine that she was not experiencing any immediately debilitating effects of the earlier trauma in her life (i.e., no symptoms of PTSD and no suicidal or homicidal ideation). Beth summarized the stressors she had heard from Clara, beginning with Clara's childhood difficulties of losing her parents at a young age, followed by her sister's addiction, June's addiction, Clara's health problems, and her husband's health problems. She suspected that there were other difficulties that Clara had not had time to mention. She expressed amazement at Clara's resilience, making the point that many people would have given up if they had been through what Clara had.

Beth then summarized the strengths and supports she saw contributing to Clara's resilience: Clara's relationships with her grandparents (now deceased), her current relationships with women friends and her husband, the Church, and her faith. Beth inquired about fun activities, and Clara said that she enjoyed sewing. When Beth asked about specific culturally related activities by naming them, Clara said yes, she enjoyed berry picking, fishing, and simply being outdoors. She said that she did not use cleansing or purifying rituals nor did she do drumming, and although she would have liked to dance, she said she did not feel up to it.

Beth asked whether there were any personal qualities that Clara liked about herself. With tears in her eyes, Clara modestly shrugged and said nothing. Beth knew that modesty is a traditional value, so she then asked the question in a different way: "What do your best friends like about you?" Clara said, "They say I'm a good listener." Beth asked what Clara's husband would say, and she said, "He says I take good care of him." This information gave Beth a good list of Clara's strengths and supports to draw from later. The assessment ended with Beth's explanation of how counseling might be helpful to Clara by building on her current strengths and supports and possibly adding some additional ones. She also stated that she (Beth) could help Clara solve the problem of what to do about June. Clara agreed that this would be helpful.

Problem Solving

At the second session, Beth asked for an update on Clara's situation. June had called, and Clara had sent her $50 that June said she needed for food. Clara said she knew June would probably use it for drugs. Beth asked questions aimed at helping Clara articulate her confused feelings of hurt, anger, fear, and love. She validated these feelings as understandable given her relationship with June and June's behavior. Beth then asked several questions aimed at helping Clara move into the initial stages of problem solving. This included the exploration of Clara's (a) perception of the problem, (b) attributions or beliefs about the causes of the problem, (c) appraisal of the problem's significance in her life, (d) perception of control regarding the problem (i.e., whether it was solvable, and whether she was capable of solving it), and (e) the amount of time and effort involved in making the situation better and her willingness to put forth this time and effort (D'Zurilla & Nezu, 2001).

Clara perceived the problem to be June's loss of and conflicting feelings toward her mother and father, compounded by the harmful relationships she developed in connection with her alcohol and drug abuse. Clara saw June's alcohol and drug behaviors as symptomatic (i.e., the result rather than the cause) of June's emotional and spiritual pain. When Beth asked, Clara could also see that part of the problem was within Clara—that is, Clara's pain and emotional difficulties regarding June. Clara said that she had hope and faith that things could get better, but she was at a loss as to how to make this happen. She was willing to come to counseling on a weekly basis if it would help, and her history suggested that she was capable of sustaining good effort toward making things better.

Beth initiated a discussion of the parts of the problem that were external to Clara (i.e., June's behavior) and the parts that were internal to Clara (Clara's feelings and thinking about the problem). This led to a discussion of possible solutions for these different parts. Regarding the external part, Clara could not think of any practical actions or changes that she had not already tried, so Beth made a couple of suggestions. One of these concerned June's request for money. Clara was clear that she could not let June starve and was afraid to take the risk of not giving her money when June sounded so desperate. Beth did not pressure her on this point because she recognized the cultural and personal importance of family to Clara and the need for Clara to keep a connection with June. Instead, Beth suggested finding a way to pay for the food directly—for example, by an arrangement with the grocery store that June frequented. Beth also helped Clara develop a list of social service resources with phone numbers that Clara could periodically give to June when June called. Clara liked these ideas because they allowed her to continue to help June (which was an expression of hope for her) without contributing to June's addiction. (For more on the importance of hope in physical and psychological healing, see Lopez, 2014, and Groopman, 2003.)

Cognitive Restructuring

As Beth worked with Clara on resolving the external parts of this situation, she listened for statements that might reflect thoughts that were contributing to or exacerbating Clara's internal conflict and pain. In her explanation of cognitive restructuring (without using the term), she explained that a certain amount of frustration, fear, and pain was understandable when someone you love is on such a hurtful path. This validation of Clara's negative feelings was important to avoid the self-blame that is so often reinforced by the dominant culture. At the same time, Beth explained how changing some of Clara's negative thoughts could help her feel better and stronger.

Remembering that Clara had said her grandparents taught her traditional values, Beth asked whether they had talked about the relationship between one's thoughts, attitudes, and behaviors. Clara said yes, she knew about the importance of holding "right attitudes" particularly when hunting and fishing. She knew that if one behaves respectfully toward animals and the environment, "things will work better." For example, she said, "If you act respectfully toward the fish, it will give itself to you." As they talked more about this idea, Beth made the connection between the Yup'ik beliefs and the cognitive behavioral idea that "what you think affects how you feel, and how you think and feel affect your behavior." Building on Clara's example, Beth said,

> If you think to yourself, "I'll never catch this stupid fish," you will probably feel discouraged and a little angry, and this will lead you to be sloppy in how you fish, whether you're setting a net or using a dip net or a line. This sloppy, disrespectful behavior will decrease the chances that you will catch the fish. However, if you respect the fish and the river and yourself, you will be careful and thoughtful in what you do, and your chances of catching a fish will be greater.

Clara added that it is possible that the fish knows that you are being respectful and is thus more willing to give itself. Beth and Clara then talked about how one's attitude and thoughts could help or hinder a person's well-being. Regarding Clara's thoughts about June, Beth gave an example of one thought she had heard Clara state, which Beth thought might be hurtful to Clara:

> If I don't give June money, she won't be able to eat, and she could get into even worse trouble. She could have to stay with bad men, she could kill herself because she gives up, or one of those bad people could kill her.

This statement illustrates the problem with using the cognitive behavioral concept of rationality as a way to categorize the helpfulness or unhelpfulness of a thought. Namely, definitions of what is rational and irrational are culture specific and situational. Whereas a middle-class European American might judge Clara's statement to be an irrational "jumping to conclusions," it is just as likely that Clara's assessment of what might happen is quite rational. It is clear that the more therapists know about a client's cultural context, the more able they will be to figure out how rational the feared thought is. However, there is still the problem of judgmentalism that can creep into one's beliefs about what is rational, particularly when the therapist is of the dominant culture and the client is not. The therapist can use the concept of helpfulness rather than that of rationality to avoid this problem (i.e., asking the client, "Is it helpful to think this?"). From a theoretical perspective, this approach can be conceptualized as challenging the utility of the thought rather than its validity (Beck, 2011).

Beth began directing Clara toward the process of cognitive restructuring by asking her how she felt when she thought about this statement. Clara acknowledged, with tears in her eyes, that she felt "very bad and very sad." There was a long silence as they both experienced the sadness of her thought. Beth asked Clara, "Is there anything that you tell yourself, that helps you to feel better about the situation with June?" Clara said yes, that when she feels low, she tells herself, "God doesn't give you more than you can handle." Beth allowed for another silence to indicate her appreciation of this statement and then said, "Well, God sure must think you're strong!" which made both of them laugh. Beth then asked questions aimed at helping Clara to elaborate on this helpful thought (i.e., adding information regarding the evidence for it and other helpful thoughts). This led Clara to articulate the following beliefs:

> I'm a strong person. I've been through a lot, and with God's help, I've survived and helped other people and even had good times along the way. I can't control June's behavior, but I will still love her and help her when I can. I'm doing my best.

Subsequent sessions focused on this cognitive restructuring process, reinforcing Clara's helpful thoughts about herself and June. Beth pointed out how counseling served as a reminder for Clara throughout the week to pay attention to her thoughts because she knew that Beth would be asking her about them. Beth also frequently called attention to Clara's strengths to reinforce Clara's awareness of her positive qualities and the supports around her.

A person's problems are never easily compartmentalized, and the internal and external aspects of Clara's pain overlapped throughout therapy sessions. At times, there was more focus on cognitive restructuring, at times on solving problems arising in the latest encounters with June, and at times on strengthening and adding to the self-nurturing activities in Clara's life. The external aspects of Clara's problem changed little during the course of therapy (i.e., June continued to drink, use drugs, and call and ask her for money). However, Clara began to feel stronger, and although each call from June brought her some sadness, Clara reported feeling less distressed on an ongoing daily basis and more able to enjoy the pleasurable activities and relationships in her life.

CONCLUSION

With its emphasis on client empowerment, practical problem solving, the development of positive coping skills, and the reinforcement of strengths and supports, CBT offers therapists tools for working effectively with Alaska Native people in treatment. However, for CBT to be truly helpful with Native people, it must be combined with culture-specific knowledge, flexibility, and creativity. This chapter discussed only a few of the many possibilities in the development of culturally responsive CBT with Alaska Native people.

REFERENCES

Alaska Conservation Foundation. (2003). *Guide to Alaska's cultures.* Anchorage, AK: Author.

Alaska Department of Health and Social Services, Division of Public Health. (2001). *Healthy Alaskans 2010: Vol. 1. Targets and strategies for improved health.* Juneau, AK: Author.

Alaska Department of Natural Resources, Division of Forestry. (2016). *What's bugging Alaska's forests? Spruce bark beetle facts and figures.* Retrieved from http://forestry.alaska.gov/insects/sprucebarkbeetle

Alaska Native Epidemiology Center. (2009). *Alaska Native health status report.* Anchorage, AK: Author. Retrieved from http://anthctoday.org/epicenter/publications/Reports_Pubs/2009_anai_health_status_report.pdf

Alaska Native Science Commission. (n.d.). *Impact of climate change on Alaska Native communities.* Retrieved from http://www.nativescience.org/pubs/Impact%20of%20Climate%20Change%20on%20Alaska%20Native%20Communities.pdf

Alaska Native Tribal Health Consortium. (2017). *The LEO network.* Retrieved from https://anthc.org/what-we-do/community-environment-and-health/leo-network/

Alaska Native Tribal Health Consortium Epidemiology Center. (2017). *Alaska Native health status report* (2nd ed.). Retrieved from http://anthctoday.org/epicenter/publications/HealthStatusReport/AN_HealthStatusReport_FINAL2017.pdf

Allen, J. (1998). Personality assessment with American Indians and Alaskan Natives: Instrument considerations and service delivery style. *Journal of Personality Assessment, 70,* 17–42. http://dx.doi.org/10.1207/s15327752jpa7001_2

Allen, J., Mohatt, G. V., Fok, C. C., Henry, D., & Burkett, R. (2014). A protective factors model for alcohol abuse and suicide prevention among Alaska Native youth. *American Journal of Community Psychology, 54,* 125–139. http://dx.doi.org/10.1007/s10464-014-9661-3

American Psychological Association. (2003). Guidelines on multicultural education, training, research, practice, and organizational change for psychologists. *American Psychologist, 58,* 377–402. http://dx.doi.org/10.1037/0003-066X.58.5.377

American Psychological Association. (2004). Guidelines for psychological practice with older adults. *American Psychologist, 59,* 236–260. http://dx.doi.org/10.1037/0003-066X.59.4.236

American Psychological Association, Div 44, Committee on Lesbian, Gay, and Bisexual Concerns Task Force. (2000). Guidelines for psychotherapy with lesbian, gay, and bisexual clients. *American Psychologist, 55,* 1440–1451. http://dx.doi.org/10.1037/0003-066X.55.12.1440

Atkinson, J., Smith, C., Tew, L., Heath, K., Reed, D., & Miller, J. (2014, July 10). *Promotion, prevention, and preparedness for Alaskans with disabilities: Alaska's disability & health program: Needs assessment report.* University of Alaska Anchorage

Center for Human Development. Retrieved from http://dhss.alaska.gov/dph/wcfh/Documents/disability/CompleteNeedsAssessmentReport(Accessible_2).pdf

Beaver, J. C. (2006). *U.S. international borders: Brief facts.* https://fas.org/sgp/crs/misc/RS21729.pdf

Beck, J. S. (2011). *Cognitive therapy: Basics and beyond.* New York, NY: Guilford Press

De Coteau, T., Anderson, J., & Hope, D. (2006). Adapting manualized treatments: Treating anxiety disorders among Native Americans. *Cognitive and Behavioral Practice, 13,* 304–309.

DeCou, C. R., Skewes, M. C., López, E. D., & Skanis, M. L. (2013). The benefits of discussing suicide with Alaska native college students: Qualitative analysis of in-depth interviews. *Cultural Diversity and Ethnic Minority Psychology, 19,* 67–75. http://dx.doi.org/10.1037/a0030566

D'Oro, R. (2015, September 22). Nearly 3 dozen Alaska villages still lack basic plumbing infrastructure. *Anchorage Daily News.* Retrieved from https://www.adn.com/rural-alaska/article/nearly-3-dozen-alaska-villages-still-lack-basic-plumbing-infrastructure/2015/09/22/

Droby, R. M. (2000). *With the wind and the waves: A guide for non-Native mental health professionals working with Alaska Native communities.* Nome, AK: Norton Sound Health Corporation, Behavioral Health Services.

Dunham, M. (2016, September 29). *Anchorage is Alaska's biggest Native "village," census shows.* https://www.adn.com/alaska-news/article/anchorage-alaskas-biggest-native-village-census-shows/2011/07/11/

D'Zurilla, T. J., & Nezu, A. M. (2001). Problem-solving therapies. In K. S. Dobson (Ed.), *Handbook of cognitive-behavioral therapies* (pp. 211–245). New York, NY: Guilford Press.

Fienup-Riordan, A. (2000a). Continuity and change in southwestern Alaska. In A. Fienup-Riordan, W. Tyson, P. John, M. Meade, & J. Active (Eds.), *Hunting tradition in a changing world: Yup'ik lives in Alaska today* (pp. 3–28). New Brunswick, NJ: Rutgers University Press.

Fienup-Riordan, A. (2000b). Mixed metaphors in the new Catholic Church. In A. Fienup-Riordan, W. Tyson, P. John, M. Meade, & J. Active (Eds.), *Hunting tradition in a changing world: Yup'ik lives in Alaska today* (pp. 109–141). New Brunswick, NJ: Rutgers University Press.

Fisher, D. G., Lankford, B. A., & Galea, R. P. (1996). Therapeutic community retention among Alaska Natives. *Journal of Substance Abuse Treatment, 13,* 265–271. http://dx.doi.org/10.1016/S0740-5472(96)00060-8

Freitas-Murrell, B., & Swift, J. K. (2015). Predicting attitudes toward seeking professional psychological help among Alaska Natives. *American Indian and Alaska Native Mental Health Research, 22*(3), 21–35.

Gerjevic, S. (2004, April). Native language classes teach manners in addition to words. *Canku Ota* [Many Paths]. Retrieved from http://www.turtletrack.org/IssueHistory/Issues04/Co04032004/CO_04032004_New.htm

Groopman, J. (2003). *The anatomy of hope*. New York, NY: Random House.

Haycox, S. (2002). *Alaska: An American colony*. Seattle: University of Washington Press.

Hays, P. A. (2012). *Connecting across cultures: The helper's toolkit*. Thousand Oaks, CA: Sage.

Hays, P. A. (2016). *Addressing cultural complexities in practice: Assessment, diagnosis, and therapy* (3rd ed.). Washington, DC: American Psychological Association.

Hootch v. Alaska State-Operated School System, 536 P.2d 793 (Alaska 1975).

Inuit Circumpolar Council–Alaska. (2016). *I am Inuit*. Retrieved from http://iccalaska.org/media-and-reports/

Jackson, A. P., & Turner, S. (2004). Counseling and psychotherapy with Native American clients. In T. B. Smith (Ed.), *Practicing multiculturalism: Affirming diversity in counseling and psychology* (pp. 215–233). New York, NY: Pearson Education.

Jans, N. (1993). *The last light breaking: Living among Alaska's Iñupiat Eskimos*. Anchorage, AK: Alaska Northwest Books.

Kawagley, O. A. (2006). *A Yupiaq worldview: A pathway to ecology and spirit*. Prospect Heights, IL: Waveland Press.

Krauss, M. E. (Cartographer). (1982). *Native peoples and languages of Alaska* [Map]. Fairbanks: University of Alaska Fairbanks, Alaska Native Language Center.

Langdon, S. J. (2002). *The Native people of Alaska*. Anchorage, AK: Great Land Graphics.

Lardon, C., Wolsko, C., Trickett, E., Henry, D., & Hopkins, S. (2016). Assessing health in an Alaska native cultural context: The Yup'ik Wellness Survey. *Cultural Diversity and Ethnic Minority Psychology, 22*, 126–136. http://dx.doi.org/10.1037/cdp0000044

Lopez, S. (2014). *Making hope happen*. New York, NY: Atria Press.

Lord, N. (2011). *Early warming: Crisis and response in the climate-change north*. Berkeley, CA: Counterpoint Press.

Malchiodi, C. A., & Rozum, A. L. (2012). Cognitive–behavioral and mind–body approaches. In C. Malchiodi (Ed.), *Handbook of art therapy* (2nd ed., pp. 89–102). New York, NY: Guilford Press.

McClanahan, A. J., & Bissett, H. L. (2002). *Na'eda: Our friends*. Anchorage, AK: The Cook Inlet Regional Foundation.

Napoleon, H. (1996). *Yuuyaraq: The way of the human being*. Fairbanks: University of Alaska, Alaska Native Knowledge Network.

Pomerville, A., Burrage, R. L., & Gone, J. P. (2016). Empirical findings from psychotherapy research with Indigenous populations: A systematic review. *Journal of Counseling and Clinical Psychology, 84*, 1023–1038. http://dx.doi.org/10.1037/ccp0000150

Rivkin, I. D., Johnson, S., Lopez, E., Trimble, J., Quaintance, T. M., & Orr, E. (2017). Yup'ik understanding of stress within the context of rapid cultural change. *Journal of Community Psychology, 45,* 33–52. http://dx.doi.org/10.1002/jcop.21831

Roysircar, G., Arredondo, P., Fuertes, J. N., Ponterotto, J. G., & Toporek, R. L. (2003). *Multicultural counseling competencies 2003.* Alexandria, VA: American Counseling Association.

Schoellhorn, J. (2010). Decline in the birth prevalence of fetal alcohol syndrome in Alaska. *State of Alaska Epidemiology Bulletin.* Retrieved from http://www.epi.alaska.gov/bulletins/docs/b2010_03.pdf

Stewart, T. J., Swift, J. K., Freitas-Murrell, B. N., & Whipple, J. L. (2013). Preferences for mental health treatment options among Alaska Native college students. *American Indian and Alaska Native Mental Health Research, 20*(3), 59–78. http://dx.doi.org/10.5820/aian.2003.2013.59

Swan Reimer, C. (1999). *Counseling the Iñupiat Eskimo.* Westport, CT: Greenwood Press.

Swift, J. K., Mayra, J., Justice, C., & Freitas-Murrell, B. (2015). The influence of an Alaska Native accent and reputation on perceived therapist credibility. *American Indian and Alaska Native Mental Health Research, 22,* 27–41. http://dx.doi.org/10.5820/aian.2201.2015.27

Townsend, L. (2017, February 8). Presbyterian Church formally apologizes to North Slope Natives for denouncing culture. *Alaska Public Media.* Retrieved from http://www.alaskapublic.org/2017/02/08/presbyterian-church-formally-apologizes-to-north-slope-natives-for-denouncing-culture/

U.S. Census Bureau. (2017). *Quick facts: Alaska.* Retrieved from https://www.census.gov/quickfacts/fact/table/AK/PST045217

U.S. Environmental Protection Agency. (January 13, 2017). *Climate impacts in Alaska: Alaska Natives.* Retrieved from https://19january2017snapshot.epa.gov/climate-impacts/climate-impacts-alaska_.html

Wenzel, A., Dobson, K. S., & Hays, P. A. (2016). *Cognitive behavioral therapy techniques and strategies.* Washington, DC: American Psychological Association. http://dx.doi.org/10.1037/14936-000

Wolforth, C. (2005). *The whale and the supercomputer.* San Francisco, CA: North Point Press.

Wolforth, C. (2016, May 17). Photographer depicting LGBT Natives is coming out herself. *Anchorage Daily News.* Retrieved from https://www.adn.com/commentary/article/photographer-depicting-transgender-natives-coming-out-herself/2016/04/23/

Wood, P. S., & Mallinckrodt, B. (1990). Culturally sensitive assertiveness training for ethnic minority clients. *Professional Psychology: Research and Practice, 21,* 5–11. http://dx.doi.org/10.1037/0735-7028.21.1.5

Zak, A. (May 24, 2016). Obama signs measure to get rid of the word "Eskimo" in federal laws. *Alaska Dispatch News,* p. A1.

3

COGNITIVE BEHAVIOR THERAPY WITH LATINXS

KURT C. ORGANISTA

In her classic writings on the Latinx family, Celia Falicov (2014) used the term *culture* to refer to a community of people that partially share the same meaning systems used to describe and ascribe meaning to the world and our place within it (e.g., values, norms, social roles). In describing how each individual varies regarding major cultural themes and norms, she emphasized the role of the person's ecological niche and its unique combination of contexts, which includes characteristics such age, gender, race or skin color, sexual orientation, and so forth. The quality of the ecological niche (e.g., social networks, built environment) influences the individual's development of feelings, behaviors, and cognitions given the person's varying degrees of access to the power and resources necessary for healthy development. This sufficiently complex definition of culture accounts for within-group similarities as well as variations from central cultural tendencies.

http://dx.doi.org/10.1037/0000119-004
Culturally Responsive Cognitive Behavior Therapy, Second Edition: Practice and Supervision, G. Y. Iwamasa and P. A. Hays (Editors)

With this in mind, Organista and Muñoz (1996) described Latinxs as follows:

> We fully recognize that each Latino is in some ways like no other Latino, and that there are subgroups of Latinos that are quite different from one another. Nevertheless, there are elements of shared history, of language, customs, religion and moral values, and of self-identity and identity attributed by others, which define, however imperfectly, a recognizable subgroup in society which must be properly served. The more clinicians know about a particular subgroup of Latinos (e.g., Mexican Americans, Puerto Ricans), the more they can conceptualize and treat the mental health problems of that group in a culturally sensitive manner. (p. 255)

In addition to this cultural framing, therapists' Latinx-related knowledge should also take into account the client's sociodemographic (e.g., socioeconomic status [SES]) profile, as described in the next section. Therapists should also be aware of the diverse acculturation histories of the Latinx group(s) with whom they practice. Organista and Muñoz (1996) further noted,

> Latinos are individuals with personal and family roots in Latino American countries. Many Latinos speak Spanish and most partake of the blended cultural traditions of the Spanish colonists and the indigenous peoples of the Americas. Latinos may belong to any racial group including those with roots in Europe, Africa, Asia, and the Middle East. (p. 256)

SOCIODEMOGRAPHIC PORTRAIT OF U.S. LATINXS

Intimations of psychosocial and health status, including mental health status, can be gleaned by reviewing sociodemographic and acculturation profiles of different U.S. Latinx groups. For example, the well-documented inverse relation between psychopathology and SES (e.g., Kessler et al., 2005) should cue us to the mental health needs of Latinxs, who are frequently over-affected by poverty and ethnic minority challenges to adjusting to the United States.

As of 2014, Latinxs numbered over 55 million or 17.3% of the U.S. population (Brown & Stepler, 2016), with Mexican Americans composing almost two thirds of Latinxs (64%), followed by Puerto Ricans (9.6%); Salvadorans (3.8%), who have just surpassed Cubans (3.7%); and growing Dominican (3.2%) and Guatemalan (2.4%) populations, which are followed by smaller groups from Central and South America. Table 3.1 emphasizes the socioeconomic disparities between Latinx and non-Hispanic White

TABLE 3.1
Sociodemographic Profiles of Major U.S. Latinx Groups
and Non-Hispanic Whites

Group	% Foreign born	Median household income	% No health insurance	% In poverty	% High school or more	% College graduation or more
Latinxs	35	$42,200	24	24	65	14
Mexicans	33	$40,000	31	26	59	10
Puerto Ricans	1	$38,900	14	27	77	18
Cubans	57	$40,500	25	20	79	25
Salvadorans	59	$44,060	37	20	52	8
Dominicans	55	$33,900	21	28	68	17
Guatemalans	64	$38,200	45	28	45	9
Non-Latinx Whites	4	$59,200	8	10	92	34

Note. Data from Brown and Stepler (2016), Lopez (2015a, 2015b, 2015c, 2015d, 2015e), and Lopez and Patten (2015).

families, as well as between Latinx groups. As can be seen, the pattern of disparity between Latinxs and Hispanic Whites is especially pronounced for Dominicans, Guatemalans, and Puerto Ricans, followed by Mexicans, with Cubans closest yet still disparate from their White counterparts (e.g., twice the rate of poverty, two thirds of family income).

Thus, in addition to anticipating different levels of SES-related mental health needs, the percentage of immigrants in each Latinx group also cues us to the probability of acculturation and adjustment challenges. For example, although a third of all Latinxs are immigrants (Mexicans being prototypical), the range for the remaining groups is between 55% and 64%, with the exception of Puerto Ricans, who possess citizenship status. Hence, Latinxs continue to actively acculturate to the United States, often in ways consistent with their diverse acculturation histories.

LATINX ACCULTURATION AND MENTAL HEALTH

In my historical analysis of Latinx acculturation (Organista, 2007a) and its relation to mental health (Organista, 2007b), two patterns predominated. The first showed between-group differences in mental health that run parallel to the different levels of SES noted earlier. That is, mental health problems such as major depression and alcohol abuse were consistently higher in Puerto Ricans and Mexican Americans compared with Cuban Americans. Unfortunately, fewer data are available for Dominicans and

Central Americans. Although more research is needed, Latinx group differences in mental health also reflect the second pattern—that is, differences in acculturation histories. These vary considerably in terms of the group's degree of acculturative stress, minority–majority group conflict, and challenges to adaptation to the United States.

For instance, Puerto Ricans have experienced a "double legacy of conquest and colonization," followed by racialized discrimination and hypersegregation similar to African Americans and decades of Puerto Rican protest and resistance (Duany, 2017; Organista, 2007a, p. 21). In contrast, the first wave of predominantly elite, professional, and racially White Cubans who fled the new Castro regime benefited from a generous open-door refugee policy replete with resettlement programs that maximized adaptation to the United States. Subsequent waves of upper- and middle-class Cubans, mostly relatives of the first wave, benefited from the same reception through the 1960s and 70s, and further consolidated today's thriving ethnic enclave in South Florida (Sweig, 2016). Interestingly, a small wave of poorer and racially darker Cubans, called *Marielitos* because they fled Cuba from the Port of Mariel, received a harsh reception during the 1980s (i.e., they were subject to military detention centers, "tent city" encampments, and deportations), although most eventually received refugee status and were absorbed into Miami's vibrant Cuban enclave.

For Mexican Americans, acculturation is consistently related to higher levels of stress-related disorders such as depression, anxiety, and alcohol and substance use disorders (Organista, 2007b). This pattern has been attributed to an ethnic minority experience characterized by stigma and discrimination, labor force participation in the service sector of the working poor, consequent segregation and poverty, and the breakdown of traditional cultural supports such as extended family and community. Interestingly, Cook, Alegría, Lin, and Guo (2009) analyzed data from a nationally representative sample of Latinxs that not only revealed the positive relationship between acculturation and diagnosable mental disorders but also demonstrated that family conflict and perceived discrimination were the two significant pathways related to the increase in anxiety and depressive disorders with increased time in the United States. Hence, such acculturation-related problems should be assessed and addressed in therapy as needed.

Thus, although the mental health needs of Latinxs vary between and within major Latinx groups, they are increasingly significant and warrant concerted efforts on the part of mental health professionals to conduct the necessary outreach, assessment, development, and evaluation of culturally competent Latinx-focused services, including cognitive behavior therapy (CBT).

ADVANTAGES OF COGNITIVE BEHAVIOR THERAPY

Although there is little comparative evidence to suggest that some forms of psychotherapy are superior to others when working with Latinxs, various dimensions of CBT are compatible with many of the cultural characteristics and social experiences of Latinx clients, as described next.

Educational and Didactic Therapy Based on Social Learning Theory

The didactic emphasis in CBT is helpful in orienting Latinx clients to therapy by educating them about how mental disorders are conceptualized (e.g., in the *Diagnostic and Statistical Manual of Mental Disorders, Fifth Edition* [American Psychiatric Association, 2013] or the *International Classification of Diseases, Tenth Revision, Clinical Modification* [World Health Organization, 2015]) and treated with CBT. Not only is an educational approach helpful in "demystifying" psychotherapy for the less familiar, but it is also consistent with what Orlinsky and Howard (1986) called "role preparation," in which clients unfamiliar with therapy learn about what they can expect and what will be expected of them as a way of enhancing treatment outcome. Consider the example of a traditionally oriented Latinx client who meets criteria for depression yet defines her symptoms as *nervios* (nerves) or a culture-bound idiom of distress in response to overwhelming problems, particularly grief, threat, and familial conflict, characterized by dysphoria and multiple somatic symptoms (Guarnaccia, 1993). CBT can offer this client an acceptable understanding of her distress and a treatment approach that does not necessarily negate her understanding of the problem (e.g., by increasing meaningful activities, changing unhelpful thoughts, improving relationships). CBT also seems less abstract than some other forms of therapies (e.g., psychodynamic) and thus easier for clients to grasp.

Helps to Decrease Stigma Attached to Mental Health Services

The typical use of therapy manuals, homework assignments, and in-session chalkboard work helps Latinx clients to think of therapy as more of a classroom experience, thus decreasing the stigma so often attached to therapy. For example, many of the Latinx clients with whom the author has worked over the years have referred to their CBT depression group as *la clase de depresión* [the depression class]. These predominantly Mexican immigrant and Central American refugee clients frequently shared that mental health services in their countries of origin were scarce and reserved mostly for *personas locas* [crazy people] in mental institutions. We respond to such comments by acknowledging that this is true for a few in the United States as well but that most people in therapy use it to decrease distress and to improve problems in living. We even joke that it is crazy not to take advantage of helpful treatments.

Consistent With Traditional Cultural Expectations of Helping Professionals

Less acculturated Latinxs often expect their doctors and other health professionals to prescribe medications or to recommend courses of action to improve their health and well-being. Professionals are viewed as authority figures who are sanctioned to be active and directive in providing services, and such expectations are more readily met in CBT than in nondirective forms of therapy.

Consistent With Low Socioeconomic Status Experiences of Many Latinxs

Given that CBT is short term and problem-solving oriented and focuses on the here and now, it often fits better with the lives of low-income people who are overly affected by poverty-related problems, frequent crises, and limited resources. CBT can be flexibly applied to such multiple problems even when they are not the immediate focus of treatment. For example, therapy may center on helping a client cope with panic disorder while simultaneously helping her improve related problems in domains such as family, work, and school. Such flexible applications of CBT to clients' pressing concerns help them to feel that therapy is responsive to their immediate lives.

LIMITATIONS OF COGNITIVE BEHAVIOR THERAPY

Cultural competence includes being able to consider how well an intervention may or may not fit with a client's social and cultural reality. In the case of Latinxs, advantages, as well as a few possible disadvantages, of CBT are considered next.

Cognitive Behavior Therapy Outcome Research With Latinxs

Well-documented evidence of the efficacy of CBT for a variety of mental disorders (e.g., mood and anxiety disorders) has continued to accrue (e.g., A Guide to Treatments That Work, Fourth Edition, Nathan & Gorman, 2015), including a few recent CBT outcome studies with Latinxs. For example, Alegría et al. (2014) conducted a multisite randomized controlled clinical trial comparing outpatient CBT, telephone-delivered CBT augmented by case management, and treatment for depression as usual in a sample of 257 low-income Latinxs receiving primary care from eight community health clinics in Boston (67.5% Central American, 11.9% South American, 11.1% Puerto Rican) and San Juan, Puerto Rico (85% Puerto Rican, 15% Dominican). Results revealed that both CBT modalities decreased depression and improved functional impairment compared with treatment as usual (i.e., antidepressant medication, mental health referrals, watchful waiting).

Alegría et al. (2014) adapted their telephone CBT plus case management treatment from a pilot study conducted by Dwight-Johnson et al. (2011), who found it to be superior to a control condition at 6-month follow-up in a sample of 101 Mexican Americans from a rural family medical clinic, resulting in decreased depression, improved functioning, and greater patient satisfaction. Although they did not focus solely on CBT, Cabassa and Hansen (2007) reviewed randomized clinical trials (RCTs) on the treatment of depression in Latinxs in primary care and concluded that collaborative care models were more effective than treatment as usual in decreasing depression, improving functioning, and increasing access to care. Evidence-based treatments included in the collaborative care models reviewed included CBT, interpersonal therapy, and antidepressant medication.

One of the RCTs included in the review compared group CBT for depression with and without case management in a sample of 199 low-income primary care patients, about 40% of whom were Latinxs (Miranda, Azocar, Organista, Dwyer, & Arean, 2003). Results showed that participants in the CBT plus case management condition had lower dropout rates than those receiving only group CBT. Social workers provided comprehensive case management services that addressed client needs and also participated as CBT group cofacilitators (see Organista & Dwyer, 1997). Miranda et al. (2003) found that group CBT plus case management was associated with greater improvements in depression and general functioning compared with CBT alone, but only for the 77 Spanish-speaking Latinx patients in the sample.

Although these studies demonstrated the efficacy of culturally competent CBT with Latinxs, Benuto and O'Donohue (2015) offered the following recommendations for improvement on the basis of their review of the literature on this topic: (a) there should be more consensus regarding the regularities of culture that should be integrated into treatment and which aspects of CBT should be culturally modified; and (b) both client level of acculturation, as well as other relevant intersectional dimensions, have to be consistently assessed and integrated into treatment as needed.

Individual Versus Social Change

One limitation of CBT to consider is that it emerges from the behavioral science tradition of emphasizing a focus on individual-level variables (e.g., cognitions, skills, behaviors) to effect therapeutic change. Although clients can be empowered with new knowledge, deeper understanding, and self-efficacy enhancing skills, their behavior may still be considerably influenced by structural–environmental, social, and cultural contexts that pattern problems and behaviors in ways that may at times be outside an individual's volitional control. Macrosocial change (e.g., laws, policies, institutional arrangements, and national norms and society-wide values) is also needed to improve Latinx mental health in addition to micro-level therapeutic interventions.

For example, in a recent analysis of state-level immigration policy climate on Latinx mental health, Hatzenbuehler et al. (2017) created a multisectoral policy climate index composed of 14 policies across the Latinx-relevant domains of immigration, language, race or ethnicity, and agricultural worker protections. Next, they examined the relation of the policy climate index to self-reported mental health in Latinxs from 31 states in the 2012 Behavioral Risk Factor Surveillance System, a population-based health survey of noninstitutionalized individuals aged 18 years or older. Results showed that individuals in states with a more exclusionary immigration policy climate reported higher rates of poor mental health days than those in states with a less exclusionary policy climate. Further, the association between state policies and poor mental health days was significantly higher among Latinxs versus non-Latinxs, and Latinxs in states with a more exclusionary policy climate had a 14% higher rate of poor mental health days than those in states with a less exclusionary policy climate. Examples of exclusionary policies include disallowing things like in-state tuition or driver's licenses to the undocumented while requiring law enforcement to check the legal status of people suspected of being undocumented. Thus, therapists have to be mindful of Latinx-relevant state policies while assessing their potential impact on the mental health of their Latinx clients.

Although it is not usually an explicit part of training or supervision, therapists and agencies working with Latinx populations should consider ways they can promote Latinx mental health at the mesocommunity and macrosocietal levels. An example would be making work authorization more available to literally millions of undocumented Latinxs who report

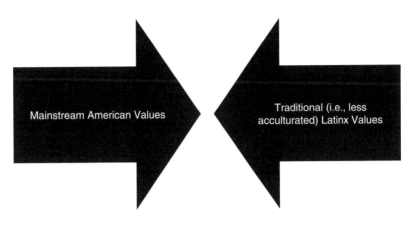

Mainstream American Values	Traditional (i.e., less acculturated) Latinx Values
Individualistic orientation	Collective/familial orientation
Verbal expressiveness Expression of feelings	Stoicism Resignation Control of emotions Nonverbal communication
Assertiveness	Traditional communication protocol based on deference to those higher in status (older vs. younger; professional vs. nonprofessional; male vs. female, etc.) Cultural script of *sympatia* [sympathy] Goal of smooth vs. confrontational relations Indirect communication through relatives to avoid direct confrontation
Egalitarian Democratic relationships	Nonegalitarian gender and age group roles based on traditional hierarchy
Scientific Intellectual reasoning	Religious faith Importance of emotions

Figure 3.1. Sampling of mainstream American values inherent in cognitive behavior therapy contrasted with traditional Latinx values.

considerable stress and anxiety related to the imminent threat of deportation (Organista & Hernandez, 2014).

Mainstream American Versus Traditional Latinx Values in Cognitive Behavior Therapy

Figure 3.1 lists a number of mainstream American and traditional Latinx cultural values that if not considered and creatively negotiated could undermine the flow and effectiveness of CBT with Latinx clients. Obviously, such values and role prescriptions are broad cultural norms, and thus considerable variation exists across Latinx clients as well as therapists. However, because they often emerge, advanced preparation and vigilance are important, as discussed next.

PRACTICAL SUGGESTIONS FOR ADAPTING COGNITIVE BEHAVIOR THERAPY

Suggestions for adapting CBT to Latinx clients are listed next, briefly followed by illustrations in a case vignette.

Use a Traditional Latinx Relationship Protocol to Engage Clients

Successful engagement in therapy is a fundamental first step that can be enhanced with Latinx clients by incorporating the salient Latinx value of *personalismo* into a culturally sensitive relationship protocol. *Personalismo* refers to a valuing of and responsiveness to the personal dimension of relationships, including task-oriented professional relationships such as medical visits and psychotherapy. As such, the mainstream practice of immediately focusing on the presenting problem can be perceived as impersonal by Latinx clients, especially if it is at the expense of the small talk needed to build rapport and *confianza*, or trust.

Because *personalismo* is not informality, it would be a mistake to come across too casually or as overly friendly. As described by Roll, Millen, and Martinez (1980), the task of the culturally sensitive psychotherapist is to find a balance between task-oriented formality and warm and caring attention to the client. To achieve such balance, it is necessary for the therapist to engage in sufficient *plática*, or small talk, that includes judicious self-disclosure.

Pretherapy Orientation

Taking the time to orient clients to therapy before they begin can also enhance engagement. At the hospital-based depression clinic where I worked, therapy preparation videos were developed in both Spanish and English by Gayle Iwamasa (the first editor of this volume). These films depict the process of therapy beginning with the referral made by medical staff trained by the clinic director to screen for symptoms of depression. In addition, a mock group therapy session is shown, described by the film's narrator and later discussed by actual clients. Actual clients discuss how they felt before and after therapy, the types of problems addressed, and how helpful they found therapy. The films have been shown in the waiting room of the general medical clinic, as well as used with patients referred for therapy following psychological evaluation.

Recognize and Address Values Underlying Cognitive Behavior Therapy as Well as Traditional Latinx Culture

As noted in Figure 3.1, being conscious of the many implicit values underlying both CBT and Latinx culture can facilitate open discussions of these issues as they arise and can result in finding the bicultural middle ground for intervention modifications:

- Advocate activity schedules for the client with and without other family members versus only for the client. Rationales such as "You need to take care of yourself first" are not as culturally appealing as those that link self-care to family care: "You can take better care of your family by taking care of yourself." Also, make sure to generate a list of enjoyable, inexpensive activities (e.g., free admission to museums first Wednesday of the month, walk in the park, visit with friends, have a cup of coffee in a cafe) for lower income folks.
- Streamline cognitive restructuring by using the "Yes, but" technique in which unhelpful thoughts and beliefs are empathically considered half-truths that have to be made into whole truths, rather than labeling client thinking as irrational or distorted (see Organista, 1995).
- Conduct culturally sensitive assertive training in ways that are mindful of the culture-based protocols for communication between people at different levels of traditional social status (e.g., older vs. younger; bosses and professionals vs. employees, men vs. women). For example, Comas-Díaz and Duncan (1985) described how to preface assertive communication in ways that convey traditional forms of respect while still being assertive: "With all due respect," and "Would you permit me to express how I feel about that?"

CASE STUDY OF A DEPRESSED AND ANGRY
LATINO MAN WITH CHRONIC PAIN

The client was a middle-aged, first-generation, married Mexican American man who spoke mainly Spanish and a little English (i.e., he was born in Mexico and immigrated to the United States as a young man). Thus, he was an individual low in acculturation, whom I will refer to as Mr. Lopez (not his real name).[1] He was referred to the depression clinic at San Francisco General Hospital by the pain clinic for suspected depression and because he was not following through with physical therapy, which he believed was too painful and physically harmful to perform. The client had been referred to the pain clinic as part of his medical treatment plan, which had included back surgery to alleviate back pain following a work-related injury the year before when he had fallen and damaged two spinal discs. The lack of bilingual Latinx staff in the pain clinic only added to the problem of "noncompliance." The depression clinic was located within the division of psychosocial medicine and staffed by bilingual and bicultural clinicians and staff who contacted the client by phone to set up the appointment.

The client and his wife had emigrated from a small rural city in Mexico and adhered strongly to traditional Mexican culture. The client's wife had mainly been a homemaker but began working full time at a local restaurant shortly after the client's accident. Although the client did not like his wife working, he recognized the financial necessity because his only source of income was disability insurance.

Client Strengths and Challenges

Mr. Lopez's strengths were that he was intelligent and communicative despite having little formal education (e.g., 8 years). He was also likable and responsive to being treated with respect and kindness. He also stated that he was committed to "finishing what he begins," including the new experience of therapy, about which he was unsure.

His challenges were that he felt extremely angry about his physical disability and the related chronic pain and inability to continue working as an auto mechanic. His anger and depression would often result in withdrawing from family activities, as well as angry outbursts during which he would yell at his wife and adult son and strike or break objects in the home. On one occasion, he punched his son in the shoulder for not doing an automotive task to his satisfaction. Recently he had even fractured the small finger on his right

---

[1]Case material in this chapter has been disguised to protect client confidentiality.

hand after punching a wall in anger. The client also appeared to be overly controlling in family activities (e.g., he would insist that the family return home from outings if his pain became intense).

Client Social Support

The client had an extended family in the Latinx Mission District of San Francisco, consisting of two adult married daughters with young children, in addition to the single adult son living at home. The client socialized with coworkers while healthy and working but had little contact with these friends during the year following his injury.

There were many Latinx-oriented centers and activities in the client's community, but he claimed to be physically unable to avail himself of these activities. However, although the community was rich in Latinx cultural resources, it was also a typical low SES environment with high crime statistics, rendering the client especially vulnerable and needing to take extra precautions (e.g., staying in more at night, doing more activities in the company of others).

Client Risk Versus Protective Factors

With regard to risk factors, the client's limited work skills, education, and English greatly diminished the possibility of nonlabor-intensive work. He said he was open to speaking English and to taking computer classes, but his pain did not allow him to sit for long. With regard to protective factors, the client's extended family offered many forms of social support, but they were growing weary of his negativism and disruptions of family activities.

Engaging the Client

Especially with less acculturated and presumably more traditional Latinx clients, emphasis should be placed on enacting a traditional Latinx relationship protocol based on the values of *respeto* [respect] and *personalismo*. Although clients higher in acculturation may need less of such traditional engagement, it seems best to err in the direction of this cultural regularity.

For example, I went out to meet Mr. Lopez in the waiting room by formally addressing him by his last name and shaking his hand in a manner that acknowledged the respect that his older age accorded. I also asked whether he had any trouble finding the clinic and whether he would like a glass of water or coffee. He agreed to a cup of coffee, and we made small talk about the pleasure of *un cafesito* [a small coffee], a Spanish term of endearment for coffee, as I joined him in a cup.

I asked Mr. Lopez where he was from, and when he answered Jalisco, Mexico, I smiled and told him that my family came from the same state and that I still visited cousins there. We spent the next few minutes talking about the capital city of Guadalajara and some of our favorite places to visit, such as Lake Chapala and the arts and crafts town of Tlaquepaque (just being able to pronounce the latter confers a degree of ethnic authenticity!).

Eventually, I mentioned the concerns of his doctor at the pain clinic about his adjustment to his severe back injury and chronic pain and his decision to discontinue physical therapy. I also assured the client that I had read his medical chart and empathized with his predicament (i.e., ruptured spinal discs, loss of work, chronic pain) by noting that it was quite serious or *muy grave*. The client felt reassured that I did not think the pain was "in his head" but still questioned the need for psychotherapy for a physical problem. I explained that the therapy we practiced could be helpful in teaching him how to better cope with chronic pain as well as decrease his *corage* (which roughly translates to *angst*). The client replied that if he did not have the pain and injury, then he would not be upset, and to illustrate the pain, he held out a tightly clenched and slightly tremulous fist. Such if–then thinking is common under stress and a prime target for cognitive restructuring. The nonverbal image of the fist was also worth noting for future use.

Before he left our first meeting, I told Mr. Lopez that I had worked with many clients with similar medical conditions who had different levels of adjustment, ranging from anger, depression, and self-neglect to being able to live as good a life as possible under the circumstances. I asked him to think about why some people have better and worse adjustment to similar medical conditions.

Therapist–Client Differences in Acculturation and Values

Although both the client and I are of Mexican ancestry, our acculturation differences were evident in our language use, which for my part involved speaking Spanish like an English-dominant Mexican American (i.e., occasional literal translations of thoughts from English into Spanish, mixing English and Spanish as in terms such as *chequiar*, a corruption of the English verb "to check"). I dealt with the language differences by letting Mr. Lopez know up front that I spoke Spanish like a *pocho* [poached, slang for a half-baked Mexican]. Like the majority of my clients, Mr. Lopez laughed and was quick to compliment my Spanish with sincere appreciation of having a member of the staff with whom he could communicate.

Mr. Lopez was as respectful of my professional status as I was of his higher age status, yet there were other acculturation differences of which to remain mindful. For example, although I could understand the client's traditional orientation to family life, my own orientation as a third-generation American of Mexican descent has become more egalitarian (e.g., with regard to sharing household chores, child care, and decision making). Thus, our considerable mutual respect was later tested by angry outbursts on his part and limit setting on mine.

The Central Role of Empathy

Research on CBT has documented the considerable therapeutic effect of empathy, an element traditionally lacking in the CBT literature, which implicitly conveys that if you apply the right techniques to the problem, a positive outcome follows. For example, Burns and Nolen-Hoeksema (1992) found that depressed patients who rated their cognitive behavior therapists the warmest and most empathic improved significantly more than patients who rated therapists as less empathic, even when controlling for factors such as initial depression severity and homework compliance.

With chronic pain, generous amounts of empathy have to be communicated for clients to feel they are being understood. It was not difficult to empathize with the client's anger and depression in response to his pain and disability given the high value he placed on working. He was, in a sense, culturally as well as physically dislocated.

STREAMLINING COGNITIVE RESTRUCTURING

Small Steps Toward Pain Tolerance

Enacting the aforementioned culture-based relationship protocol helped the client to feel comfortable and respected, thereby enhancing engagement. The client also became more open to the idea of using therapy to manage his chronic pain and depression better. Although he initially insisted that his severe pain was constant and intolerable (i.e., "*No puedo soportarlo!*" ["I can't stand it!"]), self-monitoring revealed that it was more severe when attempting physical tasks and that he paid less attention to the pain when absorbed in interesting activities such as watching a movie or reading. I spent time in the first couple of sessions teaching the client some relaxation techniques (e.g., deep breathing), with the rationale that if his body were less tight, his pain would be less bothersome. We used his own nonverbal symbol of his back pain to promote relaxation by having him tightly clench his fist and then slowly relaxing it along with deep breathing and verbal cues such as "calm" or "*tranquilo*" [tranquil; a popular Mexican Spanish term of choice for describing the state of being relaxed].

Finally, we discussed how "automatic" it is for us to think, "I can't stand this!" when experiencing intense pain but how such thoughts can actually exacerbate pain. We discussed countering such automatic thoughts with those that help us cope, such as "It feels like I can't stand it, but I can" and "This pain is very uncomfortable but not intolerable." After the first week of therapy, the client reported "a little" improvement in his back pain consistent with his daily self-monitoring scores, which were beginning to drop a couple of points from the maximum pain rating.

Addressing Anger-Related Pain

Addressing the client's anger was touchy, but I began by empathizing with the seriousness of his physical problems and noting how understandable it was that he felt frustrated and angry about his predicament. Next, I asked him to describe how getting angry affected his body, and he was able to describe muscle tightness that made his back pain worse. I also added that if he expressed his anger by striking objects, he also ran the continued risk of increasing his physical injuries such as his fractured finger. Here the empathic logic was, "Look, you already have enough pain and physical problems. You don't have to add to them by hurting yourself when angry."

Thus, we agreed that less anger would be beneficial to his health, although he could not see how to escape the vicious cycle of pain causing anger and vice versa. I empathized that reaching this goal would not be easy but that it was possible. I asked him to continue with the relaxation training but also to monitor situations and thoughts related to his anger. In addition to "I can't stand it!" another troublesome automatic thought identified was "I can't do anything!" Cognitive structuring with this thought proceeded by using what I call the "Yes, but" technique, in which unhelpful thoughts are described to the client as "half-truths" that are partly but not completely true. The beauty of this technique is that it conveys empathy while raising client curiosity about the part of their thinking that may not be true.

The "Yes, But" Technique

To teach the client how to change such unhelpful thoughts, I asked him to complete the following thought: "Yes, my pain does make it very difficult to do many things, but . . . ," to which the client eventually responded, "But I guess I can do some things." He was instructed to use the new restructured thought to counter the negative automatic thought whenever the latter emerged and to convey how changing his thinking made him feel. Here it is important to explain that although restructuring thinking may not provide immediate relief, consistent practice can provide relief by the end of the day or over the course of a few days (i.e., the positive effects tend to be cumulative).

Restructuring the two thoughts was also helpful in increasing the client's daily activities to reduce symptoms of depression further. He agreed to experiment with trying to do more daily activities on his own, such as walking two blocks to a cafe near his home to have coffee in the morning. He reported that this was difficult, that he had to stop many times along the way, but that he did enjoy his *cafesito*. We discussed this as an important lesson to take many breaks when trying to do ordinary things that are no longer easy to perform (e.g., washing dishes).

Less Bothersome Pain Versus Less Pain

By about midway through our 16 weeks of therapy, the client began to accept how his pain, anger, and depression were affected by his activities, thinking, and interactions with family members. However, on days when his pain was particularly severe or when a lack of activities led to ruminating about his limitations, Mr. Lopez seriously questioned the extent to which therapy would help him adjust to his pain and disability. We would discuss adjustment to disability as a lifelong process requiring not perfect but consistent practice of new skills to manage his difficult situation. He accepted the idea that the goal of his therapy was to try to live as good a life as possible under the circumstances.

Mr. Lopez's depression had dropped from severe to moderate, as indicated by weekly Beck Depression Inventory (Beck, Steer, & Brown, 1996) scores, but his pain ratings remained high. Because he seemed closed to ever admitting to less pain, we discussed how it would be better for him to do daily ratings of how much his pain bothered him. That is, without challenging the client's claim of constant pain, we could assess his coping in terms of being less bothered by the pain because of activities (i.e., distractions) and thinking patterns.

Addressing the Client's Sense of Uselessness

Although his thoughts were relatively easy to identify, core beliefs are by definition more central and less consciously available to clients. Often, they are activated only during stressful events, can elicit catharsis when identified, and require considerable assistance identifying them and their role in causing and maintaining psychological distress. To begin identifying such core beliefs, I asked Mr. Lopez perhaps the most probing question in therapy: Could he help me understand what the hardest part about living with his pain and disability was? He quickly answered, "*Porque ya no sirvo para nada!*" [Because I am no longer good for nothing!] and "*No valgo!*" [I do not have any worth or value]. On exploring the roots of such a belief, it came up that Mr. Lopez's father had frequently made similar statements when talking about manhood and its relation to hard work and providing for the family, and we both discussed how common this belief was in Mexican culture and among those who perform physical labor. We also sketched out on paper the relation between such a belief and depression in the event of injury and disability.

I asked the client in a manner that made him laugh what we should do with men in our families who can no longer work: "*Debemos echarlos pa' fuera?*" ["Should we throw 'em out?"]. However, when the laughter subsided, Mr. Lopez became teary eyed and asked, "What good is such a man?" I answered that everybody becomes unable to work eventually yet can remain valuable to others. I then asked him to consider the value of retired elderly family members, and he was able to name some of their important functions, such as giving advice to younger family members and being good *compañeros* [companions] to spouses and friends. I strategically amplified his answer by adding that they also serve as examples of how to cope with problems such as chronic illnesses to which younger family members eventually succumb. I then asked him to think about what he wanted to teach his son at home about coping with chronic pain and disability.

Giving the central value of *familismo* in Mexican and Latinx culture and the respect accorded to elders in the family, this reasoning made cultural sense to the client, and we eventually constructed a counter to his core beliefs "I'm not good for anything" and "I don't have any value," such as the following: "Yes, it's true that I can no longer work and earn money like before my injury, but . . ." (How would the reader complete an adaptive counter belief?).

To give the restructuring of his problematic core beliefs a "testing ground," we wrote up a behavioral contract in which he was assigned to stop by the auto shop where he used to work to visit some of his old friends. I told him that he could expect his negative core belief to interfere with attempting this assignment but that he was now prepared, given the positive counter belief that we had written on an index card for him to carry in his shirt pocket and practice during the week. In addition, we did some role playing in which he practiced responses to questions that his friends were likely to ask, such as what was wrong with him, whether he is going to recover, and what he is doing now.

CULTURALLY SENSITIVE ASSERTIVENESS TRAINING

Limit Setting With Client

At first, the client was happy to see me and on two occasions brought small 4-ounce cans of Folgers coffee for me to try at home because it was his favorite. I graciously accepted these gifts in a manner consistent with Latinx culture. However, as therapy became more difficult in challenging the client to do more activities to lift his mood and to help out at home, he often became angry.

At one point in therapy, Mr. Lopez again balled his fist but this time struck my desk when he felt I was suggesting something unreasonable (i.e., we were discussing his need for more physical therapy). I recall having to monitor and control my impulse to admonish him so that I could seize the moment to illustrate the role his thoughts played in driving his anger and hostility, which could result in physical harm to himself as well as others. I said, "I see that you're very angry, but instead of hitting my desk, can you help me understand what I said that made you so angry?" When the client answered that I did not understand how painful physical therapy was for him, I sketched out on paper how such a belief would make anybody in his position angry but that there might be other ways to interpret my comment (e.g., concern).

The incident also made me consider the possibility that Mr. Lopez was expressing anger at me in a manner similar to the way he behaved toward his adult son at home. As such, I had to think about how to assertively set limits with him as a prelude to addressing such family issues.

Family-Focused Interventions

The client described how he would get angry with his adult son whom he would ask to do things but who was either too busy to do them immediately or could not do them to his father's satisfaction (e.g., car and home repairs). There appeared to be few challenges to the client from wife, son, and other family members. Midway through treatment, I asked the client to invite his wife and son to therapy so that I could better assess and address family dynamics.

In response to my suggestion, the client brought his wife and adult son to two sessions of therapy. To accommodate their work schedules, I had to arrange two evening sessions in which I was able to gain more information regarding my hypothesis about the client's possible secondary gain (i.e., attention) for complaining about his pain. Although our clinic is not set up for family therapy per se, it is important in working with Latinx clients to be open to inviting key family members to therapy sessions.

Mrs. Lopez and her son, Hector, expressed considerable concern for Mr. Lopez but also expressed some exasperation about how to help. Mrs. Lopez's biggest frustration was dealing with her husband breaking things in anger when she asked him to help with household chores. The son similarly expressed frustration with his father's anger when he could not do tasks to Mr. Lopez's satisfaction or as quickly as his father desired. In both cases,

I saw the need for assertive limit setting with Mr. Lopez's anger but realized that the wife and son ran the risk of being perceived as rude and disrespectful. The potential culture clash here is that American assertiveness training is based on democratic principles and a personal (equal) "right" to express one's thoughts and feelings that can run counter to the nondemocratic, traditional hierarchy of many Latinx families. Hence, I had to teach assertiveness in a culturally sensitive manner, and I relied on the informative work of Comas-Díaz and Duncan (1985) to pursue this strategy.

I began by informing Mrs. Lopez and Hector that anger makes Mr. Lopez's pain worse and that although his frustration and irritability are understandable, he could use their help in managing his anger. I then asked Mr. Lopez whether he would "permit" his wife and son to help him by occasionally giving their opinions on family matters and by expressing their feelings to him about how he is handling difficult situations. Phrased this way, he could hardly say no because the term *permit* within Latinx culture acknowledges the respect he deserves as head of the family (i.e., permitted vs. unsolicited criticism).

Next, I tried to model culturally sensitive assertiveness by reminding Mr. Lopez of the time he struck my desk with his fist, asking him to role play this event. With an embarrassed smile, he pretended to strike the desk, and I said to him, "*Con todo respeto, Papá, por favor no pegas mi escritorio. No es bueno para tu salud y también me hace sentirme mal cuando prefería sentirme bien contigo*" ["With all due respect, Dad, please do not hit my desk. It is not good for your health, and it makes me feel bad when I would prefer to feel good with you"]. Note how this communication begins with an acknowledgment of respect before making a request and expressing one's reactions to the father's hostile behavior.

When I asked Mr. Lopez how he felt about such a communication, he said that it was okay. After helping the son to practice the communication, we also did a little added problem solving such as suggesting to the son that he give his father an alternate time when he could do a chore if he was too busy to do it when requested. I also told Mr. Lopez that nobody was going to do things for him to his satisfaction until he became less frustrated with his diminished ability to do things (i.e., that perhaps he was taking his frustration out on his wife and son).

With regard to secondary gain for disrupting family outings with his pain, I addressed this topic with Mrs. Lopez and Hector, and they noted that if Mr. Lopez experiences great pain during a drive or while at a family gathering he insists they all return home. This demand was typically met by unsuccessful attempts to console Mr. Lopez. I asked the family whether they could think of a way to achieve "balance" between taking care of Mr. Lopez and taking care of the family's need to relax and spend time together. The son offered the idea of taking two cars to such events in case Mr. Lopez felt the need to leave (he still drove, albeit with pain and effort). I asked everybody whether this was acceptable, and they agreed to try it out.

I also emphasized that Mrs. Lopez and Hector should continue encouraging Mr. Lopez's involvement with family activities but should resist being overly attentive to his bouts of pain and discomfort because sometimes too much attention can increase irritability (i.e., sometimes paying less attention to a chronic problem is better). I added that they should also not wait until a severe bout of pain to check in with Mr. Lopez to see how he is doing. Again, I checked this out with everybody, and all were agreed to implement this new strategy. I warned them that this would take practice because it was not the natural way that they dealt with things.

In the ensuing weeks, Mr. Lopez reported less complaining at family gatherings and on one occasion leaving a gathering early by himself in his car. Although he continued to report being irritable, he had stopped breaking things and was permitting his wife and son to express their opinions on his behavior. We discussed how important it was for him to promote more open communication given his family's need to be more bicultural in the United States (with assertiveness being an important skill for his son and wife to have in their places of work, etc.). Here the emphasis was not on replacing Latinx communication styles with American styles but on enhancing bicultural skills for maximum flexibility.

ACTIVITY INTERVENTIONS

Mr. Lopez came to our next session smiling about completing the behavioral contract to visit his former workplace. He shared how enjoyable it was to talk with his former coworkers whom he had visited a couple of days before our session. He even recalled giving some advice and guidance on an automotive problem that a former coworker was trying to solve. I asked Mr. Lopez how "bothersome" his pain was on the day he visited his old job, and he rated it a 6 on the 10-point scale ranging from *pain not bothersome* (1) to *pain very bothersome* (10), his lowest rating yet.

Resuming Physical Therapy

Toward the latter part of therapy, I opened up the topic of resuming physical therapy by trying to use an analogy that my client as a mechanic might appreciate. I told him that I realized that there were problems with his physical therapy but that just as it is important to maintain a car regularly; it would be in the best interest of his health to resume physical therapy. The client immediately became red faced, raised his voice, and said that they requested too much of him in the pain clinic. I asked Mr. Lopez to forget about the pain clinic for a moment and to consider what happens to a car when its owner goes on vacation and stops using it for weeks. He noted how the battery might go dead, and we continued to discuss mechanical problems that could occur over the course of months of inactivity. Next, I conveyed his physical therapists' concern that without such therapy he could wind up with more pain and disability. Thus, the argument for physical therapy was pitched more in terms of "cutting losses" rather than improvement per se. With respect to Mr. Lopez's concern about the painfulness of exercising, we discussed the analogy of dental visits, which can be painful at the moment but which prevent more pain and problems in the long run.

I offered to meet with the client and his physical therapist "just to discuss areas of disagreement." I told him that before he decided whether to return, it would be important to make sure all parties involved understood each other (especially given the language differences). In preparation for the meeting, I pressed Mr. Lopez to consider other ways of looking at his physical therapists' insistence that he do some difficult exercises. Although he insisted they could not feel and understand his pain, he was able to acknowledge the possibility that they were concerned about his health and wanted to prevent him from becoming inactive and worse.

I reminded Mr. Lopez that the pain clinic was providing a service to him and that as a consumer he could express his thoughts and desires to them. We again did some role playing in which we practiced communications that he could use with his physical therapists. Such communications included the request for an explanation of the day's exercises, as well as responses to requests that he perceived as too demanding. Role playing was expedited by replaying his last encounter at the pain clinic in which he claimed that certain exercises landed him in bed for a couple of days. I asked him to role play the therapist's requests and modeled sample assertive responses (in broken English) such as the following: "Can we slow down please?" "What is this exercise for?" and "Can we try it another way?"

The meeting with pain clinic staff went fairly well, with the former eventually being able to convey their sincere concerns about Mr. Lopez's health and the client asserting his worry about hurting himself. In the beginning, however, things almost went awry when a frustrated pain clinic staff member unintentionally challenged Mr. Lopez's machismo by saying, "If you don't do your physical therapy, your back is going to get worse!" to which Mr. Lopez argued that it was his business. When I asked the staff person the motivation behind his statement, he said he wanted Mr. Lopez to get better, and he knew he could be helpful to him.

All eventually agreed to a "trial" return to the clinic in which exercises would be thoroughly explained and where Mr. Lopez could elect not to attempt certain exercises (i.e., have some control over the situation). This particular intervention is an example of the flexibility required of therapists working with clients with multiple problems that need support and "culture brokering" from therapists who are overly accustomed to providing only an hour of weekly, in-session assistance.

Culturally Appropriate Termination

During our last month of treatment, I began to prepare Mr. Lopez for termination by reviewing our problem list and therapeutic strategies. The client was generally positive about the CBT treatment plan as applied to his pain, depression, and anger. He had no trouble "buying" the important role of behaviors and activities in the management of his situation and the lifelong need to continue these techniques after terminating therapy. The posttreatment evaluation revealed mild to moderate depression, a clinically significant gain for the depression clinic's low-income, frequently overwhelmed, and severely depressed patient population.

With regard to termination, we routinely tell our clients that they are free to drop by and say hello, and in the case of Mr. Lopez, treat me to a *cafesito*. This flexible approach to termination is related to our hospital-based location, where we frequently see our many clients coming in for various medical appointments. However, it is also based on Latinx relationship protocol in which it would seem abnormal to terminate a positive and personalized relationship completely.

Although most clients do not stop by, Mr. Lopez did eventually return and offer to buy me a cup of coffee downstairs in the hospital cafeteria. Although busy at the moment, I graciously accepted the offer and asked whether we could meet at a nearby cafe that brewed extra good coffee. He responded that the cafe was a bit out of his way but that if the coffee were really that good, it would be worth it.

CONCLUSION

As a logically cohesive and didactic set of techniques, CBT is relatively straightforward and lends itself to empowering clients with effective ways to prevent and mitigate painful and debilitating signs and symptoms of distress and mental disorders. To maximize the reach of CBT across diverse cultural populations such as Latinxs, it is important to continue adapting CBT to cultural and social backgrounds and realities of our increasingly diverse client population. In response to this exciting challenge, this chapter provided a set of specific recommendations, based on years of clinical experience, illustrated with a detailed case study. As recommended in Benuto and O'Donohue's (2015) review of the literature on CBT with Latinxs, this chapter highlighted regularities in Latinx culture that can be integrated into treatment (i.e., relationship protocols based on core traditional values to enhance engagement and trust, engaging family members where relevant) and identified aspects of CBT that can be modified to be more culturally (i.e., culturally sensitive assertiveness training, streamlined cognitive restructuring, less rigid termination) and socially (i.e., activity schedules mindful of low income backgrounds) competent. As such, culturally competent CBT can more effectively alleviate human suffering, maximize adjustment, and unleash unlimited human potential.

REFERENCES

Alegría, M., Ludman, E., Kafali, E. N., Lapatin, S., Vila, D., Shrout, P. E., . . . Canino, G. (2014). Effectiveness of the Engagement and Counseling for Latinos (ECLA) intervention in low-income Latinos. *Medical Care, 52,* 989–997. http://dx.doi.org/10.1097/MLR.0000000000000232

American Psychiatric Association. (2013). *Diagnostic and statistical manual of mental disorders* (5th ed.). Arlington, VA: Author.

Beck, A. T., Steer, R. A., & Brown, G. K. (1996). *Manual for the BDI–II.* San Antonio, TX: The Psychological Corporation.

Benuto, L. T., & O'Donohue, W. (2015). Is culturally sensitive cognitive behavioral therapy an empirically supported treatment? The case for Hispanics. *International Journal of Psychology and Psychological Therapy, 15,* 405–421.

Brown, A., & Stepler, R. (2016). *Facts on U.S. immigrants, 2015: Statistical portrait of the foreign-born population in the United States.* Retrieved from Pew Research Center website: http://www.pewhispanic.org/2016/04/19/statistical-portrait-of-the-foreign-born-population-in-the-united-states-key-charts/

Burns, D. D., & Nolen-Hoeksema, S. (1992). Therapeutic empathy and recovery from depression in cognitive-behavioral therapy: A structural equation model. *Journal of Consulting and Clinical Psychology, 60,* 441–449. http://dx.doi.org/10.1037/0022-006X.60.3.441

Cabassa, L. J., & Hansen, M. C. (2007). A systematic review of depression treatments in primary care for Latino adults. *Research on Social Work Practice, 17,* 494–503. http://dx.doi.org/10.1177/1049731506297058

Comas-Díaz, L., & Duncan, J. W. (1985). The cultural context: A factor in assertiveness training with mainland Puerto Rican women. *Psychology of Women Quarterly, 9,* 463–476. http://dx.doi.org/10.1111/j.1471-6402.1985.tb00896.x

Cook, B., Alegría, M., Lin, J. Y., & Guo, J. (2009). Pathways and correlates connecting Latinos' mental health with exposure to the United States. *American Journal of Public Health, 99,* 2247–2254. http://dx.doi.org/10.2105/AJPH.2008.137091

Duany, J. (2017). *Puerto Rico: What everyone needs to know.* New York, NY: Oxford University Press.

Dwight-Johnson, M., Aisenberg, E., Golinelli, D., Hong, S., O'Brien, M., & Ludman, E. (2011). Telephone-based cognitive-behavioral therapy for Latino patients living in rural areas: A randomized pilot study. *Psychiatric Services, 62,* 936–942. http://dx.doi.org/10.1176/ps.62.8.pss6208_0936

Falicov, C. J. (2014). *Latino families in therapy* (2nd ed.). New York, NY: Guilford Press.

Guarnaccia, P. J. (1993). *Ataques de nervios* in Puerto Rico: Culture-bound syndrome or popular illness? *Medical Anthropology, 15,* 157–170. http://dx.doi.org/10.1080/01459740.1993.9966087

Hatzenbuehler, M. L., Prins, S. J., Flake, M., Philbin, M., Frazer, M. S., Hagen, D., & Hirsch, J. (2017). Immigration policies and mental health morbidity among Latinos: A state-level analysis. *Social Science & Medicine, 174,* 169–178. http://dx.doi.org/10.1016/j.socscimed.2016.11.040

Kessler, R. C., Berglund, P., Demler, O., Jin, R., Merikangas, K. R., & Walters, E. E. (2005). Lifetime prevalence and age-of-onset distributions of DSM–IV disorders in the National Comorbidity Survey Replication. *Archives of General Psychiatry, 62,* 593–602. http://dx.doi.org/10.1001/archpsyc.62.6.593

Lopez, G. (2015a). *Hispanics of Cuban origin in the United States, 2013: Statistical profile.* Retrieved from Pew Research Center website: http://www.pewhispanic.org/2015/09/15/hispanics-of-cuban-origin-in-the-united-states-2013

Lopez, G. (2015b). *Hispanics of Dominican origin in the United States, 2013: Statistical profile.* Retrieved from Pew Research Center website: http://www.pewhispanic.org/2015/09/15/hispanics-of-dominican-origin-in-the-united-states-2013/

Lopez, G. (2015c). *Hispanics of Guatemalan origin in the United States, 2013: Statistical profile.* Retrieved from Pew Research Center website: http://www.pewhispanic.org/2015/09/15/hispanics-of-guatemalan-origin-in-the-united-states-2013/

Lopez, G. (2015d). *Hispanics of Mexican origin in the United States, 2013: Statistical profile.* Retrieved from Pew Research Center website: http://www.pewhispanic.org/2015/09/15/hispanics-of-mexican-origin-in-the-united-states-2013/

Lopez, G. (2015e). *Hispanics of Salvadoran origin in the United States, 2013: Statistical profile.* Retrieved from Pew Research Center website: http://www.pewhispanic.org/2015/09/15/hispanics-of-salvadoran-origin-in-the-united-states-2013/

Lopez, G., & Patten, E. (2015). *Hispanics of Puerto Rican origin in the United States, 2013: Statistical profile.* Retrieved from Pew Research Center website: http://www.pewhispanic.org/2015/09/15/hispanics-of-puerto-rican-origin-in-the-united-states-2013/

Miranda, J., Azocar, F., Organista, K. C., Dwyer, E., & Arean, P. (2003). Treatment of depression among impoverished primary care patients from ethnic minority groups. *Psychiatric Services, 54*, 219–225. http://dx.doi.org/10.1176/appi.ps.54.2.219

Nathan, P. E., & Gorman, J. M. (Eds.). (2015). *A guide to treatments that work* (4th ed.). New York, NY: Oxford University Press. http://dx.doi.org/10.1093/med:psych/9780195304145.001.0001

Organista, K. C. (1995). Cognitive-behavioral treatment of depression and panic disorder in a Latina patient: Culturally sensitive case formulation. *In Session: Psychotherapy in Practice, 1*, 53–64.

Organista, K. C. (2007a). The Americanization of Latinos: Patterns of acculturation and adjustment in the United States. In K. C. Organista (Ed.), *Solving Latino psychosocial and health problems* (pp. 3–38). Hoboken, NJ: Wiley.

Organista, K. C. (2007b). Latino mental health. In K. C. Organista (Ed.), *Solving Latino psychosocial and health problems* (pp. 215–244). Hoboken, NJ: Wiley.

Organista, K. C., & Hernandez, M. (2014). The mental health needs of the undocumented. In L. A. Lorentzen (Ed.), *Hidden lives and human rights in the United States: Understanding the controversies and tragedies of undocumented immigration* (Vol. II, pp. 321–353). Santa Barbara, CA: Praeger.

Organista, K. C., & Muñoz, R. F. (1996). Cognitive behavioral therapy with Latinos. *Cognitive and Behavioral Practice, 3*, 255–270. http://dx.doi.org/10.1016/S1077-7229(96)80017-4

Organista, K. C., & Dwyer, E. V. (1997). Clinical case management and cognitive-behavioral therapy: Integrated psychosocial services for depressed Latino primary care patients. In P. G. Manoleas (Ed.), *The cross-cultural practice of clinical case management in mental health* (pp. 119–143). New York: The Haworth Press.

Orlinsky, D. E., & Howard, K. I. (1986). Process and outcome in psychotherapy. In S. L. Garfield & A. E. Bergin (Eds.), *Handbook of psychotherapy and behavior change* (3rd ed., pp. 311–381). New York, NY: Wiley.

Roll, S., Millen, L., & Martinez, R. (1980). Common errors in psychotherapy with Chicanos: Extrapolations from research and clinical experience. *Psychotherapy: Theory, Research & Practice, 17*, 158–168. http://dx.doi.org/10.1037/h0085906

Sweig, J. E. (2016). *Cuba: What everyone needs to know.* New York, NY: Oxford University Press.

World Health Organization. (2015). *International classification of diseases, tenth revision, clinical modification.*

4

COGNITIVE BEHAVIOR THERAPY WITH AFRICAN AMERICANS

SHALONDA KELLY

African Americans are one of the largest minority groups in the United States, comprising 13.3% of the U.S. population (U.S. Census Bureau, 2017), and their common challenges are unique. Africans had founded advanced agricultural kingdoms such as Timbuktu but were enslaved and forcibly brought to the United States, and attempts were made to eradicate their culture and break up their families after their arrival. Such acts provided their White slave owners the convenience and profit of using their labor to build the cotton industry that established the economic infrastructure of the United States (Black & Jackson, 2005; Coates, 2014). After the end of slavery in 1870, racially hostile laws and practices continued, such as the dehumanizing Jim Crow laws of the late 1800s, lynchings that lasted into the 1930s, and forced segregation into inferior schools until 1954 (Black & Jackson, 2005). Into the mid-1900s, many African Americans migrated from the rural South to the urban North to gain employment and escape brutality

http://dx.doi.org/10.1037/0000119-005
Culturally Responsive Cognitive Behavior Therapy, Second Edition: Practice and Supervision, G. Y. Iwamasa and P. A. Hays (Editors)

and segregation, resulting in wide-scale disruption of their families and communities. African Americans continued to be denied basic rights until the Civil Rights and Voting Rights Acts in the 1960s. From the 1980s to the present, there has been the widespread practice of race-related mass incarceration of African Americans (Higgins, Ricketts, Griffith, & Jirard, 2013). During the housing crisis of the early 2000s, predatory subprime loans were disproportionately given to African Americans compared with their White counterparts of the same socioeconomic status (Wesley, 2017).

These interconnected and systematic laws, policies, and practices that disadvantage African Americans at all ecological levels across U.S. history constitute structural racism. African Americans continue to experience systematic discrimination in employment (e.g., Coleman, 2003), housing (e.g., Wesley, 2017), education (e.g., Gregory, Skiba, & Noguera, 2010), the justice system (e.g., Higgins et al., 2013), and the media (e.g., Coltrane & Messineo, 2000). They also experience inferior mental and physical health services and high morbidity rates (e.g., Wesley, 2017).

These systems of structural racism are legitimized through negative stereotypes, segregation, and socioeconomic stratification. For example, the average well-meaning person often observes African American low social status across situations. From these observations, the person develops implicit racial bias in unfairly applying automatic negative stereotypes and perceiving African Americans' skin color as a marker for pathology and poverty. Moreover, such biases prevent the acknowledgment of systematic discrimination by members of the dominant White culture (e.g., Sampson & Raudenbush, 2004). Such stigma legitimizes dehumanization and likely relates to the disproportionate number of racial hate crimes that African Americans face at the microsystemic level (U.S. Department of Justice—Federal Bureau of Investigation, 2015), as well as frequent microaggressions—that is, cumulative discrimination in the form of small racial slights and insults (D. W. Sue et al., 2007). Some African Americans may internalize negative stereotypes of themselves, which are associated with individual distress and poor relationship quality (e.g., Kelly, 2004; Kelly & Floyd, 2006).

COMMONALITIES RELEVANT TO TREATMENT

Experiences, Worldviews, and Culture-Related Behaviors

African Americans' experiences of structural racism are highly relevant to treatment. African Americans report significantly more perceived racial and ethnic discrimination than other racial and ethnic groups (e.g., Chou, Asnaani, & Hofmann, 2012). Their perceptions of racial discrimination are associated with disorders such as depression (e.g., Matthews, Hammond, Nuru-Jeter, Cole-Lewis, & Melvin, 2013). In fact, a meta-analysis of 66 studies found that perceived racism is positively associated with psychological distress for African Americans, particularly regarding specific psychiatric symptoms common to trauma victims (Pieterse, Todd, Neville, & Carter, 2012). Moreover, after controlling for demographics in a large-scale study, for only those reporting perceived racial and ethnic discrimination, African Americans experience higher rates of panic disorders and posttraumatic stress disorder than their Asian American and Latino counterparts (Chou et al., 2012). The relationship between perceived racism and psychological functioning remains when demographics and/or stressors are controlled (e.g., Schulz et al., 2000). Notably, the mental health field historically has contributed to the pathologizing, deficit view of African Americans (Wesley, 2017).

Anger at perceived racism and discrimination is one of the primary reasons many African Americans seek therapy (Clark, 2000). African Americans' experiences of inequity and stress can lead to particular treatment presentations. Many African Americans experience rage that may be expressed toward White therapists or even therapists of color who are seen as representatives of the dominant culture. Anger may also be directed toward family members because they are safer targets or because family members fail to support one another—for example, arguing over who experiences the worst racism or how racist incidents should be handled (e.g., Kelly, 2003). Generations of oppression has resulted in a deep distrust of Whites by many African Americans, which often is referred to as a "healthy cultural paranoia" (Boyd-Franklin, 2003). Unsurprisingly, in one study, African Americans attended fewer therapy sessions and discussed fewer racially stigmatized topics, such as substance abuse, when they were not matched with an African American therapist (Ibaraki & Hall, 2014).

African Americans may also present with worldviews related to the pain of oppression. For example, some may exhibit internalized racism as manifested in negative in-group statements and a preference for White therapists, who some may perceive as more competent than African American therapists (Boyd-Franklin, 2003; Kelly, 2003, 2004). Some African Americans become demoralized by racism, which leads to feelings of nihilism, an external locus of control, or a fatalistic perspective. Some therapists misinterpret these worldviews and coping responses as blaming others, being self-pitying, or lacking motivation. Laszloffy and Hardy (2000) described such an example:

> In the first session between a therapist and an 11-year-old African American boy diagnosed with conduct disorder, the child described his misbehavior as related to his dislike of his White teacher, who he felt was racist. After hearing his examples, the therapist, who was [also] White, told him that he may have misunderstood the teacher's intentions and

actions, and that his anger was no excuse to break the rules. Moreover, the predominantly White supervisory team behind the two-way mirror agreed with the therapist; they all viewed his behavior through the lens of his disorder, and none considered race or racism in their discussion. Not surprisingly, the child and his family discontinued treatment. (p. 43)

Several common cultural tendencies among African Americans may present challenges to traditional psychotherapy. Beliefs that "the future will wait" and experiences with social services that require people to wait for hours may foster excessive lateness and missed appointments (Hardy, 2004). In valuing direct experience in deciding whom to trust, African Americans may ignore a therapist's academic degrees and suggestions until they are sure of the feeling or "vibes" they get from the therapist (Boyd-Franklin, 2003). Another potential issue for therapists is that despite their training against corporal punishment (American Psychological Association, 1975), data from large samples show that it is not associated with negative outcomes in African American communities where it is prevalent (Simons et al., 2002) and children do not view it as a sign of caregiver rejection (Rohner, Bourque, & Elordi, 1996). Therapists must carefully consider their approach when corporal punishment issues arise in treatment, including the severity of corporal punishment because corporal punishment involving the need for medical treatment would not be acceptable in the African American community. In a related vein, many African Americans may cope with hard life experiences by being tough or perfectionistic (Kelly & Hudson, 2017). Toughness has the benefit of resilience in the face of adversity, yet it may make it more difficult for them to bond with the therapist or even with their own family members. Striving for perfection can lead to success, yet it may add to one's stress burden, consistent with the folk tale of John Henry, an African American man who used active high-effort coping to succeed but died from it (e.g., Matthews et al., 2013). Finally, therapists may misinterpret emotional expressiveness, nonverbal communication, and nonstandard language as an inability to regulate emotions and communicate effectively (e.g., Boyd-Franklin, 2003; Kelly & Boyd-Franklin, 2005).

Cultural Strengths

Cultural strengths and supports among African Americans can help to offset the adverse effects of racism and discrimination (e.g., Kelly, Maynigo, Wesley, & Durham, 2013). An important source of strength and support originating in African cultures is the extended family, which can include blood kin, such as cousins, and "fictive kin," who are unrelated by blood (e.g., a "play mama"; Boyd-Franklin, 2003). The extended family may engage in reciprocal assistance with money, goods, and services that increase the economic viability of African American families (Taylor, Chatters, & Jackson, 1997). Extended family members may share their homes with each other for short-term stays during times of financial hardship or for longer periods, as in the case of informal adoption (e.g., Boyd-Franklin, 2003). Extended family members may also serve as mediators, judges, or networkers, flexibly adopting these roles as needed. African American parents also prepare their children for the race-related struggles they will encounter. Findings show that increased parental racial socialization increases the likelihood that African American youth will explore and commit to their racial identity (Seaton, Yip, Morgan-Lopez, & Sellers, 2012). Overall, surveys show that proximity, subjective closeness, and frequency of kinship interaction contribute to the physical and emotional well-being of African Americans (Taylor et al., 1997).

Religion and spirituality are additional sources of strength for African Americans, and data have consistently demonstrated greater levels of religiosity and spirituality for African Americans compared with other ethnic groups (e.g., Pew Research Center, 2009). African American churches provide formal and informal supports such as childcare and educational programs that help improve the welfare of African Americans (e.g., Kelly & Hudson, 2017). Churches enable African Americans to obtain the leadership roles, status, and skills that compensate for the relative lack of opportunities and status in the dominant culture. Many African Americans seek help from the church, rather than from mental health professionals, for mental health and family support (Chatters, Taylor, Bullard, & Jackson, 2008). Data also show that African American religiosity fosters relationship stability (Cutrona, Russell, Burzette, Wesner, & Bryant, 2011), which can be used in treatment to improve their couple relationships (Beach et al., 2011).

A positive racial or ethnic identity is another source of strength for African Americans. The National Survey of American Life surveyed 3,570 African Americans nationwide and found that, on average, these African Americans have a strong and positive racial identity (Hughes, Kiecolt, Keith, & Demo, 2015). They identify highly with their own group, endorse feeling between fairly and very close to other African Americans of all backgrounds, and endorse more positive than negative attributes about African Americans as a group (Hughes et al., 2015). Those participants who identify more with their racial group and evaluate it more positively have higher self-esteem, greater mastery, and fewer depressive symptoms. Conversely, for those who evaluate African Americans negatively, a strong identification with the group is associated with lower mastery and more depressive symptoms, which the authors attributed to internalized racism (Hughes et al., 2015).

INDIVIDUAL DIFFERENCES AMONG
THOSE OF AFRICAN DESCENT

Many demographic factors including but not limited to skin color, gender, and socioeconomic status (SES) profoundly affect the experiences of African Americans (Celious & Oyserman, 2001). Data show that socio-economic gaps between light and dark African Americans are of the same magnitude as the gap between Whites and Blacks in America. Those who are light may be considered prettier, are often more affluent, and receive better treatment in the broader society. Still, both very light and very dark African Americans can experience bias. For example, those who are dark are sometimes prized within the community because they are considered to be racially pure (Celious & Oyserman, 2001). Societal stereotypes of African American men elicit fear and hostility (e.g., fear of them being violent criminals), whereas those of African American women elicit derision and sexual intrigue (e.g., stereotypes of them being welfare queens and Jezebels). Data supports the existence of both types of stereotypes (Torres-Harding, Andrade, & Romero Diaz, 2012). Such treatment results in differing experiences for each gender (Celious & Oyserman, 2001). African Americans also are among the poorest racial groups (e.g., Wickrama, Noh, & Bryant, 2005), and even at higher income levels, there are large wealth and resource gaps between the wealthiest African Americans and the wealthiest Whites (Saegert, Fields, & Libman, 2011). African Americans of greater SES tend to report experiencing greater discrimination because they have greater contact with the larger society (Cutrona et al., 2003). Clearly, it is important to note the individual differences that exist among African Americans.

Although African Americans are the focus of this chapter, there are notable differences between African Americans and immigrants from the African diaspora. Many Black immigrants have not experienced American slavery and racism or the loss of as many cultural connections. Many Black immigrants (e.g., West Indians and Africans) are the majority group in their country, so they may define race more broadly than African Americans and often do not experience it as an indicator of success or social mobility. Often, these groups immigrate voluntarily to partake in the American dream, and many have the option of maintaining ties with home or returning home (Stephenson, 2004). Finally, although all Blacks share an African cultural legacy, Black immigrants also have unique cultures related to their country and its history of colonization.

Initially, these differences often result in less awareness of racism, more beliefs in meritocracy, more positive feelings about White Americans, and more varied notions of identity compared with those of African Americans (Phinney & Onwughalu, 1996; Stephenson, 2004). Thus, when confronted with racism, some Black immigrants may experience shock, may distance themselves from African Americans because of their differing national identities, and/or circumvent the adoption of what they view as a restrictive, inferior status (Stephenson, 2004).

This lack of identification and experience with oppression in the first generation may be why Caribbean Blacks and other recent Black immigrants have socioeconomic advantages such as higher household incomes, more prestigious jobs, and higher levels of educational achievement than their African American counterparts (Thornton, Taylor, & Chatters, 2013). They also have mental health advantages in the form of self-reported emotional and physical well-being (Thornton et al., 2013), as well as higher marital satisfaction (Bryant, Taylor, Lincoln, Chatters, & Jackson, 2008) compared with their African American counterparts. Still, data show that American-born children of Black immigrants and the immigrants who stay in America for long periods often develop racial identities and stances that are more similar to those of African Americans (Phinney & Onwughalu, 1996; Stephenson, 2004).

Often, African Americans with the same backgrounds may behave in radically different ways, as determined by their differing levels of acculturation and racial identities. *Acculturation* refers to the extent of adopting the dominant culture versus one's indigenous culture (Klonoff & Landrine, 2000). In mental health treatment, knowledge of acculturation can indicate the likelihood that a given African American client might present in ways more common to African Americans and/or in ways more common to mainstream U.S. culture. Acculturation levels often account for more variance in African American behavior than education and income combined (Klonoff & Landrine, 2000).

> Jim, a White male therapist, had his first session with Larry,[1] an African American male in his early 20s, who was born and raised in Los Angeles, California. In his attempt to develop a rapport with Larry, Jim mentioned how the West Coast was "really cool" because West Coast rappers made the best hip-hop music. To Jim's surprise, Larry said, "I have no idea what you are talking about. I play the cello and study classical music." Jim told his supervisor, who gave him readings on acculturation theory and other aspects of diversity among African Americans, which they then discussed. After that, Jim learned to ask questions aimed at obtaining a better understanding of his clients' levels of acculturation.

Like acculturation, consideration of racial identity is important in treatment because it also involves each client's and each therapist's orientation toward the person's ingroup and toward the dominant group. Therapists of

---

[1]Case material in this chapter has been disguised to protect client confidentiality.

color who see African American clients may receive questions as to their competence, responses conveying distance or dissimilarity, or responses conveying feelings of similarity and/or connection (Boyd-Franklin, 2003). White therapists commonly encounter reluctance to receive treatment, anger related to oppression, or deference (Boyd-Franklin, 2003). The clients' racial identity can explain these observations; racial and ethnic identity predict the degree of preference for African American versus other therapists (e.g., Townes, Chavez-Korell, & Cunningham, 2009). Cross's (1971) seminal racial identity model has undergone much development, but at its core and across model updates, it proposes that in the context of U.S. oppression, African Americans undergo stages of identifying with their race, which range from adhering to Whites' standards, values, and beliefs, and also viewing being Black as something to distance oneself from or something to be degraded, to having a positive sense of their own Blackness, which may take on African-centered or multiculturalist overtones (Kelly & Hudson, 2017). Although this chapter focuses on African Americans and Black racial identity, similar models explain the racial identity of people of color and Whites, whose racial identity processes also begin with holding the dominant White group's standards, values and beliefs (Jernigan, Green, & Helms, 2017).

Helms's social interaction model (SIM) brings each of these racial identity models into the treatment setting; it predicts racial identity challenges for therapists of any race with African American and other clients (Jernigan et al., 2017). This model asserts that when the therapist has a progressive or advanced state of racial identity, such as when the therapist has progressed to having a positive and realistic sense of his or her own race, the therapist will have enough knowledge and sensitivity to model responsiveness to race and other sociodemographic backgrounds. Thus, the therapist can help the client progress to a more advanced state of racial identity. If both the therapist and client have parallel or similar racial identity levels, the relationship will be agreeable due to their having similar racial views and ideologies, but the relationship may not necessarily produce the client's growth in regard to racial identity. If the therapist has a regressive or less advanced racial identity than the client, there is a greater likelihood of opposition, anger, and psychological withdrawal in their interactions. If the therapist and client racial identities are at odds or in direct opposition, they lack a shared framework regarding psychosocial identities, but if the therapist's identity is the one that is more advanced, it can lead to the client's greater self-exploration. Overall, the SIM suggests that developing one's racial identity would be beneficial in working with African American clients, consistent with findings that treatment tailored to the needs of African Americans and other diverse groups yields greater effect sizes (e.g., Griner & Smith, 2006). In addition, one mechanism that yields these effect sizes is the ability of the therapist to tailor treatment to the worldview of the client (Benish, Quintana, & Wampold, 2011).

THE USEFULNESS OF COGNITIVE BEHAVIOR THERAPY WITH AFRICAN AMERICANS

Advantages

With its emphasis on tailoring therapy to the particular individual, cognitive behavior therapy (CBT) has the potential to address African Americans' treatment needs positively. CBT adheres to a functional-analytic approach in which its contingencies shape behavior; therapists seek to understand the function of either problematic or desired behavior by identifying the antecedents and consequences that serve to maintain it (Epstein & Baucom, 2002). CBT also adheres to ideographic assessment data, which are assessment data that are tailored to and maximally relevant for the individual. Thus, functional-analytic ideographic assessment data tailor treatment both to clients and to their relevant, diverse contexts, such as SES and extended families (Kelly, Bhagwat, Maynigo, & Moses, 2014). A CBT approach also can help therapists to avoid a judgmental stance toward differences because observable behavior should never be explained by unobservable mentalistic events such as motivation or intelligence but, rather, be understood in light of their environmental consequences (Fudge, 1996). Instead, as a structured, evidence-based treatment, a CBT approach applies social learning and functional-analytic principles that have been shown to work and which uniquely can be tailored to clients' lives (e.g., Kelly et al., 2013).

The second advantage of CBT with African Americans is the collaborative nature of the treatment; the therapist is the expert on the treatment, but clients are the experts on themselves and their problems. For example, regardless of whether they are seeing individuals, couples, or families, therapists collaborate with clients to ensure shared conceptualization, goals, and interventions by all, and they encourage clients to take a hypothesis-testing stance regarding their issues (Sayers & Heyman, 2003). Cognitive behavior therapists also provide clients with the skills to facilitate change related to the problems defined by the clients. Clients have control over the duration of treatment because it ends when they report that their symptoms are no longer a problem. This emphasis on a collaborative set was speculated to be the reason that observers in one study rated CBT significantly higher on the therapeutic alliance than psychodynamic treatments (Raue, Goldfried, & Barkham, 1997).

The third potentially beneficial characteristic of CBT with African Americans is its emphasis on empowerment. CBT empowers African

American clients by helping them build strengths, supports, and skills to meet their goals more effectively (e.g., Sayers & Heyman, 2003). Therapists actively help clients to build on and expand social support and recognize coping skills that have worked for them in the past and may work again (Epstein & Baucom, 2002). Clients also are taught to look for and expect evidence of ongoing improvement and to use behavioral experiments that provide evidence to replace their cognitive distortions with realistic, noncatastrophic appraisals (e.g., Epstein & Baucom, 2002).

In sum, the advantages of CBT with African Americans include an emphasis on nonjudgmental, collaborative problem solving and empowerment of the client through skill building and strengthening of natural support systems. Note these key components in the following example:

> Peter was an African American first-generation college freshman who sought treatment at the university clinic for depression and difficulties completing schoolwork. His therapist was John, a White, third-generation Italian American. Because Peter was attending college locally, part of his problem involved the racial differences between him and his college peers and the pressure he felt from his high school friends who had not "made it" to college. His friends gave him messages to "keep it real and stop acting like those stuck up White boys." John avoided the assumption that Peter's friends were bad. Nor did he imply that these friendships were deficient or try to break Peter's friendships by raising the pros and cons of ending those relationships or encouraging him to behave more like his White college peers. Instead, John encouraged Peter to talk about his friendships and normalized his experiences by suggesting that it is not an uncommon coping mechanism for friends to denigrate experiences they have not had together, as a way of preventing the loss of the friendship. Following John's normalizing, psychoeducational reframe, Peter described several instances in which his high school peers had applauded his academic efforts. They then solved the problem of how to maintain his old friendships as a means of improving his depression and academic performance.

Limitations

Many cognitive behavior therapists and researchers claim that CBT is a neutral and universally applicable approach due to its scientific orientation (e.g., Kelly et al., 2014). S. Sue (1999) challenged this myth by noting researchers' and therapists' selective enforcement of the scientific principles of skepticism and convincingness, as when they lack skepticism about the validity of generalizing findings found with White Americans to ethnic minorities. Conversely, many have claimed that findings obtained from ethnic minorities are not generalizable if they lack a White control group when they do not require the reverse. Another bias is the assumption that one must take a "colorblind" approach. The erroneous belief that such an approach is value neutral hinders consideration of cultural influences on human behavior and thus hinders fair treatment of ethnic minorities (e.g., Kelly et al., 2014).

Fudge (1996) also noted that science continues to sanction the use of nonscientific concepts to explain African Americans' behavior. For example, subjective assertions of negative innate or genetic tendencies have long been asserted about African Americans, and often deficit models regarding African Americans' differences from Whites are readily believed and investigated. For example,

> Shannon, an African American student, began treatment at a local counseling center because of the stress of her first year of graduate school in biology. In an early session describing her feelings of alienation on campus, she complained to her therapist that one of her professors described research investigating genetic causes of Black violence, as if African Americans were inferior and genetically prone to violence. Although her White female therapist empathized with her, being a cognitive behavioral scientist–practitioner, the therapist tried to explain the teacher's perspective by saying, "It may help you to know that in the pursuit of knowledge, scientists should be able to study any topic." The student was offended and angrily quipped, "Well, I never heard about studies of a gene for violence in Whites back when they were lynching and conquering everybody."

Beyond the therapist's discounting of her client's experience of oppression, this vignette highlights the Eurocentrism embedded in CBT and in the research base on which it is founded. African Americans are underrepresented as research participants and as researchers (Ginther et al., 2011) and, as such, exert little influence on the topics, direction, and value placed on areas of psychotherapy research. The psychotherapy research that does exist regarding African Americans is still at the descriptive and understanding phases, far behind the prediction and control phases of research regarding White Americans. Although data have begun to show the effectiveness of culturally adapted treatments overall, much less is known about adaptations to African Americans in particular, even though data have shown that such specific tailoring yields greater effect sizes (e.g., Griner & Smith, 2006).

Eurocentrism is also a problem in some applications of cognitive behavioral theory. For example, the emphasis on rational thinking can be interpreted in ways that devalue African Americans' spirituality and tendencies toward emotional expressiveness.

> One African American client reported that her depression would increase if she could not cry and let out her emotions periodically. This sounded illogical and too much like a catharsis for her therapist, who

challenged her belief and encouraged the client to regulate her emotions at those times. The client then felt chastised and began to try to hold in her tears, though they functioned to relieve stress in her life.

Similarly, mainstream U.S. values regarding the importance of personal independence and autonomy (e.g., Smith, 2010) tend to be reinforced by cognitive behavioral orientations. Cognitive behavior therapists who fail to recognize the importance of family and community for their African American clients may be seen as reinforcing dominant individualistic cultural values (Kelly et al., 2014). They may overlook how the community may serve as social support, yield empowerment via community service that addresses structural issues related to their presenting problems, and offer experiences consistent with an Afrocentric perspective and a positive racial and ethnic identity. From a behavioral perspective, involvement in the community can help African Americans to actively change the contingencies in their environment that maintain their current symptoms of distress (e.g., Fudge, 1996).

In summary, it is only fair to note that many of the preceding criticisms pertain less to the theory of CBT than to those who practice it without cross-cultural knowledge and awareness. Although CBT can be tailored flexibly to African Americans without sacrificing its theoretical principles, those who practice CBT and other orientations typically and erroneously assume that therapists can identify, understand, and address diversity factors without being specifically trained to do so (Kelly et al., 2014). Moreover, although African American therapists initially may have unearned ascribed credibility due to their skin tone, being a therapist of color is no guarantee against cultural biases. Therapists of color receive the same training as White American therapists, and treatments in the United States often are exported internationally.

MODIFYING COGNITIVE BEHAVIOR THERAPY FOR AFRICAN AMERICANS

Therapists must ensure that they use widely agreed-on elements of cultural competence and use them to bridge differences between themselves and African American clients. The elements of therapists' cultural competence (S. Sue, 2006) are (a) knowledge about diversity that is relevant to each client, (b) dynamic sizing or the understanding of when to generalize this knowledge to each client and when to individualize client experiences, (c) treatment skills, and (d) therapists' awareness of their own identities, biases, and their relationship to structural oppression. Kelly et al. (2014) theorized that cultural competence works through four potential mechanisms that bridge differences in areas often overlooked by treatment as usual. These are (a) differences in worldviews and values between the therapist, client, and family members; (b) differences in their experiences and contexts; (c) differences in the power they wield in and out of the therapy session; and (d) the palpable felt distance related to all other differences experienced in the sessions.

Awareness and Knowledge

The first essential modification of CBT involves therapists building their awareness and knowledge through self-exploration and education to be able to bridge differences in therapist and client worldviews. Such differences often result when therapists lack awareness of the Eurocentric biases embedded in cognitive behavioral research and theory, along with common documented diagnostic and treatment biases regarding African Americans (e.g., Whaley & Geller, 2007). Awareness includes exploration of one's racial and cultural identity and reveals that Eurocentric values of logic and individualism stem from one lens among many viable worldviews.

In addition, research on implicit racial bias has suggested that structural factors such as segregation and socioeconomic stratification result in disproportionate poverty and adverse life situations for African Americans and fuel common stereotypes and misperceptions that African Americans are inferior, without malicious intent. In fact, data show that Whites have significantly less knowledge of the history of slavery and racism than their African American counterparts and thus are more likely to deny or minimize the existence of racism. Moreover, this denial is exacerbated by their lower perceptions of the relevance of racial identity (Nelson, Adams, & Salter, 2013). White therapists, as well as others, can build their knowledge about these realities. They also can become aware that such perceptions, White privilege, power, and the prioritization of Eurocentric worldviews (e.g., McIntosh, 1998), may lead to microaggressions toward African Americans within the therapy session (e.g., D. W. Sue et al., 2007). Awareness and knowledge also are facilitated by exposure to those of African descent in real-world settings in which the therapist's status is not higher than that of their African American counterparts so that they have greater exposure to normative, successful models of African Americans. Supervision and case consultation may be helpful when therapists lack knowledge of culturally acceptable and normative behaviors and beliefs (e.g., Kelly, 2003).

Once a therapist recognizes the reality of racism in African Americans' lives, she or he will be better prepared to join with African American clients to form a collaborative therapeutic alliance and bridge the felt distance in the room. This joining must occur early in treatment if it is to prevent dropout, which is significantly higher among African Americans than among Whites

(Fudge, 1996). Therapists are encouraged to be overtly warm and authentic and to decrease jargon and give every indication of respect to African Americans via supportive, noncritical statements. Nonthreatening psychoeducation regarding the purposes, course, and process of therapy, along with clear expectations regarding therapist and client roles, can help to increase the therapeutic alliance. Also important is to avoid affiliation with agencies with negative reputations in the community.

Assessment Through Dynamic Sizing Facilitates Use of Appropriate Treatment Skills

Therapists must gain the courage to raise the topic of race and ethnicity (as well as other forms of diversity) in a way that is comfortable for them and friendly and supportive to their clients and to communicate that African American clients have strengths and values that are important and that anything can be discussed (e.g., Kelly & Hudson, 2017). In some cases, the therapist may choose to identify his or her own racial, ethnic, and cultural background and then ask the client to do the same. Cultural genograms (Kelly et al., 2014) and the Cultural Formulation Interview in the *Diagnostic and Statistical Manual of Mental Disorders* (fifth ed., American Psychiatric Association, 2013) can be used to guide therapists in asking about the importance of African Americans' worldviews, values, experiences, and contexts and how these may relate to their symptoms and problems. Questionnaires aimed at assessing racial identity, level of acculturation, or Afrocentricity can provide information regarding individual differences and the extent to which clients participate in their ethnic traditions and those of the broader American culture. When working with couples and families, the therapist should make such assessments for each individual, noting similarities and differences between family members.

A good assessment enables modifications of CBT that bridge differences related to experiences and contexts that are common for many African Americans, such as being stigmatized and experiencing discrimination. Examples of these differences lie in the foregoing cases in which therapists, in their attempts to be helpful, gave their clients benign interpretations of the experiences that the clients believed were racist. When therapists dismiss clients' beliefs about the presence of racism, they prevent themselves from conducting a full functional analysis of the client's behavior. Furthermore, they decrease clients' willingness to disclose further how racism and racial or cultural values are related to their problems. At times, African American clients may be reluctant themselves to consider how racism may be related to their symptoms because it can be a reminder of stigma. Thus, it is crucial to discuss race-related incidents, with the supposition and labeling of the racism or unfair disparities involved, as well as to validate the client's experience of such incidents and assess how they are relevant to the problem. Fink, Turner, and Beidel (1996) showed the relevance of such an understanding:

> An African American female physician was diagnosed with social phobia. She initially shared her fears of speaking in front of her colleagues, because they would see her as stupid and not cut out to be a physician. These facts were used in an imaginal exposure intervention. Early exposure sessions did not produce the expected arousal levels, indicating that the presented cues were not salient in invoking her symptoms. Further exploration revealed that she was the only African American resident at her job, and she reported that her symptoms were primarily elicited in situations involving middle-aged White male colleagues. In particular, she reported beliefs that they saw her as incompetent and undeserving of being a physician largely because of her race; she reported beliefs that they thought she only got into medical school because she was African American. The authors noted, "racially relevant cues enhanced the social-evaluative, fear-producing quality of the scene as reflected by the patient's verbal report, behavior, and an index of arousal." (p. 208)

Moreover, racial cues were used systematically in her in vivo homework exercises, with positive long-term effects. The authors attributed these effects to their success in extinguishing her core racially based fear.

Such assessments lead to modifications involving the culturally competent factor of *dynamic sizing* (e.g., Kelly, 2017), wherein the therapist can assess the degree to which aspects common to many African Americans fit for each client. Thus, therapists will not err as the therapist did in one of the foregoing examples in assuming each factor exists in every African American client's life. These modifications also enable therapists to bridge power differentials between themselves and their African American clients by identifying client strengths and values that can be used to enhance treatment success. For example, a therapist may identify strong religious values within a genogram and then use that value to help the client find the support of a "church home."

Overall, bridging differences by working within African American clients' worldviews, considering their values and experiences, empowering them, and decreasing felt distance in the room is consistent with S. Sue and Zane's (2009) assertions about the goals of any cultural modifications. They asserted that such modifications should serve the goal of making the therapist and interventions credible to each African American client and help them feel as if they were given something helpful in treatment. The following is an example:

> A good friend recommended that Judy, an African American, seek treatment from Carol, a White therapist. In the first session, Judy was initially

nervous, but she admitted to Carol that much of her problem stemmed from the microaggressions, or subtle forms of racism and disrespect, she experienced at her job. She stated that she had begun to doubt her abilities. Carol told Judy how sorry she was that Judy was victimized by racism and made genuine statements affirming Judy's worth. During treatment, Carol did self management and self-advocacy training with Judy to enhance her effectiveness in managing and connecting with her coworkers. Notably, Carol did not imply deficiencies in Judy, nor did she ignore or excuse any racism. Carol also helped Judy to challenge her self-doubts via positive statements about her race and culture. In hearing that Judy coped with the situation by working long hours and praying, Carol's interventions included asking Judy to put the work that she could not get done in the "something-for-God-to-do" box and pray on it. By the end of treatment, Judy reported a decrease in her stress and depression, and stated that her relationships with the people that she managed were "much better."

COGNITIVE BEHAVIOR THERAPY THAT CONSIDERS AFRICAN AMERICAN COUPLES, FAMILIES, AND COMMUNITIES

Jacobson and Christensen (1996) noted that couples made up of partners of different racial or cultural backgrounds might not recognize when their conflicts stem from differing cultural norms and that these conflicts can be exacerbated during times of stress. They asserted that CBT could be helpful with couples through attention to the environmental (i.e., cultural) influences on the couple. Conflicts can be reframed as at least partially related to broader social stressors affecting the couple and to how each partner's views have been shaped by their cultural heritage (Jacobson & Christensen, 1996). This attention to larger, external influences can help to decrease client defensiveness and increase therapist understanding, thus facilitating collaborative problem solving.

Even when family members are both African American, such conflicts can easily arise due to individual differences in how each perceives and copes with racism and stigma (e.g., Kelly, 2003; Kelly & Boyd-Franklin, 2005). In addition, each may have different learning histories related to parental racial socialization, their own experiences of racism, the stimulus value of their varying skin tones, and more. Boyd-Franklin and Franklin (1998) suggested using the reframe that clients are "letting racism win" instead of uniting together to fight against it.

Kim and Terrance were an African American couple who sought therapy because of their frequent fights involving finances. Kim reported that Terrance did not bring her flowers, as some of her White cowork-ers' partners did at their workplace. Terrance angrily replied that Kim was "always wanting something and testing my manhood." Sheila tried a communication intervention that met with limited success in reduc-ing the couple's blaming of one another. Although she commonly used reframing to normalize stress for couples who were new parents, Sheila did not normalize the socioeconomic stressors of this couple. Nor did they think about their periodic unemployment as a chronic socioeco-nomic stressor.

In this case, the therapist might have been more effective if she had reframed the problem. She also could have observed that Kim and Terrance were letting racism win by turning their frustration regarding limited eco-nomic opportunities on each other. Further, she could have encouraged them to work together and support mutual coping and thriving in the face of struc-tural racism.

The idea of working together and supporting one another fits well with CBT's emphasis on building strengths and supports. Toward this end, thera-pists may respectfully ask African Americans to share aspects of their heritage and background of which they are proud, and then acknowledge and validate those strengths (e.g., Kelly & Hudson, 2017). It is also important to elicit information regarding strengths and supports that may have been disrupted over time but can be reinstated or rebuilt—for example, reconnecting with a "church family" or relatives.

Incorporating clients' natural support systems may involve the inclu-sion of elders or other respected family members and clergy to collaborate in treatment (e.g., Boyd-Franklin, 2003). For some clients, forming an alliance with the person's pastor or religious leader can enhance treatment outcomes and provide additional therapeutic leverage. Therapists have to be aware of the supports offered by local African American churches and mosques, including couple and family ministries. Home visits, outreach to commu-nity organizations, and the identification of community role models can be helpful in developing realistic goals and supporting positive change. Some African Americans are spiritual but not involved in organized religion; thera-pists should ask about the role of spirituality in their lives and build on these beliefs in therapy.

Research has indicated that a negative racial identity is strongly asso-ciated with greater personal distress (e.g., Kelly, 2004). Given the chronic influences of racism and socioeconomic stressors in many African Americans' lives, therapists have to assess the degree to which their African American clients internalize racist and self-blaming societal messages. At times, clients may spontaneously express negative internalized stereotypes, as in the afore-mentioned case when Terrance stated that Kim was testing his manhood.

Unfortunately, the therapist did not recognize this statement as a common negative stereotype that depicts African American women as psychologically castrating of African American men.

In the case example of an African American man being treated for substance abuse, Fudge (1996) identified several key themes that revealed the client's negative racial identity. These included "being Black means I'll never be good enough" and "being Black means acting in a particular [negative] way" (p. 328). To counter such myths, the therapist used standard rational emotive therapy (RET) to help the client develop more realistic and positive self-statements. In addition, the therapist provided the client with culturally relevant readings (*The Autobiography of Malcolm X* [1965], and Gordon Park's autobiography, *A Choice of Weapons* [1966]) that were integrated into RET as bibliotherapy. These materials provided examples to which the client could relate, demonstrated African American men's transition from a negative to a positive racial identity, and helped the client to shift his racial identity to a more positive direction. The therapist also empowered the client by encouraging him to take action on larger social factors that he felt were related to his problem. This work involved problem solving, coaching, and role playing, and eventually resulted in the client talking with the teens who drank and disturbed the residents in his building to decrease their noise level (Fudge, 1996).

CONCLUSION

CBT's theory, philosophy, and use of idiographic data make it supportive of and suitable for use with African Americans. However, CBT is conducted within mainstream America, which endorses a Eurocentric framework that is oppressive and damaging to African Americans. As a result, CBT has been tainted by myths of neutrality and universality that promote White privilege and justify the failure to include African Americans in clinical research. The literature demonstrates the need for therapists to gain knowledge about and experience with African Americans. By using elements of cultural competence to counter therapist and systemic biases and call attention to and address the unique experiences and strengths of African Americans, this training can help cognitive behavior therapists to bridge cultural differences and improve the efficacy of their treatment of African American clients.

REFERENCES

American Psychiatric Association. (2013). *Diagnostic and statistical manual of mental disorders* (5th ed.). Arlington, VA: Author.

American Psychological Association. (1975). *Corporal punishment*. Retrieved from http://www.apa.org/about/policy/corporal-punishment.aspx

Beach, S. R. H., Hurt, T. R., Fincham, F. D., Franklin, K. J., McNair, L. M., & Stanley, S. M. (2011). Enhancing marital enrichment through spirituality: Efficacy data for prayer focused relationship enhancement. *Psychology of Religion and Spirituality, 3*, 201–216. http://dx.doi.org/10.1037/a0022207

Benish, S. G., Quintana, S., & Wampold, B. E. (2011). Culturally adapted psychotherapy and the legitimacy of myth: A direct-comparison meta-analysis. *Journal of Counseling Psychology, 58*, 279–289. Advance online publication. http://dx.doi.org/10.1037/a0023626

Black, L., & Jackson, V. (2005). Families of African origin: An overview. In M. McGoldrick, J. Giordano, & N. Garcia-Preto (Eds.), *Ethnicity and family therapy* (pp. 77–86). New York, NY: Guilford Press.

Boyd-Franklin, N. (2003). *Black families in therapy: Understanding the African American experience* (2nd ed.). New York, NY: Guilford Press.

Boyd-Franklin, N., & Franklin, A. J. (1998). African American couples in therapy. In M. McGoldrick (Ed.), *Re-visioning family therapy: Race, culture, and gender in clinical practice* (pp. 268–281). New York, NY: Guilford Press.

Bryant, C. M., Taylor, R. J., Lincoln, K. D., Chatters, L. M., & Jackson, J. S. (2008). Marital satisfaction among African Americans and Black Caribbeans: Findings from the National Survey of American Life. *Family Relations, 57*, 239–253. http://dx.doi.org/10.1111/j.1741-3729.2008.00497.x

Celious, A., & Oyserman, D. (2001). Race from the inside: An emerging heterogeneous race model. *Journal of Social Issues, 57*, 149–165. http://dx.doi.org/10.1111/0022-4537.00206

Chatters, L. M., Taylor, R. J., Bullard, K. M., & Jackson, J. S. (2008). Spirituality and subjective religiosity among African Americans, Caribbean Blacks, and non-Hispanic Whites. *Journal for the Scientific Study of Religion, 47*, 725–737. http://dx.doi.org/10.1111/j.1468-5906.2008.00437.x

Chou, T., Asnaani, A., & Hofmann, S. G. (2012). Perception of racial discrimination and psychopathology across three U.S. ethnic minority groups. *Cultural Diversity and Ethnic Minority Psychology, 18*, 74–81. http://dx.doi.org/10.1037/a0025432

Clark, R. (2000). Perceptions of interethnic group racism predict increased vascular reactivity to a laboratory challenge in college women. *Annals of Behavioral Medicine, 22*, 214–222. http://dx.doi.org/10.1007/BF02895116

Coates, T. (2014, June). The case for reparations. *The Atlantic*. Retrieved from http://www.theatlantic.com/magazine/archive/2014/06/the-case-for-reparations/361631/

Coleman, M. G. (2003). Job skill and Black male wage discrimination. *Social Science Quarterly, 84*, 892–906. http://dx.doi.org/10.1046/j.0038-4941.2003.08404007.x

Coltrane, S., & Messineo, M. (2000). The perpetuation of subtle prejudice: Race and gender imagery in 1990s television advertising. *Sex Roles, 42*, 363–389. http://dx.doi.org/10.1023/A:1007046204478

Cross, W. E., Jr. (1971). Negro-to-Black conversion experience: Toward a psychology of Black liberation. *Black World, 20*, 13–27.

Cutrona, C. E., Russell, D. W., Abraham, W. T., Gardner, K. A., Melby, J. N., Bryant, C., & Conger, R. D. (2003). Neighborhood context and financial strain as predictors of marital interaction and marital quality in African American couples. *Personal Relationships, 10*, 389–409. http://dx.doi.org/10.1111/1475-6811.00056

Cutrona, C. E., Russell, D. W., Burzette, R. G., Wesner, K. A., & Bryant, C. M. (2011). Predicting relationship stability among midlife African American couples. *Journal of Consulting and Clinical Psychology, 79*, 814–825. http://dx.doi.org/10.1037/a0025874

Epstein, N. B., & Baucom, D. H. (2002). *Enhanced cognitive-behavioral therapy for couples: A contextual approach.* Washington, DC: American Psychological Association. http://dx.doi.org/10.1037/10481-000

Fink, C. M., Turner, S. M., & Beidel, D. C. (1996). Culturally relevant factors in the behavioral treatment of social phobia: A case study. *Journal of Anxiety Disorders, 10*, 201–209. http://dx.doi.org/10.1016/0887-6185(96)00005-9

Fudge, R. C. (1996). The use of behavior therapy in the development of ethnic consciousness: A treatment model. *Cognitive and Behavioral Practice, 3*, 317–335. http://dx.doi.org/10.1016/S1077-7229(96)80021-6

Ginther, D. K., Schaffer, W. T., Schnell, J., Masimore, B., Liu, F., Haak, L. L., & Kington, R. (2011). Race, ethnicity, and NIH research awards. *Science, 333*, 1015–1019. http://dx.doi.org/10.1126/science.1196783

Gregory, A., Skiba, R. J. & Noguera, P. A. (2010). The achievement gap and the discipline gap: Two sides of the same coin? *Educational Researcher, 39*, 59–68. http://dx.doi.org/10.3102/0013189X09357621

Griner, D., & Smith, T. B. (2006). Culturally adapted mental health intervention: A meta-analytic review. *Psychotherapy: Theory, Research, Practice, Training, 43*, 531–548. http://dx.doi.org/10.1037/0033-3204.43.4.531

Hardy, K. V. (2004, June). *Worlds apart: Family therapy with low-income and minority families.* Paper presented at the meeting of the American Family Therapy Academy, San Francisco, CA.

Higgins, G. E., Ricketts, M. L., Griffith, J. D., & Jirard, S. A. (2013). Race and juvenile incarceration: A propensity score matching examination. *American Journal of Criminal Justice, 38*, 1–12. http://dx.doi.org/10.1007/s12103-012-9162-6

Hughes, M., Kiecolt, K. J., Keith, V. M., & Demo, D. H. (2015). Racial identity and well-being among African Americans. *Social Psychology Quarterly, 78*, 25–48. http://dx.doi.org/10.1177/0190272514554043

Ibaraki, A. Y., & Hall, G. C. N. (2014). The components of cultural match in psychotherapy. *Journal of Social and Clinical Psychology, 33,* 936–953. http://dx.doi.org/10.1521/jscp.2014.33.10.936

Jacobson, N. S., & Christensen, A. (1996). *Integrative couple therapy: Promoting acceptance and change.* New York, NY: Norton.

Jernigan, M. M., Green, C. E., & Helms, J. E. (2017). Identity models. In S. Kelly (Ed.), *Diversity in couple and family therapy: Ethnicities, sexualities, and socioeconomics* (pp. 363–392). Santa Barbara, CA: Praeger.

Kelly, S. (2003). African American couples: Their importance to the stability of African American families, and their mental health issues. In J. S. Mio & G. Y. Iwamasa (Eds.), *Culturally diverse mental health: The challenge of research and resistance* (pp. 141–157). New York, NY: Taylor & Francis.

Kelly, S. (2004). Underlying components of scores assessing African Americans' racial perspectives. *Measurement and Evaluation in Counseling & Development, 37,* 28–40. http://dx.doi.org/10.1080/07481756.2004.11909748

Kelly, S. (Ed.). (2017). *Diversity in couple and family therapy: Ethnicities, sexualities, and socioeconomics.* Santa Barbara, CA: Praeger.

Kelly, S., Bhagwat, R., Maynigo, T., & Moses, E. (2014). Couple and marital therapy: The complement and expansion provided by multicultural approaches. In F. T. L. Leong (Ed.), *APA handbook of multicultural psychology, Vol. 2. Applications and training* (pp. 479–497). Washington, DC: American Psychological Association.

Kelly, S., & Boyd-Franklin, N. (2005). African American women in client, therapist, and supervisory relationships: The parallel processes of race, culture, and family. In M. Rastogi & E. Wieling (Eds.), *The voices of color: First person accounts of ethnic minority therapists* (pp. 67–90). Thousand Oaks, CA: Sage. http://dx.doi.org/10.4135/9781452231662.n5

Kelly, S., & Floyd, F. J. (2006). Impact of racial perspectives and contextual variables on marital trust and adjustment for African American couples. *Journal of Family Psychology, 20,* 79–87. http://dx.doi.org/10.1037/0893-3200.20.1.79

Kelly, S., & Hudson, B. N. (2017). African American couples and families and the context of structural oppression. In S. Kelly (Ed.), *Diversity in couple and family therapy: Ethnicities, sexualities, and socioeconomics* (pp. 3–32). Santa Barbara, CA: Praeger.

Kelly, S., Maynigo, P., Wesley, K., & Durham, J. (2013). African American communities and family systems: Relevance and challenges. *Couple and Family Psychology: Research and Practice, 2,* 264–277. http://dx.doi.org/10.1037/cfp0000014

Klonoff, E. A., & Landrine, H. (2000). Revising and improving the African American acculturation scale. *Journal of Black Psychology, 26,* 235–261. http://dx.doi.org/10.1177/0095798400026002007

Laszloffy, T. A., & Hardy, K. V. (2000). Uncommon strategies for a common problem: Addressing racism in family therapy. *Family Process, 39*, 35–50. http://dx.doi.org/10.1111/j.1545-5300.2000.39106.x

Malcolm X, & Haley, A. (1965). *The autobiography of Malcolm X*. New York, NY: Ballantine Books.

Matthews, D. D., Hammond, W. P., Nuru-Jeter, A., Cole-Lewis, Y., & Melvin, T. (2013). Racial discrimination and depressive symptoms among African-American men: The mediating and moderating roles of masculine self-reliance and John Henryism. *Psychology of Men & Masculinity, 14*, 35–46. http://dx.doi.org/10.1037/a0028436

McIntosh, P. (1998). White privilege: Unpacking the invisible knapsack. In M. McGoldrick (Ed.), *Re-visioning family therapy: Race, culture, and gender in clinical practice* (pp. 147–152). New York, NY: Guildford Press.

Nelson, J. C., Adams, G., & Salter, P. S. (2013). The Marley hypothesis: Denial of racism reflects ignorance of history. *Psychological Science, 24*, 213–218. http://dx.doi.org/10.1177/0956797612451466

Parks, G. (1966). *A choice of weapons*. St. Paul: Minnesota Historical Society Press.

Pew Research Center. (2009). *African-Americans and religion*. Retrieved from Pew Research Center website: http://www.pewforum.org/2009/01/30/african-americans-and-religion/

Phinney, J. S., & Onwughalu, M. (1996). Racial identity and perception of American ideals among African American and African students in the United States. *International Journal of Intercultural Relations, 20*, 127–140. http://dx.doi.org/10.1016/0147-1767(95)00040-2

Pieterse, A. L., Todd, N. R., Neville, H. A., & Carter, R. T. (2012). Perceived racism and mental health among Black American adults: A meta-analytic review. *Journal of Counseling Psychology, 59*, 1–9. http://dx.doi.org/10.1037/a0026208

Raue, P. J., Goldfried, M. R., & Barkham, M. (1997). The therapeutic alliance in psychodynamic-interpersonal and cognitive-behavioral therapy. *Journal of Consulting and Clinical Psychology, 65*, 582–587. http://dx.doi.org/10.1037/0022-006X.65.4.582

Rohner, R. P., Bourque, S. L., & Elordi, C. A. (1996). Children's perceptions of corporal punishment, caretaker acceptance, and psychological adjustment in a poor, biracial southern community. *Journal of Marriage and the Family, 58*, 842–852. http://dx.doi.org/10.2307/353974

Saegert, S., Fields, D., & Libman, K. (2011). Mortgage foreclosure and health disparities: Serial displacement as asset extraction in African American populations. *Journal of Urban Health, 88*, 390–402. http://dx.doi.org/10.1007/s11524-011-9584-3

Sampson, R. J., & Raudenbush, S. W. (2004). Seeing disorder: Neighborhood stigma and the social construction of "broken windows." *Social Psychology Quarterly, 67*, 319–342. http://dx.doi.org/10.1177/019027250406700401

Sayers, S. L., & Heyman, R. E. (2003). Behavioral couples therapy. In G. P. Sholevar (Ed.), *Textbook of family and couples therapy: Clinical applications* (pp. 462–500). Washington, DC: American Psychiatric Publishing.

Schulz, A., Williams, D., Israel, B., Becker, A., Parker, E., James, S. A., & Jackson, J. (2000). Unfair treatment, neighborhood effects, and mental health in the Detroit metropolitan area. *Journal of Health and Social Behavior, 41,* 314–332. http://dx.doi.org/10.2307/2676323

Seaton, E. K., Yip, T., Morgan-Lopez, A., & Sellers, R. M. (2012). Racial discrimination and racial socialization as predictors of African American adolescents' racial identity development using latent transition analysis. *Developmental Psychology, 48,* 448–458. http://dx.doi.org/10.1037/a0025328

Simons, R. L., Lin, K.-H., Gordon, L. C., Brody, G. H., Murry, V., & Conger, R. D. (2002). Community differences in the association between parenting practices and child conduct problems. *Journal of Marriage and Family, 64,* 331–345. http://dx.doi.org/10.1111/j.1741-3737.2002.00331.x

Smith, T. B. (2010). Culturally congruent practices in counseling and psychotherapy: A review of research. In J. G. Ponterotto, J. M. Casas, L. A. Suzuki, & C. M. Alexander (Eds.), *Handbook of multicultural counseling* (3rd ed., pp. 439–450). Thousand Oaks, CA: Sage.

Stephenson, E. (2004). The African diaspora and culture-based coping strategies. In J. L. Chin (Ed.), *The psychology of prejudice and discrimination: Racism in America* (Vol. 1, pp. 95–118). Westport, CT: Praeger.

Sue, D. W., Capodilupo, C. M., Torino, G. C., Bucceri, J. M., Holder, A. M., Nadal, K. L., & Esquilin, M. (2007). Racial microaggressions in everyday life: Implications for clinical practice. *American Psychologist, 62,* 271–286. http://dx.doi.org/10.1037/0003-066X.62.4.271

Sue, S. (1999). Science, ethnicity, and bias: Where have we gone wrong? *American Psychologist, 54,* 1070–1077. http://dx.doi.org/10.1037/0003-066X.54.12.1070

Sue, S. (2006). Cultural competency: From philosophy to research and practice. *Journal of Community Psychology, 34,* 237–245. http://dx.doi.org/10.1002/jcop.20095

Sue, S., & Zane, N. (2009). The role of culture and cultural techniques in psychotherapy: A critique and reformulation. *Asian American Journal of Psychology, S,* 3–14. http://dx.doi.org/10.1037/1948-1985.S.1.3

Taylor, R. J., Chatters, L. M., & Jackson, J. S. (1997). Changes over time in support network involvement among Black Americans. In R. J. Taylor, J. S. Jackson, & L. M. Chatters (Eds.), *Family life in Black America* (pp. 293–316). Thousand Oaks, CA: Sage.

Thornton, M. C., Taylor, R. J., & Chatters, L. M. (2013). African American and Black Caribbean mutual feelings of closeness. *Journal of Black Studies, 44,* 798–828. http://dx.doi.org/10.1177/0021934713516978

Torres-Harding, S. R., Andrade, A. L., Jr., & Romero Diaz, C. E. (2012). The Racial Microaggressions Scale (RMAS): A new scale to measure experiences of racial microaggressions in people of color. *Cultural Diversity and Ethnic Minority Psychology, 18*, 153–164. http://dx.doi.org/10.1037/a0027658

Townes, D. L., Chavez-Korell, S., & Cunningham, N. J. (2009). Reexamining the relationships between racial identity, cultural mistrust, help-seeking attitudes, and preference for a Black counselor. *Journal of Counseling Psychology, 56*, 330–336. http://dx.doi.org/10.1037/a0015449

U.S. Census Bureau. (2017). *Population estimates, July 1, 2017*. Retrieved from https://www.census.gov/quickfacts/fact/table/US/PST045216

U.S. Department of Justice—Federal Bureau of Investigation. (2015). *Uniform crime report: Hate crime statistics, 2014*. Retrieved from https://www.fbi.gov/about-us/cjis/ucr/hate-crime/2014/topic-pages/victims_final.pdf

Wesley, K. (2017). Disparities in mental health care and homeownership for African Americans and Latinos in the United States. In S. Kelly (Ed.), *Diversity in couple and family therapy: Ethnicities, sexualities, and socioeconomics* (pp. 393–419). Santa Barbara, CA: Praeger.

Whaley, A. L., & Geller, P. A. (2007). Toward a cognitive process model of ethnic/racial biases in clinical judgment. *Review of General Psychology, 11*, 75–96. http://dx.doi.org/10.1037/1089-2680.11.1.75

Wickrama, K. A. S., Noh, S., & Bryant, C. M. (2005). Racial differences in adolescent distress: Differential effects of the family and community for blacks and whites. *Journal of Community Psychology, 33*, 261–282. http://dx.doi.org/10.1002/jcop.20053

5

COGNITIVE BEHAVIOR THERAPY WITH ASIAN AMERICANS

GAYLE Y. IWAMASA, CURTIS HSIA, AND DEVON HINTON

At the time of this book's first edition, there was limited literature on cognitive behavior therapy (CBT) and evidence-based psychotherapies for Asian Americans. Since that time, interest has increased and some progress has been made in examining evidence-based approaches to mental health care for Asian Americans. This chapter provides an updated summary of the research to date, including general information and considerations for CBT with Asian Americans and a case example demonstrating how CBT can be customized for Asian Americans. Information regarding specific South Asian cultures is addressed in Chapter 6.

Asian Americans are one of the most diverse and fastest growing ethnic groups in the United States, having grown 43% between 2000 and 2010 (U.S. Census Bureau, 2012). Asian Americans consist of over 30 different ethnic groups, constituting approximately 4.8% of the U.S. population (14.7 million), and they are expected to continue growing in number

http://dx.doi.org/10.1037/0000119-006
Culturally Responsive Cognitive Behavior Therapy, Second Edition: Practice and Supervision, G. Y. Iwamasa and P. A. Hays (Editors)
Copyright © 2019 by the American Psychological Association. All rights reserved.

(U.S. Census Bureau, 2012). Asian Americans are the most likely of any racial or ethnic group to live in mixed-ethnic neighborhoods and marry across ethnic groups, with about 74% born abroad and 50% who speak English fluently (Pew Research Center, 2013).

Despite this diversity, researchers often lump together Asians of diverse cultures, and as a result, the generalizability of these studies is limited (Pan, Huey, & Hernandez, 2011). Furthermore, participants in such studies are often English-speaking students attending U.S. universities—a group that is not representative of Asian Americans as a whole. Acknowledging these limitations, some researchers have identified similarities across Asian ethnic groups that can be useful to clinicians. In addition, awareness of the marked cultural, political, and environmental differences among and within groups may assist therapists in providing culturally competent treatment. However, it must be stressed that each culture, as well as each individual, has unique characteristics that have to be fully explored and understood; this chapter merely serves as a guide.

In the United States, Asian Americans are often viewed homogenously as either a model minority (Gupta, Szymanski, & Leong, 2011; Kiang, Huynh, Cheah, Wang, & Yoshikawa, 2017) or "forever foreign" (Zhou, 2004). Unfortunately, both views work against the provision of culturally competent care. Assuming that a client is a model minority member can lead the therapist to overlook significant stressors, whereas viewing the client as forever foreign may cause the therapist to assume the client is incapable of healthy adaptations. Competent clinicians recognize the heterogeneity of Asian Americans, including differences related to language (i.e., preferred spoken language, fluency, multilingual abilities), religion and spirituality, gender roles, education and employment status, identity, generational status, and immigration history (including intergenerational experiences as refugees or immigrants).

HISTORICAL AND CULTURAL BACKGROUND

The histories of many Asian countries overlap because of their proximity and mutual conquests. For example, part of the Japanese language is based on the Chinese language, and many still use the Asian lunar calendar. Some negative sentiment remains between some Asian countries because of past political conflicts (e.g., Japan and China) and current ones (e.g., North Korea and South Korea). Culturally competent care requires awareness of the potential for such histories to affect an Asian American client's perceptions, beliefs, and behaviors. A comprehensive review of the histories of specific Asian American cultures is beyond the scope of this chapter, and readers are encouraged to consult Hall and Okazaki (2002) and Leong et al. (2007).

Immigration

Some Asian Americans, such as Japanese Americans, have been established in the United States for many generations, whereas others, such as the Hmong Lao, are relatively new (Pew Research Center, 2013). Asian immigrants have recently surpassed Hispanics as the largest group of immigrants to the United States (Pew Research Center, 2013). As a whole, Asian immigrants are also the most highly educated immigrant group to the United States, with 61% of adult immigrants ages 25 to 64 having at least a bachelor's degree. Particularly among first- and second-generation Asian Americans, it is essential to consider how the client's pre-, during, and postmigration experiences may be related to the current level of distress.

Asian American immigration to the United States has occurred in large waves, mainly in response to economic and political issues. The first Asian immigrants were the Chinese, who were recruited to build railroads and work in agriculture in the mid-1800s. The 1882 Chinese Exclusion Act barring further Chinese immigration was enacted when the Chinese began to settle in the United States and prosper by owning businesses and land (National Archives, 2018). Subsequently, Caucasian businesses and landowners, who demanded cheap labor, began recruiting workers from other Asian countries. This continued until the 1924 Asian Exclusion Act, which barred all Asian immigration, again because some of the workers of Asian descent began settling in the United States and acquiring property (Office of the Historian, n.d.).

The 1965 Immigration Act was specifically designed to increase European immigration, but it also allowed for an increase in immigration from Asian countries (Kammer, 2015). The mid-1970s saw the beginning of Southeast Asian immigration, mainly Vietnamese refugees, followed by voluntary immigration of Koreans and Asian Indians in the 1980s. The 1980 Refugee Act provided states with funding for refugee assistance programs (National Archives Foundation, 2018), and in 1987 the Amerasian Homecoming Act was established (Civic Impulse, 2018). This act allowed those Asian children born to U.S. military personnel between 1962 and 1976 (and some family members) to apply for U.S. visas before 1990.

Clinicians should be aware of the differences between immigrants and refugees (Chung & Bemak, 2007). *Immigrants* typically desire and plan to move to the United States. They often have family members who already live in the United States, higher levels of education, and greater financial resources, particularly more recent Chinese immigrants to the United States and Canada (Keister, Agius Vallejo, & Aronson, 2016). Many of these individuals have familiarity with the United States, including the English language, and are more likely to immigrate with their entire family and have support for employment and housing when they arrive. They often settle in areas near family, sometimes in or near an already established ethnic community in which others speak their native language and where culturally familiar foods, activities, and events are readily available.

Refugees typically have no previous interest in or experience with the United States and leave their homes without planning, mainly due to political and social violence and upheaval. Many of these individuals are less educated and poor and often leave their homes with only the clothes they are wearing. They are often separated from loved ones and come to the United States with no resources. They often speak little to no English, and this, in combination with their lack of formal education and skills, results in difficulty obtaining employment or adequate housing. Many refugees find themselves living with other refugees from their same village and in places unfamiliar with Asian culture (e.g., the Hmong Lao in Minnesota). Economic opportunities for them are limited, and because of this, they also tend to live in communities where poor U.S. ethnic minority groups live. In addition to experiencing racism and discrimination from the dominant U.S. society, many Asian refugees experience racism and discrimination from other ethnic minorities, many of whom are ignorant of their traumatic experiences and erroneously believe that the refugees are unfairly supported and subsidized by the U.S. government.

Culture-Specific Values and Traditions

It is important for clinicians to understand several culture-specific issues in the lives of many Asian Americans. These include religion and spirituality, family structure and roles, gender roles, acculturation, ethnic and racial identity, values, language and cognitive styles, health beliefs, and social behaviors. We discuss each briefly in the following sections.

Religion and Spirituality

The Pew Research Center (2013) reported that 42% of Asian Americans identified as Christians. In addition, many religious belief systems in Asia are not specific to any geographical area. As in Europe, many ideas and ideologies spread across Asia, resulting in myriad belief systems. Asian Americans may also vary in their depth of faith, and some do not identify with any religion at all (e.g., in China, where the official state religion is atheism). For an excellent summary of the range of religious and spiritual beliefs among

Asian Americans, see Ai, Bjork, Appel, and Huang (2013). Many Asian Americans are active in their local church or temple and consider religion to be an important part of their lives (see Tan & Dong, 2014, for a summary of the history of Asian American churches and spiritual traditions).

A major spiritual theme in traditional Asian religions is balance. Most widely known in the West are the concepts of yin and yang and the need to balance them (Tseng, 2003). Whereas *yin* represents passivity, *yang* represents activity (Kazarian & Evans, 2001). This concept permeates all domains of traditional Chinese, Japanese, and Vietnamese society, from the conception of the body (as noted by the need to balance the intake of food with yin and yang qualities) to emotions, society, and the environment (Spector, 2004). To achieve balance, an individual is expected to practice moderation in all things, as in Buddhism, and avoid engaging in any one area to excess (e.g., exercising to exhaustion; Spector, 2004).

Collectivism, Family Structure, and Roles

Many traditional Asian societies are collectivistic, with the size of the collective ranging from the nuclear family to the extended family, village, city, and even country. In contrast to most Western societies, the focus is not on the rights of the individual but rather the good of the group (Marín & Gamba, 2003). For example, a popular American phrase is "The squeaky wheel gets the grease," whereas a well-known Japanese proverb is "The protruding nail will be pounded down." *Individual-level collectivism* refers to an individual's personal sacrifice for the good of the group. For example, a young adult who wishes to attend a distant college may instead decide to attend college nearby to allow her to help at home with younger siblings or a family business.

In keeping with this collectivist orientation, one's "ingroup" extends beyond the nuclear family, often encompassing the extended family and close friends who have been "adopted" into the family and given titles such as "aunt" or "uncle" (D. Sue, 2005). It is not uncommon to have three generations living in one house, with many relatives living within walking distance (Pew Research Center, 2013). This pattern may originate from Asian countries, where in some areas whole villages could consist of one family group. Historically and currently, most traditional Asian cultures are best characterized by a patriarchal authoritarian system also known as *familism* (Yang, 2006). The father (and to a lesser extent the mother) makes decisions for the family often without the input of the children because it is assumed that parents have greater wisdom and will be able to make better decisions, even after the children reach adulthood (Wu, 2001). In addition, each person in the family has a specific role they are expected to fulfill (Yeh, 2003). For example, the typical role of the father is to provide financially and make decisions for the family but not be involved in the day-to-day operations of the household because this is the domain of the mother. The mother's role can include preparing the food, cleaning and caring for the house, managing finances, and rearing the children. Children are expected to help with daily chores, especially the daughters, who are taught how to manage their own home for the future.

In general, traditional Asian American parents do not display their emotions or affection to their children as openly as do Western parents. It is expected that children understand that their parents love them by providing for them and not through overt expressions of affection. This may be in part due to the emphasis on harmony and the importance of the group over individuals, where the functioning of the family overall is the priority (Yee, DeBaryshe, Yuen, Kim, & McCubbin, 2007).

Lee (1996) described five common types experienced by many Asian American families: traditional, cultural conflict, bicultural, American, and interracial. *Traditional* families follow the traditional patriarchal structure described earlier. *Cultural conflict* families are those in which parents and children are of different generational status and, thus, may have differing opinions and expectations of family roles (Wu, 2001). *Bicultural* families are those who engage in both traditional Asian and "American" activities and combine the value systems in family life. *American* families are those that do not integrate traditional Asian practices and roles into everyday family life. Finally, *interracial* families are those in which one parent is of Asian heritage and the other parent is not.

Although it is less common than in the 1980s and 90s, therapists should be aware of the phenomenon of *parachute kids*, minor children, typically from Taiwan, mainland China, South Korea, and Southeast Asia, sent unaccompanied to the United States. Most of these kids start off as exchange students similar to American kids who study abroad. However, some kids from wealthy families have homes and vehicles bought for them by their parents rather than living with a sponsoring family (arranged through the school). Similarly, *astronaut families* are those in which the father typically remains in the country of origin while the mother and "satellite" kid reside in the United States. Obviously, family roles and values are affected in these nontraditional situations. Mok (2015) briefly reviewed some of the challenges experienced by individuals in these situations, including navigating in a new culture with different languages, foods, norms, and customs, as well as the learning to survive economically and form new social ties while often lacking adequate adult supervision.

Intergenerational conflict is common, related to generational differences in values and responsibilities (Wu, 2001), as in the example of differing levels of commitment to the family. Often the older generation, being more collectivistic, expects that the younger generation will take care of the elders (e.g., go to college near home, move back home after college, and stay near home after marrying). The younger generation, being more individualistic, may feel unfairly imposed on by the older generation, believing that certain responsibilities to their parents have ended. However, recent research on Asian American families has also focused on more positive family-related factors, such as identification of strengths (Wong, Wong, & Obeng, 2012), family ethnic socialization (Nguyen, Wong, Juang, & Park, 2015), and resiliency (Yee et al., 2007).

Being part of a collectivistic society, the Asian American client may experience one of two extremes: (a) not wanting anyone to know they are in therapy or (b) being from a family that wants to be active and involved in the therapy. In the former case, it is important to reassure the client of confidentiality, often across several sessions. If the family is involved in treatment, sometimes reframing the presenting problem as a physiological disorder with a behavioral solution (e.g., depression is a chemical imbalance in the brain that can be treated with behavioral activation and challenging irrational thoughts) is a more culturally acceptable conceptualization for both the client and the family. It may not be unusual for an Asian American client to want his or her entire family, including aunts, uncles, and grandparents, to participate in treatment. When this occurs, it is important to remember that deference and respect should be shown to the elders. Family members may have questions, and the therapist might have to budget extra time to spend with the entire family. If an interpreter is used, the client, not the interpreter, should be addressed directly. The effectiveness and ethics of using interpreters for non-English speakers in therapy are beyond the scope of this chapter, and readers who encounter such situations should be familiar with the research and issues in these situations. For a summary of these issues, see Angelelli and Geist-Martin (2005).

Therapists should be aware of how collectivistic values influence their clients' everyday lives and be cognizant that stressing independence and individual problem solving may not be culturally appropriate. For instance, it may not be in the best interest of the individual to disregard the family's wishes and go away to college. Therapists should be able to assist clients with being able to evaluate the consequences of the decisions that they make, keeping in mind familial and cultural values and ethnic and gender roles, so that clients will be comfortable with and aware of the results of their choices.

Gender Roles

As might be expected, individuals from more traditional Asian families are more likely to adhere to traditional gender roles. As discussed in Chin's (2000) groundbreaking edited volume, *Relationships Among Asian American*

Women, many myths continue to exist regarding the "mystique about Asian American women, and stereotypes that objectify and disempower them remain" (p. 6). Until recently, discussions about gender roles and the experiences of Asian American women were largely absent from many of the primary sources in Asian American psychology (Wang & Iwamasa, 2017). However, therapists must be aware of how media portrayals affect societal perceptions and stereotypes of Asian American women, how immigration and refugee experiences affect Asian American women and their children, how relationships between Asian American mothers and daughters change over time, and how ethnic identity and the acculturation process influence dating and marriage practices. In addition, therapists should be aware that the likelihood that Asian American women will marry outside their ethnic and racial group is twice that of Asian American men (Pew Research Center, 2013).

Liu, Iwamoto, and Chae's (2010) edited volume, *Culturally Responsive Counseling With Asian American Men*, also demonstrates the increasing attention professional psychology has focused on Asian American men's issues. Their volume provides readers with additional historical background and cultural context in which Asian American men live. Some considerations for therapists to be aware of when working with Asian American men include the effects of the intersection of masculinity and racism, and stereotypes of Asian American men, including the impact of the model minority myth. Additional areas to consider include health behaviors, cultural values, substance use, and help-seeking.

Acculturation and Ethnic and Racial Identity

In the Asian American psychology literature, major advances have been made in examining the concepts of acculturation, enculturation, ethnic identity, and racial identity (Zhang & Moradi, 2013). These concepts are briefly reviewed so that clinicians can be aware of how such processes and personal identity issues may affect the client and the therapy process. Of particular importance is the erroneous assumption that these concepts can be used interchangeably (Iwamasa & Yamada, 2001). Recent research indicates that these constructs can predict and affect multiple psychological variables such as problems in youth, particularly among Korean Americans (Choi, Kim, Pekelnicky, Kim, & Kim, 2017).

Acculturation is often defined as the process of change over time when individuals encounter a different culture (Moyerman & Forman, 1992). Importantly, it is not just the individual who undergoes acculturation; individuals in the dominant culture also undergo change as a result of interacting with someone from a different cultural background.

Enculturation is the socialization and maintenance process of adherence to norms of one's indigenous culture, including connection to the values and concepts of the indigenous culture (Herskovits, 1948). Thus, Asian Americans may be engaging in acculturation and enculturation simultaneously. Both have been linked to various psychological variables such as attitudes toward help-seeking, psychological functioning, and family issues. (See Zhang & Moradi, 2013, for a more thorough list of research examining the relationship of acculturation and enculturation with psychological variables.)

Ethnic identity is often defined as a sense of belonging based on beliefs, communication styles, values, attitudes, and behavioral norms shared by a group (Phinney, 2003). It is both self- and other-defined. The development of ethnic identity is influenced by factors such as cognitive development, age, and experiences with one's ethnic group, exposure to other ethnic groups, and experiences of racism and discrimination. Ethnic identity is believed to develop over time and tends to remain strong throughout the acculturation process (Phinney, 2003).

Helms and Talleyrand (1997) defined *racial identity* as one's identification with one's racial group and includes how individuals recognize and overcome the psychological effects of racial oppression as a result of being identified racially by others. The concept of racial identity incorporates the experience of negative societal messages regarding one's race into the identity formation process, whereas ethnic identity tends to be viewed as an internal and individualistic process. The culturally competent clinician understands that these concepts may be important to the client and thus considers them accordingly (Helms, 1992).

Language Issues and Cognitive Styles

Language plays a significant role in how an individual views the world. How concepts are expressed varies from one language to the next, and some languages do not contain concepts present in other cultures. In translating from one language to another, words or concepts that do not exist in one language often have to be constructed or further explained to make sense in another language. There are many words and ideas not easily expressed in English that exist in Asian languages and vice versa (Hannas, 1997). For example, a common linguistic mistake made by Mandarin speakers occurs in the use of *he* and *she*. In spoken Mandarin, there is no differentiation between *he*, *she*, or *it*, and therefore, when Mandarin speakers use English, there may be confusion regarding the gender of the pronoun. Clinicians should be aware that clients for whom English is a second language may engage in a process of translating what has been said into their first language, thinking about it, then translating it back into English, with the possibility that some concepts will have to be clarified or explained. As an example, the Western conceptualization of psychology does not always translate well into Asian cultures

(Guo & Hanley, 2015). Ng, Chan, Ho, Wong, and Ho (2006) noted that the Chinese word commonly used for depression (*youyu*) does not comprehensively describe major depressive disorder, but just one aspect (experience of stagnation, or being stuck), as opposed to a more comprehensive description. Although subtle, linguistic differences can lead to significant misunderstandings of symptomology that can affect diagnosis and treatment.

Apart from linguistic issues, there can be cognitive differences as well. Some Asian Americans may not think in a cause-and-effect manner as do Westerners. As part of the yin–yang concept, one's well-being involves harmony with the world. If one is not in balance with others (i.e., family, friends, or nature), the result can be an imbalance in health. Western thought is often mechanistic and reductionistic (e.g., looking for a direct cause by observing a system and reducing it to its smallest parts), whereas many traditional Asian cultures view systems holistically, often focusing on indirect causes for a result (Shiraev & Levy, 2004). Thus, although a therapist may see a direct causal link between a thought and an action, an Asian American client may take into consideration additional causes that may not have occurred to the therapist but that are valid and make sense to the client.

A related issue is locus of control. In the dominant individualistic U.S. society, people are often assumed to have an internal locus of control, and this focus is believed to be the healthiest. However, in Asian American cultures, the opposite may be true. For example, it is more common for Chinese people to have an external locus of control and, when certain events occur, to believe that the source was an outside factor and that their own actions had a minimal effect. Therapists must be aware of this when using cognitive approaches that stress cause and effect (Park & Kim, 1998). What the therapist may see as a logical outcome may not be as clear to an Asian American client, and vice versa. For instance, although an illogical thought pattern may seem obvious to the therapist, the client may be taking into account how their thoughts and behaviors also affect the family.

Health Beliefs

In contrast to Western culture, traditional Asian cultures have a different understanding of medicine and health. Similar to the collectivist emphasis on relationships with others, traditionally oriented individuals also believe they are interconnected with the universe (Wang & Iwamasa, 2017). One's health is related not only to direct causes as seen by Western medicine (e.g., influenza caused by a virus) but also to disharmony within the world (Spector, 2004). This includes relationships with other people, the earth, and the environment. It may also include how one thinks about the world and the forces beyond one's control (e.g., luck).

On the basis of a presenting problem, many different traditional treatments may be suggested, ranging from dietary changes, acupuncture, coining, cupping, and medicinal herbs. An example of coining is provided in the case example that follows. *Cupping* is the placing of a cup (sometimes heated) on the body and suctioning of air so that the skin is drawn up into the cup. The practice is believed to stimulate blood flow and relieve pain and is often used in acupuncture. Many traditional Asian Americans do not view their physiological well-being separately from other parts of their life (Spector, 2004). It is interesting to note that this is similar to the biopsychosocial model of health. With this in mind, understanding traditional Asian medical approaches and incorporating them into the therapy may be useful for some Asian American clients. For example, progressive muscle relaxation, often used to treat generalized anxiety disorder, may be paired with or replaced by meditation, tai chi, or yoga.

For clients who would benefit from integrating indigenous complimentary approaches, connecting them with indigenous practitioners within Asian American communities can be quite helpful. In addition, working within the Asian American community itself can be a way to limit the stigma associated with psychological treatment. This can be done by interacting with the community nonprofessionally (e.g., spending time at the community center or ethnic churches) and by gaining the trust of those within the community.

Social Behaviors

For a number of reasons, Asian Americans may be perceived as less interpersonally active and verbal than their Western counterparts in various settings, including meetings, class, work, and therapy. For clients who speak English as a second language, it is important to assess the individual's language ability because the client may not understand the therapist's vocabulary, especially psychological terminology. Asian American clients may also ask fewer questions and interact less with the therapist because of cultural norms. For example, in many Asian cultures, it is considered inappropriate to question elders or authorities because it may be perceived as doubting their abilities. Furthermore, it is possible that a client may verbally or nonverbally agree (e.g., nod) to what is being said while actually being in disagreement. This may be done to avoid confrontation and to maintain a harmonious relationship with the therapist. For example, after being assigned homework, the client may agree to do the task yet not have any intention of completing it. Querying the client about the feasibility of the homework is useful in assessing the likelihood of it being completed. It is also helpful for the client to understand clearly why the assignment is important to complete and how it is directly connected to the therapy goals. Keep in mind that acculturation and enculturation levels likely mediate social behaviors; thus, therapists should be prepared to observe significant diversity amongst Asian American clients in their nonverbal behaviors. If a therapist observes behaviors they believe pose a challenge to developing rapport, then an open and supportive inquiry about the behaviors would likely be beneficial rather than assuming pathology on the part of the client.

COGNITIVE BEHAVIOR THERAPY AND ASIAN AMERICANS

There is a growing research literature examining CBT with culturally diverse populations (Bernal, Jimenez-Chafey, & Domenech Rodriguez, 2009), including the work of Wei-Chin Hwang (2006) with ethnic minorities and Chinese Americans and Hinton and Patel (2017) with Southeast Asian refugees. Hwang's work includes the development of the theory-based "top-down" psychotherapy adaptation and modification framework that identifies domains of adaptations to assist therapists with developing skills to work more effectively with culturally diverse populations. These domains include understanding that culture is dynamic and complex, orienting clients to therapy and providing psychoeducation, understanding clients' culturally based beliefs about psychological dysfunction and treatment, understanding the therapy relationship, understanding culturally based expressions of psychological distress, and being aware of cultural issues and values specific to ethnically diverse clients. Hwang later developed a formative method for adapting psychotherapy (Hwang, 2009), a community-based "bottom-up" approach that provides a framework for adapting evidence-based practices such as CBT, as well as non–evidence-based treatments.

The following section focuses on clinical considerations in using CBT with Asian Americans but does not comprehensively include specific components of Hwang's (2006, 2009) ideas, such as deep structure adaptations to evidence-based practices. Readers are referred to Hwang's (2016a, 2016b) primary sources for in-depth review and discussion. Next, and particularly in the case study section, we illustrate how Hinton and Patel (2017) developed a method of assessment and CBT treatment particularly appropriate for traumatized Southeast Asian refugee groups; these include the "multiplex models" that demonstrate how somatic-focused distress is generated.

Advantages and Disadvantages of Cognitive Behavior Therapy

CBT is advantageous in the treatment of Asian Americans for several reasons. Its individualized, short-term, problem-focused orientation is appealing because many Asian Americans seek treatment for a specific acute problem that is currently interfering with their ability to function. CBT's focus on addressing specific symptoms with specific interventions and breaking down goals into small, doable steps is also helpful. Most Asian Americans would not be comfortable with long-term or open-ended therapy and would likely see such therapy as a failure. They may wonder if it takes so long for improvement to occur, why continue? CBT's emphasis on contextual factors also makes it a culturally consistent treatment approach. An additional advantage is that given the importance of harmony and respect for authority, Asian American clients may be more amenable to following directions and engaging in assigned readings and homework.

However, CBT's solution-focused treatment may result in clinicians initially attending more to the problem behaviors rather than ensuring the establishment of a strong therapeutic alliance. As indicated previously, for many Asian American clients, such an alliance is crucial to establishing the therapist's credibility (S. Sue & Zane, 1987). CBT's reductionistic approach to solving problems may also result in miscommunication and misunderstanding if the therapist seeks to solve problems in what they believe to be the most efficient and linear way. An additional limitation of CBT is its emphasis on individualism and an internal locus of control, in contrast to the Asian American emphasis on the family unit, collectivism, and spirituality. A final limitation for non-native English-speaking Asian Americans is CBT's reliance on written assignments, such as daily activity scheduling and thought records, as well as on reading and reviewing handouts and self-help books. Reliance on interventions such as these for those Asian Americans for whom English is a second language or who have had little or no formal education in the United States may be inappropriate.

Recently, Hwang et al. (2015) conducted a randomized controlled trial comparing CBT and culturally adapted CBT with Chinese American adults who were severely depressed and found that participants who received culturally adapted CBT had a greater decrease in depressive symptoms. However, although all participants showed a significant decrease in depressive symptoms, they did not reach remission by the end of treatment. The authors suggested that more intensive treatment might be required for Chinese Americans with severe depression. Although research on the effectiveness of CBT with Asian Americans is limited, Hall and Eap (2007) also found that CBT was helpful with Asian Americans, as have all three authors of this chapter.

Therapist Issues

Ibaraki and Hall (2014) found that having an ethnically matched therapist increased the length of treatment but that content of treatment (e.g., types of problems and issues discussed) depended on the client's perception of shared beliefs, attitudes, and values. Ethnic matching of the therapist and client, although preferred by many ethnic minority individuals, is unlikely to occur given the small proportion of ethnic minority therapists available to Asian American clients. For this reason, cross-cultural competence is especially important.

Hwang and Wood (2007) argued that cultural competence is difficult to define and that, even with education, therapists may not actually be culturally competent if one defines cultural competence as having cultural self-awareness, knowledge, and skills that improve care delivery to culturally diverse clients. The authors argued that sensitivity and awareness are not enough—one must actually have skills to develop effective working relationships. Culturally competent therapists are those who can take broad generic information, think critically and integrate this information with clinical issues and individualize and customize treatment for a particular client (Hwang, 2016a). Self-awareness, including awareness of how one's reactions affect one's clinical judgment, is particularly important (Yon, Malik, Mandin, & Midgley, 2017). Indeed, Wang and Kim (2010) found that Asian American college students rated therapists demonstrating multicultural competence higher in developing a therapeutic alliance and empathy than therapists who did not demonstrate multicultural competence.

Most Asian Americans have experienced racism sometime during their lives, be it overt racism (e.g., verbal abuse, physical beatings) or more subtle forms such as the "bamboo ceiling" (i.e., exclusion from the highest levels of a company; Zhou & Lee, 2017). Consequently, non-Asian therapists (especially older White men) should be aware that they may be seen as an unfriendly figure or at least viewed as an outsider who is unable to understand the client's situation (Kiselica, 1998).

Assessment

In beginning mental health treatment, it is always helpful for the therapist to explain the process of CBT. Informing a potential client of what to expect and how one plans to work assists both the client and therapist to determine whether they will be able to develop a good working relationship. Rather than the simple open-ended question "What brings you here today?" which often causes anxiety and discomfort in people, for Asian American clients, it is often helpful to take the lead in explaining the structure and content you have planned for the initial assessment session and provide an opportunity for the client to ask questions. Some of this may be provided in your first contact with clients, on your professional website, and in written materials such as practice brochures and your informed consent for treatment. Following a brief description of CBT and what it entails, therapists can explain their need to gather background information to have an understanding of the client's decision to enter therapy at this time.

As noted previously, Asian Americans are a diverse group who vary significantly in religion, cultural and historical experiences, and beliefs. A fourth-generation Japanese American college student living in Hawaii who only speaks English has different needs than a first-generation Filipino immigrant who is currently learning English and working full-time as a laborer.

The goal of an assessment is universal, regardless of culture: Identify the issue(s) causing interference and distress, identify relevant strengths that will assist the therapy, and identify potential barriers that may hinder the therapy process. There are many well-researched instruments for assessing clinical symptoms, but the most widely used ones were not developed with Asian Americans in mind (e.g., the Beck Depression Inventory–II, the Anxiety Disorder Interview Schedule).

In this volume, Hays (see the Introduction) describes the ADDRESSING framework, which can also be used to consider cultural influences on Asian Americans. Another assessment approach designed to capture culturally relevant information for cognitive behavior therapists is the Culturally Informed Functional Assessment (CIFA) interview (Tanaka-Matsumi, Seiden, & Lam, 1996). The CIFA aims to increase the cultural relevance of a case formulation by generating detailed, culturally relevant information regarding observable events that are potentially connected to the client's presenting problem. The CIFA involves eight successive stages:

1. assessment of the client's cultural identity and level of acculturation;
2. assessment of the client's presenting problems;
3. elicitation of the client's conceptualization of the problems and possible solutions;
4. functional analysis of the antecedent–target–consequence sequence;
5. negotiation of similarities and differences between the functional analysis and the client's causal explanation of the problems;
6. development of a treatment plan that is acceptable to all parties involved, including culturally different individuals and reference groups;
7. data gathering that facilitates ongoing assessment of the client's progress; and
8. discussion of treatment duration, course, and expected outcome.

Throughout the assessment process, the therapist continually considers the perspectives of the client, the family, and cultural reference groups in developing a case formulation (Tanaka-Matsumi et al., 1996). Use of the CIFA has been found to increase the therapist's knowledge regarding a client's cultural norms and definition of the problem, resulting in a more beneficial treatment plan for the client (Okazaki & Tanaka-Matsumi, 2006).

Readers interested in a more comprehensive summary are pointed to Kinoshita and Hsu's (2007) review of assessment issues for Asian Americans. In addition to reviewing Hays's ADDRESSING framework, these authors provide information on the use of interpreters in treatment, family systems approaches to assessment, standardized and adapted assessment measures with Asian Americans, and neuropsychological assessment. Finally, it is important to note that inquiring about any of the areas identified in the ADDRESSING framework and CIFA can and should occur throughout the course of therapy (not solely in an initial assessment) because target behaviors, goals, interventions, and homework must be informed by an accurate understanding of the client's context, which may change during the course of treatment.

INITIAL SESSIONS

Initial therapy sessions should focus on assessment, development of rapport, goal setting, psychoeducation, and achieving success with short-term goals. In the first session it is important to communicate to the client that you understand the presenting issue. *Essence reflection*, whereby you reflect the content of what you heard, may be a useful tool to reassure both yourself and the client that the problem is understood and that you are able to treat it. Therapists should discuss the treatment plan and schedule in an interactive manner, asking the client, "At the end of treatment, what would you like to have accomplished?" In this way, unrealistic goals may be discussed and more reasonable goals determined. This also helps when it is necessary to set longer term goals for therapy that are clearly understood by both therapist and client.

With Asian American clients, one should inquire about the presence of any problems in addition to the initially presented problem because the client may be reticent about sharing other areas of dysfunction. Clients may not be forthcoming regarding contextual information, especially if it may cause embarrassment to the family. In making judgments about how the client is functioning, it is important to keep in mind that what may seem maladaptive in the therapist's culture may be adaptive and useful in the client's culture. Along these lines, it is also important to examine the functionality of a behavior in its context. This means that the therapist may have to ask questions about whether a behavior is specific to the person and their culture. Asking questions about the client's cultural values and practices demonstrates an interest and willingness to learn on the part of the therapist.

Once longer term goals have been agreed on, it is important to discuss the short-term goals so that the client understands the therapy process and the idea that longer term goals are achieved through the short-term goals. If the treatment plan is clearly laid out, the client will likely feel more comfortable, which will enhance therapy attendance and participation.

During the first few sessions, success is imperative to reassure the client that therapy is beneficial. An Asian American client unaccustomed to counseling may expect something akin to herbal or Western medicine in which the problem is quickly assessed and addressed. Setting achievable short-term goals will increase the likelihood that the client will return. Engaging in behaviors that are successful and useful to the client will build trust and rapport. Examples include behavioral activation for clients with depression, interoceptive conditioning for panic disorder, and systematic desensitization for phobias. Each can be done in the first few therapy sessions, in or out of the therapy session.

If language is an issue, it may be prudent to rely more on behavioral interventions. For example, the second author (Hsia) has limited skills with Cantonese and worked successfully with a Cantonese-speaking client who had limited English skills and was diagnosed with obsessive–compulsive disorder (contamination issues) by focusing on systematic desensitization. Even with a language barrier, the client saw success by decreasing his anxiety in handling "contaminated" items and, thus, regularly attended therapy.

Psychoeducation is also important in initial sessions. Many clients do not have an understanding of their disorder and experience relief when they understand the etiology of their disorder and that their problem is not unique. Sharing what you know from the empirical literature regarding the effectiveness of therapy techniques can make clients feel more at ease as they learn that their disorder is well known and researched and that a viable solution exists. Teaching clients the CBT model and how it will address their problems increases comfort with therapy and enables Asian American clients to anticipate what therapy will be like. It is useful to ask clients about their beliefs about the problem because this will help the therapist better understand how the client perceives the problem and the underlying issues that support behaviors.

Because gift giving is a common practice among Asian Americans, giving a small gift at the end of the initial assessment can help build the working relationship. For example, the therapist might give the client a card with a phrase identified during the session that illustrates one of the client's strengths (Hwang, Wood, Lin, & Cheung, 2006).

MIDDLE SESSIONS

The focus of middle sessions should be on continued behavioral interventions, cognitive challenging, preparation for in vivo exposure if necessary, and preparation for termination. If good rapport has been established, it is not uncommon during the middle sessions for other issues to arise. Once the client has observed the effectiveness of therapy and experienced a decrease in symptoms along with an increase in quality of life, the Asian American client may become more open about other problems. For example, after a few successful sessions, a Chinese client divulged to the therapist that she was in the United States illegally, currently living with her mother, and needed help finding alternative housing. In such a situation, it is necessary to make some decisions: Does the new problem interfere to such an extent that treatment for the initial problem should be put on hold? Can someone else (family, friends) help with the new problem? Should treatment continue?

This decision-making process should be nonconfrontational and collaborative, with the therapist and client together reviewing the original treatment plan and deciding whether it should be altered to address more immediate problems. Although it is important to help the client learn new skills, it is also imperative that the client does not feel like he or she is being lectured or shamed or is losing face (Hwang et al., 2006). It can be helpful to remind the client that as one problem becomes resolved, typically other problems also resolve without the direct focus of therapy. The therapist can emphasize how such a process indicates the client's increased ability to generalize and apply skills learned in treatment.

The hallmark of the middle sessions, once behavioral interventions have been successful, is a focus on learning cognitive skills. Both in terms of ease of use and language issues, cognitive challenging can be simplified and thus more easily remembered and used. One approach is to focus on three areas:

- Core cognitions: "What is your underlying concern?"
- Probability overestimation: "What is the likelihood of your underlying concern occurring?"
- Catastrophizing: "If your underlying concern does occur, will it really be that horrible?"

The therapist can have the client practice these statements so that it becomes second nature to ask him- or herself such questions. Ideally, these cognitive tools will become ingrained to such an extent that, in any situation, the client can critically assess the problem and select the necessary action, thus increasing the client's ability to cope on his or her own after therapy ends.

In cognitive challenging with Asian Americans, if the client speaks English as a second language, they may approach situations differently than clients for whom English is their first language. Whereas American English makes significant use of slang, many Asian languages (e.g., Chinese) express thoughts through the use of idioms. Thus, it may be useful to learn some idioms or proverbs from the client's background to use as examples in therapy. In addition, Asian Americans may not always approach situations on the basis of whether it is a logical choice. They may take into consideration how decisions will affect their family and others around them. Even if an action seems logical to the therapist, an Asian American may perceive it as potentially embarrassing or as bringing shame to the family and refuse the suggestion. If this occurs, or if the client objects to the intervention, a different approach should be taken.

Clinicians have to assess how the client has dealt with the problem behavior and discuss why such approaches may not have been successful. The therapist can then suggest a new approach to the problem by critically assessing the problem and breaking it down into more manageable steps that can be addressed individually. Once this is done, the relational aspects of changing one's behavior and how this might affect others may be discussed. A helpful cognitive reframe is that, without change, the whole family will experience some level of dishonor because the client's difficulties are not being addressed, but by addressing the problem, harmony and honor for the family can be achieved. Some compromises may have to be made, especially in implementing in vivo practices, because of possible concerns about looking foolish in public. If the client and therapist can discuss what is helpful and what is not working well in therapy, it is likely that acceptable alternative approaches can be found.

During the middle sessions, it is also important to begin laying the groundwork for the client's final sessions and beyond. Therapy should focus on the cognitive skills learned while training the client to become their own therapist.

END SESSIONS

The last few sessions should focus on the practice of behavioral and cognitive skills, continued preparation for termination, and assisting the client to increase his or her social support. In particularly challenging situations, practicing "dry runs" or role plays will increase the likelihood of success in the real situation. For in vivo practice, one may have to begin with imaginary exposures and build toward in vivo exposures. The therapist may have to be inventive in finding sites for in vivo practice away from locations where other community members may see the client. In addition, it is suggested that the client either be given notes during treatment or that the client take notes and create a notebook that includes not only notes but also handouts and readings that can be used for reference after treatment has ended.

If the client is reluctant to engage in behaviors seen as potentially embarrassing, another approach is to address the consequences if no change occurs. Using the "What if" approach and asking the client to brainstorm the positives and negatives about changing the behavior can be useful. Although the client may want to avoid short-term shame, long-term consequences may become more problematic. Discussing what aspects of the intervention make it embarrassing and examining its pros and cons will provide the therapist with more information about how to revise the intervention to make it more comfortable for the client.

Therapists should discuss termination and what to expect after treatment ends. Although the client may indicate that he or she does not want any further interaction, the therapist should still stress future availability regardless of circumstances. An Asian American client may feel that if gains are not maintained, they have failed and experience shame in admitting problems after therapy has ended. Emphasizing realistic expectations will help the client understand that life will continue to be stressful and that experiencing future difficulties is normal.

In ending therapy with Asian American clients, three steps are suggested. The first is to increase the time between final sessions. The second is, after termination and if the client agrees, to maintain contact through several monthly follow-up phone calls. During these calls, the therapist will remind the client that life will continue to have its ups and downs and that difficulties are common and should be expected. This way, when clients encounter problems, they may be more willing to contact the therapist if a problem exceeds their coping abilities. Finally, encouraging the client to explain what they have learned in therapy to a trusted friend or family member can reinforce the client's learning because it also reinforces their social support.

CASE EXAMPLE

To provide culturally sensitive treatment, the therapist must understand the culture and history of the client's ethnic group and how it may influence the experience and expression of psychological distress. For example, for Cambodian and Vietnamese refugees, unique forms of panic attacks may occur, such as *orthostatic panic* (i.e., dizziness on standing that causes a panic attack) and *neck-focused panic* (i.e., neck sensations that cause a panic attack; Hinton, Um, & Ba, 2001). Research has shown that in such cases, panic attacks combine posttraumatic stress disorder (PTSD) characteristics (e.g., flashbacks) and those of panic disorder (e.g., fear of death from physiological dysfunction; Hinton, So, Pollack, Pitman, & Orr, 2004).

The multiplex model of panic generation (see Figure 5.1) can be used to explain how panic attacks are generated among Southeast Asian refugees (Hinton & Simon, 2015; Hinton et al., 2004). According to the model, a panic attack may begin after the induction of an *arousal-reactive symptom*— that is, a symptom made worse by arousal (e.g., dizziness; Taylor, Koch, & McNally, 1992). The symptom may be induced by various causes, such as a worry episode, hyperventilation, exertion, anger, overeating, head rotation, or thinking about a traumatic event.

The arousal-reactive sensation may activate one or more fear networks: (a) trauma associations, (b) catastrophic cognitions, (c) metaphoric associations, and (d) interoceptive conditioning leading directly to somatic and psychological fear. Anxiety generated by the activation of one or more of these four types of fear networks aggravates the arousal-reactive symptom, which leads to further activation of the fear networks. Through this positive feedback loop, an escalating spiral of arousal may ensue, leading to a panic attack. When all four types of fear networks are simultaneously activated and create an escalating spiral of panic, it may be called a TCMIE *panic attack* (*T* for trauma associations, C for catastrophic cognitions, M for metaphoric associations, *I* for interoceptive conditioning of an arousal-reactive sensation to psychological and somatic fear, and *E* for escalating arousal). The following is a case description of a Cambodian refugee with orthostatically induced panic, based on the TCMIE model.

On initial presentation to a psychiatric clinic, 59-year-old Chan[1] was experiencing hour-long orthostatic panic attacks three times a week. During the attacks, on standing, he experienced severe dizziness, along with cold hands, palpitations, and neck soreness. He would immediately sit down, fearing "wind overload." Cambodians consider "wind" to be an air-like substance that runs in the body alongside blood, which may surge upward in the body, with disastrous results (Hinton et al., 2004). Chan also worried about cardiac arrest, neck vessel rupture, and stroke. During a third of these panic

---

[1]Case material in this chapter has been disguised to protect client confidentiality.

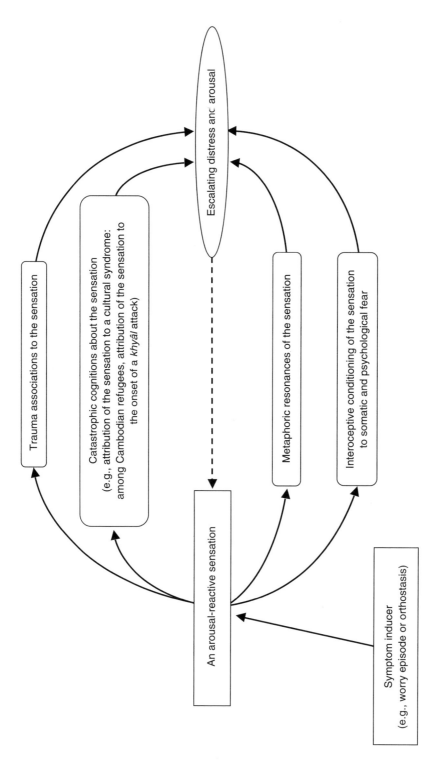

Figure 5.1. The generation of the TCMIE (multiplex) panic attack. T = trauma associations; C = catastrophic cognitions; M = metaphoric associations; I = interoceptive conditioning of an arousal-reactive sensation to somatic and psychological fear; and E = escalating arousal and panic.

Within the figure:

- Trauma associations to the sensation
- Catastrophic cognitions about the sensation (e.g., attribution of the sensation to a cultural syndrome: among Cambodian refugees, attribution of the sensation to the onset of a *khyâl* attack)
- Escalating distress anc arousal
- Metaphoric resonances of the sensation
- Interoceptive conditioning of the sensation to somatic and psychological fear
- An arousal-reactive sensation
- Symptom inducer (e.g., worry episode or orthostasis)

attacks, Chan had flashbacks of either his brothers' execution or stacks of body parts.

To relieve the symptoms, Chan would "coin" himself to remove excessive inner wind. Chan considered cold extremities, dizziness, and other symptoms to result from the blockage of vessels in the limbs and an inner accumulation of wind. Coining is thought to remove wind and restore proper blood and wind flow in the vessels. One takes a coin, dips the edge in wind oil, and drags the coin's edge in a proximal to distal direction, either along the ribs of the front or the back of the body, along the limbs, or both, resulting in streaks. The color of the streaks reveals how much wind has accumulated in the body.

In the Khmer Rouge period, Chan worked 12 hours a day under a hot sun. Twice a day he was fed a watery rice broth. The work was mainly of two types: digging and carrying dirt in a bucket and rice transplantation. Chan had often felt dizzy, especially after bending over, and he saw many people collapse while doing the work. In the Pol Pot period, Chan, like most Cambodians, contracted severe malaria. Malaria may predispose individuals to panic disorder by forming a trauma association to symptoms of autonomic arousal such as dizziness and by causing interoceptive conditioning of fear to sensations of autonomic arousal such as chills, dizziness, and palpitations (Hinton, Hinton, Pham, Chau, & Tran, 2003). Chan had malaria attacks every day for 6 months. These episodes essentially formed a "cold" panic attack lasting 45 minutes and were marked by rigors and palpitations, followed by 30-minute "hot" panic attacks marked by palpitations, headache, extreme dysphoria, and severe dizziness. As were most Khmer, Chan was frequently accused of feigning illness. Consequently, even after a malarial attack commenced, he was forced to work. Chan would struggle to work and, suddenly dizzy, would often collapse.

Just before the Vietnamese invasion of his village, Chan and his two brothers were farming rice about an hour's walk from their village. Six Khmer Rouge suddenly arrived and arrested them. The soldiers knew Chan's brothers had served as soldiers before the Khmer Rouge invasion. Chan was charged with the crimes of being related to a soldier and not revealing his brothers' identities to the authorities. Three soldiers escorted Chan's brothers a distance away while the other three guarded Chan. One of the guards lit a cigarette and, while exhaling smoke into Chan's face, told him they would kill and eviscerate his two brothers and consume their livers. Chan was forced to watch his brothers being bound, shot in the chest, and then eviscerated. Chan was overcome with panic, nausea, dizziness, and leg weakness. The soldiers released him, saying that this would be his fate if he committed any errors. On arriving at his village, Chan found the Khmer Rouge assembling the villagers to view the corpses of two people who tried to escape. A pile of limbs, severed at the knee and elbow, was next to the two heads. When the Vietnamese invaded his village a few hours later, he escaped and managed to reach the Thai border.

Once the therapist understood the etiology of Chan's panic attacks, the treatment plan could be established. Seven core elements were stressed during Chan's treatment:

- psychoeducation—provision of information about PTSD and panic disorder, such as how trauma reminders and catastrophic cognitions generate panic attacks;
- training in muscle relaxation and diaphragmatic breathing procedures, including relaxation techniques;
- framing relaxation techniques as a form of mindfulness, while attending to specific sensory modalities (i.e., muscular tension and the kinesthetics of breathing);
- cognitive restructuring of fear networks, especially trauma memories and catastrophic misinterpretations of somatic sensations including culture-related fears;
- interoceptive exposure (including reassociation) to anxiety-related sensations to treat panic attacks generated by catastrophic cognitions, interoceptive conditioning, and trauma associations to such sensations;
- provision of an emotional processing protocol to use during times of trauma recall (e.g., flashbacks), bringing about a shift from an attitude of pained acceptance to one of mindfulness; and
- specifically exploring orthostatic panic, both the investigation of initiation sequences and the determination of catastrophic cognitions and trauma associations.

Following the initial assessment and efforts to establish rapport, the CBT process and concepts were explained. Chan was asked whether he had questions to ensure that he understood the connection between the techniques and his treatment goals. In addition, the therapist described the TCMIE conceptualization of panic attacks and trauma-related disorders and explained how fright could generate symptoms such as cold extremities or dizziness.

In the middle sessions, Chan's catastrophic cognitions regarding somatic symptoms were discussed, including his traumatic associations to dizziness and other symptoms elicited by standing. Cognitive restructuring was used to help change these catastrophic cognitions. Behavioral relaxation techniques were framed as mindfulness, and Chan practiced various techniques until he was comfortable with initiating them "in the moment." Chan was also offered and agreed to take an antidepressant medication (paroxetine). By the end of treatment, Chan had experienced complete resolution of his panic attacks and a substantial decrease in his PTSD severity, such that his symptoms no longer met diagnostic criteria for either disorder. He developed a number of skills and was able to articulate various techniques that worked well for him. Chan reported he was confident that he could use the tools he acquired in CBT if he needed to in the future.

CONCLUSION

This chapter summarized issues related to conducting CBT with Asian Americans. The heterogeneity among Asian Americans, including their historical context and immigration history, was briefly presented. In addition, we provided information on culture-specific issues such as religion, family structure and roles, gender roles, acculturation, ethnic and racial identity, values, language and cognitive styles, health beliefs, and social behaviors and how these cultural factors may influence clients' behaviors and perceptions of therapy and the therapist. We also discussed the advantages and disadvantages of CBT with Asian American clients. Finally, a case example of successful CBT with an Asian American client was presented. The case demonstrates the utility of understanding the client's culturally influenced experiences and integrating that assessment information into a conceptualization that assists with the development of a focused treatment plan. Treatment plans should include psychoeducation regarding the client's specific symptoms and individually tailored behavioral and cognitive interventions that directly address the client's symptoms.

REFERENCES

Ai, A. L., Bjork, J. P., Appel, H. B., & Huang, B. (2013). In K. I. Pargament (Ed.), *APA handbook of psychology, religion, and spirituality: Vol 1. Context, theory, and research* (pp. 581–598). Washington, DC: American Psychological Association. http://dx.doi.org/10.1037/14045-032

Angelelli, C., & Geist-Martin, P. (2005). Enhancing culturally competent health communication: Constructing understanding between providers and culturally diverse patients. In E. Ray (Ed.), *Health communication in practice: A case study approach* (pp. 271–283). Mahwah, NJ: Erlbaum.

Bernal, D., Jimenez-Chafey, M. I., & Domenech Rodriguez, M. M. (2009). Cultural adaption of treatments: A resource for considering culture in evidence-based practice. *Professional Psychology: Research and Practice, 40,* 361–368. http://dx.doi.org/10.1037/a0016401

Chin, J. L. (Ed.). (2000). *Relationships among Asian American women*. Washington, DC: American Psychological Association. http://dx.doi.org/10.1037/10349-000

Choi, Y., Kim, T. Y., Pekelnicky, D. D., Kim, K., & Kim, Y. S. (2017). Impact of youth cultural orientation on perception of family process and development among Korean Americans. *Cultural Diversity and Ethnic Minority Psychology, 23,* 244–257. http://dx.doi.org/10.1037/cdp0000093

Chung, R. C., & Bemak, F. (2007). Asian Immigrants and Refugees. In F. T. L. Leong, A. Ebreo, L. Kinoshita, A. G. Inman, L. H. Yang, & M. Fu (Eds.), *Handbook of Asian American psychology* (2nd ed., pp. 227–244). Thousand Oaks, CA: Sage.

Civic Impulse. (2018). *H.R. 3568: Amerasian Homecoming Act.* Retrieved from GovTrack website: https://www.govtrack.us/congress/bills/100/hr3568

Guo, F., & Hanley, T. (2015). Adapting cognitive behavioral therapy to meet the needs of Chinese clients: Opportunities and challenges. *PsyCh Journal, 4,* 55–65. http://dx.doi.org/10.1002/pchj.75

Gupta, A., Szymanski, D. M., & Leong, F. T. L. (2011). The "Model Minority myth": Internalized racialism of positive stereotypes as correlates of psychological distress, and attitudes toward help-seeking. *Asian American Journal of Psychology, 2,* 101–114. http://dx.doi.org/10.1037/a0024183

Hall, G. C. N., & Eap, S. (2007). Empirically supported therapies for Asian Americans. In F. T. L. Leong, A. Ebreo, L. Kinoshita, A. G. Inman, L. H. Yang, & M. Fu (Eds.), *Handbook of Asian American psychology* (2nd ed., pp. 449–467). Thousand Oaks, CA: Sage.

Hall, G. C. N., & Okazaki, S. (Eds.). (2002). *Asian American psychology: The science of lives in context.* Washington, DC: American Psychological Association. http://dx.doi.org/10.1037/10473-000

Hannas, W. (1997). *Asia's orthographic dilemma.* Honolulu: University of Hawaii Press.

Helms, J. E. (1992). *A race is a nice thing to have: A guide to being a White person or understanding the White persons in your life.* Topeka, KS: Content Communication.

Helms, J. E., & Talleyrand, R. (1997). Race is not ethnicity. *American Psychologist, 52,* 1246–1247. http://dx.doi.org/10.1037/0003-066X.52.11.1246

Herskovits, M. J. (1948). *Man and his works: The science of cultural anthropology.* New York, NY: Knopf.

Hinton, D., Hinton, S., Pham, T., Chau, H., & Tran, M. (2003). "Hit by the wind" and temperature-shift panic among Vietnamese refugees. *Transcultural Psychiatry, 40,* 342–376. http://dx.doi.org/10.1177/13634615030403003

Hinton, D., So, V., Pollack, M., Pitman, R., & Orr, S. (2004). The psychophysiology of orthostatic panic in Cambodian refugees attending a psychiatric clinic. *Journal of Psychopathology and Behavioral Assessment, 26,* 1–13. http://dx.doi.org/10.1023/B:JOBA.0000007451.85942.42

Hinton, D., Um, K., & Ba, P. (2001). *Kyol goeu* ("wind overload"): Part I. A cultural syndrome of orthostatic panic among Khmer refugees. *Transcultural Psychiatry, 38*, 403–432. http://dx.doi.org/10.1177/136346150103800401

Hinton, D. E., & Patel, A. (2017). Cultural adaptations of cognitive behavior therapy. *Psychiatry Clinics of North America, 40*, 701–714. http://dx.doi.org/10.1016/j.psc.2017.08.006

Hinton, D. E., & Simon, N. M. (2015). Somatization, anxiety disorders (GAD, Panic Disorder, and PTSD), and the arousal complex in cultural context: The multiplex model and the cultural neuroscience of anxiety disorders. In L. J. Kirmayer, R. Lemelson, & C. Cummings (Eds.), *Revisioning psychiatry: Cultural phenomenology, critical neuroscience, and global mental health* (pp. 343–374). Cambridge, England: Cambridge University Press. http://dx.doi.org/10.1017/CBO9781139424745.017

Hwang, W.-C. (2006). The psychotherapy adaptation and modification framework: Application to Asian Americans. *American Psychologist, 61*, 702–715. http://dx.doi.org/10.1037/0003-066X.61.7.702

Hwang, W.-C. (2009). The Formative Method for Adapting Psychotherapy (FMAP): A community-based developmental approach to culturally adapting therapy. *Professional Psychology: Research and Practice, 40*, 369–377. http://dx.doi.org/10.1037/a0016240

Hwang, W.-C. (2016a). Culturally adapting evidence-based practices for ethnic minority and immigrant families. In N. Zane, G. Bernal, & F. T. L. Leong (Eds.), *Evidence-based psychological practice with ethnic minorities: Culturally informed research and clinical strategies* (pp. 289–309). Washington, DC: American Psychological Association. http://dx.doi.org/10.1037/14940-014

Hwang, W.-C. (2016b). *Culturally adapting psychotherapy for Asian heritage populations: An evidence-based approach.* San Diego, CA: Academic Press.

Hwang, W.-C., Myers, H. F., Chiu, E., Mak, E., Butner, J. E., Fujimoto, K., . . . Miranda, J. (2015). Culturally adapted cognitive-behavioral therapy for Chinese Americans with depression: A randomized controlled trial. *Psychiatric Services, 66*, 1035–1042. http://dx.doi.org/10.1176/appi.ps.201400358

Hwang, W.-C., & Wood, J. J. (2007). Being culturally sensitive is not the same as being culturally competent. *Pragmatic Case Studies in Psychotherapy, 3*, 44–50. http://dx.doi.org/10.14713/pcsp.v3i3.906

Hwang, W.-C., Wood, J. J., Lin, K. M., & Cheung, F. (2006). Cognitive-behavioral therapy with Chinese Americans: Research, theory, and clinical practice. *Cognitive and Behavioral Practice, 13*, 293–303. http://dx.doi.org/10.1016/j.cbpra.2006.04.010

Ibaraki, A. Y., & Hall, G. C. N. (2014). The components of cultural match in psychotherapy. *Journal of Social and Clinical Psychology, 33*, 936–953. http://dx.doi.org/10.1521/jscp.2014.33.10.936

Iwamasa, G. Y., & Yamada, A. M. (2001). Asian American acculturation and ethnic/racial identity: Research innovations in the new millennium. *Cultural Diversity and Ethnic Minority Psychology, 7*, 203–206. http://dx.doi.org/10.1037/1099-9809.7.3.203

Kammer, J. (2015). *The Hart-Celler Immigration Act of 1965*. Retrieved from the Center for Immigration Studies website: https://cis.org/Report/HartCeller-Immigration-Act-1965

Kazarian, S., & Evans, D. (2001). *Handbook of cultural health psychology*. San Diego, CA: Academic Press.

Keister, L. A., Agius Vallejo, J., & Aronson, B. (2016). Chinese immigrant wealth: Heterogeneity in adaptation. *PLoS One, 11*(12), e0168043. http://dx.doi.org/10.1371/journal.pone.0168043

Kiang, L., Huynh, V. W., Cheah, C. S. L., Wang, Y., & Yoshikawa, H. (2017). Moving beyond the model minority. *Asian American Journal of Psychology, 8*, 1–6. http://dx.doi.org/10.1037/aap0000070

Kinoshita, L. M., & Hsu, J. (2007). Assessment of Asian Americans: Fundamental issues and clinical applications. In F. T. L. Leong, A. Ebreo, L. Kinoshita, A. G. Inman, L. H. Yang, & M. Fu (Eds.), *Handbook of Asian American psychology* (2nd ed., pp. 409–428). Thousand Oaks, CA: Sage.

Kiselica, M. S. (1998). Preparing Anglos for the challenges and joys of multiculturalism. *The Counseling Psychologist, 26*, 5–21. http://dx.doi.org/10.1177/0011000098261001

Lee, E. (1996). Asian American families: An overview. In M. McGoldrick, J. Giordano, & J. Pearce (Eds.), *Ethnicity and family therapy* (pp. 227–248). New York, NY: Guilford Press.

Leong, F. T. L., Ebreo, A., Kinoshita, L., Inman, A. G., Yang, L. H., & Fu, M. (Eds.). (2007). *Handbook of Asian American psychology* (2nd ed.). Thousand Oaks, CA: Sage.

Liu, W. M., Iwamoto, D. K., & Chae, M. H. (2010). *Culturally responsive counseling with Asian American men*. New York, NY: Routledge.

Marín, G., & Gamba, R. (2003). Acculturation and changes in cultural values. In K. M. Chun, P. B. Balls-Organista, & G. Marín (Eds.), *Acculturation: Advances in theory, measurements, and applied research* (pp. 83–93). Washington, DC: American Psychological Association. http://dx.doi.org/10.1037/10472-007

Mok, T. A. (2015). A long-term therapeutic journey with an Asian "parachute kid." *Asian American Journal of Psychology, 6*, 281–288. http://dx.doi.org/10.1037/a0039378

Moyerman, D. R., & Forman, B. D. (1992). Acculturation and adjustment: A meta-analytic study. *Hispanic Journal of Behavioral Sciences, 14*, 163–200. http://dx.doi.org/10.1177/07399863920142001

National Archives. (2018). *Chinese Exclusion Act records at the National Archives at Seattle*. Retrieved from the National Archives website: https://www.archives.gov/seattle/finding-aids/chinese-exclusion-act#aboutcea

National Archives Foundation. (2018). *Refugee Act of 1980*. Retrieved from National Archives Foundation website: https://www.archivesfoundation.org/documents/refugee-act-1980/

Ng, S., Chan, C. L. W., Ho, D. Y. F., Wong, Y.-Y., & Ho, R. T. H. (2006). Stagnation as a distinct cultural syndrome: Comparing 'yu' (stagnation) in traditional Chinese medicine with depression. *British Journal of Social Work, 36*, 467–484. http://dx.doi.org/10.1093/bjsw/bcl008

Nguyen, C. P., Wong, Y. J., Juang, L. P., & Park, I. J. K. (2015). Pathways among Asian Americans' family ethnic socialization, ethnic identity, and psychological well-being: A multigroup mediation model. *Asian American Journal of Psychology, 6*, 273–280. http://dx.doi.org/10.1037/aap0000026

Office of the Historian. (n.d.). *The Immigration Act of 1924 (The Johnson-Reed Act)*. Retrieved from https://history.state.gov/milestones/1921-1936/immigration-act

Okazaki, S., & Tanaka-Matsumi, J. (2006). Cultural considerations in cognitive–behavioral assessment. In P. A. Hays & G. Y. Iwamasa (Eds.), *Culturally responsive cognitive–behavioral therapy: Assessment, practice, and supervision* (pp. 247–266). Washington, DC: American Psychological Association. http://dx.doi.org/10.1037/11433-011

Pan, D., Huey, S. J., Jr., & Hernandez, D. (2011). Culturally adapted versus standard exposure treatment for phobic Asian Americans: Treatment efficacy, moderators, and predictors. *Cultural Diversity and Ethnic Minority Psychology, 17*, 11–22. http://dx.doi.org/10.1037/a0022534

Park, Y., & Kim, U. (1998). Locus of control, attributional style, and academic achievement: Comparative analysis of Korean Chinese and Chinese students. *Asian Journal of Social Psychology, 1*, 191–208. http://dx.doi.org/10.1111/1467-839X.00013

Pew Research Center. (2013). *The rise of Asian Americans*. Retrieved from http://www.pewsocialtrends.org/2012/06/19/the-rise-of-asian-americans/

Phinney, J. S. (2003). Ethnic identity and acculturation. In K. M. Chun, P. B. Organista, & G. Marín (Eds.), *Acculturation: Advances in theory, measurement, and applied research* (pp. 63–81). Washington, DC: American Psychological Association. http://dx.doi.org/10.1037/10472-006

Shiraev, E., & Levy, D. (2004). *Cross-cultural psychology*. Boston, MA: Allyn & Bacon.

Spector, R. (2004). *Cultural diversity in health and illness*. Upper Saddle River, NJ: Prentice Hall.

Sue, D. (2005). Asian American/Pacific Islander families in conflict. In W. George (Ed.), *Race, culture, psychology, and law* (pp. 257–268). Thousand Oaks, CA: Sage. http://dx.doi.org/10.4135/9781452233536.n17

Sue, S., & Zane, N. (1987). The role of culture and cultural techniques in psychotherapy: A critique and reformulation. *American Psychologist, 42*, 37–45. http://dx.doi.org/10.1037/0003-066X.42.1.37

Tan, S., & Dong, N. J. (2014). Psychotherapy with members of Asian American churches and spiritual traditions. In P. S. Richards & A. E. Bergin (Eds.), *Handbook of psychotherapy and religious diversity* (2nd ed., pp. 423–450). Washington, DC: American Psychological Association. http://dx.doi.org/10.1037/14371-017

Tanaka-Matsumi, J., Seiden, D., & Lam, K. (1996). The Culturally Informed Functional Assessment (CIFA) Interview: A strategy for cross-cultural behavioral practice. *Cognitive and Behavioral Practice, 3*, 215–233. http://dx.doi.org/10.1016/S1077-7229(96)80015-0

Taylor, S., Koch, W. J., & McNally, R. J. (1992). How does anxiety sensitivity vary across the anxiety disorders? *Journal of Anxiety Disorders, 6*, 249–259. http://dx.doi.org/10.1016/0887-6185(92)90037-8

Tseng, W. S. (2003). *Clinician's guide to cultural psychiatry*. San Diego, CA: Academic Press.

U.S. Census Bureau. (2012). *The Asian population: 2010*. Retrieved from https://www.census.gov/prod/cen2010/briefs/c2010br-11.pdf

Wang, S., & Kim, B. S. K. (2010). Therapist multicultural competence, Asian American participants' cultural values, and counseling process. *Journal of Counseling Psychology, 57*, 394–401. http://dx.doi.org/10.1037/a0020359

Wang, S. C., & Iwamasa, G. Y. (2017). Indigenous healing practices and Asian immigrant women. *Women & Therapy, 41*, 149–164. http://dx.doi.org/10.1080/02703149.2017.1330917

Wong, A., Wong, Y. J., & Obeng, C. S. (2012). An untold story: A qualitative study of Asian American family strengths. *Asian American Journal of Psychology, 3*, 286–298. http://dx.doi.org/10.1037/a0025553

Wu, S. (2001). Parenting in Chinese-American families. In N. Webb (Ed.), *Culturally diverse parent–child and family relationship: A guide for social workers and other practitioners* (pp. 235–260). New York, NY: Columbia University Press.

Yang, K. S. (2006). Indigenized conceptual and empirical analyses of selected Chinese psychological characteristics. *International Journal of Psychology, 41*, 298–303. http://dx.doi.org/10.1080/00207590544000086

Yee, B. W. K., DeBaryshe, B. D., Yuen, S., Kim, S. Y., & McCubbin, H. I. (2007). Asian American and Pacific Islander Families: Resiliency and life-span socialization in a cultural context. In F. T. L. Leong, A. Ebreo, L. Kinoshita, A. G. Inman, L. H. Yang, & M. Fu (Eds.), *Handbook of Asian American psychology* (2nd ed., pp. 69–86). Thousand Oaks, CA: Sage.

Yeh, K. (2003). The beneficial and harmful effects of filial piety: An integrative analysis. In K. S. Yang, K. K. Hwang, P. B. Pederson, & I. Daibo (Eds.), *Progress in Asian social psychology: Conceptual and empirical contributions* (pp. 67–82). Westport, CT: Praeger.

Yon, K., Malik, R., Mandin, P., & Midgley, N. (2017). Challenging core cultural beliefs and maintaining the therapeutic alliance: A qualitative study. *Journal of Family Therapy, 40*, 180–200. http://dx.doi.org/10.1111/1467-6427.12158

Zhang, S., & Moradi, B. (2013). Asian American acculturation and enculturation: Construct clarification and measurement consolidation. *The Counseling Psychologist, 41*, 750–790. http://dx.doi.org/10.1177/0011000012456882

Zhou, M. (2004). Are Asian Americans becoming "White?" *Contexts, 3*, 29–37. http://dx.doi.org/10.1525/ctx.2004.3.1.29

Zhou, M., & Lee, J. (2017). Hyper-selectivity and the remaining of culture: Understanding the Asian American achievement paradox. *Asian American Journal of Psychology, 8*, 7–15. http://dx.doi.org/10.1037/aap0000069

6

COGNITIVE BEHAVIOR THERAPY WITH SOUTH ASIAN AMERICANS

SHEETAL SHAH AND NITA TEWARI

According to the 2010 U.S. Census Bureau, 3.4 million South Asian Americans live in the United States. The term *South Asian* denotes a common identity, bringing together diverse populations on the basis of a shared culture and history (Shankar & Srikanth, 1998). South Asian Americans include people who immigrated to the United States from Bangladesh, Bhutan, India, Maldives, Pakistan, Nepal, and Sri Lanka. Indians are the largest segment of the South Asian community, making up over 80% of the total population, followed by Pakistanis, Bangladeshis, Nepalis, Sri Lankans, Bhutanese, and Maldivians (U.S. Census Bureau, 2010). South Asian Americans are the fastest growing population among all major ethnic groups in the United States. The largest South Asian American populations in the United States are in California, New York, New Jersey, Texas, and Illinois, and the populations of South Asian Americans in these states continue to grow (Pew Research Center, 2013; Shankar & Srikanth, 1998). Although shared region, culture, and history help bring South Asian Americans into an identified group, it is

http://dx.doi.org/10.1037/0000119-007
Culturally Responsive Cognitive Behavior Therapy, Second Edition: Practice and Supervision, G. Y. Iwamasa and P. A. Hays (Editors)

161

important to know that South Asian Americans are a heterogeneous group, diverse in ethnic identities, immigration histories, languages, religious practices, cultural values, socioeconomic status, and acculturation levels (Das & Kemp, 1997; Tewari, 2009).

In the first part of this chapter, we review historical and cultural factors influencing South Asian Americans, including intersections of identities and culturally specific concerns, acculturation, bicultural stress, and more. Following the cultural overview of South Asian Americans as a population, we present cognitive behavior therapy (CBT) treatment considerations, interventions, and assessment for this population. We provide a case example using CBT with a South Asian American client as well, highlighting cultural factors when applying CBT interventions, using assessments, and providing therapy to individuals from this population.

In a review of the psychological literature, we found a lack of research on therapeutic interventions with South Asian Americans in general and an absence of articles specifically referencing CBT with South Asian Americans. Horrell (2008) conducted a review of the effectiveness of CBT for ethnic minority populations by examining 12 studies with individuals of African, Asian, and Hispanic descent. She found that CBT is effective but noted that only five studies included Asian Americans, and South Asian Americans were not a represented group. Although there is a dearth of empirically based literature summarizing the implementation of CBT with South Asian Americans, cultural understanding can help in tailoring CBT to South Asian American clients.

HISTORICAL AND CULTURAL OVERVIEW OF SOUTH ASIAN AMERICANS

To understand the complexity of clients that identify as South Asian American, clinicians must ask themselves what, aside from country of origin, makes an individual South Asian American? Although an individual may identify as such, each South Asian American has ties not only to his or her heritage culture and country (or family's country) of origin but also to languages spoken, religious beliefs, and cultural practices. The next section highlights historical and cultural considerations of intersecting identities pertaining to South Asian American clients.

Immigration

The experience of immigrating to and settling in the United States varies for South Asian American individuals and families. Initial waves of

South Asians immigrating to the United States began in 1898, largely from India, present-day Pakistan, and Bangladesh (Ibrahim, Ohnishi, & Sandhu, 1997). This first wave of immigrants from South Asia were laborers and often worked in the agricultural sector (Ibrahim et al., 1997). National origin quotas were subsequently established by the United States government in 1921, limiting immigration from Asian and Arab countries (Zong & Batalova, 2016). It was not until the United States government passed the 1965 Immigration and Nationality Act that immigration from this region was again allowed (Kurien, 2005). Following the 1965 act, a large percentage of South Asians who immigrated to the United States were professionals, including doctors, engineers, scientists, academicians, and students seeking professional degrees in American universities. The 1980 Reunification Act brought a later wave of less-educated South Asian immigrants, who were less fluent in English and who were often lower wage earners (Sandhu & Madathil, 2007).

Currently, South Asia is the primary region from which international students and temporary H-1B visa holders (i.e., temporary workers who plan to return to their country) originate. India is the country with the second highest number of international students in the United States; 70% of H1-B visa holders come from India (Zong & Batalova, 2016). International students and temporary workers have unique experiences in the United States because adjustment is fast but also time limited given their visa status. The concerns of this population may overlap with the struggles of South Asian Americans, but given that they do not identify as American and their typical stay in the United States is time limited, their experiences may differ. However, individuals from this population may also undergo a unique cultural adjustment and struggle with isolation during their time in the United States.

Language

The primary languages spoken by South Asians include Hindi in India, Urdu in Pakistan and Bangladesh, and Singhalese in Sri Lanka, with English (due to Britain's colonization) spoken in most countries (Shankar & Srikanth, 1998). However, each country within South Asia has multiple languages spoken in different regions. India, for example, has states with unique dialects, including Gujarati, Punjabi, Bengali, Tamil, Kannada, Arabic, Urdu, Malayalam, and others. Most individuals who immigrate to the United States are bilingual or have a cursory understanding of their regional language.

Language can be a strong link to maintaining a relationship to cultural identity and connection to family. However, generational differences and acculturation levels among South Asian Americans influence language proficiency and use. For example, first-generation immigrants (who have immigrated from their native country) can communicate in their heritage language. In contrast, the second generation (born in the United States) may be able to speak their heritage language in the home but may be limited in verbal fluency and written communication. The third generation are more removed and may not speak or fully understand his or her heritage language.

Religion

South Asian American religious views inform an individual's value system and understanding of the world. Knowledge of these views and religious traditions can help in understanding a client's family life, ethnic affiliation, and cultural practices (Inman & Tewari, 2003). There are many religious affiliations in South Asia including, but not limited to, Hinduism, Islam, Sikhism, Buddhism, Christianity, Judaism, and Jainism. Historically, Pakistan and Bangladesh were a part of India until 1947 when India gained independence from Great Britain, resulting in a religious split separating Muslim (Pakistan and Bangladesh) and Hindu (India) countries. Three religions, Hinduism, Islam, and Sikhism, are highlighted in this section because they are the most practiced religions amongst South Asians. Hinduism and Islam are the top two religions amongst South Asian Americans, and Sikhism is a religion unique to South Asians.

Hinduism

Hinduism is often viewed as a polytheistic religion (Juthani, 2001). However, it is in fact a monotheistic one; followers believe in the Brahma, or one divine being (Van Der Veer, 2002). Many gods and goddesses (in the form of deities) represent aspects of divinity and are worshipped at one's home or in a temple or mandir (Juthani, 2001). In Hinduism, there are three main depictions of God that are worshipped: Brahma (creator of the universe), Vishnu (preserver of the universe), and Shiva (destroyer of the universe). Varying names also exist for Hindu gods and goddesses according to language, region, and family traditions. In many families, there are traditions of orally passing down stories about gods between generations.

Hindus believe in reincarnation and the roles of *karma* (the belief that one has control over their actions and reactions in life) and *dharma* (religious duties that help guide moral and family life). Hindu worshipping may be a collective approach; members of family and community come together at a temple for services, songs, and rituals. On an individual level, Hindus have idols at home and engage in private (or family) worship of idols. Another form of worship is meditation, reciting mantras or *shloks* (prayers) and fasting.

Hinduism encourages the forming of spirituality along with religious practices (Juthani, 2001). A person who identifies with Hinduism commonly believes that things happen for a reason and they can control their own actions but trust God's reason or plan. Hindus also believe that God resides within oneself, so honoring one's mind, body, and soul also honors God.

Islam

As followers of a monotheistic religion, Muslims believe in one God (Allah) and that He is the creator (Podikunju-Hussain, 2006; Pridmore & Pasha, 2004). Muslims follow the teachings of prophets, including Muhammad, who is believed to be the last prophet (Ali, Liu, & Humedian, 2004). In Islam, believers hope to live a life free of sin and offer themselves to God to attain a place in paradise (Podikunju-Hussain, 2006). Many followers of Islam engage in ritual prayer five times daily and fasting on holy days, such as during the month of Ramadan. However, many Muslims may not follow Islam in a ritualistic or formal sense but may attend religious services or engage in fasting or use religious values as their moral compass. Families often attend mosque services together and engage in religious learning together, such as reading the Quran. Prayer is often seen as an individual's connection to God. A common belief often held by Muslims is that "God does not give one anything one cannot handle." This belief can be used as a basis for understanding clients' core beliefs and can be identified as a strength and used to instill hope and progress in therapy.

Sikhism

Established in the 15th century in the Punjab region of India, Sikhism holds the principle that all people are children of God, regardless of caste, status, or history. The founder of Sikhism, Guru Nanak Dev, aimed to use Sikhism to emphasize "a casteless society in which there will be mutual coexistence and cooperation" (Singh, 2008, p. 35) and defined *Sikh* to mean "disciple" (Singh, 2008). Sikhs believe in the formless concept of God and suggest that the best way to salvation is living a good family life based on the principles of work, worship, charity, and meditation. Practicing Sikhs will often engage in morning and evening prayers and meditation. They may do this in their home or at a local gurdwara or temple. Many Sikhs attend gurdwaras on Sundays or during holidays, gathering as a community to listen to kirtans, or religious talks, or to meditate, sing, and pray together. In addition, baptized Sikh males often have uncut hair and wear turbans. As a principal of the faith, *Kesh*, or uncut hair, symbolizes the way of nature. Cutting hair is seen as a form of interfering with nature, and therefore, practicing Sikhs choose to not cut their hair. Furthermore, Sikhism advocates for an ideology of optimism and hope and focuses on doing good deeds as good for the soul (Singh, 2008).

Understanding an individual's religious beliefs may help a clinician assess their South Asian American client's assumptions and worldviews and how the client may interpret "why things happen." An examination of the saliency of religion and spirituality specific to the personal beliefs and family expectations and their influence on the client's well-being assists mental health providers with developing a culturally informed conceptualization of the client's cognitions and behaviors.

VALUES: COLLECTIVISM, ACCULTURATION, AND FAMILY

A cognitive behavior therapist working with a South Asian American should consider the influence of culture on a person's interpersonal and intra-personal experiences, including values orientation, acculturation status, family dynamics, relationships, and dating (Inman & Tewari, 2003). South Asian American culture tends to be group focused (Durvasula & Mylvaganam, 1994), or *allocentric*, placing greater importance on the group or family than on the individual. An individual with a more collectivistic orientation is more likely to take a group-centered approach to decision making, considering the psychological impact of personal decisions on their family and social systems. Level of acculturation and generational status affect collectivistic values orientation and influence an individual's values. When South Asian individuals and their families immigrate to the United States, they are expected to adapt to their new environment, learn the language of their new home, and adopt the values, beliefs, and customs of the dominant culture. Essentially, this involves balancing the two cultures, also known as *acculturation* (Cabassa, 2003). The process consists of social and psychological interactions between individuals of different cultures (Berry, 1997; Ryder, Alden, & Paulhus, 2000). Typically, less acculturated individuals maintain more traditional, interdependent, and collectivistic views of themselves and others.

The process of acculturation begins as soon as immigrants and their families come in contact with the dominant culture, creating different choices for parents and their children. In using CBT, counselors should assess their client's values and the family's immigration process and socialization, the level of connection with both the ethnic and dominant cultures, and their social and familial support in the United States. Research has indicated that parents tend to acculturate and adapt to the mainstream or dominant culture at a slower rate in comparison with their children who are in school and may have more frequent and varied interactions with people of different cultures (Phinney, Ong, & Madden, 2000). Because rates of acculturation vary between a parent and child, intergenerational discrepancies in cultural values are unavoidable and tend to cause conflict (Phinney et al., 2000). Second-generation South Asian American children, those born and raised in the United States, deal with many of the same acculturation issues as their foreign-born parents. However, their interpretations and experiences are likely different because they were socialized and educated in the host society rather than in their heritage culture (Berry, Phinney, Sam, & Vedder, 2006).

Some South Asian Americans experience bicultural stress as a part of the acculturation experience. *Bicultural stress* is "the perception of stress due to everyday life stressors as a result of pressure to adopt the majority culture in addition to adopting the minority culture" (Romero, Carvajal, Valle, & Orduña, 2007, p. 520). Stressors of acculturation include intergenerational family conflict, discrimination, language brokering, value conflicts, and cultural pressure from both sides. However challenging it is to navigate two cultures, many South Asian Americans must balance more than one cultural identity (Chen, Benet-Martínez, & Bond, 2008). Bicultural stress is exemplified in, for example, making choices about food. In the home, there may be stricter rules about food, such as eating only vegetarian or halal food. However, outside the home, these foods may not exist, or there may be a desire to try other food options. An individual may feel bicultural stress in having to make choices regarding what is expected by one's family while at home and what he or she may experience outside the home.

Traditional South Asian American families follow a patriarchal system (Durvasula & Mylvaganam, 1994) in which the head of the family is typically the eldest male of the household (Juthani, 2001). The husband or father in the family is often the wage earner and the primary decision maker, with women taking on caretaking roles and making decisions related to the household and the raising of children (Durvasula & Mylvaganam, 1994). Qualities such as generational interdependence, obedience, conformity, obligation, and sharing are valued in South Asian American families and are emphasized in raising children. The degree to which families adhere to these values depends on the acculturation levels and generational status of family members. Furthermore, children in South Asian families are often viewed as the culmination of the parents' life work. For traditional South Asian parents, the goal of parenting is to provide children with sufficient skills and to instill in them a sense of obligation and duty through which they may attain and maintain spirituality.

Depending on immigration histories of family members, it is not uncommon for South Asian families to have three generations living in the same household, including grandparents, parents, and children (Inman & Tewari, 2003), resulting in a hierarchy among family members (Juthani, 2001). In adulthood, South Asians are responsible for taking care of their parents, a concept known as *filial piety* (Kim, Atkinson, & Yang, 1999). Elders and older siblings often have the most influence in South Asian families, which demonstrates respect for age but which can also cause frustration for younger siblings who may feel ignored. The extended family, such as aunts and uncles, is usually important to South Asians, with regular contact between households. Despite the hierarchical context, boundaries among family members may appear enmeshed, with parents expecting to know "everything" in which their child is involved or expecting their children to share their life's details with them.

RELATIONSHIPS: DATING AND SEXUALITY

Dating and intimate relations can be complex and full of conflict for many South Asian Americans. Dating raises issues related to sex, which is perceived as an "American" concept, resulting in a lack of discussion or acknowledgment of sexuality in the South Asian culture. However, one medium in which sexuality is more openly portrayed in South Asian culture is through Indian, or Bollywood, films. Sex and sexuality have traditionally been associated with the villain (male or female) who has a Western name and wears revealing Western clothes, whereas the hero or heroine in the films is often portrayed as adhering strongly to South Asian cultural values (Sandhu & Madathil, 2007).

Public displays of affection, premarital sexual relations, and physical intimacy are unacceptable in the South Asian cultural context (Sandhu & Madathil, 2007). South Asian American parents raising their children in an American cultural context that involves social gatherings such as proms and homecoming dances often view these events as distracting, encouraging preoccupation with sexual behavior, and creating a potential risk of poor academic achievement, less successful career pursuits, and limited future marriage prospects (Mehta, 1998). These activities are further viewed as unnecessary by parents who expect their children to participate in arranged marriages.

Arranged marriage (i.e., the expectation for marriage partners to be from the same geographical region in South Asia, religion, level of education, socioeconomic status, and caste) is a tradition that poses significant challenges for both generations in South Asian American communities (Sandhu & Madathil, 2007). Arranged marriages can differ in philosophy. A more traditional approach to arranged marriages involves parents finding matches for their children based on family, caste, education level, and other characteristics. Once a match for marriage is identified, it is assumed that the marriage will be agreed to or fixed. The assumption with the traditional form of arranged marriage is that you marry a person chosen for you, then fall in love with the person you marry. A less traditional approach to arranged marriages is one in which the parents may introduce their child to potential partners and allow them to date but with openness and some expectation that a match will be made. This approach is more common in the United States. The former option has limited opportunities for dating, whereas the latter option allows for some dating. The former option assumes one marries and then falls in love, and the latter option allows more room to fall in love first and then get married. Parental involvement in their child's dating activities can range from family introductions to potential spouses with limited dating to introductions followed by an extended courtship leading to marriage (Tewari, 2009). Parent involvement and expectations about marriage are often made known to the child and can be a source of conflict when the child's desire for dating and marriage based on love conflict with parental expectations for an arranged marriage.

Given the emphasis on heterosexuality in South Asian culture and the predominance of traditional cisgender roles and domestic households, coming out as lesbian, gay, bisexual, transgender, or queer can be difficult for South Asian Americans (Sandhu & Madathil, 2007). Families, especially parents, often have negative attitudes and biases toward those in the queer community (Rosario, Schrimshaw, & Hunter, 2004). Family structure and adherence to religion play large roles in coming to terms with one's sexual orientation and the coming out process for lesbian, gay, bisexual, transgender, and queer or questioning South Asians. Social desirability and conformity are important, and someone struggling with sexual orientation issues may fear being shunned or rejected. A study by Bhugra (1997) found that siblings are more likely to be used as confidants regarding sexual orientation but that there are significant struggles in coming out to parents and extended family members. An important component when working with individuals who hold intersecting identities related to ethnicity, sexual orientation, religion, and other cultural influences is distinguishing between external stressors (i.e., familial, society, and environmental) and those that stem from maladaptive thoughts about the self. In both cases, it is important to validate a South Asian American's unique experience in their coming out process and assess sources of support and discord and their impact on the client's thought process.

EXPERIENCES OF DISCRIMINATION

Racial discrimination has been, and continues to be, a constant part of American society. Historically, South Asians immigrating to the United States at the turn of the 20th century faced discrimination and struggled with being accepted by mainstream American society (Mio, Nagata, Tsai, & Tewari, 2007). Antimiscegenation laws (laws against interracial marriages) existed, as did exclusionary policies prohibiting mass immigration. The sociopolitical climate regarding immigration continues to be a debated topic in mainstream American society. As this chapter was being formulated, the Trump Administration issued an executive order on January 27, 2017, preventing citizens from seven Muslim-majority countries from entering the United States (Trump, 2017). The order was challenged in courts and revised and reissued, only to be challenged in the judicial system, and at this time, it is still under review. Although it is yet unclear what this law will mean for immigration, a cognitive behavior therapist should be aware of such events. An individual who is an immigrant or a child of an immigrant may experience anti-immigrant and anti-Muslim sentiments and discrimination, be viewed as a potential terrorist, and be a target of violence and anger.

The events of September 11, 2001, in New York City had not only a tremendous impact on the United States but also led to increased discrimination toward the South Asian community (Inman, Yeh, Madan-Bahel, & Nath, 2007; Mio et al., 2007). Many South Asians were mistakenly identified as Arabs. South Asians and Muslims became the targets of anti-Arab and Islamophobic feelings in the country. Such suspicions and fears in the post-9/11 atmosphere continue to exist and have taken a psychological toll on South Asians.

A recent report released by South Asian Americans Leading Together (2017) suggested that the current spike in hate violence and rhetoric is similar to levels seen following the September 11th attacks, with a 7% increase in hate crimes since 2014. In particular, there was a 23% increase in religion-based hate crimes and a 67% increase in anti-Muslim hate crimes across the country. Post-9/11 United States has seen a surge of Islamophobia, which has affected individuals who identify as Muslim or may appear to be Muslim (Ali et al., 2004; Mio et al., 2007), especially those whose physical appearance marks their identity, such as Sikh men who wear turbans, Muslim women who wear hijabs, and Muslim men who maintain a beard or wear traditional garb (Ali et al., 2004). A therapist working with South Asian Americans must keep in mind that over the decades, there has been a loss of ethnic and cultural identity because South Asian Americans have not felt safe enough to express themselves in dress, religion, and culture, fearing being targets of verbal and physical attacks (Mio et al., 2007; Tewari, 2009). A cognitive behavior therapist must assess the potential impact of racist experiences, microaggressions, and sociopolitical environments because these experiences may affect their clients' thought processes, perceptions, assumptions, and behaviors and may have implications in therapy.

In addition, therapists working with South Asian Americans should know that there are historical animosities between Indians and Pakistanis as a result of postcolonial rule and the partition of India. The two dominant religions influencing people from these countries are Hinduism and Islam. Although the antipathies are less relevant to those born in the United States, one must be aware of these negative feelings among elder immigrants (Mio et al., 2007) because they are points of potential stress in the diaspora.

It is important to keep in mind that discrimination is not always overt, and people of color often experience subtle forms of discrimination, known as *microaggressions*. Sue and colleagues (2007) identified eight microaggressions experienced by Asian Americans, which also apply to South Asians: (a) being considered alien in one's own land, (b) being thought of as lacking intelligence, (c) being exoticized as Asian women, (d) having interethnic differences invalidated, (e) having racial reality denied, (f) having cultural values and communication styles pathologized, (g) being thought of as having a second-class citizenship, and (h) being considered invisible. These microaggressions affect the everyday experiences of many people of color, who often feel othered, marginalized, or invalidated.

Tummala-Narra, Alegria, and Chen (2012) sampled 169 individuals to study the experiences of discrimination and acculturative stress and their potential role in depression among South Asians. The researchers found that perceived discrimination was positively associated with depression for South Asians, and family support was found to moderate the relationship between perceived discrimination and depression. Historically, and even currently, experiences of discrimination and racism have influenced many parents to push their children toward prestigious, highly respected, autonomous professions such as medicine or engineering, in the hopes of seeing their children live financially secure lives (Mehta, 1998). Many South Asian Americans believe that higher education, wealth (financial security), and a respectable profession will help minimize the prejudicial experiences that numerous South Asian immigrants have faced.

Some South Asian immigrants may be low-income individuals struggling, for example, to keep their restaurant, motel, or grocery store businesses afloat, often barely making ends meet. As a result of discrimination, success among these immigrants may be attributed to family cooperation and contribution to the family business, not to educational and financial successes. Second-generation South Asian Americans growing up in these families may feel conflicted about family loyalties obliging them to work in the family business rather than obtaining an education to pursue other careers. Thus, expectations about education, financial stability, and success and business involvements should be assessed with South Asian clients as well.

CLINICAL CONSIDERATIONS IN COGNITIVE BEHAVIOR THERAPY WITH SOUTH ASIANS

In this chapter we have thus far discussed how an individual's cultural identity influences thought processes, beliefs, assumptions, and behaviors, all of which are essential components in using CBT effectively with South Asian Americans. In this section, we explore clinical considerations, such as the therapeutic relationship, advantages and disadvantages of using CBT, and assessment with South Asian American clients.

The Therapeutic Relationship

Building a collaborative, trusting relationship is essential to the work of a cognitive behavior therapist (Beck, 2011). To start building a strong therapeutic relationship, therapists have to be conscious of how their clients' names are correctly pronounced. Ethnic names can easily be mispronounced, and correcting the therapist can feel awkward for the client given the perceived power differential inherent to therapy. Repeated mispronouncing of an individual's name can make the client feel devalued and has the potential to create distance in the relationship. The therapist should typically use first names but should be mindful of respect for clients who are elders, using first names only if directed to do so. A therapist may consider asking the origin of the client's name or what the name means to help establish interest and gather more information. For example, a client may say, "My name in Punjabi means . . . ," giving the therapist a chance to not only understand the name and how to pronounce it but also an opportunity to discuss the client's culture and ethnicity.

South Asian Americans who pursue therapy prefer an active, direct, and goal-oriented approach that focuses on practical tasks (Tewari, 2009), which is consistent with CBT. South Asian American clients may search for and feel most comfortable with a therapist who is warm, directive, and interested in establishing a therapeutic alliance similar to a relationship they may have with a respected and educated elder in the community (Das & Kemp, 1997).

Depending on the client's exposure and experience with therapy, it is important to be prepared to discuss expectations of the therapist and treatment. Clients may have to be educated on the therapeutic process, CBT, and expectations of therapy, such as completing homework and actively participating during sessions. Clients may seek therapy as a form of advice seeking or may assume it is a quick process and not understand the typical process of CBT.

Strengths of Cognitive Behavior Therapy

Using CBT and similar therapeutic approaches, such as behavioral modification and mindfulness, to increase cognitive, behavioral, affective, and environmental awareness is congruent with South Asian Americans' daily lifestyles (Tewari, Inman, & Sandhu, 2003). For example, these approaches are consistent with religious and spiritual practices and beliefs such as karma or having control of one's actions, with meditation as an important religious component. A therapist could identify such practices and use CBT techniques as a way to integrate them into already existing practices and thoughts (Hays, 2009). For example, the importance of prayer and its purpose in expressing gratitude toward the creator can be an important therapeutic tool and may serve as a grounding process during a time of struggle.

CBT's structured, time-limited approach, emphasis on problem solving and increasing awareness of one's thought processes, and focus on the present are strengths in working with the South Asian American population. Clients may see results and improvements in their functioning more rapidly, instilling hope and increasing motivation to continue focusing on therapeutic work (Rathod, Kingdon, Pinninti, Turkington, & Phiri, 2015). Therapists may focus on being present in the here and now, complimenting the philosophy of being mindful, controlling what the client has power over, being grounded in increasing awareness, and making active shifts in thinking and behavior. Last, by identifying therapy goals, clients can learn to feel empowered and accomplished, especially as they track progress (Rathod et al., 2015).

Limitations of Cognitive Behavior Therapy

Although there are numerous advantages to implementing CBT with South Asian Americans, several potential disadvantages should also be considered. CBT's solution-focused and goal-oriented approach may decrease attention to the experience of being in therapy and reflecting on the self (Hall & Ibaraki, 2015). CBT has a focus on individualism, which can overlook the relational aspects of therapy and potentially discount a client's collectivistic values (Durvasula & Mylvaganam, 1994; Rathod et al., 2015). For example, individuals may feel the need to prioritize their family's needs over their own. A common dissonance between collectivist and individualistic decision making for South Asian Americans is career-oriented decisions (Tewari et al., 2003). A person may focus on finding jobs and/or pursuing a career based on family needs and expectations versus personal goals and dreams. Another disadvantage of CBT is the emphasis on rationality, internal locus of control, and examination of evidence. In contrast, South Asian Americans may believe that things may happen outside their control (Carter & Rashidi, 2003) due to fate, luck, and/or God's will.

A major component of CBT is understanding and modifying maladaptive thinking and beliefs. A potential dilemma that could arise is a misunderstanding regarding intermediate or core beliefs stemming from cultural values (Rathod et al., 2015). For example, asking a client to make a decision "for themselves" versus "their family" can be especially conflicting for individuals who have a collectivistic values orientation. CBT may also involve doing homework or exercises outside the session, which may be challenging for some South Asian Americans. Shame or worry that others may know or ask about therapy or lack of privacy and time at home, school, or work may prevent the individual from completing homework assignments. In addition, CBT terms do not always translate well into other languages, and the nuances of words and words with similar meaning can create misunderstandings.

Assessment

During assessment and case formulation, a cognitive behavior therapist must consider how ethnic identification, immigration history, language, religion, values, relationships, experiences with discrimination, and other factors affect the thoughts, feelings, and behaviors of the client (Ibrahim et al., 1997). Clients' views of themselves and their psychological distress influence how they seek help, engage in services, and consider treatment goals. A therapist must also keep in mind that there continues to be a stigma in the South Asian diasporic community associated with mental health problems or seeking mental health support. An individual seeking counseling may be hesitant to be open in therapy and may even deny having problems (Carter & Rashidi, 2003).

Assessment in CBT is ongoing (Beck, 2011; Tewari et al., 2003), with cognitive behavior therapists constantly engaging in case conceptualization, goal setting, and collaboration with clients. Hays (2009) discussed cognitive behavioral assessment as having two categories: first, understanding a client's environment and, second, understanding the stressors in a client's cognitively based problems. A cognitive behavior therapist working with a South Asian American client should consider how culture affects both environmental and cognitive problems. For South Asian Americans, generational status, immigration history, religiosity, collectivism, acculturation status, family dynamics, dating life, sexuality, and intersecting identities are all salient aspects of the client's environment and environmental stressors. When considering cognitive problems (e.g., negative self-talk), a cognitive behavior therapist must consider how a person's worldview and culture shape one's cognitive thought process, behaviors, and beliefs. In addition, the therapist should assess clients for strengths and ways they have used these strengths in the past, especially during hardship.

Given that CBT can be tailored to meet the unique strengths and needs of an individual (Hays, 2009), finding congruence with a client's daily practices (i.e., daily prayer ritual) and belief system (i.e., Islamic faith) can be straightforward. For example, if a cognitive behavior therapist wants to introduce anxiety-reduction tools, linking them to already established daily prayer may be seamless. Clients may have a hard time explaining how they experience distress, so asking the client to discuss physical, emotional, and behavioral factors and thought processes related to stressors is important for the therapist. The therapist may use a distressing situation disclosed by the client to explore these areas further. Last, the therapist should assess each client's commitment to therapy and making a change. One way to do this is to help the client identify and set goals. Another way is to use a scale and have clients assess where they fall on the scale—for example, "On a scale of 1 to 5, with 5 being *extremely ready*, how ready are you to . . .?"

A therapist can also work with a client to engage in self-assessment via the use of thought journals, worksheets, scales, and review of goals. The understanding that assessment is a continual process in CBT may help clients feel empowered and increase the likelihood they will be active collaborators in identifying and working toward their goals.

Finally, the therapist has to be aware of his or her beliefs about family structure and relationships and adherence to religious beliefs and practices when interpreting a client's struggles (Hall & Ibaraki, 2015). A culturally responsive therapist invites the integration of cultural factors in assessment, treatment considerations, and application of CBT techniques. The following case example highlights clinical considerations.

CASE EXAMPLE

Bina[1] is a 21-year-old, single, heterosexual, second-generation Hindu Asian Indian woman, currently in her third year of college. Bina was referred to individual therapy by her academic advisor, who noted that Bina was on academic probation for failing two classes the previous quarter. At the time of intake, Bina lived at home with her parents, the eldest of two siblings.

Bina's parents are first-generation immigrants to the United States from the northwestern part of India. Bina grew up in a close-knit family where she had weekly, if not daily, interactions with members of her large extended family in addition to her nuclear family. Coming from a background in which

---

[1]Case material in this chapter has been disguised to protect client confidentiality.

she and her siblings and cousins were pushed to be achievement oriented placed much pressure on them to be successful. Bina had difficulty reconciling expectations placed on her by her parents with wanting to explore her desires, goals, and self, like her mainstream peer group.

Bina had trepidation about and questioned her academic path and future career plans. She was majoring in business but was interested in pursuing a major in education. Bina's family operated a family business and hoped Bina would join it once she graduated. However, Bina stated she felt "put off by the business world." She also reported not having many friends.

Bina commuted to campus after having lived on campus during her freshman year. Her move back home was precipitated by her parents' need for help in caring for her younger brother because they were spending more time on the family business. Her parents did not know about her academic struggles or that she was attending therapy. Bina expressed shame and worry about her parents finding out about her falling grades or that she was struggling in general. Bina stated she was coming to counseling to address anxiety about her future, her frustrations with parents, and her self-reported symptoms of depression (feelings of sadness, isolation, loss of interest in activities, low motivation, increased sleep, and increased appetite).

To help orient Bina to therapy and began building a therapeutic relationship, the therapist provided Bina with psychoeducation about CBT, collaboratively set objectives and goals for the first session, invited open dialogue and feedback, and highlighted the limits of confidentiality. In addition, given that this was her first time in counseling and because she was choosing not to share it with her family, the therapist spent some time discussing the stigma and shame Bina felt about counseling, privacy, and "saving face."

During the initial session, the therapist also focused on understanding Bina's multiple identities and how she was experiencing her current symptoms and life circumstances, with an aim of helping to set goals for treatment. Bina explored being the first generation to be brought up in the United States and how she struggled with navigating the two worlds in which she lives (home and school). Bina shared that at home there were daily Hindu religious rituals practiced in the mornings and evenings. Her family mainly spoke Gujarati and was conservative, which meant that her family was patriarchal and she had strict gender roles to adhere to while at home. For example, Bina shared that she and her mother were responsible for household chores and cooking, and Bina was expected to "take care" of her brother. Bina described often fearing disappointing or angering her father, which resulted in her behaving obediently and being quiet at home.

The assessment of Bina focused on understanding the presenting concerns, symptoms, and cultural factors affecting her. The client noted she started feeling more depressed 6 months before returning home after having lived on campus. When living in the dorms, Bina reported having lots of friends. However, since she moved home, she found it hard to sustain friendships outside the classroom, partially because social activities were mostly in the evening, when she would have to be home. After a while, she started feeling more isolated. In addition, Bina's academic path was confusing because she stated her father had "chosen" her major, although she had always hoped to go into teaching.

Bina struggled with having college goals different from her parents' goals for her, and she was also distressed by the acculturation differences between her and her parents. As a result, Bina felt as though she could not fully express herself or her needs to her parents because she did not want to be disrespectful or violate familial norms. She also worried about letting her parents down, which led her to feel shame.

By the end of the initial session, there was a mutual understanding of Bina's symptoms, intersecting identities, and cultural context. The main issues to consider for CBT treatment planning were to (a) help Bina increase awareness about her own beliefs, thought process, and behaviors; (b) reconcile expectations of family and managing bicultural stress; (c) help Bina consider ways to understand her goals and how she could work toward them; and (d) help reduce symptoms of depression.

Sessions two to four focused on exploring Bina's current mood, thought process, and reactions. Bina explored the feeling of having no agency in making important decisions. Bina spent time noticing her automatic thought process and reactions, often identifying a thought pattern that mimicked "What's the point?" or "I don't care." Bina was able to notice that her thinking seemed fatalistic or hopeless, and she often lacked confidence in her actions. Bina identified feeling as though she had no say in her major life decisions and was often held to a measure of success defined by others and not herself. Not having her own ways of feeling successful or happy, Bina started disconnecting and reacting with a "what's-the-point" attitude. Bina explored what it would be like to challenge her family's expectations of her and how to recognize "getting stuck" in a negative thought process that was forcing her to give in or give up.

In exploring her Hindu beliefs, Bina responded to the idea of karma. Bina noted that for her, karma meant "action." Integrating religious cognitions as a part of the therapeutic process was important in the treatment plan and helped with behavioral activation. Bina explored whether karma meant she could take action according to what she felt was right for her but that she could not control the outcome of what would happen. Behavioral activation techniques were used to increase Bina's motivation and focus on improving her academic involvement because there was a fear she would fail two of her current classes. Bina started making lists and taking "baby steps" to start accomplishing tasks on her list. For homework assignments, she was asked to track her progress with these baby steps, noting her goals, objectives, and progress. She also kept a thought journal to reflect on her reactions to perceived stressors or tasks. The homework assignments helped Bina increase positive behavioral changes because she was aware of her progress. She was also able to explore areas in which she felt stuck by using her thought journal to reflect on these areas, identifying her thought patterns and assumptions about being stuck.

Sessions five to six focused on reinforcing Bina's progress, positive changes, and baby steps, as well as managing her bicultural stress and family dynamics because she said that she was often pulled to pursue her own happiness but then felt equally pulled to be a good daughter and do what was best for the family. Bina explored what it would be like to find more balance between the two cultural pulls. She started considering how to engage in conversations with her parents about career options and setting limits at home. The therapist wanted to help Bina balance her collectivistic values orientation, the cultural factors in family communication style, and her self-described goals. As Bina focused on engaging in conversations, she was better able to manage feelings of sadness and anxiety and accept that although conversations such as these were uncomfortable, the focus was on what she wanted to change. The conversations in therapy were congruent with Bina's idea about collectivism and helped her feel a stronger sense of belonging in the family while also challenging her negative thought process of "what is the point?"

By the end of the seventh session, Bina was able to be more open with parents about her struggles making and maintaining friendships due to her strict schedule. Her parents decided to allow Bina to live with roommates but asked that she be home on the weekends, which was a comfortable compromise for both Bina and her parents. In addition, Bina's parents were open to Bina double majoring in business and education, which would require that Bina take an extra year of school to complete. This was framed as allowing Bina to have more career options in the future. At the end of therapy, although Bina was undecided about engaging in the family business, she felt more comfortable with the idea of having a choice. Moreover, by the end of therapy, Bina identified ways to engage in more self-care and continued to explore how she reacted to different situations she encountered.

CONCLUSION

In this chapter, we highlighted considerations for cognitive behavior therapists working with a largely heterogeneous South Asian American community and ways that therapists can use this knowledge to engage in deeper work with South Asian American clients. Understanding the individual's family's country (or countries) of origin and the experiences of immigrating and settling in the United States is an important factor when working with South Asian Americans. Equally important is understanding clients' generational status, acculturation process, languages spoken in the home, and attempts to balance dominant and heritage cultural values. The cognitive behavior therapist should also know clients' religious identity and how their religious experiences influence their value system, family life, ethnic affiliation, and cultural practices (Inman & Tewari, 2003). Last, the cognitive behavior therapist should consider how culture affects both environmental and cognitive problems for their South Asian American clients.

Because assessment in CBT is ongoing, therapists may have to work hard to understand clients' unique and intersecting identities and their influence on clients' thought processes, beliefs, and assumptions. This understanding can assist in a deeper case conceptualization and collaborative relationship with the client because therapists can use this knowledge to enhance their understanding of the client, the client's struggles, and ways culture can be integrated into treatment. Furthermore, with a deeper understanding of a client's culture, a therapist can identify practices congruent with South Asian Americans' daily lifestyles and use CBT techniques as a way to integrate these practices into existing practices. If a therapist is successful in increasing the understanding and assessment of the client through a cultural lens, therapeutic work and subsequent changes in thought and behavior can be more meaningful to the client.

REFERENCES

Ali, S. R., Liu, W. M., & Humedian, M. (2004). Islam 101: Understanding the religion and therapy implications. *Professional Psychology: Research and Practice, 35,* 635–642. http://dx.doi.org/10.1037/0735-7028.35.6.635

Beck, J. S. (2011). *Cognitive behavior therapy: Basics and beyond.* New York, NY: Guilford Press.

Berry, J. W. (1997). Immigration, acculturation, and adaptation. *Applied Psychology, 46,* 5–34.

Berry, J. W., Phinney, J. S., Sam, D. L., & Vedder, P. (2006). Immigrant youth: Acculturation, identity, and adaptation. *Applied Psychology, 55,* 303–332. http://dx.doi.org/10.1111/j.1464-0597.2006.00256.x

Bhugra, D. (1997). Coming out by South Asian gay men in the United Kingdom. *Archives of Sexual Behavior, 26,* 547–557. http://dx.doi.org/10.1023/A:1024512023379

Cabassa, L. J. (2003). Measuring acculturation: Where we are and where we need to go. *Hispanic Journal of Behavioral Sciences, 25,* 127–146. http://dx.doi.org/10.1177/0739986303025002001

Carter, D. J., & Rashidi, A. (2003). Theoretical model of psychotherapy: Eastern Asian-Islamic women with mental illness. *Health Care for Women International, 24,* 399–413. http://dx.doi.org/10.1080/07399330390212180

Chen, S. X., Benet-Martínez, V., & Bond, M. H. (2008). Bicultural identity, bilingualism, and psychological adjustment in multicultural societies: Immigration-based and globalization-based acculturation. *Journal of Personality, 76,* 803–838. http://dx.doi.org/10.1111/j.1467-6494.2008.00505.x

Das, A. K., & Kemp, S. F. (1997). Between two worlds: Counseling South Asian Americans. *Journal of Multicultural Counseling and Development, 25,* 23–33. http://dx.doi.org/10.1002/j.2161-1912.1997.tb00313.x

Durvasula, R. S., & Mylvaganam, G. A. (1994). Mental health of Asian Indians: Relevant issues and community implications. *Journal of Community Psychology, 22,* 97–108. http://dx.doi.org/10.1002/1520-6629(199404)22:2%3C97::AID-JCOP2290220206%3E3.0.CO;2-%23

Hall, G. C. N., & Ibaraki, A. Y. (2015). Multicultural issues in cognitive-behavioral therapy: Cultural adaptations and goodness of fit. In C. M. Nezu & A. M. Nezu (Eds.), *The Oxford handbook of cognitive and behavioral therapies* (pp. 465–481). New York, NY: Oxford University Press. http://dx.doi.org/10.1093/oxfordhb/9780199733255.013.14

Hays, P. A. (2009). Integrating evidence-based practice, cognitive–behavior therapy, and multicultural therapy: Ten steps for culturally competent practice. *Professional Psychology: Research and Practice, 40,* 354–360. http://dx.doi.org/10.1037/a0016250

Horrell, S. C. V. (2008). Effectiveness of cognitive–behavioral therapy with adult ethnic minority clients: A review. *Professional Psychology: Research and Practice, 39,* 160–168. http://dx.doi.org/10.1037/0735-7028.39.2.160

Ibrahim, F., Ohnishi, H., & Sandhu, D. S. (1997). Asian American identity development: A culture specific model for South Asian Americans. *Journal of Multicultural Counseling and Development, 25,* 34–50. http://dx.doi.org/10.1002/j.2161-1912.1997.tb00314.x

Inman, A. G., & Tewari, N. (2003). The power of context: Counseling South Asians within a family context. In G. E. Roysircar, D. S. E. Sandhu, & Bibbins, V. E., Sr. (Eds.), *Multicultural competencies: A guidebook of practices* (pp. 97–107). Alexandria, VA: Association for Multicultural Counseling & Development.

Inman, A. G., Yeh, C. J., Madan-Bahel, A., & Nath, S. (2007). Bereavement and coping of South Asian families post 9/11. *Journal of Multicultural Counseling and Development, 35,* 101–115. http://dx.doi.org/10.1002/j.2161-1912.2007.tb00053.x

Juthani, N. V. (2001). Psychiatric treatment of Hindus. *International Review of Psychiatry, 13,* 125–130. http://dx.doi.org/10.1080/09540260125005

Kim, B. S., Atkinson, D. R., & Yang, P. H. (1999). The Asian Values Scale: Development, factor analysis, validation, and reliability. *Journal of Counseling Psychology, 46*, 342–352. http://dx.doi.org/10.1037/0022-0167.46.3.342

Kurien, P. A. (2005). Being young, brown, and Hindu: The identity struggles of second-generation Indian Americans. *Journal of Contemporary Ethnography, 34*, 434–469. http://dx.doi.org/10.1177/0891241605275575

Mehta, S. (1998). Relationship between acculturation and mental health for Asian Indian immigrants in the United States. *Genetic, Social, and General Psychology Monographs, 124*, 61–78.

Mio, J. S., Nagata, D. K., Tsai, A. H., & Tewari, N. (2007). Racism against Asian/Pacific Island Americans. In F. T. L. Leong, A. Ebreo, L. Kinoshita, A. G. Inman, L. H. Yang, & M. Fu (Eds.), *Handbook of Asian American psychology* (pp. 341–361). Thousand Oaks, CA: Sage.

Pew Research Center. (2013). *The rise of Asian Americans.* Retrieved from Pew Research Center website: http://www.pewsocialtrends.org/2012/06/19/the-rise-of-asian-americans/

Phinney, J. S., Ong, A., & Madden, T. (2000). Cultural values and intergenerational value discrepancies in immigrant and non-immigrant families. *Child Development, 71*, 528–539. http://dx.doi.org/10.1111/1467-8624.00162

Podikunju-Hussain, S. (2006). Working with Muslims: Perspectives and suggestions for counseling. In G. R. Walz, J. Bleuer, & R. K. Yep (Eds.), *VISTAS: Compelling perspectives on counseling* (pp. 103–106). Alexandria, VA: American Counseling Association.

Pridmore, S., & Pasha, M. I. (2004). Psychiatry and Islam. *Australasian Psychiatry, 12*, 380–385. http://dx.doi.org/10.1080/j.1440-1665.2004.02131.x

Rathod, S., Kingdon, D., Pinninti, N., Turkington, D., & Phiri, P. (2015). *Cultural adaptation of CBT for serious mental illness: A guide for training and practice.* Hoboken, NJ: Wiley. http://dx.doi.org/10.1002/9781118976159

Romero, A. J., Carvajal, S. C., Valle, F., & Orduña, M. (2007). Adolescent bicultural stress and its impact on mental well-being among Latinos, Asian Americans, and European Americans. *Journal of Community Psychology, 35*, 519–534. http://dx.doi.org/10.1002/jcop.20162

Rosario, M., Schrimshaw, E. W., & Hunter, J. (2004). Ethnic/racial differences in the coming-out process of lesbian, gay, and bisexual youths: A comparison of sexual identity development over time. *Cultural Diversity and Ethnic Minority Psychology, 10*, 215–228. http://dx.doi.org/10.1037/1099-9809.10.3.215

Ryder, A. G., Alden, L. E., & Paulhus, D. L. (2000). Is acculturation unidimensional or bidimensional? A head-to-head comparison in the prediction of personality, self-identity, and adjustment. *Journal of Personality and Social Psychology, 79*, 49–65. http://dx.doi.org/10.1037/0022-3514.79.1.49

Sandhu, D. S., & Madathil, J. (2007). South Asian Americans. In G. McAuliffe (Ed.), *Culturally alert counseling: A comprehensive introduction* (pp. 353–387). Thousand Oaks, CA: Sage.

Shankar, L. D., & Srikanth, R. (1998). *A part, yet apart: South Asians in Asian America.* Philadelphia, PA: Temple University Press.

Singh, K. (2008). The Sikh spiritual model of counseling. *Spirituality and Health International, 9,* 32–43. http://dx.doi.org/10.1002/shi.331

South Asian Americans Leading Together. (2017). *This week in hate—October 11: The spatial spread of hate violence pre and post election.* Retrieved from the SAALT website: http://saalt.org/?s=2017+a+recent+report+hate+crimes&submit=Search

Sue, D. W., Capodilupo, C. M., Torino, G. C., Bucceri, J. M., Holder, A. M., Nadal, K. L., & Esquilin, M. (2007). Racial microaggressions in everyday life: Implications for clinical practice. *American Psychologist, 62,* 271–286. http://dx.doi.org/10.1037/0003-066X.62.4.271

Tewari, N. (2009). Seeking, receiving, and providing culturally competent mental health services: A focus on Asian Americans. In N. Tewari & A. N. Alvarez (Eds.), *Asian American psychology: Current perspectives* (pp. 575–606). New York, NY: Routledge/Taylor & Francis.

Tewari, N., Inman, A., & Sandhu, D. S. (2003). South Asian Americans: Culture, concerns, and therapeutic strategies. In J. S. Mio & G. Y. Iwamasa (Eds.), *Culturally diverse mental health: The challenges of research and resistance* (pp. 191–209). New York, NY: Brunner-Routledge.

Trump, D. J. (2017). *Order protecting the nation from foreign terrorist entry into the United States.* Retrieved from The White House website: https://www.whitehouse.gov/the-press-office/2017/01/27/executive-order-protecting-nation-foreign-terrorist-entry-united-states

Tummala-Narra, P., Alegria, M., & Chen, C. N. (2012). Perceived discrimination, acculturative stress, and depression among South Asians: Mixed findings. *Asian American Journal of Psychology, 3,* 3–16. http://dx.doi.org/10.1037/a0024661

U.S. Census Bureau. (2010). *The Asian population: 2010.* Retrieved from https://www.census.gov/prod/cen2010/briefs/c2010br-11.pdf

Van Der Veer, P. (2002). Transnational religion: Hindu and Muslim movements. *Global Networks, 2,* 95–109. http://dx.doi.org/10.1111/1471-0374.00030

Zong, J., & Batalova, J. (2016). *Asian immigrants in the United States.* Retrieved from https://www.migrationpolicy.org/article/asian-immigrants-united-states

7

COGNITIVE BEHAVIOR THERAPY WITH PEOPLE OF ARAB HERITAGE

PAMELA A. HAYS AND NUHA ABUDABBEH

When this book chapter was first published in 2006, there were few publications regarding psychotherapy with Arab people. This paucity of research has persisted and is especially problematic in the United States, as strong anti-Arab sentiment currently fuels misconceptions and stereotypes. Using the terms *Arab* and *psychology* to search the Social Science Citation Index from 1989 to 2014, Harb (2016) found only 73 studies. To our knowledge, there are only three English-language books that address psychotherapy with Arab people: *Handbook of Arab Psychology* (Amer & Awad, 2016), *Counseling and Diversity: Arab-Americans* (Nassar-McMillan, Choudhuri, & Santiago-Rivera, 2010), and *Cross-Cultural Counseling: The Arab-Palestinian Case* (Dwairy, 1998). In addition, there are a few psychotherapy books regarding Muslims that also address Arab populations (Ahmed & Amer, 2012; Badri, 2013; Dwairy, 2006; Rassool, 2015).

We thank Jawed Zouari and Germine Awad for their helpful feedback regarding this chapter.

http://dx.doi.org/10.1037/0000119-008

Culturally Responsive Cognitive Behavior Therapy, Second Edition: Practice and Supervision, G. Y. Iwamasa and P. A. Hays (Editors)

Not surprisingly, publications regarding cognitive behavior therapy (CBT) are even scarcer. The few articles we found concern posttraumatic stress disorder (PTSD) with Iraqi refugees (Hijazi et al., 2014), with Egyptians (Jalal, Samir, & Hinton, 2017), and in "global settings" including Arab populations (Hinton & Jalal, 2014). In this chapter, we draw from some of these sources as well as our own experiences working with people of Arab heritage, with a focus on Arab Americans.

UNDERSTANDING ARAB CULTURES

There are approximately 300 million Arabs in the world (American–Arab Anti-Discrimination Committee, 2009), and Arab cultures represent enormous diversity. A common definition of Arab identity is that of ethnic, cultural, or linguistic heritage that can be traced to the originally nomadic tribes of Arabia—a definition that is broad enough to include second-, third-, and later-generation Arab Americans who do not speak Arabic. A common misconception regarding Arab people is that all Arabs are Muslim when, in reality, the two identities are quite distinct.

In the United States, the majority of Arab people are of Christian heritage, not Muslim. A survey conducted by the Arab American Institute Foundation in 2002 found that 63% of Arab Americans identified as Christian (including 35% Roman/Eastern Catholic, 18% Eastern Orthodox, and 10% Protestant); 24% identified as Muslim (including Sunni, Shia, and Druze); and 13% identified as "other" or reported no religious affiliation (in Amer & Kayyali, 2016, p. 50). As Harb (2016) noted, it is inaccurate to refer to Arab nations as "Islamic countries" in the same way that it is inaccurate to describe Western nations as "Christian countries." With the exception of the Kingdom of Saudi Arabia (and Iran, which is not an Arab country), all other majority-Muslim countries "follow a complex set of laws and constitutions that combine, to various degrees, both secular and Qur'an-inspired legislative systems" (Harb, 2016, p. 4).

Although large Arab Christian populations can be found in Lebanon, Egypt, Syria, Jordan, and Palestine, the majority of Arabs worldwide are Muslim. The word *Islam* means "submission," and a Muslim is "one who submits [to God]" (Amer & Kayyali, 2016, p. 52). There are two main divisions within Islam, the Sunni and the Shia, a split that occurred after the death of the Prophet Mohammed in 632 AD and was related to who would be his successor in leading the religious community. The Druze and Alawite religious communities, located primarily in Lebanon, Syria, and Israel, are considered offshoots of Shia Islam (Amer & Kayyali, 2016).

Before the Prophet Mohammed, the people of the Arabian Peninsula worshiped pagan gods, women were considered property, and only male descendants were recognized for inheritance purposes. The Prophet called on the people to unite in the name of Islam, and introduced social reforms considered extraordinary at the time including the obligation of husbands to provide for their wives and children, inheritance rights for women as well as men, financial independence for wives, and rights for women after divorce or the death of their husband (Lamchichi, 2003).

From the seventh through the 10th centuries, Islam and the Arabic language spread into the continents of Asia, Europe, and Africa (Dwairy, 2006). This period was known as the Golden Era of Islam, owing to the extraordinary cultural advances that occurred, including the development of Arabic literature, poetry, philosophy, architecture, mathematics, science, hospitals, and medical practices (Ashrif, 1987; Hourani, 1970). This flourishing of Arab Muslim culture occurred at the same time that the period known as the Dark Ages was occurring in Europe. Later, during the European Renaissance, many of the scientific and literary developments of the Arabs and Muslims were claimed as European, a practice that persists to the present day in academia and public education (Ashrif, 1987).

The last Muslim empire was that of the Ottomans, with its capital in Istanbul, which reached its zenith during the 16th century and thereafter began to decline. During the late 1800s and early 1900s, the decline accelerated as European powers began colonizing the Middle East and North Africa (e.g., Algeria, Tunisia, and Morocco by France; Egypt by England; and Libya by Italy). In 1916, the British and French divided the remaining area into zones of permanent influence via the Sykes-Picot Agreement, and the British took control of Palestine and pledged in the Balfour Declaration of 1917 to support a Jewish national home in Palestine "provided this did not prejudice the civil and religious rights of the other inhabitants of the country" (Hourani, 1970, p. 318). During and after World War II, Jewish immigration to Palestine increased dramatically, as Jewish refugees fled Nazi persecution. In 1947, the United Nations General Assembly voted to partition Palestine into an Arab and a Jewish state. Britain ended its protectorate status over Palestine and withdrew. The Jewish population declared the existence of the independent state of Israel in 1948. The Arab population rejected the partition, and war ensued. During this period, more than 70% of Palestinians were expelled from their homeland and became refugees to the Israeli military–occupied territories of the West Bank and Gaza; the surrounding Arab countries of Jordan, Syria, Lebanon, and Egypt; and other countries around the world (Dwairy, 1998).

Since the 1991 U.S.-led coalition against the Iraqi invasion of Kuwait (i.e., the Gulf War), there has been a cascade of sociopolitical events profoundly affecting Arab people both directly as casualties of war and indirectly by fomenting anti-Arab prejudice and discrimination. After the attacks on the World Trade Center and the Pentagon on September 11, 2001 (henceforth 9/11), the FBI reported a 17-fold increase over the previous year in hate crimes against Arab Americans, Muslims, and Sikhs (Leadership Conference on Civil and Human Rights, 2017). In the book *Homeland Insecurity: The Arab American and Muslim American Experience After 9/11*, Cainkar (2009) provided documentation of this, which she discussed further in a later work: "Arabs and Muslims were directly or indirectly targeted by 25 of 37 U.S. government security measures," and

> At least 100,000 Arabs and Muslims were personally affected by these initiatives, which included FBI interviews, wiretapping, mass arrests, secret and indefinite detentions, closed hearings, secret evidence, government eavesdropping attorney-client conversations, removal of aliens for technical feasibility, and mandatory special registration . . . [and] some 1,200 citizens and noncitizens, most of Arab and South Asian descent, were rounded up and detained based on their physical appearance or names. (Cainkar, 2016, p. 25)

Adding to all of this, unilateral actions by the U.S. government (e.g., the U.S. invasion of Iraq without seeking United Nations support) have been perceived by many as symbolic of the arrogance of a world power that acts mainly with its own interests in mind

In 2010, within many Arab countries, antigovernment protests began (now known as the Arab Spring), starting with the self-immolation of a Tunisian man that led to the overthrow of the Tunisian president Zine El Abidine Ben Ali. In 2011, protests erupted against Egyptian President Hosni Mubarak, who was forced to resign, followed by protests against Libya's Colonel Muammar al-Qaddafi, who was captured and killed subsequent to North Atlantic Treaty Organization intervention. Also in 2011, the Yemeni president, Ali Abdullah Saleh, stepped down to make way for a transitional government, while Al-Qaeda began seizing territory in the south, and as of 2018, the country remains highly unstable. In Syria, protests against the repressive government of Bashar al-Assad, who responded with brutality, has resulted in a civil war that has killed nearly half a million people and displaced another 11 million from their homes (Boghani, 2016; Manfreda, 2016).

In the United States, another surge in hate crimes occurred in 2015, with 5,818 reported hate crimes against minority members, the biggest increase being on Muslims, who experienced a jump of hate crimes by 67% over the previous year. Hate crime monitors including the Southern Poverty Law Center have also reported an increase in verbal and physical assaults aimed at other minority members, as the fear and hatred of Arabs and Muslims spread even to non-Arab and non-Muslim people of color who were assumed by attackers to be Arab or Muslim (see Leadership Conference on Civil and Human Rights, 2017; Lichtblau, 2016). President Donald Trump's attempts in the first years of his presidency to ban refugees from Muslim-majority countries reflect and have fueled anti-Arab and anti-Muslim sentiments in the United States.

ARAB AMERICANS

The 2011 U.S. Census Bureau's American Community Survey estimated the Arab American population to be approximately 1.8 million (Brown, Guskin, & Mitchell, 2012), although due to differences in definitions of ethnicity and calculation methods, other estimates are as high as 3.7 million (Asi & Beaulieu, 2013; Brown, Guskin, & Mitchell, 2012). The largest specific Arab American population is Lebanese, who comprise about one half million Arab Americans. Remaining groups (from larger to smaller populations, although not exclusively these) include Egyptian, Syrian, Palestinian, Moroccan, Iraqi, Jordanian, and Yemeni (Asi & Beaulieu, 2013). The largest number of Arab Americans live in Detroit/Dearborn, Los Angeles, New York/New Jersey, Chicago, and the Washington D.C. area (Brown, Guskin, & Mitchell, 2012). Compared with the general U.S. population, Arab Americans have a higher proportion of college and graduate degrees, higher employment rates, higher incomes, and greater proportion of people employed in management, professional, and related occupations (U.S. Census Bureau, 2000).

The first wave of Arab immigration to the United States occurred between 1890 and 1940 and consisted mainly of merchants and farmers who emigrated primarily from Lebanon and Syria for economic reasons. They were mostly Christian, poor, and uneducated, and were less likely to identify themselves as Arabs (Abudabbeh, 2005). These individuals assimilated into U.S. culture with less difficulty than did subsequent immigrants (Suleiman, 1999).

The second wave of Arab immigrants began after World War II and consisted of many university students and professionals seeking refuge in the United States after the creation of the state of Israel or for other political reasons. This group included a larger percentage of Palestinians and Muslims who also had a stronger Arab identity (Abudabbeh, 2005).

A third wave began after the 1967 Arab–Israeli war. These individuals came from a variety of Arab countries primarily to escape political conflict in their countries of origin. They included more Lebanese (as a result of the civil war that lasted 17 years) and Iraqis following the Gulf War. They too have tended to hold a strong Arab identity that, along with the multicultural movement in the United States, the Arab–Israeli conflict, and U.S.-led war on Iraq, contributed to the increasing cultural separateness of Arab Americans (Abudabbeh, 2005).

Arab people have played an important role in American politics and include activists Ralph Nader and the founder of Mothers Against Drunk Driving (MADD) Candy Lightner; members of Congress Nick Joe Rahall II of West Virginia, Ray LaHood of Illinois, Charles Boustany of Louisiana, Darrell Issa of California, John E. Sununu of New Hampshire, and the former congressman and governor of Maine John Baldacci; and the longest serving secretary of health and human services, Donna Shalala. Successful Arab Americans in science and medicine include the schoolteacher Christa McAuliffe, who lost her life in the Space Shuttle *Challenger* crash; Michael DeBakey, who invented the heart pump; and Ahmed Zewail, a professor of physics at the California Institute of Technology and Elias Corey of Harvard, both of whom won the Nobel Prize for chemistry. The best-known business-person is the late Steve Jobs, whose biological father was a Syrian Muslim immigrant. Other successful businesspeople include Jacques Nasser, former president and CEO of Ford Motor Company; the late Stephen Yokich, who served as president of the International United Auto Workers union; and John Mack, who served as CEO of Morgan Stanley, one of the largest invest-ment banking firms in the United States. This is just a small number of a much larger list compiled by the Arab American Institute (see http://www.aaiusa.org/famous-arab-americans).

Cultural Values and Beliefs

A number of ethnographic studies and polls point to the commonality of several values among Arab people: religion, morality, honor, generosity, hospitality, and the centrality of family (Harb, 2016). Traditionally, the Arab family has been patriarchal and organized hierarchically by age and gender (Ajami, Rasmi, & Abudabbeh, 2016). Final authority rests with the father; however, both men and women are expected to contribute to the support and maintenance of the family unit. In many families, fathers are considered the authority with regard to the outside world, while the mother takes care of the home. Fathers are expected to provide for the family, mothers to care for their husbands and children, and children to honor their parents. In Arab coun-tries, the extended family often provides a great deal of emotional, social, and financial support. The actions of one family member reflect on the entire family. Members are expected to place the family's welfare above their own, and family values often include self-sacrifice and the pursuit of satisfaction through the happiness of others (Abudabbeh, 1996).

Although family cohesion has been challenged by rapid social change, it continues to be the primary socioeconomic unit in Arab cultures, including among Arab Americans (Barakat, 1993). Outside the Western world, arranged marriage is still the norm, with parents choosing their child's future spouse. Ideally, this process involves input from both the young woman and man and is intended to ensure that the two families are as well matched as the individuals. A dowry is paid by the man to his future wife, which is interpreted by some to be a form of financial insurance for her in the case of divorce. However, in practice, the dowry is frequently given to the wife's family and thus provides her with little security. Moreover, in most Arab countries, it is relatively easy for a man to divorce his wife but nearly impossible for a woman to divorce her husband without his consent (Barakat, 1993).

Within Islam, a Muslim man is allowed to marry a non-Muslim woman as long as she belongs to the "people of the Book" (i.e., is Jewish or Christian). Traditionally, women join the family of their husband, and it is assumed that the woman will become Muslim. A Muslim woman is not allowed to marry a non-Muslim man (Esposito, 1982), although a non-Muslim man can convert to marry a Muslim woman. The Qur'an gives a man the option to have more than one wife as long as he can treat all of them equally; however, it also states that a man can never maintain fairness and equality between women no matter how hard he tries. Thus, polygyny is controversial, with some arguing that the Qur'an supports it and others countering that the Qur'an discourages it. (*Polygyny* refers to the right of a man to have more than one wife; *polygamy* refers to either spouse's right.) Although polygyny is legal in most Arab countries (with the exception of Tunisia), in practice it is now relatively rare (Barakat, 1993, p. 112).

Within the marriage, the husband holds the ultimate authority and connection to the outside world; however, the wife can wield a great deal of power within the family. This is particularly true when polygyny is not an option and divorce is considered shameful for both parties. For example, in Tunisia, divorce may be seen as a sign that a man is unable to "satisfy" his wife. A woman may express disagreement with her husband's behavior by going to her parents' house for a day (or several days, depending on the severity of his transgression) without first fixing dinner for him and, if she is especially angry, without taking the children with her (Hays & Zouari, 1995). In tightly knit rural communities where few behaviors are private, the wife's brief departure serves as an embarrassment (or source of public amusement) that pressures the husband to make amends. Erickson and Al-Timimi (2001) cited a similar example in which an Arab American homemaker briefly left home at mealtime without fixing the family's dinner in response to their complaints about the meal being overdone the night before. The family recognized this as a nonverbal communication that they needed to be more respectful of her contributions. The point here is that therapists need to be cautious about assuming powerlessness on the part of Arab women (Friedman & Pines, 1992; Hays, 2007).

Children are considered an essential part of marriage and one of the primary joys of family life. Child-rearing is relatively lax compared with European American norms, with young children frequently indulged, and boys often favored. Common forms of discipline include shaming, instilling fear that something bad will happen if the child misbehaves, and physical punishment. Children are expected to obey their parents, and it is not uncommon to observe parents lecturing children rather than inviting them to discuss a problem. Rote learning is valued over innovative forms of self-expression. Children are encouraged to maintain close ties with their families through adulthood and are not encouraged to be individualistic or separate from their parents. An exception to this pattern can be found in rural Bedouin families in which children are encouraged to be more individualistic (Barakat, 1993). Younger children spend more time with their mother than with their father and are likely to be more open with her, at times using her as the messenger or go-between with their father (Abudabbeh, 1996).

Identity and Acculturation

Although the values described earlier are common among Arab people, therapists need to be aware of within-group differences related to national identity and social status. Each Arab country (i.e., those in which a majority of the inhabitants are of Arab heritage) has its own unique constellation of values, beliefs, and traditions. These differences have emerged in the context of particular geographic locations, natural resources, and political histories. For example, the French colonization of Morocco, Algeria, and Tunisia contributed to the strong French influence in these countries and the greater tendency for individuals to immigrate to France or French-speaking Québec than to the United States. In contrast, the British colonization of Iraq, Jordan, Egypt, and the Arabian Peninsula has resulted in closer economic ties and greater immigration to the United Kingdom and United States.

Social status in Arab societies is linked to social class; however, social class involves a more complex and dynamic set of variables that include but extend beyond income, occupation, and education (Barakat, 1993). Land ownership and occupational autonomy (i.e., working for oneself, for example, as a business owner) have traditionally conferred a higher status, and currently, particular professions hold an especially high status (e.g., engineer, physician, attorney). Greater respect is typically given to and expected by individuals who are older, well-educated, wealthier, and religious, as well as to those who belong to a family that has "a good name" (i.e., a reputation for integrity based on benevolent works or religiousness). The practice of arranged marriages tends to reinforce class differences.

In recent decades, oil revenues have contributed to the socioeconomic differentiation of Arab cultures. For example, the relatively rapid growth of the economies of Qatar, the United Arab Emirates, Kuwait, and Saudi Arabia has led to increased urbanization, opportunities for international travel, and greater exposure to Western ideas, goods, and media for middle- and upper-middle-class citizens of these countries. The disparity in wealth has resulted in the loss via emigration of many well-educated and skilled laborers from the poorer countries (e.g., Morocco, Algeria, Tunisia, Egypt, Jordan, and Palestine) to the United States, Canada, Europe, and the wealthier Arab nations (Barakat, 1993).

Within the United States, Arab ethnic identity is complex. Amer and Kayyali (2016) cited several studies demonstrating the close connection between religious and cultural identity for both Christian and Muslim Arabs. In one example, religion became a primary way for Christian Jordanian women and Egyptian Copts in Washington, DC, to maintain the continuity of their ethnic culture in the face of pressures to assimilate. In another example, the desire of Muslim Arab Americans to read the Qur'an led them to learn Arabic (see Amer & Kayyali, p. 53, for the specific studies). As Hakim-Larson and Menna (2016) explained, Christian Arabs "endorse some values that stem from the Middle East's predominantly Islamic history, while Muslim Arabs have incorporated some traditions and values stemming from the Abrahamic ancestry (Old Testament of the Bible)" (p. 35), and both Christian and Muslim Arabs who emigrate to the United States may adopt Western values such as the Protestant work ethic and an emphasis on individual autonomy and independence.

People's ethnic identities may also be strongly influenced by their generational status (i.e., how far back their roots in the United States extend) and the degree of connection to their country of origin. It is not uncommon to find Arab Americans whose family members immigrated several generations ago (during the first wave from Syria or Lebanon) and who are assimilated into European American culture; these individuals tend to be Republican and conservative in their political affiliation (Erickson & Al-Timimi, 2001). In contrast, more recently immigrated individuals may identify strongly with their national origins.

Within the United States, identity may be influenced by surrounding sociocultural events as well. Stereotypes and discrimination certainly existed before the events of 9/11, but both have increased dramatically since then, increasing the vulnerability of Arab American Muslim youth who are exposed to a nearly continuous stream of negative images and news via Internet regarding Arabs and Muslims (Hakim-Larson & Menna, 2016). As Germine Awad noted, Christian Arab Americans also experience a great deal of discrimination because of the assumption that they are Muslim (in Clay, 2017, p. 38). Studies suggest that among Arab American youth, psychological distress is negatively correlated with ethnic identity, that is, those with stronger ethnic identities experience less psychological distress (Hakim-Larson & Menna, 2016).

Given the negative portrayal of Arab people on television, in films, news reports, and, most recently, by President Trump, therapists should not be surprised if Arab clients appear distrustful. In addition to U.S. governmental actions, autocratic leadership and the abuse of civil rights in clients' countries of origin may contribute to distrust that can extend to the therapist who is seen as an authority figure or assumed to hold the same attitudes as the dominant culture (Bushra, Khadivi, & Frewat-Nikowitz, 2007). Furthermore, when a client's refugee status is a result of direct U.S. intervention or the use of U.S. resources to facilitate the collapse of their country, as in the case of Iraq, it should not be surprising that clients feel angry toward the United States and toward the American therapist (Nassar-McMillan & Hakim-Larson, 2003).

Because political histories and current events can strongly affect clients' attitudes toward therapy, it is essential that therapists consider the interaction of their own identities with those of their clients. For example, the initial feelings and beliefs held by a recently immigrated Christian Palestinian client toward a European American Christian therapist will be different from those of a fourth-generation Syrian Muslim client toward a European American Jewish therapist. In some cases, a similar identity (e.g., when both therapist and client are Arab or Muslim or Christian) can create a sense of connection; however, therapists must also be aware of the possibility of overemphasizing similarities and missing important differences (Chin, 1994). In sum, the more the therapist knows about the political history of and current events in a client's specific culture, the more able he or she will be to understand and address the client's concerns and reservations regarding the therapist and therapy.

COGNITIVE BEHAVIORAL ASSESSMENT AND THERAPY

CBT with Arab clients requires a number of special considerations to be sure that the assessment is accurate and therapy is helpful. This includes pretherapy work therapists need to do regarding their own attitudes toward and knowledge of people of Arab heritage, recognition of the advantages and disadvantages of CBT with Arab people, knowledge of how to establish a respectful and caring relationship including knowledge of Arab customs and expectations, familiarity with commonly presented problems, and consideration of the appropriateness and inappropriateness of tests and measures.

Advantages and Disadvantages of CBT With Arab Clients

Several authors have articulated the characteristics of CBT that make it well suited for work with Arab people. These include CBT's structured educational approach, its emphasis on problem-solving, and its focus on the here and now (Abudabbeh & Aseel, 1999; Erickson & Al-Timimi, 2001; Nassar-McMillan & Hakim-Larson, 2003). CBT has also been described as congruent with many aspects of Islamic culture and beliefs (Jalal et al., 2017). In addition, CBT is adaptable for work with couples and families, which is especially important given the importance of family relationships among Arab Americans. Finally, CBT's emphasis on the enhancement and reinforcement of strengths and social supports also fits well with Arab values regarding family involvement. The latter communicates an appreciation of Arab culture, which is especially important during this time when Arab Americans face negative portrayals of their culture in the media on a daily basis (Hays, 2007).

Therapists also need to be aware of the potential limitations of CBT with Arab people. The term itself, *cognitive behavior therapy*, emphasizes the cognitive and behavioral aspects of the situation and thus may be interpreted by Arab clients as overlooking areas of life that they consider central—namely, family and religion. In addition, CBT is permeated with European American cultural norms, including the high value placed on personal independence and autonomy, behavioral change, and rationality (Hays, 2016). In contrast, many Arab clients place a higher priority on family interdependence and harmony, patience, acceptance, and faith. Finally, cognitive restructuring may be seen as offensive and disrespectful if it is conducted in a confrontational manner or if it is aimed at challenging core cultural beliefs.

Preassessment Work

The need for therapists to examine their own attitudes is as important with Arab people as with any other group. However, given the pervasiveness of anti-Arab sentiment in the United States today, along with the lack of clinical information regarding Arab populations, non-Arab U.S. therapists will have to work extra hard to obtain information that is accurate and helpful. Toward this goal, several suggestions are offered. First, therapists are advised to engage in an ongoing process of individually oriented work that includes introspection, self-questioning, research, and reading across disciplines. This individually oriented work is necessary but not sufficient for uncovering one's own biases and knowledge gaps.

A second suggestion involves the use of critical thinking about one's sources of information. The following questions can help to facilitate this process: Who wrote (or directed or funded) this website, article, or program? What is its purpose or goal? Who is represented in this report, and who is not? What voices are heard or not heard? An additional source of information that can facilitate critical thinking is supervision by or consultation with an Arab or Arab American therapist.

A third suggestion is to seek out experiences and relationships with people of Arab heritage, if this is a possibility in the therapist's social environment. It is often only through close relationships with people that one learns the subtleties of individual and family variations within a culture. At the same time, it is important to remember that power differentials can affect what and how much a person will share. In relationships with people who are in a less powerful position than oneself (e.g., clients, students, support staff), the person in the less powerful position may feel less able to speak openly. Some of the best learning comes from intimate relationships in which both parties hold enough power to honestly and safely share their feelings and thoughts (Hays, 2016).

Assessment

As is true in many other groups, mental illness carries a heavy stigma in Arab cultures. In more traditional households, attempts to hide psychological problems may be related to a desire to protect the family's reputation or concern about a young person's marriage opportunities if the problem becomes known by others (Al-Darmaki & Sayed, 2004). Individuals may also be unaware of mental health treatment options, particularly those who have emigrated from countries where psychological services were unavailable.

Whatever the case, Arab Americans tend to seek help from family, friends, and religion before considering mental health services (Al-Krenawi & Graham, 2016). For this reason, it is important to consider incorporating a family systems approach, along with consultation and collaboration with religious leaders when appropriate. For example, Al-Krenawi and Graham (2016) described the case of a young woman who was referred to an Arab male psychologist after she attempted suicide when her family found out she was having an affair. During therapy, the client began acting in a sexualized manner toward the therapist, so the therapist adopted a traditional Arabic brother role, repeatedly referring to her as "my sister" and consulting with elders and religious leaders on how to use religious and culturally normative themes in his work with her. He also included her mother (with whom there was a great deal of tension) initially via guided imagery exercises and then later in joint sessions with the client and her mother.

Given the cautiousness with which many Arab people will approach an assessment and counseling, establishing a positive, caring relationship is especially important. Because respect is a central value, knowledge of and respect for cultural expectations regarding social interactions and etiquette is important (Mahmood & Ahmed, 2016). Questions about the therapist's marital status, children, country of origin, or family name (if the latter two appear Arab) are to be expected. Turning down a gift, shrugging off a hug, or refusing to answer such questions will often be perceived as rejection or arrogance (Bushra et al., 2007). Arab people pride themselves on their generosity and hospitality. These values often enter the therapy relationship in the form of clients giving the therapist small gifts or inviting the therapist to the client's home for a meal. Within-gender physical touch and kissing on both cheeks as a form of greeting are common (i.e., with women touching only women, men touching only men, the exception being within the family wherein men and women may also use this form of greeting). Therapists are advised to be responsive to these preferences and flexible in their adaptation of mainstream procedures. For example, Abudabbeh and Aseel (1999) suggested that therapists be willing to go to clients' homes, and in cases of family therapy in which one family member does not want to attend, to call and attempt to persuade that family member to join the family session.

When Arab people do come to an initial assessment, it is often with the expectation that the therapist will be in an authoritative position, offering specific suggestions and providing help with problem-solving. In countries where few psychological services exist, people will often present with somatic complaints to their physician. However, in contrast to the common assumption that somatization is more common in Eastern than in Western cultures, a World Health Organization study found this assumption to be false; somatization was related primarily to lower levels of education (Gureje, Simon, Ustun, & Goldberg, 1997).

Among Arab Americans seeking mental health services, commonly presented problems include the following (Abudabbeh, 1996):

- generational conflict between parents who expect their children to follow traditional norms of behavior and children who feel pulled between these expectations and the norms of their U.S. peers;
- gender-related conflicts between spouses, as women become exposed to a wider range of lifestyles, behaviors, and opportunities;
- struggles between parents and adult children over the choice of a spouse, with parents insisting on their right to choose for

their child, and the dilemma when a child is in love with someone the parents do not choose;

- cross-cultural marriages that often involve conflicts over
  child-rearing practices, spousal responsibilities, and behavioral
  expectations;
- legal entanglements related to diverse problems, such as asylum
  seeking, competency to stand trial, or sexual abuse; and
- trauma before, during, and after immigration.

Nassar-McMillan and Hakim-Larson (2003) noted the increasing number of Arab Americans diagnosed with PTSD. In a survey of therapists working at a community services agency serving a large Arab American population,
many individuals were reported to be exhibiting severe postwar trauma. These
individuals were primarily Iraqi refugees and immigrants from the Lebanese
civil war. Similarly, Dwairy (1998) described high rates of trauma among
Palestinian children, noting that 40% of the Palestinians killed during the
Intifada were children.

In an overview of the many types of trauma experienced by Arab people,
Kira and Wrobel (2016) noted that like people everywhere, Arab people
may have experienced abandonment, child maltreatment, and sexual and
physical abuse. However, in addition, they may also have experienced
severe collective identity and secondary traumatization, including "historical traumas, oppression by dictatorships and police states, discrimination as
minorities, and gender discrimination" (p. 190). Even after having moved
to the United States, trauma can be an ongoing experience, not simply a
one-time event. At the same time, these authors noted that resilience and
posttraumatic growth are notable among Arab people and that at present,
there are several gaps in the literature on stress and trauma among Arab
Americans, including the oppression of sexual minorities and the psychological effects of gender discrimination.

When an assessment suggests the use of psychological tests and measures, caution is advised, particularly with immigrants and individuals who
do not speak English as a first language. Although Arabic translations
exist of the major cognitive tests such as the Wechsler scales (Wechsler,
2008) and the Stanford–Binet Intelligence Scales (Binet & Terman, 2003),
Mahmood and Ahmed (2016) noted that "as an Arab American examinee
gets culturally and linguistically further away from the European American
groups that most U.S.-based instruments were designed for, the cross-
cultural construct validity of the test decreases or may vanish altogether"
(p. 280). The same applies in the use of personality tests such as the Minnesota
Multiphasic Personality Inventory (Butcher, Mosch, Tsai, & Nezami, 2006)

and projective tests. Language is an enormously important factor with such tests, and the clinician needs to know whether the translation of a particular tool matches the client's Arabic dialect. Studies show that even for bilingual individuals, expressing emotions in one's nondominant language can be difficult, especially when in distress, and may result in a distorted presentation. Failure to account for a client's language preferences and abilities is likely to result in an inaccurate diagnosis and assessment.

Therapeutic Adaptations

In keeping with the American Psychological Association Presidential Task Force on Evidence-Based Practice (2006) definition of evidence-based practice, the adaptation of cognitive behavioral techniques with Arab clients involves attention to the client's particular characteristics, culture, and preferences. In an excellent illustration of specific adaptations, Jalal et al. (2017) described their work with Muslim Egyptians who had experienced significant trauma. Beginning with a thorough understanding of each client's local ethnopsychology and ethnophysiology, the authors emphasized the "grounding" of cognitive behavioral techniques in the culture. The following are some examples of the ways in which they accomplished this:

- To decrease the stigma associated with mental health treatment, the psychologists used a common Egyptian term for PTSD (which translates into English as "instability after being traumatized"), while simultaneously emphasizing that this did not mean the person was "crazy."
- To increase positive expectancy, treatment was described in terms of cultural practices and metaphors—for example, comparing the treatment process to the making of a special dish that requires multiple culinary steps and takes time to complete.
- To teach mindfulness and attentional control, they incorporated *salah* (a ritualistic form of prayer involving the physical movements of prostration, bowing, and standing) and the practice of chanting God's many names (e.g., The Ever Most Merciful, the Ever Most Loving, the Grantor of Security, the Protector).
- For a visual imagery exercise, rather than using the imagery of a warm light (which they noted works well with Latino clients), they used water and cooling (e.g., "imagine love flowing from your heart, like a cooling water") because the imagery of water and cooling appear frequently in the Qur'an.

- To teach self-soothing and helpful self-talk, they used Qur'anic verses, for example, "Allah does not burden the soul beyond that it can bear" (Qur'an: 2:286) and "In the remembrance of God the heart finds rest" (Qur'an: 13:28).

These are just a few of the specific adaptations that can make CBT more culturally responsive. The following case example includes additional suggestions.

CASE EXAMPLE

Fatima[1] was a 35-year-old married Arab American woman who presented with symptoms of depression (poor sleep, decreased appetite, irritability, and a sense of foreboding regarding the future). At the time of the assessment, she was 5 months pregnant with her first child. Her husband, Ahmed, accompanied her to the appointment. The Arab American therapist noted that Ahmed was dressed in Western clothes, and Fatima was wearing a long-sleeved shirt, long skirt, and headscarf.

Fatima told the therapist that she was the youngest daughter in a family of six children, all of whom were married with children. Her Palestinian parents had immigrated to the United States before she was born, and she grew up in a large Midwestern city, attended public schools, was an honor student, and completed a bachelor's degree in science education. She worked as a teacher for several years before marrying her Palestinian husband. He had come to the United States as a college student on scholarships and obtained permanent residency after they married.

Fatima and Ahmed had been married approximately 6 months when she became pregnant. Fatima had just ended her teaching year, and they agreed that she would not renew her contract. During the summer, they moved out of her parents' home into their own house in a city approximately 2 hours away. Both she and her husband defined themselves as devout Muslims and before moving had maintained an active connection to a local mosque. Fatima said that her family was "not very religious," but she considered them close and missed seeing them on a daily basis. Her husband's family was living in Jordan, and they spoke occasionally by phone.

Ahmed's commute after the move took the same amount of time that it had before they relocated. He worked long hours in a biotech company and enjoyed his work, but this meant that Fatima was alone much of the time.

---

[1]Case material in this chapter has been disguised to protect client confidentiality.

They both acknowledged missing her family and neither had friends in the new place; since the move, they had begun having arguments. Fatima was not looking forward to the baby's birth, although Ahmed said that he thought things would improve because she would be busier with the baby. Still, he was concerned that she was not happy and had difficulty carrying out her normal activities of housecleaning, cooking, and grocery shopping.

At the end of the assessment, the therapist summarized her perspective beginning with the stressors she had heard from Fatima and Ahmed, along with those that she inferred on the basis of her knowledge of Arab Muslim culture. These included the stress of a new marriage with all of the interpersonal adaptations required, the pregnancy (a physical and possibly psychological stressor), the move to a new city, and the losses of Fatima's family's daily support, their involvement with the mosque of their former town, and Fatima's work and collegial friendships. The three of them talked about the stressful nature of these changes. Fatima and Ahmed had not previously recognized the degree of stress involved because, as they noted, many of the changes involved good things.

Next, the therapist described the strengths and supports she saw in their lives, namely, their concern for one another; their caring families; their financial stability, which she attributed to a sense of family responsibility; their faith; and their strong identities as Muslims, including their connection to the Muslim community. With regard to the last, she did not say "former connection" because although they were no longer involved in the mosque of their prior home, they still had a strong sense of connection to the *umma*, or worldwide community of Muslims. Fatima and Ahmed seemed to appreciate the therapist's recognition of these positive aspects of their lives, particularly those related to their faith.

The therapist then described her approach as one that involved "problem-solving regarding those things that a person can change, and learning to cope better with those things that you can't or choose not to." Regarding the former, she said, "Practical problem-solving often involves figuring out a way to change something in your environment to make the problem less stressful." She used the example of their current lack of social support and emphasized how important interactions with family and friends are for people to be happy and healthy. She said that counseling could be useful in helping them figure out ways to increase their support.

Regarding problems that cannot be solved by changing something in one's environment, she explained how cognitive restructuring works without using the term itself. She said, "One thing we know in psychology is that what we think affects the way we feel. Often, people are unaware of what they're thinking and how their thoughts are affecting their stress level." She gave an example in which a wife calls her husband when he is at work, and the husband is short with her, saying that he has to get back to work.

> If the wife thinks to herself, "He'd rather be at work than with me, I know he doesn't really love me," she will probably feel pretty low, and the more she tells herself this, the worse she will feel to the point that she may be all upset and crying by the time he gets home. On the other hand, if she tells herself, "He must be feeling really pressured at work. I must have caught him at a bad time," she may feel some concern for him but will not work herself into such an emotional state that she starts questioning her marriage and his love for her.

The therapist asked Fatima and Ahmed if this made sense to them. They both said yes, and Fatima added, "I know I do that." The therapist continued,

> Well, we all have tendencies to say these kinds of things to ourselves sometimes, especially when we're under a lot of stress or experiencing some big transitions in our lives. Counseling can be helpful because it gets people to start to recognize the negative and hurtful things that may be pulling them down or increasing their anxiety. It can also help in figuring out more positive and helpful things to say to yourself. Now this may sound pretty easy, and in my experience most people are able to do this part, but the hard part comes in keeping it up. And that's another place that counseling can be helpful. You know that you're coming back in a week so you're more apt to practice it during the week, because you know that I'm going to ask you whether it helped or not.

The therapist explained to Fatima and Ahmed that she could work together with them as a couple or individually with Fatima, and that her recommendation was to try two to three couple sessions first, then if it felt appropriate, she would meet alone with Fatima for three to four sessions. She said that she did not recommend an evaluation for medication at this point given Fatima's pregnancy and the possibility that counseling might help without it. However, she said, after the pregnancy, medication could be an option if the depression persisted. Fatima and Ahmed agreed to follow her suggestions and returned together the next week.

Environmental and Behavioral Interventions

In the first counseling session, the therapist helped Fatima and Ahmed to generate a broad range of possible solutions to their need for more support. It was explained that this increased support could help to improve their relationship and Fatima's mood. Their ideas included moving back to live with Fatima's parents, Ahmed looking for a different job that would require fewer hours, or Ahmed decreasing his hours at the current job. The therapist asked questions aimed at helping them to look at the advantages and disadvantages of each possible change. Ahmed insisted that decreasing his hours was not possible given the type of job he had, and he did not want to look for another job. Fatima was accepting of his decision on this. Through the questioning process, they remembered the reasons they had decided to move out of her parents' home (not enough physical space for them and a baby, along with some times of irritation because of the lack of privacy). They did not rule out moving back to the area in which her parents lived but decided that for the time being this would not be a sound financial decision given the purchase of their new house. (Another financial responsibility they had both committed to was sending money on a monthly basis to Ahmed's family in Jordan.)

Through the course of this brainstorming process, Fatima and Ahmed recognized their need to find a new mosque, a task that they were able to accomplish within a couple of weeks. However, it was clear that although making friends would be helpful, Fatima still missed her family. Attention was given to ways that she might increase her family connections without moving. They came up with a plan whereby Fatima would visit her family overnight once during the week when Ahmed was working long hours anyway. Ahmed was quite self-sufficient when it came to preparing his own meals because he had lived in the United States as a single young man for several years before marrying, and cooking had been one of the most enjoyable ways he stayed connected to his culture. In addition, Fatima's mother came to stay with them every other week on a weeknight so that Fatima and Ahmed still had some time alone together on weekends. Fatima and Ahmed continued to visit her family for celebrations and family dinners at least once a month.

It is important to note that the therapist did not push Fatima and Ahmed to decrease their connections with her family. Whereas a mainstream European American perspective might have emphasized the need for this young couple to "individuate," this therapist recognized that they needed more support and that enlisting her family's support was the most culturally congruent strategy, particularly in that the family was able and willing to be involved. Obviously, the couple's plan was possible because the physical distance was not too great. Yet even if the family had been much farther away, the point would still be the same: That is, the therapist would have helped the couple to enlist greater family support rather than discourage it.

Similarly, the therapist raised questions for Ahmed and Fatima to think about regarding his commitment to his job, but once they made their preferences clear, she did not push either of them on this point. Although the therapist preferred the economic independence she had in her own marriage, she did not want to impose her value priorities on Ahmed and Fatima. Rather, she accepted their more traditional relationship. She was aware that in such relationships, couples often have more realistic expectations regarding what needs their spouses can and cannot meet. Such realism is rooted in traditional Arab marriages in which each spouse's social needs are met primarily within the family, by other same-gender family members. Although immigration and the exportation of Western values into Arab countries are changing this pattern, it was still a preferred mode for Fatima and Ahmed, and it was possible given the proximity of her family.

Cognitive Restructuring

Regarding the second part of the therapist's approach (i.e., learning to cope better with those things that do not have an environmental solution), she met individually with Fatima to find out more about her feelings and thoughts regarding marriage, her role as wife and mother, and the loss of her work outside the home. Fatima shared that she had always expected to stay home with her children as her mother had done. She added that for many years, she had felt strong pressure to marry and have children, and now at age 35, she was long past the "ideal" age. However, her mother had never been to college or worked outside the home, but Fatima found that she enjoyed her studies and work. At the same time, she said that her mother strongly encouraged her career, and Fatima had the feeling that her mother experienced a great deal of vicarious satisfaction through Fatima's professional accomplishments.

As the therapist asked questions aimed at helping her to articulate these expectations, Fatima was able to recognize the strongly conflicting messages she had received from her family and culture. These included: "As a wife and mother, I should be devoted to my husband's and children's well-being" and "As an Arab American woman, I have to take advantage of all the opportunities that were never available to my mother, and I should achieve as much as possible to make my parents proud."

The therapist did not challenge the idea that these were good or acceptable things to want (i.e., the validity of the beliefs) but rather asked questions that raised Fatima's awareness of the subtle imperative in these statements (i.e., what is implied by "should" and "have to"). In addition, she questioned the helpfulness of such absolute expectations. They talked about the variety of adaptations Fatima saw other women making, including women doing career-oriented work outside and inside the home, single mothers, and women focused on homemaking. The therapist asked if Fatima could think of any women she knew who were completely devoted to their families but not particularly happy. Fatima could think of one such woman and was able to make a link to the idea that one needs to take care of oneself to be a better mother and wife. She eventually reworded her earlier statement to say,

"I want to be a loving wife and mother who cares for her husband and children, and I need to take care of my spiritual, physical, and social needs to be a good wife and mother."

The therapist encouraged Fatima to think about the ways in which she might take better care of herself in each of the domains she mentioned. Regarding her spirituality, Fatima said now that she was going to the new mosque, she was praying more regularly again and felt that this was good spiritual self-care. Regarding her physical self, she said that she ate healthy food according to Muslim dietary rules, but she acknowledged her need for more exercise. However, she did not want to make a change in this area at the time, and the therapist did not push her to do so.

Regarding her social needs, Fatima expressed a desire to talk about the loss of her work and friends. She had not thought about the possibility that she would miss her work and coworkers until after she was gone. However, now she could see that she missed the social activity as well as the sense of accomplishment. Regarding the latter, it was apparent to her and the therapist that she had a strong achievement orientation, as do many Arab Americans, particularly first- and second-generation immigrants.

As Fatima explored her beliefs about what exactly would be involved in being a good mother and wife, she recognized that she could probably be both, and work outside the home, at least part time. As this idea became more real to her and as she talked more about it, her mood began to improve. She knew it would be several months until she could seriously explore part-time work possibilities (because of the upcoming birth), but having the goal in mind gave her something to look forward to. She talked with Ahmed, and he agreed on the condition that she wait until the baby was a year old. She preferred 6 months but agreed to wait with the intention that she would begin exploring possibilities before then. In the final session held with Ahmed and Fatima about 2 months before the baby's birth, they were regularly attending services at the new mosque, Fatima had met a new friend at the mosque who was also pregnant, the visitation plan with her family was working well, and Fatima was looking forward to returning to part-time work in a year. Ahmed continued to work long hours but felt more satisfied with Fatima and the marriage.

CONCLUSION

This case illustrates some of the key components of culturally responsive CBT with people of Arab heritage. The first component involves a focus on the present and on specific problems as presented by clients. This focus reflects and includes respect for the clients' assessment of their own situation and needs. An educational approach will often be the most helpful, including the therapist's explanation in lay language of the relationship between stressors, social support, and mental health. Flexibility is important and requires a willingness to see the same clients individually or as couples and families (or both) depending on their needs. In most cases, the therapy will consist of both behavioral interventions aimed at addressing behavioral and environmentally based problems and cognitive interventions that help clients reconsider the helpfulness (i.e., utility) of beliefs rather than their validity.

It is clear that this is a new area that requires a great deal of clinical research to clarify what works and what does not with the diversity of people who define themselves as Arab and Arab American. This chapter has attempted to provide some beginning suggestions for this work.

REFERENCES

Abudabbeh, N. (1996). Overview on Arab families. In M. McGoldrick, J. Giordano, & J. K. Pearce (Eds.), *Ethnicity and family therapy* (2nd ed., pp. 333–346). New York, NY: Guilford Press.

Abudabbeh, N. (2005). Arab families: An overview. In M. McGoldrick, J. Giordano, & N. G. Preto (Eds.), *Ethnicity and family therapy* (3rd ed., pp. 423–436). New York, NY: Guilford Press.

Abudabbeh, N., & Aseel, H. A. (1999). Transcultural counseling and Arab Americans. In J. McFadden (Ed.), *Transcultural counseling: Bilateral and international perspectives* (pp. 283–296). Alexandria, VA: American Counseling Association.

Ahmed, S., & Amer, M. M. (Eds.). (2012). *Counseling Muslims: Handbook of mental health issues and introductions*. New York, NY: Routledge.

Ajami, J., Rasmi, S., & Abudabbeh, N. (2016). Marriage and family: Traditions and practices throughout the family lifecycle. In M. M. Amer & G. H. Awad (Eds.), *Handbook of Arab American psychology* (pp. 103–116). New York, NY: Routledge.

Al-Darmaki, F., & Sayed, M. A. (2004, July). *Practicing polymorphism in traditional gender-role Emirates: Conflicts and challenges*. Paper presented at the 112th Annual Convention of the American Psychological Association, Honolulu, HI.

Al-Krenawi, A., & Graham, J. R. (2016). Help seeking: Traditional and modern ways of knowing, and insights for mental health practice. In M. M. Amer & G. H. Awad (Eds.), *Handbook of Arab American psychology* (pp. 263–274). New York, NY: Routledge.

Amer, M. M., & Awad, G. (Eds.). (2016). *Handbook of Arab American psychology*. New York, NY: Routledge.

Amer, M. M., & Kayyali, R. A. (2016). Religion and religiosity: Christian and Muslim faiths, diverse practices, and psychological correlates. In M. M. Amer & G. H. Awad (Eds.), *Handbook of Arab American Psychology* (pp. 48–62). New York, NY: Routledge.

American–Arab Anti-Discrimination Committee. (2009, November 9). *Facts about Arabs and the Arab world.* Retrieved from http://www.adc.org/facts-about-arabs-and-the-arab-world/

American Psychological Association Presidential Task Force on Evidence-Based Practice. (2006). Evidence-based practice in psychology. *American Psychologist, 61,* 271–285. http://dx.doi.org/10.1037/0003-066X.61.4.271

Ashrif, S. (1987). Eurocentrism and myopia in science teaching. *Multicultural Teaching, 5,* 28–30.

Asi, M., & Beaulieu, D. (2013, May). *Arab households in the United States: 2006–2010* (U.S. Census Bureau American Community Survey Briefs). Retrieved from https://www.census.gov/prod/2013pubs/acsbr10-20.pdf

Badri, M. (2013). *Abu Zayd al-Balkhi's sustenance of the soul: The cognitive behavior therapy of a ninth century physician.* Herndon, VA: International Institute of Islamic Thought.

Barakat, H. (1993). *The Arab world: Society, culture, and state.* Berkeley: University of California Press.

Binet, A., & Terman, L. (2003). *Binet Intelligence Scales* (5th ed.). Stanford, CA: Springer.

Boghani, P. (2016, February 11). A staggering new death toll for Syria's war—470,000. *Frontline.* Retrieved from http://www.pbs.org/wgbh/frontline/article/a-staggering-new-death-toll-for-syrias-war-470000/

Brown, H., Guskin, E., & Mitchell, A. (2012, November 28). Arab-American population growth. *Pew Research Center.* Retrieved from http://www.journalism.org/2012/11/28/arabamerican-population-growth

Bushra, A., Khadivi, A., & Frewat-Nikowitz, S. (2007). Multiple perspectives on the Middle Eastern identity in psychotherapy. In J. C. Muran (Ed.), *Dialogues on difference: Diversity studies of the therapeutic relationship* (pp. 219–235). Washington, DC: American Psychological Association.

Butcher, J. N., Mosch, S. C., Tsai, J., & Nezami, E. (2006). Cross-cultural applications of the MMPI–2. In J. N. Butcher (Ed.), *MMPI–2: A practitioner's guide* (pp. 505–537). Washington, DC: American Psychological Association. http://dx.doi.org/10.1037/11287-018

Cainkar, L. (2009). *Homeland insecurity: The Arab American and Muslim American experience after 9/11.* New York, NY: Russell Sage Foundation.

Cainkar, L. (2016). Race and racial is Asian: Demographic trends and the process of reckoning social place. In M. M. Amer & G. H. Awad (Eds.), *Handbook of Arab American psychology* (pp. 19–33). New York, NY: Routledge.

Chin, J. L. (1994). Psychodynamic approaches. In L. Comas-Díaz & B. Greene (Eds.), *Women of color: Integrating ethnic and gender identities in psychotherapy* (pp. 194–222). New York, NY: Guilford Press.

Clay, R. A. (2017, April). Islamophobia. *Monitor on Psychology, 48*(4), 34.

Dwairy, M. A. (1998). *Cross-cultural counseling: The Arab-Palestinian case.* Binghamton, NY: Haworth Press.

Dwairy, M. A. (2006). *Counseling and psychotherapy with Arabs and Muslims: A culturally sensitive approach.* New York, NY: Teachers College, Columbia University.

Erickson, C. D., & Al-Timimi, N. R. (2001). Providing mental health services to Arab Americans: Recommendations and considerations. *Cultural Diversity and Ethnic Minority Psychology, 7,* 308–327. http://dx.doi.org/10.1037/1099-9809.7.4.308

Esposito, J. L. (1982). *Women in Muslim family law.* Syracuse, NY: Syracuse University Press.

Friedman, A., & Pines, A. (1992). Increase in Arab women's perceived power in the second half of life. *Sex Roles, 26,* 1–9. http://dx.doi.org/10.1007/BF00290121

Gureje, O., Simon, G. E., Ustun, T. B., & Goldberg, D. P. (1997). Somatization in cross-cultural perspective: A World Health Organization study in primary care. *The American Journal of Psychiatry, 154,* 989–995. http://dx.doi.org/10.1176/ajp.154.7.989

Hakim-Larson, J., & Menna, R. (2016). Acculturation and enculturation: Ethnic identity socialization processes. In M. M. Amer & G. H. Awad (Eds.), *Handbook of Arab American psychology* (pp. 34–47). New York, NY: Routledge.

Harb, C. (2016). The Arab region: Cultures, values, and identities. In M. M. Amer & G. H. Awad (Eds.), *Handbook of Arab American psychology* (pp. 3–18). New York, NY: Routledge.

Hays, P. A. (2007). A strengths-based approach to psychotherapy with Middle Eastern people: Commentary regarding Bushra et al. In J. C. Muran (Ed.), *Dialogues on difference: Diversity studies of the therapeutic relationship* (pp. 243–250). Washington, DC: American Psychological Association. http://dx.doi.org/10.1037/11500-027

Hays, P. A. (2016). *Addressing cultural complexities in practice: Assessment, diagnosis, and therapy* (3rd ed.). Washington, DC: American Psychological Association.

Hays, P. A., & Zouari, J. (1995). Stress, coping, and mental health among rural, village, and urban women in Tunisia. *International Journal of Psychology, 30,* 69–90. http://dx.doi.org/10.1080/00207599508246974

Hijazi, A. M., Lumley, M. A., Ziadni, M. S., Haddad, L., Rapport, L. J., & Arnetz, B. B. (2014). Brief narrative exposure therapy for posttraumatic stress in Iraqi refugees: A preliminary randomized clinical trial. *Journal of Traumatic Stress, 27,* 314–322. http://dx.doi.org/10.1002/jts.21922

Hinton, D. E., & Jalal, B. (2014). Parameters for creating culturally sensitive CBT: Implementing CBT in global settings. *Cognitive and Behavioral Practice, 21,* 139–144. http://dx.doi.org/10.1016/j.cbpra.2014.01.009

Hourani, A. (1970). *Arabic thought in the liberal age: 1798–1939*. London, England: Oxford University Press.

Kira, I. A., & Wrobel, N. H. (2016). Trauma: Stress, coping, and emerging treatment models. In M. M. Amer & G. H. Awad (Eds.), *Handbook of Arab American psychology* (pp. 188–205). New York, NY: Routledge.

Jalal, B., Samir, S. W., & Hinton, D. E. (2017). Adaptation of CBT for traumatized Egyptians: Examples from culturally adapted CBT (CA–CBT). *Cognitive and Behavioral Practice, 24*, 58–71. Retrieved from http://dx.doi.org/10.1016/j.cbpra.2016.03.001

Lamchichi, A. (2003, July). Claiming independence, asserting personal choice: Islam's rebel women. *Le Monde Diplomatique* [English version]. Retrieved from http://mondediplo.com/2003/07/16lamchichi?var_recherche=lamchichi

Leadership Conference on Civil and Human Rights. (2017). *Hate crimes against Arab Americans, Muslims, and Sikhs*. Retrieved from http://www.civilrights.org/publications/hatecrimes/arab-americans.html

Lichtblau, E. (2016, November 14). *Hate crimes against Arabs*. https://www.nytimes.com/2016/11/15/us/politics/fbi-hate-crimes-muslims.html?_r=0

Manfreda, P. (2016, October 9). *Arab spring uprisings, about news*. http://middleeast.about.com/od/humanrightsdemocracy/tp/Arab-Spring-Uprisings.htm

Mahmood, O. M., & Ahmed, S. R. (2016). Psychological assessment: Distinguishing the clinically relevant from the culturally unique. In M. M. Amer & G. H. Awad (Eds.), *Handbook of Arab American psychology* (pp. 275–288). New York, NY: Routledge.

Nassar-McMillan, S. C., Choudhuri, D. D., & Santiago-Rivera, A. (2010). *Counseling and diversity: Arab Americans*. Belmont, CA: Cengage Learning.

Nassar-McMillan, S. C., & Hakim-Larson, J. (2003). Counseling considerations among Arab Americans. *Journal of Counseling & Development, 81*, 150–159. http://dx.doi.org/10.1002/j.1556-6678.2003.tb00236.x

Rassool, G. H. (2015). *Islamic counseling: An introduction to theory and practice*. New York, NY: Routledge.

Suleiman, M. W. (1999). *Arabs in America: Building a new future*. Philadelphia, PA: Temple University Press.

U.S. Census Bureau. (2000). *We the people of Arab ancestry in the United States* (Special report). Retrieved from http://www.census.gov/prod/2005pubs/censr-21.pdf

Wechsler, D. (2008). *Wechsler Adult Intelligence Scale* (4th ed.). New York, NY: Psychological Corp. Pearson.

8

COGNITIVE BEHAVIOR THERAPY WITH ORTHODOX JEWS

STEVEN FRIEDMAN, CHERYL M. PARADIS,
AND DANIEL CUKOR

Little has been published concerning cognitive behavior therapy (CBT) with Orthodox Jews, a group of individuals who define themselves in terms of their religious lives. It is estimated that there are approximately 2.2 million Orthodox Jews worldwide and 600,000 in the United States (Gall, 1998). As of 2013, 10% of the 5.3 million Jews in the United States self-identify as Orthodox (Cooperman, Smith, Alper, & Cornibert, 2015). Of the 1.54 million Jews in the greater New York City area, 18.4% self-identify as Orthodox. Compared with Jews who identify as secular, Conservative, or Reform, the Orthodox Jewish community is, on average, younger (40 vs. 50) and more likely to be married (69% vs. 49%), to marry only other Orthodox Jews, and to raise their children Orthodox (98%). Twenty-seven percent are 18 years old or younger. They have an average of 4.1 versus 1.7 children per family. Among those who have had children, nearly half (48%) have four or more children. If this trend continues in the future, the majority of Jews in the

http://dx.doi.org/10.1037/0000119-009
Culturally Responsive Cognitive Behavior Therapy, Second Edition: Practice and Supervision, G. Y. Iwamasa and P. A. Hays (Editors)

United States will be Orthodox. In addition, in the United States Orthodox Jews tend to take a conservative position on many social issues. In fact, in many ways, Orthodox Jews as a group have much in common with other very religious groups such as Evangelical Christians (Cooperman et al., 2015). In our experience, Orthodox clients often consider CBT, with its emphasis on symptom reduction, as their first choice of treatment modalities. Clients are usually less interested in long-term, insight-oriented treatment.

This chapter provides an overview of the Orthodox Jewish community and reviews the many cultural issues that affect assessment and treatment, including views of mental illness, confidentiality, family relationships, collaboration with religious leaders, therapeutic alliance, and observance of the Sabbath and holidays. Many of these issues are relevant for the treatment of individuals of other faiths; thus, much of this chapter may have utility for people from other religious groups. Clinicians have long emphasized the importance of understanding, respecting, and integrating religious and cultural beliefs in treatment (Heilman & Witztum, 2000; Sperry & Shafranske, 2005; Witztum & Buchbinder, 2001). A glossary of terms is included (Table 8.1). The case examples used in this chapter involve the treatment of anxiety and depressive disorders. For information about the treatment of Orthodox Jews with psychotic disorders, we recommend Bilu and Witztum (1993); Mohr et al. (2010); Rathod, Kingdon, Phiri, and Gobbi (2010); and D. D. Rosen, Rebeta, and Rothschild (2014). To the best of our knowledge, there are no epidemiological studies looking at the incidence of psychiatric disorders in Orthodox Jewish population, but it is our clinical experience that the prevalence of psychiatric disorders is similar to the distribution in the general U.S. population.

OVERVIEW OF THE ORTHODOX JEWISH COMMUNITY

There are two main divisions within Jewish Americans: *Ashkenazi* Jews, who emigrated from Europe; and *Sephardic* Jews, who emigrated from North Africa and the Middle East (E. J. Rosen & Weltman, 1996). Sephardic Jewish immigration to the United States began in the mid-17th century. Their descendants are a small proportion of the current Jewish population in the United States of approximately 5.3 million. The earliest Ashkenazi Jewish immigrants came to the United States in the mid-1800s and were primarily from Germany. The majority of American Jews are descendants of Eastern European Jews who immigrated to the United States during the late 1800s and early 1900s. In addition, a recent wave of approximately 300,000 Jewish immigrants came from the former Soviet Union (E. J. Rosen & Weltman, 1996).

TABLE 8.1
Glossary of Terms

chumrah	An acceptable, stringent religiosity
frum	Orthodox, religious
Hassid (Chasid)	Followers of a fervent religious movement founded in the first half of the 18th century in Eastern Europe
Holocaust	The organized mass persecution and annihilation of European Jewry by the Nazis (1933–1945)
kashrut	Jewish dietary laws
kosher	Ritually permitted or restricted food and its preparation according to Jewish law; for example, meat and dairy are never mixed, no pork or shellfish are consumed
mitzvah	Refers to a commandment to perform certain deeds; also used to refer to good or charitable deeds
nidah	A woman during the period of menstruation and 7 days after its cessation when no physical contact between husband and wife is permitted
reb, rebbe	Yiddish form for rabbi, applied generally to a teacher or a Hassidic rabbi
shanda	Shame, disgrace, "marked" by a secret
synagogue	Place of worship, the center of religious and social life for Orthodox Jews
Talmud	"Teaching," the authoritative body of Jewish law and tradition codified in the third to fifth century comprising both Halacha and Aggadah ("folklore")
Torah	Scroll containing the first five books of the Bible for reading in the synagogue; can also refer to the entire body of traditional Jewish teaching
yeshiva	An academy devoted to the study of religious and rabbinic literature (in the Orthodox tradition, sexes are educated separately); currently, in these schools, children receive both religious and secular education

There are several different subgroups of Jews, including Orthodox, Conservative, Reconstructionist, Reform, and those not affiliated with any specific denomination. Individuals within both the Ashkenazi and Sephardic lineage may define themselves as Orthodox.

Shared Beliefs of Orthodox Jews

Within the Orthodox Jewish community, subgroups vary in their cultural and familial traditions; however, all hold a core set of beliefs stemming from the conviction that the Torah and the laws of God are unchangeable and nonnegotiable (Hirsch, 1967). The Torah consists of the five books of the Bible believed to have been given by God directly to Moses. The Torah and its laws are interpreted in the Talmud and other written commentaries in the rabbinical literature. These laws dictate Orthodox Jews' relationships with others and with God and include precise prescriptions for family relationships, marriage, sexual behavior, observance of the Sabbath and holidays, dietary laws, financial and business relationships, and all aspects of life.

Orthodox Jews value the religious way of life and recognize no differences between civil and religious obligations. They view their laws and requirements not as a burden but rather as a source of strength. They share important cultural and religious values that differ from those of the modern secular community. Their goals and decisions are often viewed from the position of what is good for the family and community. They also strive to lead a life that focuses on community and group solidarity, acting in the service of God.

Orthodox Jews often strive to isolate themselves from mainstream American society to maintain adherence to their cultural and religious beliefs and traditional way of life. The separation is achieved through choices regarding where they live and school their children and whom they marry. Because Jewish law forbids traveling in cars on the Sabbath and many of the holidays, individuals need to live within walking distance of their synagogue; this need favors locating the community in urban settings. Recently, there has been an expansion of Jewish Orthodox communities in the suburbs.

Orthodox Jews almost always send their children to private schools called *yeshivas*, where they are educated in Jewish studies and American school curriculum. After high school graduation, some may continue to attend religious schools, whereas others, more commonly among Modern Orthodox, pursue more mainstream college and graduate school education. Marriage to non-Orthodox Jews is not acceptable, and marriage within the community fosters separation from the secular world. Separation is also fostered by dietary restrictions. Orthodox Jews follow the laws of *kashrut*, which include dietary laws both inside and outside of the home.

Although those who consider themselves Orthodox Jews share much in common, the term *Orthodox* does not describe a monolithic group. There are many subgroups that vary in the strictness of their interpretation of Jewish law (Margolese, 1998). At one end of the continuum are the Hasidic Jews, a subgroup that includes the Lubavitch and Satmar communities. Members of this community often speak Yiddish and continue the traditions of 18th and 19th centuries in their dress. There are a variety of differences in the social mores and beliefs among Hasidic sects. For example, most Lubavitch do outreach to nonaffiliated Jews, whereas other Hasidic groups rarely interact with those outside their community. Heilman (2000) provided an extensive description of the Israeli ultra-Orthodox communities. At the other end of the spectrum are the Yeshivesh and Modern Orthodox groups. The Modern Orthodox group believes in the assimilation of secular culture into their religious framework.

It is important to recognize that religious identification can be very personal and complex. A therapist should never make assumptions about an Orthodox Jew's religious life based on his or her appearance. This overview is provided to help the therapist place the client's description of his or her religious world in context and to provide a point of reference for normative Orthodox beliefs and behaviors.

Family Relationships

Like other religious groups, Orthodox Jews place a high value on family. To be effective, the therapist must frame the CBT within traditional values of the Orthodox community. In many Orthodox Jewish families, men and women have different roles and requirements as prescribed by the Torah and tradition. Women are primarily responsible for running the household and caring for children, whereas men are primarily responsible for financial support and religious obligations including study of the Torah and certain prayers. Often, however, a young married couple is financially supported by relatives and the wife to allow the husband to continue his pursuit of Torah study.

Orthodox Jews follow rules of segregation of the sexes, and no physical contact is allowed between men and women outside the immediate family. A married couple follows the laws of *Taharat Hamishpocho*, or family purity. This includes the laws of *nidah*, which proscribes physical intimacy for the couple from the start of the wife's menstruation until 7 days after its cessation. Sexual activity is resumed after the *mikvah*, or ritual bath.

Children are educated separately by gender, and men and women do not sit together at synagogue. For Hasidic Jews, segregation by gender may be more encompassing (Silverstein, 1995). For example, Hasidic Jews may avoid the use of public transportation because of the mingling of the sexes, and many Hasidic women do not drive because it is considered immodest.

In contrast to mainstream American women, Hasidic women are less likely to work outside the home. Women in Modern Orthodox sects may pursue careers or employment, but their primary responsibility remains caring for their family. Achievement for women is also more likely to be gained through defined roles within the community, including volunteer work such as *bikor cholim* (visiting the sick) or teaching in the yeshivas (Loewenthal et al., 1995). These issues are illustrated in the following example.

A 30-year-old Orthodox mother of six entered treatment for panic disorder with a non–Orthodox Jewish therapist. She presented with depression, low self-esteem, and a perception that she "did nothing important" in her life. In addition to CBT for panic symptoms, the therapist encouraged her to seek career opportunities. The therapist was unaware of the client's core family values (Heilman & Witztum, 1997). The client experienced the therapist's suggestions as insensitive and further confirmation of her inadequate achievements. Her husband expressed the belief that the therapist did not appreciate or value the importance of his wife's role within the family. Both became resistant to behavioral homework assignments. Before the therapist made these suggestions, the woman's anxiety symptoms and the frequency of the panic attacks had lessened with a combination of relaxation training and exposure. Supervision with an Orthodox therapist helped this woman's therapist become more knowledgeable about the values of Orthodox Jews and also to examine her own beliefs about women's roles. The treatment got back on track when the primary therapist helped the client choose her own culturally acceptable work opportunities. The client began volunteer work and found it enabled her to develop leadership skills and improved her interpersonal effectiveness. Her self-esteem improved, and her depressive symptoms lessened.

ASSESSMENT CONSIDERATIONS

When working with any ethnic minority population, one must consider a variety of cultural issues as part of a careful case conceptualization. In clinical practice, the interview for 90% of CBT therapists will provide the bulk of the information gathered (Spiegler & Guevremont, 1998). With Orthodox Jewish patients, one must consider several critical issues, such as the "worldview" of the Orthodox Jewish community. As has been noted by many cross-cultural psychologists (Hays, 2001; Tanaka-Matsumi, Seiden, & Lam, 1996), Western secular culture emphasizes individuality (autonomy); in contrast, non-Western cultures may emphasize the "community" (collective group values). Orthodox Jews, as noted earlier, emphasize the community group experience.

During the assessment phase, beliefs regarding important "values" and normative "behavior" must be carefully assessed. One of the most critical issues is how does the community view "mental illness." For members of this community, their view may be divided between two extremes: "those who are psychotic versus everyone else who is healthy." The more ultra-Orthodox may use a Yiddish phrase that translates to "problems with nervin," which indicates that the person may be thought to be suffering with a "psychotic"-like experience.

Another challenge for the therapist in doing an assessment with an Orthodox Jew is having empathy for the client's internal spiritual life. This can be a challenge because the vast majority of mental health providers in the United States are much less religious than the population at large (Shafranske & Cummings, 2013). Ultimately, the narrative case conceptualization and rationale for treatment must make sense in relation to the client's worldview. This narrative will often be influenced by the client's religious life and beliefs.

One 26-year-old woman presented to treatment due to feelings of being "overwhelmed and depressed." She had been married for 4 years, was the mother of four young children, and had a small side business as a home decorator. Her husband had recently taken on additional work responsibilities. He had transitioned from being a teacher to also being a pulpit rabbi, now with a community to minister to. With this new role, there was expectation on her that she would serve as an informal advisor to many of the community's women as well as organize certain annual communal activities. She felt that she was unable to meet all of these expectations and was experiencing disappointment in herself. She was also committed to shielding her husband from her feelings because she knew he was strained as well and did not want him to feel he could not count on her.

Through the course of treatment, the client was encouraged to consider each of her responsibilities and their relative value to her. She saw serving the community as the wife of a pulpit rabbi as the most important role or value to which one could aspire. However, she consistently rated all of her multiple roles as "10 out of 10—most important," and thus she felt unable to give up responsibility for any of them. As treatment progressed, it became clearer that, due to her rapid adoption of all these roles, she had not yet fully integrated her new duties into her identity. A therapist unfamiliar with cultural norms might have been tempted to push her to choose between these competing priorities, but because the therapist endorsed the meaningfulness of these roles, he gained credibility and was ultimately able to help his client question some of her own assumptions. Once she was able to challenge some of her thoughts such as, "A rabbi's wife does . . . or never does . . . ," she realized the excessive burden she had placed on herself. Instead of feeling the need to be perfect and seamlessly meet all of the demands, she was able to ask for help as appropriate, set limits, and discovered a newfound connection with many of the women in her community due to her empathy around their struggles with balancing competing demands.

As noted earlier, Orthodox Jews tend to present for treatment due to behavioral dysfunctions. For example, in confronting issues of scrupulosity (i.e., an overly strict interpretation of what is religiously moral or proper) in Orthodox Jews, one must clarify whether the religious behavior is normative or, as is often the case, the particular area of scrupulosity goes beyond halachic requirement, often leading to neglect of other religious demands (Greenberg & Witztum, 2001). Their religious life may have taken on an overly narrow and trivial focus. The balance that people in the community strive for in devoting time to work, prayer, and family obligations may be ignored or neglected.

Additionally, in assessing for strengths and support a client may have, the therapist needs to assess the level of "reverence" that most members of the community derive from their religious beliefs. For example, in an Internet-based survey, Orthodox Jews, who reported a higher belief level about the benevolence and attentiveness of God, predicted lower depression and anxiety (Rosmarin et al., 2011). On the flipside, clients will be reluctant to discuss their belief that if only if they "had more faith," they would not be struggling with their emotional disorder. Often they may be struggling with fully accepting a psychological-learning based intervention to their problem. On some level, they still believe more praying will cure them.

Similarly, when it comes to assessing goals for treatment, one must think about clients' beliefs regarding their symptoms and behavior while assessing environmental triggers, such as family gatherings, holidays, and services. Clients may initially be uncomfortable disclosing the extent to which religious holidays, rituals, or family responsibilities are making their symptoms worse. An emotionally sensitive way to assess this may be by asking a client with obsessive-compulsive disorder (OCD) about the intensity of "panic and fear" he has rather than using the word "discomfort" regarding a religious question. This may help in sorting out normative religious questions from scrupulosity. Similarly, during the assessment phase, the therapist can ask whether "religious questions stick in your head?" or "are you searching for safety or certainty 100% of the time?"

The importance of assessing for spiritual beliefs, when developing a cognitive behavioral case formulation for religious people was demonstrated by Rosmarin et al. (2011). In an Internet-based survey study, they showed that in self-identified religious Jews and Christians, "mistrust in God," a negative spiritual belief, was associated with greater worry and intolerance of uncertainty. Their sample included a subclinical group of Orthodox Jews with anxiety who had participated in a short Internet-based spiritually integrated intervention designed to increase their trust in God. The results showed that a decrease in mistrust of God resulted in decreased worry by primarily decreasing intolerance of uncertainty. Other research has also shown that trust in God is associated with lower depression, lower anxiety, and less worry and mistrust in God with higher levels of symptoms in religious communities (Rosmarin et al., 2009).

As far as we are aware, no studies have looked at Orthodox Jews and established normative data for such common assessment instruments as the Beck Depression Inventory (second edition; Beck, Steer, & Brown, 1996) or the Beck Anxiety Inventory (Beck & Steer, 1993). Finally, as noted at various points in this chapter, a behavioral assessment is difficult to do outside the office because of concerns regarding privacy.

Family Issues

The Orthodox Jewish community places great importance on the respect of elders and parents, and it is forbidden to express criticism of parents. Concomitantly, the law against *loshon hora* (translated literally as "evil speech" and figuratively as simply gossip) can complicate the taking of a complete history during psychotherapy. An inexperienced therapist might mistake a client's desire to avoid criticism of parents as denial, avoidance, or uncooperativeness. For example, a 24-year-old Orthodox man reported that he lived at home with his parents but would not comment on their mental health, stating, "It's not for me to judge." On consultation with the family, the therapist learned that the father was in treatment for major depression. His depression affected the entire family, particularly the client, because many of the interactions within the home were marked with criticism and hostility stemming from the father's poor mood. The therapist came to view his client's reluctance to discuss his father's mental illness as culturally appropriate. The therapist also demonstrated sensitivity and awareness by not forcing him to say something critical of his father. Doing so would have disrupted the therapeutic rapport. As a strong working alliance developed, the client became increasingly able to discuss his father's depression and how it affected him. He realized that he was not merely speaking ill of his father but relaying vital information about the family dynamic that was a contributing factor to his own depression.

Dating, Marriage, and Children

Orthodox couples date primarily for the purpose of selecting an appropriate marriage partner. However, within the different subgroups, there are considerable differences in courtship and marriage practices. In Hasidic communities, the couple may only meet one to three times, and marriages are essentially arranged. A "date" may be a brief meeting in the home of the young woman, chaperoned by both sets of parents. In Modern Orthodox communities, the couple may date for a longer period of time, but usually not more than a year.

When a young man or woman reaches a certain age, he or she begins the courtship process, and parents are actively involved in finding a suitable partner. Young men may begin dating by age 20 or 21 years and young women between ages 18 and 20 years. Premarital sex or any physical contact is forbidden. Marriage is considered a lifelong commitment, and divorce is proscribed except in cases of severe abuse or continuous irreconcilable strife. Making radical changes in family dynamics is usually not a preferred focus of treatment. Because clients with anxiety disorders and marital problems are often referred to marital therapy, a more helpful focus is on improving the marital relationship. It can be especially helpful to promote intimacy through verbal communication during times of physical separation (Ostrov, 1978).

Following the Torah's commandment "Be fruitful and multiply," the Orthodox community places great value on having many children. The practice of having large families is supported by religious beliefs and the motivation to psychologically replace relatives murdered during the Holocaust (Heilman, 2000). Different subgroups of Orthodox Jews have different numbers of children according to the strictness with which this commandment is interpreted.

A large number of children may place great stress on both parents and exacerbate a variety of emotional disorders. Although large family size can serve as a stressor, therapists should not routinely encourage Orthodox women to use birth control. Although contraception may be permitted following rabbinical consultation, it is often reserved for situations in which having more children would be a threat to the mother's health.

Individuals with emotional disorders are usually reticent about discussing the exact nature of their disorder with their rabbi because of their feelings of shame and embarrassment. In treatment, we encourage our clients to honestly discuss their feelings and symptoms with their rabbi. We have found that when the rabbi has a sophisticated appreciation of the disorder and the potential impact of more children, he often encourages the client to use contraception.

TREATMENT CONSIDERATIONS

Various treatment considerations are relevant when working with the Orthodox community. These include the importance of building client trust in the therapist, the need for confidentiality, and the importance of understanding cultural mores that are similar to issues with non-Orthodox clients but should receive greater emphasis. Issues specific to working with Orthodox clients include consulting with the client's rabbi and focusing on dating and marriage issues (which are central to Orthodox communal values) and issues surrounding holiday observances. We discuss these considerations in detail in this section, as well as the advantages and limitations of CBT with this population.

Relationship With the Therapist

Orthodox clients may find it difficult to trust a therapist from outside the community and usually wonder whether even a Jewish, but non-Orthodox, therapist understands and respects their values and way of life (Cinnirella & Loewenthal, 1999; Wikler, 1986). They may ask whether the therapist is Jewish or understands Jewish law. In our experience, we have found it helpful in establishing rapport to answer these questions honestly.

It is important for the therapist to be aware of social and political events that may affect the Jewish and particularly the Orthodox Jewish community. The readily identifiable dress and traditional clothes may make Orthodox Jews, especially Hasidic Jews, vulnerable to anti-Semitism. It is also important for therapists to examine whether they hold any anti-Semitic or anti-religious biases or beliefs.

Regarding attire, therapists need to be aware that dressing modestly is perceived by Orthodox clients as a sign of respect. Laws of modesty mean a therapist should refrain from touching a client of the opposite sex, including even shaking hands. The therapist may leave their office door closed but unlocked if treating a client of the opposite sex.

Views of Mental Illness and Confidentiality

The stigma against mental illness makes it especially important to maintain confidentiality when working with Orthodox Jewish clients. It is essential that therapists not underestimate the widespread prejudice against those with mental illness in this community (Wikler, 1986). *Shanda* is a term that means "shame" or "disgrace" and is used to describe being "marked" by a secret such as intellectual disability or mental illness in the family. Open disclosure of psychological symptoms can affect the reputation of the family and marriage prospects of the client, their children, and immediate relatives.

The importance of confidentiality affects CBT in a variety of ways. Clients may refuse to do in vivo work in their neighborhood because they may be observed by neighbors. In addition, Orthodox Jewish therapists are often known within the community. A client doing in vivo work with a recognized mental health professional will be noticed, and his or her reputation may be adversely affected. If the therapist is not an Orthodox Jew, neighbors will speculate about the person's relationship with an individual who is clearly not from the community. Therapists are also advised to avoid scheduling consecutive office visits for clients within the same Orthodox community because a chance meeting could cause unnecessary embarrassment. The community is so small and close-knit that often one client may know or recognize another Orthodox client.

The stigma against mental illness also affects the help-seeking behaviors of Orthodox individuals. Some may be unlikely to discuss their anxiety or depressive symptoms or treatment with individuals outside their immediate family. Members of this community usually attempt to conceal symptoms and postpone seeking treatment, which is sought only when symptoms grossly interfere with functioning in the family, at work, or at school. Initially, individuals often seek help from family or rabbinical leaders. Rabbinical leaders may be concerned that a mental health professional, ignorant of Orthodox Jewish values and religious obligations, would recommend that the client break with the religion or community. Thus, they may recommend an Orthodox therapist or a non-Jewish therapist rather than a nonreligious assimilated Jewish therapist who is perceived as having negative attitudes or unresolved conflicts about Judaism.

Rabbinical Consultation

It is often helpful to include rabbinical consultation or collaboration in the cognitive-behavioral treatment of Orthodox clients with anxiety or depressive disorders. Collaboration can enhance treatment by educating the non-Orthodox therapist about Jewish law and clarifying misunderstandings. Collaboration with a rabbi also demonstrates to the client that the therapist is willing to work within the Orthodox value system. It will certainly lessen or alleviate the anxiety associated with some homework assignments if the client is aware that his or her rabbi has consented to the exercise.

Consultation with a rabbi can be ineffective or counterproductive if the rabbi is not accepting of mental health intervention. This may occur if he senses that the therapist does not respect religious priorities or might encourage Orthodox clients to defer from religious requirements or question their faith. One way to avoid such pitfalls is to discuss the treatment with the rabbi before meeting together with the client. During this meeting, the therapist needs to begin with psychoeducation about the CBT process. The therapist needs to emphasize the severity of the client's symptoms, explain how they interfere with religious and community obligations, and focus specifically on what the rabbi can say to the client to assist treatment. If the rabbi understands that the consultation is being done out of respect for religious values, he may be more open to establishing a collaborative relationship. It is our clinical sense that CBT approaches are generally more acceptable to Orthodox community leaders.

Collaboration is especially critical for clients with OCD who have difficulty differentiating between *chumrah* (a culturally acceptable, stringent religiosity) and scrupulosity, which is a form of OCD. Research has found that Orthodox Jewish clients with OCD experienced a greater number of religious symptoms than nonreligious symptoms (Greenberg & Shefler, 2002). Rosmarin, Pirutinsky, and Siev (2010) demonstrated that when assessing clinical vignettes regarding possible cases of scrupulosity, Orthodox Jews, in contrast to a comparison group of nonorthodox Jews, were able to recognize that the "religious" OCD symptoms required treatment. It appeared that members of the Orthodox Jewish community easily recognized the difference between normative religious thoughts and behaviors and scrupulosity.

Clients with OCD may consult with a series of rabbis, doubting their advice. Before the consultation, it is important for the therapist to encourage the client with OCD to agree to follow the advice of their chosen rabbi and avoid "rabbi shopping" (Greenberg & Witztum, 2001).

Because of their anxiety or OCD, some Orthodox clients may misinterpret halachic rules, leading to increased anxiety symptoms. For example, a 40-year-old Orthodox man had a history of OCD beginning at age of 13. During adolescence, he was "plagued by doubts about whether I had properly recited my prayers." He recited prayers that should have taken only a few minutes for hours. His rabbi referred him for CBT because "his many concerns regarding preparation for Passover are unrealistic and symptoms of a disorder." Throughout the year, the client had obsessive thoughts that crumbs of *chometz* (bread) would be dropped in his house and make it impossible to clean correctly for Passover. (Orthodox Jews remove all leaven products from their homes before Passover.) He completed numerous compulsions that involved checking for breadcrumbs that might be left on furniture and engaged in hand-washing rituals to prevent the spread of crumbs. CBT included conjoint sessions with his wife and a consultation with his rabbi. Exposure and ritual prevention exercises were effective, and his compulsive rituals decreased dramatically.

The importance of rabbinical consultation is also illustrated in the case of an 18-year-old man who had experienced a recent onset of OCD involving obsessions about his rabbi. He visualized his rabbi as an "evil person." He continually used mental compulsions to reduce anxiety and avoided prayer and study because he was convinced that it was a sin to study Torah or pray while experiencing these abhorrent obsessions. The client was resistant to treatment with exposure and ritual prevention until a rabbinical consultation was arranged. The rabbi explained that his OCD and obsessive thoughts were not a sin and did not prevent prayer and study. The rabbi instructed him to continue normal daily prayer and engage in the exposure and ritual prevention components of treatment. After the rabbinical consultation, CBT treatment was effective in eliminating compulsions and lessening the frequency and severity of his obsessive thoughts.

Dating and Marriage

An Orthodox Jewish person with a severe mental health disorder will often be deemed not ready to marry and the dating process postponed until the condition improves. In our experience, many individuals with mild to moderate anxiety or depressive disorders can fulfill their marital responsibilities. Their symptoms may only interfere with travel or participation in large religious or social gatherings.

If a client is dating, the timing of disclosure to a possible marriage partner is an important issue in treatment. Premature disclosure of the existence of an anxiety disorder, or of current or past psychological treatment, is usually not recommended until the couple is seriously considering marriage. This protects the client's reputation and future marriage prospects in the community. Again, this is an issue in which rabbinical guidance can be helpful to the client and the therapist. It is important to address these issues directly in treatment, as illustrated in the following case. A 23-year-old man presented with mild to moderate OCD. He had intrusive thoughts when he tried to pray, asking, "How do I know there really is a Supreme Being?" Intrusive thoughts in which he doubted his own commitment to Judaism would only present when he tried to pray the required three times a day. Occasionally while studying religious texts, he would also be seized with the thought that "I don't really understand the material" and compulsively reread.

Despite these moderately disturbing thoughts, even before engaging in treatment, he was often able to "allow these thoughts to stay alone and just continue to do what I have to do." He reported that he was "very functional and I don't believe that anyone knows about my thoughts." Because most men in his community begin dating by age 19 or 20, the therapist raised the issue of his not looking for an appropriate match. He reluctantly agreed that this was the prime reason for presenting for treatment. He thought he could not present himself as ready for marriage because "if I tell the matchmaker or prospective woman about my symptoms, I will be thought of as crazy and only be set up with disturbed, mentally ill women." He also believed that if he wasn't totally honest and described every possible issue that he experienced, it "would be sinful to lie and fool people into believing I am normal." He wanted to be "symptom-free and cured" before beginning the dating process.

As part of the treatment, he and the therapist had already engaged in examining some of his errors in thinking, such as "black-and-white" dichotomization, and he was able to entertain the notion that perhaps he was being unrealistic and could begin the dating process. We encouraged him to discuss the dilemma he faced with his rabbi. At first he was extremely ashamed, but with some encouragement, they had a fruitful discussion. His rabbi pointed out that he was "quite a functional, caring, and responsible person, who would make a good husband and father." The rabbi encouraged him to begin the process of looking for an "appropriate match" and also encouraged him by saying that if he responded to the CBT approach and learned the relevant skills, he was not halachically required to reveal every personal "flaw." At the same time, the rabbi encouraged him that if after a few meetings, he liked a potential partner, it would be useful and appropriate to discuss his history of having struggled with and overcome some issues described as "anxiety." The rabbi pointed out that as a husband, he would want a wife who would be caring, supportive, and nonjudgmental. At the same time, the rabbi pointed out that if he was taking medication, which this young man was not, that would have to be disclosed.

In another example, a 20-year-old man began CBT because of his avoidance of dating. His panic disorder with agoraphobia, which began at age 18, caused difficulty in attending synagogue, and he had fled on numerous occasions due to panic attacks. During treatment, he had begun to date a young woman and contemplated marriage; however, he was concerned about whether and how to discuss his anxiety disorder with her. After receiving a written release from the client, the therapist scheduled a consultation with both the client and prospective spouse. The focus of the consultation session was to educate both about the course and treatment of anxiety disorders. They both reported that this session was helpful. They felt reassured with the information that panic disorder did not indicate a severe character flaw that would require him to avoid marriage.

Clients' embarrassment about a mental health disorder may be so intense that they avoid discussing it within their family. For this reason, we have often found it necessary to include the spouse to some extent in the treatment. The importance of timing in the inclusion of family members is illustrated in the case of a 28-year-old Orthodox man who had been experiencing undiagnosed OCD his entire life but had hidden the disorder from his wife and children. When he was 14, he had discussed his problems with a trusted adult, who counseled him to "keep the bizarre thoughts and actions as hidden as possible from everyone." The client believed that he had successfully hidden his problem, despite such obvious rituals as checking the alarm clock before bed nearly 100 times or putting on and removing his shoes five times whenever he dressed. The client was terrified by the therapist's suggestion to include his spouse in treatment. After cognitive restructuring regarding beliefs about his wife's possible reaction, the patient agreed and found inclusion of his wife liberating. He was finally able to speak openly with her about his OCD. She was also relieved to be included in the treatment process and receive information regarding OCD because she had worried that her husband had a psychotic disorder.

Holidays and Sabbath

Therapists working with Orthodox clients need to be knowledgeable about the Jewish calendar and the rules and rituals associated with daily events, Sabbath, and holidays. These rituals are time-consuming and may cause additional stress for clients with anxiety disorders. However, it is essential that therapists appreciate the sense of continuity and source of joy associated with these religious observances, as well as the embarrassment and pain suffered if the person cannot perform what he or she believes to be a "simple" thing.

The Sabbath, or day of rest, begins at sundown on Friday and ends 1 hour after sundown on Saturday. This day of rest is dedicated to studying religious texts, praying in synagogue, and spending time with the family. Worldly activities including working, driving, turning on lights, and using the telephone are proscribed. Individuals are forbidden to carry any object in public unless medically required or unless the community has created an *eruv* (a ritual fence around the neighborhood that creates a private domain). These restrictions often lead to increased anxiety because clients are usually proscribed from carrying nonvital medications or any security object (e.g., a bottle of water, sucking candies, a cell phone). Individuals are also to refrain from calling their therapist for reassurance except in life-threatening situations.

Visiting family for lengthy meals and attending lengthy religious services at synagogue can also be difficult for individuals who feel trapped and experience the urge to flee when anxious. Avoiding these activities affects self-esteem and leads to social isolation. Men may be honored with requests to lead prayers or read from the Torah in front of the congregation. However, this honor can cause an increase in anxiety because the man is unable to leave the synagogue and becomes the focus of the congregation's attention (Greenberg, Stravynski, & Bilu, 2004).

The observation of Sabbath rituals can also lead to increased anxiety. For instance, a 34-year-old Orthodox woman with OCD was unable to invite guests to her home for Sabbath meals, a culturally expected gesture, owing to OCD symptoms that included hoarding and eating rituals. Her dining room had become overrun with clutter, and hosting any guests was very awkward. Furthermore, the client ate her meals in a ritualized fashion and was particular about which foods could come into contact with other foods. Her eating symptoms caused her and her family great embarrassment, and they avoided all offers to eat meals at others' homes. Treatment was not considered a success until she was both able to eat at a friend's home and then to reciprocate.

Advantages of CBT

There are many advantages of CBT for anxiety and depressive disorders with Orthodox Jews. CBT is generally shorter than insight-oriented therapy and focuses on reducing symptoms and promoting adaptive functioning, all necessary to fulfill family and community roles. By identifying goals and promoting coping skills, the therapist is able to establish a trusting relationship with the client. Clients often choose not to continue treatment, even when recommended by the therapist, after these goals are achieved (Paradis, Friedman, Hatch, & Ackerman, 1996).

Exposure and response prevention have also been found effective for Orthodox Jews with OCD because it emphasizes the return to functioning without directly challenging religious beliefs (Greenberg, 1984). The therapist may need to include a rabbinical consultation if the client has scrupulosity, a form of OCD in which, as noted earlier, the rituals exceed the requirements of religious law and lead the client to neglect their religious or community obligations (Huppert, Siev, & Kushner, 2007).

Limitations of CBT

There are some limitations specific to providing CBT to Orthodox Jewish clients. Group therapy, when incorporated into treatment, often needs to be single gender and focused on specific goals (Silverstein, 1995). Because of feelings of shame, it may be difficult to create an appropriate group, and most clients prefer individual treatment. As suggested previously, in vivo exercises need to be arranged outside of the client's neighborhood to minimize the possibility of gossip and to lessen the embarrassment of a chance encounter. In addition, it is important that the therapist not treat clients with exposure to situations proscribed by religious law. This may be an issue for clients with OCD. If unsure of the possible cultural and religious implications of an intervention, details of exposure exercises should be checked with the client's rabbi. Owing to confidentiality issues, Orthodox clients may feel isolated from others who have similar disorders, and it can be helpful to recommend readings from Orthodox Jewish clinicians as adjuncts to treatment (Twersky, 1993).

CONCLUSION

Orthodox Jews with anxiety, depression, and other psychological disorders are generally underserved by the mental health system (Trappler, Greenberg, & Friedman, 1995). Because of the stigma regarding mental illness, most avoid seeking treatment until the symptoms interfere significantly with functioning. Clients are also less open to considering psychotropic medications as an adjunct to therapy because of the fear of being seen as sick or mentally ill.

These concerns need to be addressed in treatment. In our clinical experience, CBT is quite successful when the Orthodox Jewish client's values and practices are understood, respected, and incorporated into the treatment.

REFERENCES

Beck, A. T., & Steer, R. A. (1993). *Beck Anxiety Inventory manual*. San Antonio, TX: Harcourt Brace.

Beck, A. T., Steer, R. A., & Brown, G. K. (1996). *The Beck Depression Inventory* (2nd ed.). San Antonio, TX: The Psychological Corporation.

Bilu, Y., & Witztum, E. (1993). Working with Jewish ultra-Orthodox patients: Guidelines for a culturally sensitive therapy. *Culture, Medicine and Psychiatry, 17,* 197–233. http://dx.doi.org/10.1007/BF01379326

Cinnirella, M., & Loewenthal, K. M. (1999). Religious and ethnic group influences on beliefs about mental illness: A qualitative interview study. *British Journal of Medical Psychology, 72,* 505–524. http://dx.doi.org/10.1348/000711299160202

Cooperman, A., Smith, G., Alper, B., & Cornibert, S. (2015, August). *A portrait of American Orthodox Jews: A further analysis of the 2013 Survey of U.S. Jews*. Washington, DC: Pew Research Center. Retrieved from http://www.pewforum.org/2015/08/26/a-portrait-of-american-orthodox-jews/

Gall, T. L. (Ed.). (1998). *Worldmark encyclopedia of culture and daily life: Vol. 3. Asia and Oceania*. Cleveland, OH: Eastword.

Greenberg, D. (1984). Are religious compulsions religious or compulsive: A phenomenological study. *American Journal of Psychotherapy, 38,* 524–532. http://dx.doi.org/10.1176/appi.psychotherapy.1984.38.4.524

Greenberg, D., & Shefler, G. (2002). Obsessive compulsive disorder in ultra-Orthodox Jewish patients: A comparison of religious and non-religious symptoms. *Psychology and Psychotherapy, 75,* 123–130. http://dx.doi.org/10.1348/147608302169599

Greenberg, D., Stravynski, A., & Bilu, Y. (2004). Social phobia in ultra-Orthodox Jewish males: Culture-bound syndrome or virtue? *Mental Health, Religion & Culture, 7,* 289–305. http://dx.doi.org/10.1080/13674670310001606496

Greenberg, D., & Witztum, E. (2001). Treatment of strictly religious patients. In M. T. Pato & J. Zohar (Eds.), *Current treatments of obsessive-compulsive disorders* (2nd ed., pp. 173–191). Washington, DC: American Psychiatric Press.

Hays, P. (2001). *Addressing cultural complexities in practice: A framework for clinicians and counselors*. Washington, DC: American Psychological Association. http://dx.doi.org/10.1037/10411-000

Heilman, S. C. (2000). *The defenders of the faith: Inside ultra-Orthodox Jewry*. Berkeley: University of California Press.

Heilman, S. C., & Witztum, E. (1997). Value-sensitive therapy: Learning from ultra-Orthodox patients. *American Journal of Psychotherapy, 51,* 522–541. http://dx.doi.org/10.1176/appi.psychotherapy.1997.51.4.522

Heilman, S. C., & Witztum, E. (2000). All in faith: Religion as the idiom and means of coping with distress. *Mental Health, Religion & Culture, 3,* 115–124. http://dx.doi.org/10.1080/713685606

Hirsch, S. R. (1967). *The Pentateuch*. New York, NY: Judaica Press.

Huppert, J. D., Siev, J., & Kushner, E. S. (2007). When religion and obsessive-compulsive disorder collide: Treating scrupulosity in ultra-Orthodox Jews. *Journal of Clinical Psychology, 63,* 925–941. http://dx.doi.org/10.1002/jclp.20404

Loewenthal, K., Goldblatt, V., Gorton, T., Lubitsch, G., Bicknell, H., Fellowes, D., & Sowden, A. (1995). Gender and depression in Anglo-Jewry. *Psychological Medicine, 25,* 1051–1063. http://dx.doi.org/10.1017/S0033291700037545

Margolese, H. C. (1998). Engaging in psychotherapy with the Orthodox Jew: A critical review. *American Journal of Psychotherapy, 52,* 37–53. http://dx.doi.org/10.1176/appi.psychotherapy.1998.52.1.37

Mohr, S., Borras, L., Betrisey, C., Pierre-Yves, B., Gilliéron, C., & Huguelet, P. (2010). Delusions with religious content in patients with psychosis: How they interact with spiritual coping. *Psychiatry: Interpersonal and Biological Processes, 73,* 158–172. http://dx.doi.org/10.1521/psyc.2010.73.2.158

Ostrov, S. (1978). Sex therapy with Orthodox Jewish couples. *Journal of Sex & Marital Therapy, 4,* 266–278. http://dx.doi.org/10.1080/00926237808403026

Paradis, C. M., Friedman, S., Hatch, M. L., & Ackerman, R. (1996). Cognitive behavioral treatment of anxiety disorders in Orthodox Jews. *Cognitive and Behavioral Practice, 3,* 271–288. http://dx.doi.org/10.1016/S1077-7229(96)80018-6

Rathod, S., Kingdon, D., Phiri, P., & Gobbi, M. (2010). Developing culturally sensitive cognitive behaviour therapy for psychosis for ethnic minority patients by exploration and incorporation of service users' and health professionals' views and opinions. *Behavioural and Cognitive Psychotherapy, 38,* 511–533. http://dx.doi.org/10.1017/S1352465810000378

Rosen, D. D., Rebeta, J. L., & Rothschild, S. Z. (2014). Culturally competent adaptation of cognitive-behavioural therapy for psychosis: Cases of Orthodox Jewish patients with messianic delusions. *Mental Health, Religion & Culture, 17,* 703–713. http://dx.doi.org/10.1080/13674676.2014.902923

Rosen, E. J., & Weltman, S. F. (1996). Jewish families: An overview. In M. McGoldrick & J. Giordano (Eds.), *Ethnicity and family therapy* (2nd ed., pp. 611–630). New York, NY: Guilford Press.

Rosmarin, D. H., Krumrei, E. J., & Andersson, G. (2009). Religion as a predictor of psychological distress in two religious communities. *Cognitive Behaviour Therapy, 38,* 54–64. http://dx.doi.org/10.1080/16506070802477222

Rosmarin, D. H., Pirutinsky, S., Auerbach, R. P., Björgvinsson, T., Bigda-Peyton, J., Andersson, G., . . . Krumrei, E. J. (2011). Incorporating spiritual beliefs into a cognitive model of worry. *Journal of Clinical Psychology, 67,* 691–700. http://dx.doi.org/10.1002/jclp.20798

Rosmarin, D. H., Pirutinsky, S., & Siev, J. (2010). Recognition of scrupulosity and non-religious OCD by Orthodox and non-Orthodox Jews. *Journal of Social and Clinical Psychology, 29,* 930–944. http://dx.doi.org/10.1521/jscp.2010.29.8.930

Shafranske, E. P., & Cummings, J. P. (2013). Religious and spiritual beliefs, affiliations, and practices of psychologists. In K. Pargament, A. Mahoney, & E. P. Shafranske (Eds.), *APA handbook of psychology, religion, and spirituality: Vol. 2. An applied psychology of religion and spirituality* (pp. 23–41). Washington, DC: American Psychological Association.

Silverstein, R. (1995). Bending the conventional rules when treating the ultra-Orthodox in the group setting. *International Journal of Group Psychotherapy, 45*, 237–249. http://dx.doi.org/10.1080/00207284.1995.11490775

Sperry, L., & Shafranske, E. P. (Eds.). (2005). *Spiritually oriented psychotherapy.* Washington, DC: American Psychological Association. http://dx.doi.org/10.1037/10886-000

Spiegler, M. D., & Guevremont, D. C. (1998). *Contemporary behavior therapy* (3rd ed.). Pacific Grove, CA: Brooks/Cole.

Tanaka-Matsumi, J., Seiden, D., & Lam, K. (1996). The Culturally Informed Functional Assessment (CIFA) Interview: A strategy for cross-cultural behavioral practice. *Cognitive and Behavioral Practice, 3*, 215–233. http://dx.doi.org/10.1016/S1077-7229(96)80015-0

Trappler, B., Greenberg, S., & Friedman, S. (1995). Treatment of Hassidic Jewish patients in a general hospital medical–psychiatric unit. *Psychiatric Services, 46*, 833–835. http://dx.doi.org/10.1176/ps.46.8.833

Twersky, A. J. (1993). *I am I.* Brooklyn, NY: Shar Press/Mesorah.

Wikler, M. (1986). Pathways to treatment: How Orthodox Jews enter therapy. *Social Casework, 67*, 113–118. http://dx.doi.org/10.1177/104438948606700207

Witztum, E., & Buchbinder, J. T. (2001). Strategic culture sensitive therapy with religious Jews. *International Review of Psychiatry, 13*, 117–124. http://dx.doi.org/10.1080/09540260124954

II

ADDITIONAL CULTURAL MINORITY POPULATIONS

9

COGNITIVE BEHAVIOR THERAPY WITH CULTURALLY DIVERSE OLDER ADULTS

ANGELA W. LAU AND LISA M. KINOSHITA

Currently, one in every seven Americans is 65 years or older, and the population of older Americans continues to grow. It is predicted that by 2040, the proportion of older adults in the United States will grow to 21.7% of the general population (Administration on Aging, 2016). By 2030, 28% or 21.1 million of United States elders will be from ethnic minority cultures, representing a vast increase in the older ethnic minority population (Administration on Aging, 2016). In part, this latter growth is because of post–World War II legislation that enabled ethnic minorities to immigrate to the United States in record numbers many years ago (e.g., the War Bride Act, GI Fiancée's Act, Refugee Relief Act of 1953, and U.S. Refugee Act of 1980). Also adding to the increase has been the improved mortality of ethnic minorities living in the United States and an increase in the number of adult immigrants sponsoring aging parents to come to the United States and live with them.

http://dx.doi.org/10.1037/0000119-010
Culturally Responsive Cognitive Behavior Therapy, Second Edition: Practice and Supervision, G. Y. Iwamasa and P. A. Hays (Editors)
Copyright © 2019 by the American Psychological Association. All rights reserved.

Several empirical and case studies suggest that cognitive behavior therapy (CBT) is effective with older adults (Gatz et al., 1998; Knight & Satre, 1999). CBT modified to accommodate older adults has been effective for late-life depression (Gatz et al., 1998), generalized anxiety disorder (Durham, Chambers, MacDonald, Power, & Major, 2003), and insomnia (Morin, Kowatch, Barry, & Walton, 1993). A CBT approach has been effective in reducing anxiety, anger, and depression in middle-aged and older adult caregivers of patients with dementia (Gallagher-Thompson et al., 2000). Researchers are beginning to demonstrate the utility of CBT with medically ill elders in primary care settings and skilled nursing facilities (Stanley et al., 2009). Cognitive and behavioral therapies also appear effective in treating cognitively impaired elders (Cohen-Mansfield, 2001).

However, despite the growth in CBT research with older adults, the majority of the work focuses on European American elders (Areán & Gallagher-Thompson, 1996). In a literature review, Areán and Gallagher-Thompson (1996) found that only 22% of controlled treatment outcome studies for older adults with mental disorders included ethnic minority participants. This lack of inclusion is due in part to the difficulties in recruiting and retaining older minority participants (Lau & Gallagher-Thompson, 2002). However, the results of the few studies that do include diverse elders are promising. Specifically, CBT has been found effective in the treatment of anxiety and depression in Japanese and Asian Indian elders (Gupta, 2003; Kinoshita & Gallagher-Thompson, 2004), in reducing depressive symptoms and somatic complaints in community-dwelling Chinese American elders (Dai et al., 1999), and in the treatment of depression in diverse ethnic minority elders (Areán & Miranda, 1996). Furthermore, the results of these studies emphasize the importance of understanding the interaction between age and culture within the clinical process and the need to tailor assessment and therapy to incorporate clients' traditions, worldviews, cultural practices, and beliefs (Hays, 1995).

Before embarking on a discussion of culturally diverse groups, it is important to acknowledge the variability within these populations. There is great diversity within ethnic groups in terms of culture, language, immigration, acculturation histories, and life experiences based on particular cohorts. Thus, not all members of these groups will fit into the categories that are mentioned throughout this chapter. The groupings are discussed as a model for the reader. CBT therapists are responsible for conceptualizing each of their culturally diverse clients' cases with the particular individual's life experiences and worldviews in mind. Although the focus of this chapter is on CBT with elders of ethnic minority cultures, the information presented is also relevant to elders of European American heritage, elders who identify with more than one (dominant or minority) culture, and ethnic minority elders who identify more with the dominant culture than with their ethnic minority origin.

TREATMENT ISSUES WITH ETHNIC MINORITY ELDERS

There are some treatment issues therapists should keep in mind to provide culturally responsive therapy to their ethnic minority older adults. The issues mentioned in this section are generally more apparent among immigrant or less acculturated elders of ethnic minority groups, in particular with ethnic minority older adults who have poorer English proficiency and thereby less access and cultural fluency to activate available social and mental health care resources (Gelman, 2010; Jimenez et al., 2010).

First, members of ethnic minority cultures often hold explanatory models of illness that differ from the biomedical model of the dominant U.S. culture (Kleinman, 1980). These different explanatory models contribute to distinct concepts of what constitutes appropriate treatment and functional coping strategies (Jimenez, Bartels, Cardenas, Dhaliwal, & Alegría, 2012). For example, many individuals of Chinese, Mexican, and Native American heritage believe that illnesses are the result of imbalances in one's life. Proper treatment involves restoring balance through diet, herbal remedies, religious practices, and environmental manipulation (Braun & Browne, 1998; Gallagher-Thompson, Talamantes, Ramirez, & Valverde, 1996; Henderson & Henderson, 2002). African American, Native American, and Latino/Hispanic elders are also more likely to believe spiritual or mystical forces are responsible for their maladies and therefore seek folk medicine or a spiritual practitioner rather than pharmaceutical relief or psychotherapy (Connell, Roberts, McLaughlin, & Akinleye, 2009; Harris, 1998; Henderson & Henderson, 2002; Parks, 2003).

Some ethnic minority elders believe that behavioral issues or psychological difficulties are the result of severe mental illness (Lee, Lee, & Diwan, 2010; D. Liu, Hinton, Tran, Hinton, & Barker, 2008), personal weakness, lack of discipline or willpower (Jang, Chiriboga, & Okazaki, 2009; Leong & Lau, 2001), or moral misconduct by an individual or by one's ancestors (Braun & Browne, 1998; Gallagher-Thompson, Talamantes, Ramirez, & Valverde, 1996). Such beliefs decrease the likelihood that the individual will seek mental health services because admission of these problems would bring shame and stigma to themselves or their family (Conner et al., 2010; Jimenez, Bartels, Cardenas, & Alegría, 2013). For example, a Chinese family that believes Alzheimer's disease is punishment for an individual not complying with Confucian traditions and values may not seek help for the individual with dementia. Moreover, if the dementia is considered a justified punishment by spiritual forces (e.g., ancestors, gods, spirits), family members may choose to experience the difficulties as atonement rather than seek support services to improve the condition or circumstances.

Other ethnic minority elders may believe that behavioral or psychological issues are part of the normal aging process and therefore find it unnecessary to seek assessment or treatment (Hinton, Franz, Yeo, & Levkoff, 2005; Suzuki, Goebert, Ahmed, & Lu, 2015).

Elders, especially ethnic minority elders, are also less likely to seek or accept help from "outsiders," especially mental health providers. In response to experiences of discrimination, abuse, and exploitation, minority communities have often developed their own institutions and support networks to meet the physical and emotional needs of their members. These supports can include religious communities and institutions, extended family including non–blood-related kin, and aid societies. Ethnic minority elders and their families also may strongly subscribe to cultural expectations regarding the responsibility and obligation of younger generations to care for their elders (Griffin-Pierce et al., 2008).

When ethnic minority elders do finally reach out to mainstream systems of care for emotional distress or behavioral issues, they are more likely to prefer to talk to a medical professional than to a psychologist (Gum et al., 2010; Jimenez et al., 2012) and indeed are more likely to see a medical doctor than a mental health specialist (Black, 2000). Furthermore, older adults, including ethnic minority elders, are more likely to be brought in by a concerned family member or referral from a primary care physician rather than by self-referral (Baker, 1990, as cited in Baker & Takeshita, 2001). Given the cautiousness with which many elders approach mental health services, therapists will need to take special care in the initial stages of therapy to develop rapport with and engage older clients.

Finally, regardless of culture, ethnic minority elders are often experiencing a decline in physical and cognitive functioning. Therapists must be sensitive to possible sensory losses (e.g., impaired hearing and vision), slower or impaired cognitive processes (e.g., slowed motor responding and the need for more time to recall information), and other physical changes (e.g., in sleep, appetite, and libido). Therapists should also be aware of life changes and stressors that are more common in later life, including loss (e.g., retirement, death of family members and friends), chronic and acute illness, disability caused by or exacerbated by chronic or acute medical conditions, and a shift in or renewal of interests and relationships (e.g., volunteerism, travel, friendships, romantic partnerships).

COMMON PRESENTING PROBLEMS

There are a number of mental health issues with which older clients commonly present, and being prepared for these and how different cultures understand them will aid therapists in treating these populations. These problems are shared by older adults of most cultural and ethnic groups: depression, dementia, grief, bereavement, intergenerational issues, and caregiver stress. There are also behavioral medicine issues that are common among this population. We discuss all of these issues in this section.

Depression

Depression in older adults is strongly associated with the loss in functional status resulting from physical illness or disability (Zeiss, Lewinsohn, Rohde, & Seeley, 1996). Older adults have the highest rate of suicide across all age groups; those who committed suicide were more likely to have a mood disorder as well as poor physical health (Dennis & Brown, 2011; Zhong, Chiu, & Conwell, 2016).

Therapists also need to be aware that depression can cause mild to moderate cognitive impairments (e.g., difficulty with short-term memory, impaired ability to focus and sustain attention) that may be misdiagnosed as a neurocognitive disorder. However, with successful treatment of the depression, these impairments can improve (Meyers, 1998).

Anxiety

Anxiety disorders are prevalent in older adults, affecting approximately 10% to 20% of this cohort (Cassidy & Rector, 2008). In culturally diverse populations, the lifetime prevalence of anxiety disorders ranges from 9% to 18% (National Institute of Mental Health, 2007). Specifically, in Asian older adults, the lifetime prevalence of anxiety disorders is 9%, 16% in older African Americans, and 18% in Hispanic older adults. CBT is effective in treating generalized anxiety disorder in older adult patients (Durham et al., 2003; Stanley et al., 2009). Other studies have found that modified CBT for PTSD alone, PTSD with panic attacks, and panic disorder with agoraphobia is effective with ethnic minority adults (Hinton, Chhean, et al., 2005). Treatment interventions include psychoeducation, cognitive restructuring, relaxation, and exposure. The modified CBT treatment involves bilingual therapists, psychiatric measures normed on the culturally diverse patient population, and culturally appropriate visualizations.

Dementia (or Major Neurocognitive Disorder)

Dementia is one of the most common mental disorders in older adults (Langa et al., 2017). It is estimated that in 2016, more than 10% of adults aged 65 and older have Alzheimer's disease or a related dementia, and its prevalence is expected to grow exponentially over time, tripling by 2050 (Hebert, Weuve, Scherr, & Evans, 2013). Ethnic minorities are more likely than White older adults to have Alzheimer's disease and related dementias (Alzheimer's Association, 2016). Unfortunately, ethnic minority families are also less likely to seek help for an older family member with Alzheimer's disease or a related dementia (Parveen, Peltier, & Oyebode, 2017; Shanley et al., 2012). Reasons for this reticence include the belief that cognitive impairment is a part of the normal aging process, that there is no hope for the condition, lack of knowledge about the disease and available services, and that seeking outside assistance would bring further shame and stigma to the family.

Individuals in the early stages of dementia are likely to experience depression and/or anxiety that can be successfully treated (Orgeta, Qazi, Spector, & Orrell, 2015). Early-stage dementia patients may also benefit from memory-enhancement strategies that capitalize on their existing strengths and compensate for cognitive weaknesses (Clare & Woods, 2004). Although some ethnic minority older adults will present to their primary care provider with concerns about declining memory, it is more likely that family members will bring the elder to the attention of a health care professional in the later stages of the disease, seeking assistance in managing difficult behaviors exhibited by the older adult, such as agitation, aggression, paranoia, hallucinations, wandering, or other unsafe behaviors (Mukadam, Cooper, & Livingston, 2013).

Caregiver Stress

Ethnic minority families often keep a disabled or ill elder in the community and provide care at home rather than hire a paid caregiver or place the older adult in a skilled nursing facility or other external living arrangement (McCormick et al., 1996). As a result, many caregivers are partners or adult children who are themselves older adults. Caregivers often experience social isolation and frustration from their caregiving responsibilities and the cultural expectations placed on them as caregivers (e.g., to provide care without complaint or assistance). The stress and burden of caregiving can result in depression, anxiety, anger, increased somatic complaints, and the exacerbation of existing health problems (Ory, Yee, Tennstedt, & Schulz, 2000).

Grief and Bereavement

With advancing age, it is inevitable that older adults will experience losses caused by death. Losing a spouse, relatives, friends, and even adult children becomes more common. Also, it is not unusual for an older adult to begin to experience anticipatory grief for someone who is in the dying process, has been placed outside the home, or, in the case of people with a major neurocognitive disorder, is functionally no longer the same person.

Intergenerational Issues

Ethnic minority elders who are less acculturated and abide by traditional values and role expectations are more likely to experience conflict with younger generations who have become more acculturated to Western values and worldviews. These older adults are likely to experience increased stress, anxiety, and depression as a result of the acculturative mismatch (Hwang, Wood, & Fujimoto, 2010; P. P. Liu, 2015). Unfortunately, the culture gap also may reduce the older adult's support system and ability to engage in formerly effective coping or problem-resolution strategies, particularly if the elder does not learn English, while younger generations forget their native language or never learn it. The shame of a perceived loss in authority or culturally expected role may further prevent the ethnic minority elder from seeking support from others.

The changing nature of intergenerational support and intergenerational ties can also lead to poorer mental health (Fingerman, Sechrist, & Birditt, 2013). Grandparents are increasingly providing primary caregiving to their grandchildren, resulting in poorer mental and physical health (Hadfield, 2014). An aging parent may require more physical, material, or emotional support from their adult children or grandchildren due to functional decline, widowhood, or social isolation. This change in relational dynamic can lead to caregiving burden for older adult children providing support to both their old-old parent(s) as well as to their young adult children (Fingerman et al., 2013), to emotional distress in the older parent if younger generations do not meet traditional value-based expectations of caring for family elders (Dong & Zhang, 2016), or to emotional distress related to the resulting role reversal (Plowfield, Raymond, & Blevins, 2000).

Chronic Medical Conditions

Due to improvements in preventative care and advances in medical technology and interventions, at least 80% of older adults are living with one chronic medical condition, and at least 50% have two or more comorbid medical conditions, leading to increased reports of disability and lower quality of life (Centers for Disease Control and Prevention [CDC] and the Merck Company Foundation, 2007). Common medical conditions that result in changes in functional status include diabetes mellitus, hypertension, stroke, chronic obstructive pulmonary disorder, cardiovascular disease, insomnia, cancer, sexual dysfunction, and chronic pain (Sarkisian, Hays, Berry, & Mangione, 2001). Changes in health behaviors, including improved treatment adherence, nutrition, physical activity, stress reduction, can prevent many of these medical conditions or can prevent further health decompensation (American Psychological Association Office on Aging, 2005). Helping to address chronic medical conditions is also important because physical illness, functional disability, and poor self-reported health were strongly associated with high suicide rates in older adults (Almeida et al., 2016; Erlangsen, Stenager, & Conwell, 2015; Fässberg et al., 2016).

Ethnic minority status is significantly related to lower self-reported health and poorer health outcomes as a result of a lack of preventative care and treatment, poorer quality of life (e.g., inadequate pain management, lower active life), increased disability, and increased mortality from chronic medical conditions (see Institute of Medicine, 2003; Hummer, Benjamins, & Rogers, 2004). Of note is a pattern of discrimination in the physical and mental health treatment of minority clients that cannot be attributed to known factors other than race and ethnicity (Hummer et al., 2004; Institute of Medicine, 2003). Problems with cultural competence during patient–provider interactions, challenges posed by structural barriers, issues with readiness for change, and differences in health beliefs may contribute to even poorer health outcomes for ethnic minority elders.

Mental Disorders Secondary to Physical Illness or Disability

Older adults are at greater risk for developing psychological difficulties secondary to physical illness or disability (CDC and the Merck Company Foundation, 2007). Some medical conditions may have associated psychological symptoms (e.g., Parkinson's disease, stroke, hyperthyroidism). Prescribed medications or polypharmacy can also result in neuropsychiatric symptoms (e.g., anxiety, insomnia, depression).

Symptoms of depression and anxiety are also common reactions to physical illness and losses associated with a change in functional status (Zeiss et al., 1996). It is not unusual for an older adult to experience depression due to increased social isolation loss of mobility, loss of independence, or inability to engage in previously effective coping strategies because of sensory loss or physical limitations. Perceived loss of control and loss of one's identity can also lead to feelings of shame, anxiety, depression, or anger. Refusal to accept one's circumstances and to adapt or make accommodations to maintain or improve quality of life can lead to emotional distress or behavioral disturbance that can cause further mental or physical decline.

End-of-Life Issues

Older adults may experience emotional distress as they engage in life review or may experience a developmental or existential crisis when faced with their mortality. Anxiety about one's mortality may also lead to avoidance in making decisions about life-sustaining treatment or discussing their wishes with important stakeholders.

End-of-life care preferences and decision-making are related to ethnic minority status (Burgio et al., 2016; Connolly, Sampson, & Purandare, 2012; LoPresti, Dement, & Gold, 2016; Shen et al., 2016). Ethnic minorities are less likely to enroll in hospice care, have a do not resuscitate (DNR) order, or have a documented advance directive (Burgio et al., 2016; Connolly et al., 2012; LoPresti et al., 2016). Possible contributing factors include lack of knowledge about end-of-life care options, the ethnic elder's religious beliefs (e.g., life always has value) and cultural values (e.g., discussing bad news as impolite, disrespectful, bad luck, or causing terminal illness or death; may cause hopelessness, anxiety, depression; shared decision-making), and a mistrust of the medical system (e.g., DNR status will lead to inferior care; Searight & Gafford, 2005). However, education about end-of-life care options and how providers discuss end of life with patients and their families can make a difference in an ethnic elder's decision-making at this time (LoPresti et al., 2016; Shen et al., 2016).

Cohort-Specific Problems

Therapists will also want to be aware of mental health problems within specific cohorts of ethnic minority elders. For example, many immigrant populations, including refugees from Syria, Central America, Southeast Asia, and Africa, have experienced trauma associated with political oppression, civil unrest, and war. Consequently, these individuals are more susceptible to posttraumatic stress disorder (PTSD) and its sequelae. Older ethnic minority veterans are also more likely to experience PTSD than European American veterans, possibly as a result of racial discrimination that placed them in greater danger with minimal support (Allen, 1986; Loo, 1994).

Cultural Concepts of Distress

Therapists need to be aware that certain symptom clusters are more common in particular cultures. These clusters are recognized in the *Diagnostic and Statistical Manual of Mental Disorders* (fifth ed.; *DSM–5*) as cultural concepts of distress but are not formal *DSM–5* diagnoses (American Psychiatric Association, 2013). Cultural idioms of distress are cultural variations in symptom presentation and represent the attitudes, beliefs, and illness expectations of a particular cultural group. For example, racial minorities have been found to report more somatic symptoms than Whites in the context of a depressive disorder (Bagayogo, Interian, & Escobar, 2013). Saint Arnault and Kim

(2008) found that Asian subgroups with high Beck Depression Inventory scores reported unique somatic patterns that may be related to their respective display rules or the social group norms on expressions of distress.

Although *DSM–5*, as well as the *International Classification of Diseases* (10th revision—Clinical Modification; World Health Organization, 2010) classification system, are trying to move away from the construct of a culturally bound syndrome and encourage a more conceptual lens through which to assess and comprehend an individual's presentation and understanding of distress, cultural syndromes, such as *susto*, Dhat syndrome, or Zar illness, are still widely accepted and formally recognized in many non-Western cultures (Grover et al., 2016; Mianji & Semnani, 2015). Different cohort groups may also use unique language and idioms of distress to explain their experiences to others, which will influence their help-seeking behaviors (Letamendi et al., 2013). It is important for therapists to be aware of what their ethnic elder client perceives as the cause of their problem because it will influence how they respond to psychodiagnostic questions, as well as their receptivity to mental health treatment.

STRENGTHS AND LIMITATIONS OF CBT WITH ETHNIC MINORITY ELDERS

CBT is structured, psychoeducational, oriented toward problem-solving, and directive in its treatment approach, all of which are compatible with the style of relating of many ethnic minority groups (Lin, 2002). At the same time, CBT allows for creativity in adapting each treatment plan to individual needs and resources. CBT's focus on the present, specific behaviors, goal-setting, skill practice, and evaluation can decrease clients' anxiety regarding the ambiguity and vulnerability that often arise during therapy (Lin, 2002). Further, conceptualizing therapy as "going to class" can help to decrease the stigma associated with mental health care (Gallagher-Thompson et al., 1997; Lin, 2002).

CBT emphasizes listening to the client and understanding his or her worldview. It also encourages therapists to interface with the client's environment and support network to identify appropriate change mechanisms for a successful treatment plan. This approach lends itself well to elders who hold a collective worldview and whose thoughts, feelings, and behaviors are intertwined with those of other family and community members. Working with the client's support network has the added benefit of helping the therapist gain the trust of the elder and his or her family, which in turn facilitates learning and increases the likelihood that the new behavior will be maintained over time.

CBT does present certain limitations when working with this population. For example, ethnic minority elders may lack the formal education necessary to be comfortable with the record keeping, homework assignments, and other school-related behaviors typical of a CBT treatment plan. Many immigrant elders from rural areas and developing countries will have limited literacy skills in English and their native language. Moreover, because of social and economic barriers related to segregation and racism, members of ethnic minority groups who grew up and were educated in the United States are also likely to have had less formal education than European Americans.

Another limitation of CBT is its assumption that the client holds an internal locus of control (i.e., sees himself or herself as an agent of change). An internal locus of control requires a sense of autonomy and independence in relation to the external world. In contrast, ethnic minority elders from cultures that value collectivism and interdependence often experience the world with an external locus of control and thus may have difficulty accepting and engaging with CBT.

The need to identify and address affect in CBT may also be difficult for older adults from cultures in which disclosure of one's emotions is considered a sign of weakness or shameful. Similar difficulties may arise when such elders are asked to isolate, identify, and admit to negative cognitions.

CBT WITH ETHNIC MINORITY ELDERS

A number of interventions can enhance the assessment process when working with culturally diverse older adults. In this section, we review assessment methodologies, discuss ways to adapt CBT interventions for this population, and conclude with a case example that illustrates a culturally sensitive approach to CBT.

Initial Assessment

In the initial assessment, it is important to schedule extra time to develop rapport so that the elder is more likely to openly report information and engage with therapy. In addition, obtaining elders' personal histories takes longer because elders' histories *are* longer. Elders may experience some embarrassment in revealing personal information to a stranger, and thus the therapist may wish to emphasize the confidential nature of all therapy sessions. A therapist may establish trust and a personal relationship with the client through some ritual of reciprocity (e.g., an exchange of personal information or a "gift" in the form of helpful information). For example, with a Mexican American elder, sharing some personal information while engaging in small talk (*platica*) can help to establish trust (*confianza*) with the client. At the same time, clinical information can be gathered during this informal conversation. In addition, it is important to embed a brief cognitive functioning assessment into the initial sessions. Questions geared toward long- and short-term memory (e.g., When did you move to the area? What did you do yesterday?) will assist the therapist in learning about the elder's history while also assessing cognition and building rapport. With the elder's permission, collateral sources (e.g., a partner or adult child) will be helpful in obtaining additional information about the elder's history, functioning, and cognition.

A source of discomfort for some ethnic minority elders may be the identity of the therapist. Older clients in general may have less confidence in a therapist who is significantly younger than they are. Similarly, ethnic minority elders may have difficulty trusting therapists who are ethnically different from themselves. A therapist can work to overcome this distrust by learning as much as possible about the client's culture, working to understand the elder's explanatory model of his or her illness, and, as much as possible, incorporating this model into the therapist's explanation of the problem and the treatment plan. For example, interviewing techniques such as the LEARN model (*listen* with sympathy and understanding to the patient's perception of the problem, *explain* your perception of the problem, *acknowledge* and discuss the differences and similarities, *recommend* treatment, *negotiate* agreement; Berlin & Fowkes, 1983, p. 934) and the work by Kleinman and colleagues have been used to elicit a person's explanatory model and to negotiate treatment compliance (Carrillo, Green, & Betancourt, 1999; Kleinman, Eisenberg, & Good, 1978).

Incorporating a client's cultural beliefs and vocabulary regarding feelings and emotions is crucial when working with clients who speak English as a second language. Given that individuals tend to be more comfortable expressing intense emotions in their primary language, it can be helpful to allow clients to express their feelings in their native language, although this places responsibility on the therapist for learning the meaning of the words. It may also be helpful to use analogies or stories from the client's culture, life history, or past experiences to help the elder understand the therapist's point and to engage and motivate the client in the therapy process. Therapists should keep in mind that ethnic minority elders may adopt a passive communication style when asked questions. As a result, therapists need to be careful to avoid pathologizing verbal and nonverbal responses that are acceptable within the client's context (e.g., lack of eye contact, difficulty verbalizing feelings, being overly agreeable with the therapist, denial of negative experiences).

Although confidentiality is important, in many ethnic groups the immediate and the extended family are an important aspect of the older client's worldview and value system. Therefore, with the client's consent, interviewing the client's family, friends, and other members of the support system can provide valuable information and help the therapist to better understand the client's values, beliefs, strengths, and community. Such information also helps in determining whether particular thoughts and behaviors are culturally congruent. In some cases, inclusion of a traditional healer or religious leader will enhance the elder's acceptance of therapeutic recommendations and commitment to therapy.

After rapport is established, it is important for the therapist to set a clear expectation of the client's role. In the first few sessions, the therapist should introduce the CBT model, educate the client about the importance of therapy compliance and homework, emphasize the client's active role in therapy, and explain effective agenda setting. Some clients may believe that the therapist will "fix them" like a physician. Therefore, it is helpful for the therapist to discuss his or her role in therapy as a guide and active collaborator who will coach the client throughout therapy.

Because older adults are more likely to fatigue, taking short breaks during formal cognitive assessments and extensive clinical interviews is important. This time can also be used to develop rapport with the older adult.

Standardized Assessments

The use of standardized tests with older adults requires caution for at least three reasons (Hays, 1996). First, older adults frequently experience standardized tests as intimidating, confusing, or simply irrelevant. Second, older people referred for mental health problems frequently have physical health problems that can interfere with the attention and concentration required for such tests. Finally, few standardized assessments include age-appropriate norms for older people, particularly elders of ethnic minority cultures. When a standardized assessment is necessary, written assessment tools in the client's native language can help to reduce the probability of the client misunderstanding questions in a second language.

Assessing Affect

Likert and Likert-type rating scales can be less biased in assessing mood states than formal assessment measures and can provide a less threatening medium for disclosure. For example, rating scales that use pictures to depict the anchor points have more face validity and may be perceived as a more innocuous request for information (e.g., using a continuum of happy to sad or angry faces). Another strategy for assessing affect involves asking the client to describe his or her feelings from the point of view of a third party (e.g., "If Mrs. X were [in a similar situation], how and what do you think she would feel, think, or act?"). This may allow the client to feel more distance and therefore increased comfort in talking about emotions.

Adapting CBT Interventions

Several adaptations to CBT can be helpful when working with culturally diverse elders. Given the cognitive changes that arise as a result of the aging process, adapting CBT approaches to accommodate how older adults learn and recall information has been effective (Knight & Satre, 1999). To enhance the learning of specific skills, the therapist will want to keep sessions simple and structured, with regular review of important concepts. Recall of therapy concepts can be enhanced by the use of visual aids such as boards, charts, and handouts, with enlarged print when needed. In recent years, mobile technology (i.e., electronic tablets, smartphones), websites, and apps have been used successfully to complement the therapy experience (Heron & Smyth, 2010) and can be adapted for older adults. Allowing the older adult to take notes or audiotape sessions can also facilitate the maintenance of behavior change at home. For clients who have impaired vision or hearing, the therapist may use and recommend a magnifying glass with good lighting and a pocket-talker to enhance the therapist's voice for clearer understanding.

In general, older adult clients prefer sessions during the daytime rather than the evening, when visual difficulties may make it hard to travel to and from the therapist's office. A number of older adults experience a change in their circadian rhythms that results in an advanced sleep phase pattern in which they are most alert and active in the morning (Ancoli-Israel et al., 2003). Reliance on family members or the use of public transportation means that therapists will need to be flexible regarding the scheduling of appointments. For some clients who are too physically weak or ill to travel, conducting therapy sessions in the client's home or nursing facility may be necessary.

When assigning homework, therapists need to consider what is normal within the client's cultural context and daily routine. Therapists should be careful to keep homework assignments as culturally compatible as possible, assigning tasks that fit easily into the client's existing activities. Tasks may be stigmatizing if too far outside the norms of the client's life or if they require too much external assistance to complete. However, enlisting the assistance of the client's significant others can facilitate the completion of homework.

When addressing the affective or cognitive components of CBT, using analogies, a third-party example (see the Assessing Affect section in this chapter), or examples from folktales, historic lore, or cultural proverbs may help the client to feel more comfortable and increase the person's ability to understand the concepts. Therapists may need to be more directive in the beginning of therapy to point out and provide examples of the client's maladaptive thoughts and their consequences to model and guide the client in his or her ability to attend to metacognitions.

CASE EXAMPLE

The client, AC,[1] was an 82-year-old Chinese American man referred to therapy by his primary care physician for increasing somatic complaints. Initially, AC reported that he was the primary caregiver for his wife, who was in the moderate stage of Alzheimer's disease. AC admitted that he was having difficulty caring for her, particularly when she demonstrated difficult behaviors (i.e., irritability, angry outbursts). When asked, AC denied feeling depressed but reported physical symptoms of upset stomach, low back pain, frequent headaches, insomnia, and heart palpitations. His medical history was significant for hypertension and Type II diabetes mellitus, both managed with medications. He had no prior history of mental illness or psychological treatment.

During the initial assessment, AC reported the following: He and his family had emigrated from mainland China to the United States 40 years earlier in search of better economic opportunities. In China, he had 8 years of formal education and worked as a deliveryman for various businesses. After moving to the United States, he and his family settled in San Francisco's Chinatown. AC worked as a butcher a block away from his residence and rarely left the community, even after retiring. His primary language was Mandarin, and he spoke some limited English. He denied having a hearing impairment but frequently asked the therapist to repeat herself. He required glasses when reading.

With AC's consent, his daughter Mei was included in the intake process as a source of additional information. Mei worked full time and lived in a separate house with her two teenaged children. She helped to care for her mother to the extent that she could, and AC had become increasingly dependent on her for the management of their household. Contrary to AC's self-report, Mei described him as increasingly irritable, emotionally labile, and apathetic. She reported that he frequently exhibited depressed mood, hopelessness, and passive suicidal ideation. She said that he was becoming more isolated because of his caregiving responsibilities. On the basis of AC's self-reported symptoms, Mei's description, and the therapist's observations, the therapist diagnosed AC with major depressive disorder.

Initially, AC was uncomfortable with the idea of therapy because he did not perceive the therapist as having any credibility. Although the therapist was Chinese American, he believed that she could not be competent because she was a woman and much younger than he. After the first session, AC did not attend the next scheduled session. When the therapist called to reschedule his missed appointment, she carefully listened to his concerns

---

[1]Case material in this chapter has been disguised to protect client confidentiality.

regarding his wife, gave empathic responses, and provided information regarding how behavioral interventions could help him to better manage his wife. This informational exchange was meant to be a form of gift giving aimed at building rapport and trust with AC, and it worked. After the interaction, AC began attending therapy sessions regularly. Over time, he was able to learn more about the therapist as a person and to experience her knowledge and empathy regarding his immigration experiences. To reinforce his willingness to attend sessions, the therapist was careful to accommodate AC's scheduling needs, which involved relying on his daughter for transportation. This also allowed for the opportunity to occasionally include AC's daughter in the therapy sessions.

The therapist assessed AC's comfort and proficiency with the English language and found that although AC was not fluent in English, his comfort level and grasp of the language were sufficient to continue therapy together. To better understand her client's explanatory model of illness, she asked AC what he believed caused his somatic problems and what he believed would result in their resolution. AC stated he believed that his physical problems were caused by an imbalance of his *chi* (i.e., energy or life force). He explained that he was not eating right or exercising regularly as he did before caring for his wife. He did not see how he would benefit from mental health services because he believed he could eliminate his symptoms if he made a concerted effort to eat a balanced diet and exercise daily. The therapist did not challenge his explanatory model of illness. She instead used his belief in the interaction of body and mind to describe his presenting problems, and she incorporated elements of his explanatory model (e.g., the importance of enhancing one's *chi* during times of stress) to describe the rationale for the treatment plan. Although the therapist's knowledge of the basic principles of Chinese medicine facilitated the therapeutic process, it was her solicitation of and listening to AC's explanatory model, and the incorporation of his beliefs, that resulted in AC's engagement in the therapy process.

The therapist spent four sessions educating AC about the CBT model, emphasizing the importance of homework assignments and agenda setting and discussing therapy goals. She also explained her role as his therapist. She said that the sessions would be very structured, using an agenda. They decided collaboratively that his goals would be to reduce his physical distress and to improve his ability to cope with his caregiving responsibilities. They agreed that they would focus a portion of each session on caregiving concerns (i.e., questions about behavior management regarding his wife), and the rest of the session would be dedicated to attaining his goals of reducing the physical distress and improving his coping skills.

Initially, AC's mood was assessed weekly via his verbal self-report and completion of the Chinese version of the Geriatric Depression Scale (Stokes,

Thompson, Murphy, & Gallagher-Thompson, 2002). However, his self-report and responses on the questionnaire were not congruent with his clinical presentation or with his daughter's report. Consequently, the therapist changed her approach to incorporate a Likert-type rating scale anchored by a happy face and a sad face. This method of assessment appeared to more closely reflect the therapist's observations and his daughter's reports and was incorporated into the weekly assessment of AC's stress and somatic symptoms.

Because of AC's apathy at the beginning of therapy, behavioral rather than cognitive interventions were the initial focus. The therapist asked AC to complete the Older Person's Pleasant Event Schedule (OP–PES; Gallagher & Thompson, 1981) at home. The OP–PES is a self-report measure that asks the client to rate the frequency and enjoyment of a number of activities that older people often find enjoyable (e.g., kissing, touching, showing affection, listening to birds sing). Although Mei helped translate unfamiliar words while he completed the scale, AC did not endorse many of the items because they were not culturally relevant to him. At the next session, the client and therapist collaboratively developed a list of pleasant events on the basis of his response to the OP–PES, and he was asked to complete at least three of the pleasant events on his list. The next week he reported that he did not do any of the activities. When the therapist explored his homework noncompliance, he reported that he did not like the activities listed. In the session, the therapist asked him to create a list of activities he enjoyed. This list included items such as doing tai chi and Chinese calligraphy, walking, reading the Chinese newspaper, frequenting businesses in his Chinatown neighborhood, and visiting his friends. After revising the list, his homework compliance was 100%. Within a month, his mood had improved as assessed by his daily mood ratings, his daughter's report, and the therapist's observations; he reported fewer somatic symptoms and reduced caregiver stress; and he showed an increased ability to manage his wife's problematic behaviors.

Once AC became more behaviorally engaged, the therapist began to introduce cognitive interventions into therapy. AC appeared to have several maladaptive thoughts that contributed to his depressed mood. One of these was the belief that his daughter's refusal to drop her employment and other responsibilities to provide full-time care for her parents was a reflection on his authority as head of the family. He believed that it was shameful that she was not more willing to fulfill her obligation to her parents according to Confucian laws. He expressed some catastrophic thoughts that Mei's behavior was evidence that he had lost his potency as a father and as a man and that none of his children would care for him if or when he became ill or disabled. The therapist recognized that within AC's culture, such a situation would be seen as pitiful and shameful. A related belief held by AC was that men should not be engaged in "women's work"; his difficulty performing traditionally female responsibilities in his caregiving role only added to his feelings of inadequacy.

The therapist helped AC complete thought logs that specified his beliefs, thoughts, and feelings regarding his daughter's behavior; the caregiving situation; and his role within the family. She explained how what people believe and think about something affects how they feel. She also pointed out how feelings can include emotions (e.g., his frustration with his daughter) and physical symptoms (e.g., the stomachache he experienced when frustrated). She then helped AC to look for and record evidence of the many ways in which his daughter did provide support.

In addition, with the therapist's help, AC was able to engage his other two children to assist in the caregiving responsibilities for their mother. To facilitate this, the therapist asked all three adult children to attend a family session in which the client's request for increased support was reinforced by the therapist. Finally, via several discussions of the cultural norms regarding traditional roles and responsibilities for men in AC's culture, the therapist helped AC to reframe the tasks he considered traditionally feminine as acceptable for a strong husband who wishes to provide for his wife.

At the end of his 20-week treatment, AC's depressive and somatic symptoms had decreased significantly, and he reported his caregiving role to be less stressful and burdensome. He described feeling more competent in his ability to care for his wife and to manage his household effectively. He was also receiving more help from his children.

CONCLUSION

The population of elders and particularly ethnic minority elders in the United States is growing rapidly. To provide effective care, therapists need to be culturally competent and knowledgeable regarding the diversity of older adults. This chapter offered suggestions for modifying CBT oriented assessment and interventions with culturally diverse elders. Although it may take more time, effort, and patience, working with ethnic minority elders can be a rewarding experience for both the client and the therapist.

REFERENCES

Administration on Aging. (2016). *Profile of older Americans: 2015*. Washington, DC: Author.

Allen, I. M. (1986). Posttraumatic stress disorder among black Vietnam veterans. *Hospital & Community Psychiatry, 37*, 55–61.

Almeida, O. P., McCaul, K., Hankey, G. J., Yeap, B. B., Golledge, J., & Flicker, L. (2016). Suicide in older men: The Health in Men Cohort Study (HIMS). *Preventive Medicine, 93*, 33–38. http://dx.doi.org/10.1016/j.ypmed.2016.09.022

Alzheimer's Association. (2016). 2016 Alzheimer's disease facts and figures. *Alzheimer's & Dementia, 12*, 459–509. http://dx.doi.org/10.1016/j.jalz.2016.03.001

American Psychiatric Association. (2013). *Diagnostic and statistical manual of mental disorders* (5th ed.). Arlington, VA: Author.

American Psychological Association Office on Aging. (2005). *Psychology and aging: Addressing mental health needs of older adults.* Retrieved from http://www.apa.org/pi/aging/resources/guides/aging.pdf

Ancoli-Israel, S., Cole, R., Alessi, C., Chambers, M., Moorcroft, W., & Pollak, C. P. (2003). The role of actigraphy in the study of sleep and circadian rhythms. *Sleep, 26*, 342–392. http://dx.doi.org/10.1093/sleep/26.3.342

Areán, P., & Miranda, J. (1996). The treatment of depression in elderly primary care patients: A naturalistic study. *Journal of Clinical Geropsychology, 2*, 153–160.

Areán, P. A., & Gallagher-Thompson, D. (1996). Issues and recommendations for the recruitment and retention of older ethnic minority adults into clinical research. *Journal of Consulting and Clinical Psychology, 64*, 875–880. http://dx.doi.org/10.1037/0022-006X.64.5.875

Bagayogo, I. P., Interian, A., & Escobar, J. I. (2013). Transcultural aspects of somatic symptoms in the context of depressive disorders. *Advances in Psychosomatic Medicine, 33*, 64–74. http://dx.doi.org/10.1159/000350057

Baker, F. M., & Takeshita, J. (2001). The ethnic minority elderly. In W. Tseng & J. Streltzer (Eds.), *Culture and psychotherapy: A guide to clinical practice* (pp. 209–222). Washington, DC: American Psychiatric Press.

Berlin, E. A., & Fowkes, W. C., Jr. (1983). A teaching framework for cross-cultural health care: Application in family practice. *The Western Journal of Medicine, 139*, 934–938.

Black, S. A. (2000). The mental health of culturally diverse elderly: Research and clinical issues. In I. Cuellar & F. A. Paniagua (Eds.), *Handbook of multicultural mental health: Assessment and treatment of diverse populations* (pp. 325–339). San Diego, CA: Academic Press.

Braun, K. L., & Browne, C. V. (1998). Perceptions of dementia, caregiving, and help seeking among Asian and Pacific Islander Americans. *Health & Social Work, 23*, 262–274. http://dx.doi.org/10.1093/hsw/23.4.262

Burgio, K. L., Williams, B. R., Dionne-Odom, J. N., Redden, D. T., Noh, H., Goode, P. S., . . . Bailey, F. A. (2016). Racial differences in processes of care at end of life in VA medical centers: Planned secondary analysis of data from the BEACON trial. *Journal of Palliative Medicine, 19*, 157–163. http://dx.doi.org/10.1089/jpm.2015.0311

Carrillo, J. E., Green, A. R., & Betancourt, J. R. (1999). Cross-cultural primary care: A patient-based approach. *Annals of Internal Medicine, 130*, 829–834. http://dx.doi.org/10.7326/0003-4819-130-10-199905180-00017

Cassidy, K., & Rector, N. A. (2008). The silent geriatric giant: Anxiety disorders in late life. *Geriatrics & Aging, 11*, 150–156.

Centers for Disease Control and Prevention and the Merck Company Foundation. (2007). *The state of aging and health in America.* Whitehouse Station, NJ: Merck Company Foundation.

Clare, L., & Woods, R. T. (2004). Cognitive training and cognitive rehabilitation for people with early-stage Alzheimer's disease: A review. *Neuropsychological Rehabilitation, 14*, 385–401. http://dx.doi.org/10.1080/09602010443000074

Cohen-Mansfield, J. (2001). Nonpharmacologic interventions for inappropriate behaviors in dementia: A review, summary, and critique. *The American Journal of Geriatric Psychiatry, 9*, 361–381. http://dx.doi.org/10.1097/00019442-200111000-00005

Connell, C. M., Roberts, J. S., McLaughlin, S. J., & Akinleye, D. (2009). Racial differences in knowledge and beliefs about Alzheimer disease. *Alzheimer Disease and Associated Disorders, 23*, 110–116. http://dx.doi.org/10.1097/WAD.0b013e318192e94d

Conner, K. O., Copeland, V. C., Grote, N. K., Koeske, G., Rosen, D., Reynolds, C. F., III, & Brown, C. (2010). Mental health treatment seeking among older adults with depression: The impact of stigma and race. *The American Journal of Geriatric Psychiatry, 18*, 531–543. http://dx.doi.org/10.1097/JGP.0b013e3181cc0366

Connolly, A., Sampson, E. L., & Purandare, N. (2012). End-of-life care for people with dementia from ethnic minority groups: A systematic review. *Journal of the American Geriatrics Society, 60*, 351–360. http://dx.doi.org/10.1111/j.1532-5415.2011.03754.x

Dai, Y., Zhang, S., Yamamoto, J., Ao, M., Belin, T. R., Cheung, F., & Hifumi, S. S. (1999). Cognitive behavioral therapy of minor depressive symptoms in elderly Chinese Americans: A pilot study. *Community Mental Health Journal, 35*, 537–542. http://dx.doi.org/10.1023/A:1018763302198

Dennis, J. P., & Brown, G. K. (2011). Suicidal older adults: Suicide risk assessments, safety planning, and cognitive behavioral therapy. In K. H. Sorocco & S. Lauderdale (Eds.), *Cognitive behavior therapy with older adults: Innovations across care settings* (pp. 95–123). New York, NY: Springer.

Dong, X., & Zhang, M. (2016). The association between filial piety and perceived stress among Chinese older adults in greater Chicago area. *Journal of Geriatrics and Palliative Care, 4*, 1–11.

Durham, R. C., Chambers, J. A., MacDonald, R. R., Power, K. G., & Major, K. (2003). Does cognitive-behavioural therapy influence the long-term outcome of generalized anxiety disorder? An 8–14 year follow-up of two clinical trials. *Psychological Medicine, 33*, 499–509. http://dx.doi.org/10.1017/S0033291702007079

Erlangsen, A., Stenager, E., & Conwell, Y. (2015). Physical diseases as predictors of suicide in older adults: A nationwide, register-based cohort study. *Social Psychiatry and Psychiatric Epidemiology, 50*, 1427–1439. http://dx.doi.org/10.1007/s00127-015-1051-0

Fässberg, M. M., Cheung, G., Canetto, S. S., Erlangsen, A., Lapierre, S., Lindner, R., . . . Wærn, M. (2016). A systematic review of physical illness, functional disability, and suicidal behaviour among older adults. *Aging & Mental Health, 20,* 166–194. http://dx.doi.org/10.1080/13607863.2015.1083945

Fingerman, K. L., Sechrist, J., & Birditt, K. (2013). Changing views on intergenerational ties. *Gerontology, 59,* 64–70. http://dx.doi.org/10.1159/000342211

Gallagher, D., & Thompson, L. W. (1981). *Depression in the elderly: A behavioral treatment manual.* Los Angeles: University of Southern California Press.

Gallagher-Thompson, D., Areán, P., Coon, D., Menendez, A., Takagi, K., Haley, W. E., . . . Szapocznik, J. (2000). Development and implementation strategies for culturally diverse caregiving populations. In R. Schulz (Ed.), *Handbook on dementia caregiving: Evidence-based interventions for family caregivers* (pp. 151–185). New York, NY: Springer.

Gallagher-Thompson, D., Leary, M. C., Ossinalde, C., Romero, J. J., Wald, M. J., & Fernandez-Gamarra, E. (1997). Hispanic caregivers of older adults with dementia: Cultural issues in outreach and intervention. *Group, 21,* 211–232.

Gallagher-Thompson, D., Talamantes, M., Ramirez, R., & Valverde, I. (1996). Service delivery issues and recommendations for working with Mexican American family caregivers. In G. Yeo & D. Gallagher-Thompson (Eds.), *Ethnicity and the dementias* (pp. 137–152). Washington, DC: Taylor & Francis.

Gatz, M., Fiske, A., Fox, L. S., Kaskie, B., Kasl-Godly, J. E., McCallum, T. J., & Wetherell, J. L. (1998). Empirically validated psychological treatments for older adults. *Journal of Mental Health and Aging, 4,* 9–46.

Gelman, C. R. (2010). Learning from recruitment challenges: Barriers to diagnosis, treatment, and research participation for Latinos with symptoms of Alzheimer's disease. *Journal of Gerontological Social Work, 53,* 94–113. http://dx.doi.org/10.1080/01634370903361847

Griffin-Pierce, T., Silverberg, N., Connor, D., Jim, M., Peters, J., Kaszniak, A., & Sabbagh, M. N. (2008). Challenges to the recognition and assessment of Alzheimer's disease in American Indians of the southwestern United States. *Alzheimer's & Dementia, 4,* 291–299. http://dx.doi.org/10.1016/j.jalz.2007.10.012

Grover, S., Avasthi, A., Gupta, S., Dan, A., Neogi, R., Behere, P. B., . . . Rozatkar, A. (2016). Phenomenology and beliefs of patients with Dhat syndrome: A nationwide multicentric study. *International Journal of Social Psychiatry, 62,* 57–66. http://dx.doi.org/10.1177/0020764015591857

Gum, A. M., Ayalon, L., Greenberg, J. M., Palko, B., Ruffo, E., & Areán, P. A. (2010). Preferences for professional assistance for distress in a diverse sample of older adults. *Clinical Gerontologist, 33,* 136–151. http://dx.doi.org/10.1080/07317110903551901

Gupta, R. (2003). Cognitive behavioral treatment on driving phobia for an Asian Indian male. *Clinical Gerontologist, 26,* 165–171.

Hadfield, J. C. (2014). The health of grandparents raising grandchildren: A literature review. *Journal of Gerontological Nursing, 40,* 32–42. http://dx.doi.org/10.3928/00989134-20140219-01

Harris, H. L. (1998). Ethnic minority elders: Issues and interventions. *Educational Gerontology, 24*, 309–324. http://dx.doi.org/10.1080/0360127980240402

Hays, P. A. (1995). Multicultural applications of cognitive behavior therapy. *Professional Psychology: Research and Practice, 26*, 309–315. http://dx.doi.org/10.1037/0735-7028.26.3.309

Hays, P. A. (1996). Culturally responsive assessment with diverse older clients. *Professional Psychology: Research and Practice, 27*, 188–193. http://dx.doi.org/10.1037/0735-7028.27.2.188

Henderson, J. N., & Henderson, L. C. (2002). Cultural construction of disease: A "supernormal" construct of dementia in an American Indian tribe. *Journal of Cross-Cultural Gerontology, 17*, 197–212. http://dx.doi.org/10.1023/A:1021268922685

Hebert, L. E., Weuve, J., Scherr, P. A., & Evans, D. A. (2013). Alzheimer disease in the United States (2010–2050) estimated using the 2010 census. *Neurology, 80*, 1778–1783. http://dx.doi.org/10.1212/WNL.0b013e31828726f5

Heron, K. E., & Smyth, J. M. (2010). Ecological momentary interventions: Incorporating mobile technology into psychosocial and health behaviour treatments. *British Journal of Health Psychology, 15*, 1–39. http://dx.doi.org/10.1348/135910709X466063

Hinton, D. E., Chhean, D., Pich, V., Safren, S. A., Hofmann, S. G., & Pollack, M. H. (2005). A randomized controlled trial of cognitive-behavior therapy for Cambodian refugees with treatment-resistant PTSD and panic attacks: A crossover design. *Journal of Traumatic Stress, 18*, 617–629. http://dx.doi.org/10.1002/jts.20070

Hinton, L., Franz, C. E., Yeo, G., & Levkoff, S. E. (2005). Conceptions of dementia in a multiethnic sample of family caregivers. *Journal of the American Geriatrics Society, 53*, 1405–1410. http://dx.doi.org/10.1111/j.1532-5415.2005.53409.x

Hwang, W.-C., Wood, J. J., & Fujimoto, K. (2010). Acculturative family distancing (AFD) and depression in Chinese American families. *Journal of Consulting and Clinical Psychology, 78*, 655–667. http://dx.doi.org/10.1037/a0020542

Hummer, R. A., Benjamins, M. R., & Rogers, R. G. (2004). Racial and ethnic disparities in health and mortality among U.S. elderly population. In N. B. Anderson, R. A. Bulatao, & B. Cohen (Eds.), *National Research Council (U.S.) Panel on Race, Ethnicity, and Health in Later Life* (Chapter 3). Washington, DC: National Academic Press. Retrieved from https://www.ncbi.nlm.nih.gov/books/NBK25528/

Institute of Medicine, Board of Health Sciences Policy, Committee on Understanding and Eliminating Racial and Ethnic Disparities in Health Care. (2003). In B. D. Smedley, A. Y. Stith, & A. R. Nelson (Eds.), *Unequal treatment: Confronting racial and ethnic disparities in health.* Washington, DC: National Academies Press. Retrieved from http://nap.edu/books/030908265X/html

Jang, Y., Chiriboga, D. A., & Okazaki, S. (2009). Attitudes toward mental health services: Age-group differences in Korean American adults. *Aging & Mental Health, 13,* 127–134. http://dx.doi.org/10.1080/13607860802591070

Jimenez, D. E., Alegría, M., Chen, C. N., Chan, D., & Laderman, M. (2010). Prevalence of psychiatric illnesses in older ethnic minority adults. *Journal of the American Geriatrics Society, 58,* 256–264. http://dx.doi.org/10.1111/j.1532-5415.2009.02685.x

Jimenez, D. E., Bartels, S. J., Cardenas, V., & Alegría, M. (2013). Stigmatizing attitudes toward mental illness among racial/ethnic older adults in primary care. *International Journal of Geriatric Psychiatry, 28,* 1061–1068. http://dx.doi.org/10.1002/gps.3928

Jimenez, D. E., Bartels, S. J., Cardenas, V., Dhaliwal, S. S., & Alegría, M. (2012). Cultural beliefs and mental health treatment preferences of ethnically diverse older adult consumers in primary care. *The American Journal of Geriatric Psychiatry, 20,* 533–542. http://dx.doi.org/10.1097/JGP.0b013e318227f876

Kinoshita, L. M., & Gallagher-Thompson, D. (2004). Japanese American caregivers of individuals with dementia: An examination of Japanese cultural values and dementia caregiving. *Clinical Gerontologist, 27,* 87–102. http://dx.doi.org/10.1300/J018v27n01_08

Kleinman, A. (1980). *Patient and healers in the context of culture: An exploration of the borderland between anthropology, medicine, and psychiatry.* Berkeley: University of California Press.

Kleinman, A., Eisenberg, L., & Good, B. (1978). Culture, illness, and care: Clinical lessons from anthropologic and cross-cultural research. *Annals of Internal Medicine, 88,* 251–258. http://dx.doi.org/10.7326/0003-4819-88-2-251

Knight, B. G., & Satre, D. D. (1999). Cognitive behavioral psychotherapy with older adults. *Clinical Psychologist, 6,* 188–203.

Langa, K. M., Larson, E. B., Crimmins, E. M., Faul, J. D., Levine, D. A., Kabeto, M. U., & Weir, D. R. (2017). A comparison of the prevalence of dementia in the United States in 2000 and 2012. *Journal of the American Medical Association Internal Medicine, 177,* 51–58.

Lau, A. W., & Gallagher-Thompson, D. (2002). Ethnic minority older adults in clinical and research programs: Issues and recommendations. *Behavior Therapist, 25,* 10–16.

Lee, S. E., Lee, H. Y., & Diwan, S. (2010). What do Korean American immigrants know about Alzheimer's disease (AD)? The impact of acculturation and exposure to the disease on AD knowledge. *International Journal of Geriatric Psychiatry, 25,* 66–73.

Letamendi, A. M., Ayers, C. R., Ruberg, J. L., Singley, D. B., Wilson, J., Chavira, D., . . . Wetherell, J. L. (2013). Illness conceptualizations among older rural Mexican-Americans with anxiety and depression. *Journal of Cross-Cultural Gerontology, 28,* 421–433. http://dx.doi.org/10.1007/s10823-013-9211-8

Leong, F. T., & Lau, A. S. (2001). Barriers to providing effective mental health services to Asian Americans. *Mental Health Services Research, 3,* 201–214. http://dx.doi.org/10.1023/A:1013177014788

Lin, Y. N. (2002). The application of cognitive-behavioral therapy to counseling Chinese. *American Journal of Psychotherapy, 56,* 46–58 http://dx.doi.org/10.1176/appi.psychotherapy.2002.56.1.46

Liu, D., Hinton, L., Tran, C., Hinton, D., & Barker, J. C. (2008). Reexamining the relationships among dementia, stigma, and aging in immigrant Chinese and Vietnamese family caregivers. *Journal of Cross-Cultural Gerontology, 23,* 283–299. http://dx.doi.org/10.1007/s10823-008-9075-5

Liu, P. P. (2015). Intergenerational cultural conflict, mental health, and educational outcomes among Asian and Latino/a Americans: Qualitative meta-analytic review. *Psychological Bulletin, 14,* 404–446.

Loo, C. M. (1994). Race-related PTSD: The Asian American Vietnam veteran. *Journal of Traumatic Stress, 7,* 637–656. http://dx.doi.org/10.1002/jts.2490070410

LoPresti, M. A., Dement, F., & Gold, H. T. (2016). End-of-life care for people with cancer from ethnic minority groups: A systematic review. *American Journal of Hospice & Palliative Medicine, 33,* 291–305. http://dx.doi.org/10.1177/1049909114565658

McCormick, W. C., Uomoto, J., Young, H., Graves, A. B., Vitaliano, P., Mortimer, J. A., . . . Larson, E. B. (1996). Attitudes toward use of nursing homes and home care in older Japanese-Americans. *Journal of the American Geriatrics Society, 44,* 769–777. http://dx.doi.org/10.1111/j.1532-5415.1996.tb03732.x

Meyers, B. S. (1998). Depression and dementia: Comorbidities, identification, and treatment. *Journal of Geriatric Psychiatry and Neurology, 11,* 201–205. http://dx.doi.org/10.1177/089198879901100406

Mianji, F., & Semnani, Y. (2015). Zar spirit possession in Iran and African countries: Group distress, culture-bound syndrome or cultural concept of distress? *Iranian Journal of Psychiatry, 10,* 225–232.

Morin, C. M., Kowatch, R. A., Barry, T., & Walton, E. (1993). Cognitive-behavior therapy for late-life insomnia. *Journal of Consulting and Clinical Psychology, 61,* 137–146. http://dx.doi.org/10.1037/0022-006X.61.1.137

Mukadam, N., Cooper, C., & Livingston, G. (2013). Improving access to dementia services for people from minority ethnic groups. *Current Opinion in Psychiatry, 26,* 409–414. http://dx.doi.org/10.1097/YCO.0b013e32835ee668

National Institute of Mental Health. (2007). *Collaborative psychiatric epidemiology survey program (CPES): Integrated weights and sampling error codes for design-based analysis.* Washington, DC: Government Printing Office.

Orgeta, V., Qazi, A., Spector, A., & Orrell, M. (2015). Psychological treatments for depression and anxiety in dementia and mild cognitive impairment: Systematic review and meta-analysis. *The British Journal of Psychiatry, 207,* 293–298. http://dx.doi.org/10.1192/bjp.bp.114.148130

Ory, M. G., Yee, J. L., Tennstedt, S. L., & Schulz, R. (2000). The extent and impact of dementia care: Unique challenges experienced by family caregivers. In R. Schulz (Ed.), *Handbook of dementia caregiving* (pp. 1–32). New York, NY: Springer.

Parks, F. M. (2003). The role of African American folk beliefs in the modern therapeutic process. *Clinical Psychology: Science and Practice, 10,* 456–467. http://dx.doi.org/10.1093/clipsy.bpg046

Parveen, S., Peltier, C., & Oyebode, J. R. (2017). Perceptions of dementia and use of services in minority ethnic communities: A scoping exercise. *Health & Social Care in the Community, 25,* 734–742. http://dx.doi.org/10.1111/hsc.12363

Plowfield, L. A., Raymond, J. E., & Blevins, C. (2000). Wholism for aging families: Meeting needs of caregivers. *Holistic Nursing Practice, 14,* 51–59. http://dx.doi.org/10.1097/00004650-200007000-00008

Saint Arnault, D., & Kim, O. (2008). Is there an Asian idiom of distress? Somatic symptoms in female Japanese and Korean students. *Archives of Psychiatric Nursing, 22,* 27–38. http://dx.doi.org/10.1016/j.apnu.2007.10.003

Sarkisian, C. A., Hays, R. D., Berry, S. H., & Mangione, C. M. (2001). Expectations regarding aging among older adults and physicians who care for older adults. *Medical Care, 39,* 1025–1036. http://dx.doi.org/10.1097/00005650-200109000-00012

Searight, H. R., & Gafford, J. (2005). Cultural diversity at the end of life: Issues and guidelines for family physicians. *American Family Physician, 71,* 515–522.

Shanley, C., Boughtwood, D., Adams, J., Santalucia, Y., Kyriazopoulos, H., Pond, D., & Rowland, J. (2012). A qualitative study into the use of formal services for dementia by carers from culturally and linguistically diverse (CALD) communities. *BioMed Central Health Services Research, 12,* 354. http://dx.doi.org/10.1186/1472-6963-12-354

Shen, M. J., Prigerson, H. G., Paulk, E., Trevino, K. M., Penedo, F. J., Tergas, A. I., . . . Maciejewski, P. K. (2016). Impact of end-of-life discussions on the reduction of Latino/non-Latino disparities in do-not-resuscitate order completion. *Cancer, 122,* 1749–1756.

Stanley, M. A., Wilson, N. L., Novy, D. M., Rhoades, H. M., Wagener, P. D., Greisinger, A. J., . . . Kunik, M. E. (2009). Cognitive behavior therapy for generalized anxiety disorder among older adults in primary care: A randomized clinical trial. *Journal of the American Medical Association, 301,* 1460–1467. http://dx.doi.org/10.1001/jama.2009.458

Stokes, S. C., Thompson, L. W., Murphy, S., & Gallagher-Thompson, D. (2002). Screening for depression in immigrant Chinese-American elders: Results of a pilot study. *Journal of Gerontological Social Work, 36,* 27–44. http://dx.doi.org/10.1300/J083v36n01_03

Suzuki, R., Goebert, D., Ahmed, I., & Lu, B. (2015). Folk and biological perceptions of dementia among Asian ethnic minorities in Hawaii. *The American Journal of Geriatric Psychiatry, 23,* 589–595. http://dx.doi.org/10.1016/j.jagp.2014.03.012

World Health Organization. (2010). *International statistical classification of diseases and related health problems* (10th rev.). Retrieved from http://apps.who.int/classifications/icd10/browse/2010/en

Zeiss, A. M., Lewinsohn, P. M., Rohde, P., & Seeley, J. R. (1996). Relationship of physical disease and functional impairment to depression in older people. *Psychology and Aging, 11*, 572–581. http://dx.doi.org/10.1037/0882-7974.11.4.572

Zhong, B. L., Chiu, H. F., & Conwell, Y. (2016). Rates and characteristics of elderly suicide in China, 2013–14. *Journal of Affective Disorders, 206*, 273–279. http://dx.doi.org/10.1016/j.jad.2016.09.003

10

COGNITIVE BEHAVIOR THERAPY AND PEOPLE WITH DISABILITIES

LINDA R. MONA, H'SIEN HAYWARD, AND REBECCA P. CAMERON

The American Psychological Association (APA; 2002; amended in 2010 and 2017) has included cultural competence in working with people with disabilities as a standard in its *Ethical Principles of Psychologists and Code of Conduct* since 2002. However, much work remains to achieve widespread disability cultural competence within the field of psychology, given the lack of representation of disabled people and the scarcity of formal training opportunities for conducting therapy with disabled people. The goal of this chapter is to move beyond the individually oriented deficit model frequently used in conceptualizing the difficulties experienced by clients with disabilities to discuss the utility of culturally informed and responsive cognitive behavior therapy (CBT) with disabled people. To foster this broader conceptualization, we discuss disability as a cultural identity and contrast this view with historical perspectives on disability, followed by a brief review of research on psychological resources that aid people living with disability. Finally, examples of

http://dx.doi.org/10.1037/0000119-011
Culturally Responsive Cognitive Behavior Therapy, Second Edition: Practice and Supervision, G. Y. Iwamasa and P. A. Hays (Editors)

257

behavioral and cognitive strategies that can be used to improve adjustment among persons with disabilities are described and illustrated. (Note that we have chosen to use the terms *disabled people*, *disability community*, and *people with disabilities* interchangeably. We believe that exclusively using person-first language—that is, *people with disabilities*— ignores the recognition of disability as a cultural identity and the fact that many are proud to call themselves *disabled people*.)

Traditional models of disability have assumed that psychological difficulties experienced by people with disabilities originate within the individual and reflect the person's failure to adapt to the nondisabled world (Olkin, 1999, p. 25). Clinical interventions are often geared toward changing the individual to better approximate "normal" functioning. In contrast, *interactionist* models conceptualize disability as a consequence of the interplay among physical differences or conditions and multiple potentially disabling contexts (e.g., family, housing, transportation, social situations; Olkin & Pledger, 2003). Such models offer a more comprehensive approach to working with clients, highlighting issues of person–environment fit and suggesting the use of multifaceted intervention strategies.

There is an additional, sociopolitical perspective of disability that moves beyond the interactionist viewpoint to acknowledge disability as a cultural identity (Olkin & Pledger, 2003). This cultural perspective addresses issues of identity arising from environmental and social deficits that limit full self-determination and participation by people with disabilities, recognizing the interplay among biological, sociopolitical, and environmental factors that create the disability experience.

Psychological theory, assessment, and intervention have begun to embrace the disability cultural perspective (Clemency Cordes, Cameron, Eisen, Coble-Temple, & Mona, 2017). Indeed, the APA (2012) published guidelines that incorporate cultural model tenets, calling on psychologists to consider contextual and systems-level information, to focus on capacities as well as deficits, and to include well-being in assessment and intervention. Guideline 9 evokes the minority experience and interactions among person and social variables when it indicates that "psychologists strive to learn how attitudes and misconceptions, the social environment and the nature of a person's disability influence development across the life span" (APA, 2012, p. 50). Guideline 13 states, "In assessing persons with disabilities, psychologists strive to consider disability as a dimension of diversity together with other individual and contextual dimensions" (APA, 2012, p. 52). By addressing the disability experience from a larger lens, inclusive of both medical and social variables, psychologists are encouraged to develop clinical knowledge and tools to better serve the growing disability community (Clemency Cordes, Cameron, Mona, Syme, & Coble-Temple, 2016).

One challenge to comprehensive models of disability is that the term *disability* includes the shared cultural experiences of people with a wide range of differences, including physical, sensory, psychological, intellectual, and other chronic health conditions. However, much of the research relevant to clinical work with people with disabilities is undertaken with relatively homogeneous samples of people with various physical or mental health conditions. In addition, studies of psychological functioning and psychotherapeutic intervention with disabled people have largely focused on individuals with acquired rather than lifelong disabilities and have rarely incorporated disability cultural identity variables (Banks, Brown, Mona, & Ackerman, 2014; Clemency Cordes, Cameron, et al., 2016; Craig, Hancock, Chang, & Dickson, 1998).

Although the issues we present may reference or apply to specific impairments, we present these within a broad perspective that applies across a wide range of disability experiences. We begin with a brief discussion of disability culture, followed by tenets of disability-affirmative therapy, and finally a discussion of the ways in which disability has been conceptualized within psychology and other disciplines. This sets the stage for examining CBT applications within this diverse community.

DISABILITY CULTURE

According to Gill (1995), there are eight core values that underlie political struggles, are reflected in art, are included within conversations, and become a part of the goals and the behaviors of people with disabilities. These core values shed light on the foundation of disability culture and are summarized as follows: (a) an acceptance of human variation; (b) an orientation toward using assistance and an acceptance of human vulnerability and interdependence as part of life; (c) a tolerance for living with uncertainty or less-than-desired outcomes; (d) disability humor, including the ability to laugh at the oppressor as well as one's own experiences; (e) skills in managing multiple problems; (f) a sophisticated future orientation involving the ability to realistically anticipate obstacles; (g) the ability to read others' attitudes and grasp the latent meaning in contradictory social messages; and (h) a flexible, adaptive approach to tasks and a creativity stimulated by both limited resources and experience with nontraditional modes of operating (Gill, 1995).

These values reflect the adaptive value of psychological flexibility among people with disabilities and also suggest the types of social constraints that may contribute to mental health difficulties. Many of these values are consistent with those that guide the work of cognitive behavioral therapists, particularly those values that counter rigid or perfectionistic standards for human functioning. Familiarity with these ideals of disability culture can facilitate the development of a more culturally responsive approach to CBT.

Disability culture is transmitted by means of shared life experiences. For example, political issues affecting access to resources and opportunities, such as education and employment; the availability of accessible, affordable housing, transportation, and personal assistance services; and the availability and quality of structured living facilities all greatly affect the everyday life experiences of people with disabilities (Fine & Asch, 1988; Gill, 1995). Gill (1995) discussed the benefits of identifying with disability culture, including increased self-worth and psychological resilience, greater social resources and sense of community, and positive recognition of the distinctness of disability experiences. Cultural connections can foster the development of a collective voice advocating for political change. Recognition of disability cultural strengths can help cognitive behavioral therapists to more fully support identity development and political and community solidarity as adjuncts to or goals within traditional therapeutic approaches.

Appreciation for the strengths of disability culture is only a starting point for disability cultural competence as a therapist. Exploration of one's own implicit bias regarding disability is essential to create the foundation for empowering CBT work (see Guideline 2; APA, 2012). Ways that well-meaning therapists are at risk for underaddressing the complexity of the disability experience are varied and range from infantilizing people with disabilities to viewing the experiences of disabled people through a lens of inspiration for people without disabilities (see, e.g., Shapiro, 1994, pp. 16–18). Developing self-awareness to avoid perpetuating culturally transmitted ableism (i.e., discrimination or prejudice against disabled people) is critical to avoid iatrogenic effects of therapy. Olkin (1999) provided a valuable introduction to disability-affirmative therapy that is a helpful resource for clinicians aiming to develop or improve cultural competence in working with disabled clients. For example, before beginning treatment, Olkin (pp. 154–156) suggested seven principles that can guide client assessment. These principles include (a) a framework for therapy that includes appreciation for disability as a minority experience, and for clients as participants in multilayered, interactive systems (e.g., biopsychosocial–family–sociocultural); (b) disability as a bicultural experience; (c) disability as occurring within family systems; (d) disability as a social construct with inherently political dimensions; (e) the need for additional clinical skills to address disability as it interacts with other therapy targets; (f) the need to focus on enhancing functioning beyond deficit reduction; and (g) the need to show and not just tell, that is, the need to demonstrate your cultural competence. These assumptions draw from the broader perspective that disability is a complex life experience comprising more than an impairment or specific condition. For example, therapists may find themselves responding protectively to clients whose therapeutic aims include greater autonomy and self-determination because of limited experience with independent living. It may be necessary for therapists to address their own internalized paternalistic views and become willing to challenge family systems that reinforce dependency.

HISTORICAL PERSPECTIVES ON DISABILITY

How one defines disability affects one's view of disability culture and people with disabilities. In this section, we discuss commonly used paradigms of disability that have shaped disability-related cultural discourse within psychology.

The moral model of disability is based on the assertion that disability is a physical manifestation of sin or moral lapse (Olkin, 1999). Disability may also be constructed as a test of faith or a divine opportunity for spiritual growth and increased enlightenment. As described by Longmore and Umansky (2001), the medical model is inextricably linked to modern social arrangements regarding disability. This approach places almost exclusive emphasis on the responsibility of the individual to overcome her or his disability. People with disabilities are culturally mandated by the mainstream to work as hard as possible to emulate the nondisabled norm.

The social model of disability frames disability as a social construction rather than an individual deficit. The social model rejects the definition of disability as disorder and instead frames the experiences of disabled people as similar to those of other minority groups.

Current perspectives recognize disability as a complex interaction among medical, social, environmental, and political factors (World Health Organization, 2011). Under this interpretation, *disability* is an umbrella term for functional limitations that result from the relationship between physical differences and the contextual environment (World Health Organization, 2011, p. 4). Using a biopsychosocial definition of disability facilitates a focus on improving quality of life (QOL) by reducing or removing environmental, institutional, and attitudinal barriers that interfere with people with disabilities' ability to live satisfying lives (Mona, Cameron, & Clemency Cordes, 2017).

PSYCHOSOCIAL VARIABLES

Most psychological studies of people with disabilities address adaptation to acquired disability defined by specific impairments or medical diagnoses. This approach has yielded useful data regarding adjustment to specific acquired impairments, but there are limitations in our understanding of psychological adjustment related to lifelong disability, the role of environmental factors in adjustment, and the impact of shared cultural experiences on the mental health status of disabled people. Because mental health is more than the absence of psychopathology, the literature reviewed here incorporates psychological strengths shown to be relevant to people with disabilities.

Quality of Life and Well-Being

Despite common assumptions to the contrary, high levels of QOL characterize many people with disabilities. For example, Tyc (1992) reviewed empirical studies of young adults who had lost limbs due to cancer and found high QOL and low levels of psychiatric symptoms. Andrykowski and Hunt (1993) found that patients with a life-threatening disease or disability reported a stable QOL. Further, Schulz and Decker (1985) studied adults with spinal cord injuries (SCI) and found that participants saw themselves on average as being better off than most people, with or without a disability. Taking a sociopolitical view of the disability experience, it is plausible that QOL, in this research, is reflective of empowerment, physical and logistical accessibility across life domains, and the availability of resources that allow for less stress and increased direction in life (e.g., financial resources to access personal assistance services and caregiving, durable medical equipment, and choice in housing).

However, there are sizeable minorities of disabled people who do experience negative mental health outcomes resulting in lowered QOL. Living with SCI has been associated with reduced QOL (Martz, Livneh, Priebe, Wuermser, & Ottomanelli, 2005), lower life satisfaction (Kemp & Krause, 1999), and elevations in depression and anxiety (Craig, Hancock, & Dickson, 1994; Kennedy & Rogers, 2000). Similarly, in a meta-analysis of 198 studies that compared the psychological well-being of individuals with and without visual impairments, Pinquart and Pfeiffer (2011) found that individuals with visual impairments reported lower psychological well-being scores. Again, disability-specific mediating factors may play a role in these psychological outcomes. For example, information about financial resources, assistance with activities of daily living, access to transportation to social events, and other resources or barriers that restrict participation in social gatherings would help shed light on the nature of the relationship between disability and well-being.

Appraisals

Appraisals of a difficult life experience, or the way that individuals interpret a stressful event, have a strong influence on psychological outcomes (Ferguson, Matthews, & Cox, 1999). This has been demonstrated in SCI populations, with appraisals having a long-term impact on psychological as well as functional outcomes (Chevalier, Kennedy, & Sherlock, 2009). In a study by Kennedy, Lude, Elfström, and Smithson (2010), appraisals accounted for 49.4% of the variance in a measure of functional independence. Further, in a longitudinal study of individuals who were followed from immediately after an SCI until 12 weeks postinjury, both threat appraisals (appraisal of the potential for harm) and challenge appraisals (appraisal of the potential for growth, gain, and mastery) after the event were shown to predict psychological outcomes (Ferguson et al., 1999). Greater threat appraisals predicted higher levels of anxiety and greater challenge appraisals predicted lower levels of depression (Kennedy et al., 2010). Appraisals can also influence the coping strategies that are used by people with disabilities. For example, a disabled person who views her or his situation as challenging may use information seeking or positive reframing, whereas someone who views her or his situation as threatening may deny, withdraw, or disengage (Peter, Müller, Post, van Leeuwen, Werner, & Geyh, 2015).

Cognitive appraisals have substantial effects on emotional distress associated with a chronic disease, and this association can be stronger than the effects attributable to disease symptom severity (Harkins, Elliott, & Wan, 2006). The data indicate that appraisals of personal ability to tolerate vision loss and the perceived interference of vision loss with goal-directed behavior and expected activities have greater influence on distress and subsequent predictions of disability than objective symptoms (visual acuity). Guest et al. (2015) also found a weak association between well-being and injury-related or demographic factors.

Self-Efficacy

Self-efficacy (SE), or a person's belief in his or her ability to direct or perform a behavior (Bandura, 1977), is related to a large number of positive psychosocial variables in people with disabilities. In a systematic review of individuals with SCI, Peter, Müller, Cieza, and Geyh (2012) found strong connections between SE and well-being and life satisfaction. People with high SE reported better mental health in general and were consistently less depressed or anxious; they performed better health behavior, experienced more functional independence and fewer mobility restrictions, and used fewer health care services. Health-related SE was associated with greater acceptance and fewer cognitive distortions.

Coping and Adjustment

Numerous studies have examined the relationship between various coping strategies and adjustment in individuals with disabilities. Although SCI has been associated with both reduced QOL and elevations in depression and anxiety, previous studies have shown that many people living with SCI nonetheless exhibit healthy long-term adjustment (e.g., Quale & Schanke, 2010). Studies examining coping styles and adjustment in people with SCI have found that effective coping strategies, including active coping, problem-solving, and acceptance, were predictive of positive emotional adjustment (Elliott, Godshall, Herrick, Witty, & Spruell, 1991; Kennedy et al., 2000). In contrast, the use of denial as a coping strategy was found to be ineffective, resulting in barriers to rehabilitation and adjustment (Fitzgerald, 1970). Similarly, Bonanno, Kennedy, Galatzer-Levy, Lude, and Elfström (2012) found that SCI survivors with chronic depression used greater behavioral disengagement and coping through social reliance, less acceptance, and fewer challenge appraisals. Likewise, maladaptive coping styles such as drug and alcohol use, denial, and behavioral disengagement were found by Kennedy and colleagues (2000) to correlate with higher levels of anxiety and depression post-SCI.

Self-Esteem

Self-esteem, or positive evaluation of oneself, has been shown to relate positively to numerous psychosocial variables, including life satisfaction, mastery, hope, effective coping, and sexual adjustment. It has also been negatively correlated with depression, stress, and loneliness (Peter et al., 2012). In studies of people with SCIs, self-esteem does not consistently differ from that found among nondisabled people (Peter et al., 2012). Similarly, despite the predictions of theorists that visual impairment would be associated with lower self-esteem (Papadopoulos, Montgomery, & Chronopoulou, 2013), findings are mixed. Several studies have indicated that there are no major differences between individuals with and without visual impairment, and other studies have shown that individuals with visual impairments report higher self-esteem than individuals with normal vision (Kef, 2002). High self-esteem in individuals with visual impairments is positively correlated with independence in activities of daily living (Beach, Robinet, & Hakim-Larson, 1995) and with social support (e.g., Huurre, Komulainen, & Aro, 1999). Moreover, Papadopoulos, Paralikas, Barouti, and Chronopoulou (2014) showed that self-esteem is negatively correlated with depression and anxiety among people with visual impairments.

Implications for Psychological Intervention

Collectively, these findings have implications for psychological treatment to increase the well-being of people with disabilities. Psychological interventions that focus on intrapersonal factors such as enhancing positive coping strategies and on interpersonal factors such as increasing social support, may benefit disabled people who need strengthening in these areas. However, such approaches are incomplete if they focus solely on correcting apparent deficits among people with disabilities. A broader awareness of the social and environmental context of disablement is critical for culturally competent therapy. This includes a consideration of barriers that prevent optimal coping and impede the development of social support networks among people with disabilities.

Indeed, challenges may arise in conducting CBT with disabled people. As discussed earlier, using an approach that often locates problems within people rather than in social relations and societal stigma may serve to further marginalize this population. For example, Gerry and Crabtree (2013) presented a compelling argument for not using, or else heavily modifying, CBT with people with disabilities: "There is potential for therapeutic techniques used in CBT to promote questions that invite, generate and reinforce feelings of incompetence and inability" (p. 59).

However, CBT holds promise as an effective approach for persons with SCI experiencing depression, anxiety, adjustment, and coping problems. Indeed, in a review of CBT for psychosocial issues, both group and individual formats were found to positively affect adjustment in both inpatients and outpatients. It is important to note however, that these results were strongest in those individuals who were identified pretreatment as experiencing significant adjustment challenges and depression symptoms (as opposed to mild or moderate; Mehta et al., 2011).

Dorstyn, Mathias, and Denson (2010) found evidence supporting the use of CBT for promoting psychological adjustment post-SCI in a meta-analytic review of the literature. Specifically, large and significant group differences were noted for measures of coping, SE, and QOL. These data suggest that CBT has a significant positive impact on short-term psychological outcomes following SCI (Dorstyn et al., 2010).

When CBT techniques are integrated within a disability cultural frame-work, providers are able to treat the individual's psychological concerns and also address social and political factors affecting their functioning (Mona, Romesser-Scehnet, Cameron, & Cardenas, 2006). Research has shown that strategies often employed in CBT, such as relaxation, mindfulness, motiva tional interviewing, life skills training, and psychoeducation, as well as many family-focused therapies, are effective for individuals with disabilities (Perry & Weiss, 2007). For example, CBT and mindfulness have been found to be effective in treating mood and behavioral issues for women with mild to moderate intellectual disabilities (Harper, Webb, & Rayner, 2013; Hassiotis et al., 2013).

COGNITIVE BEHAVIORAL MODEL
OF PSYCHOTHERAPY AND DISABILITY

The cognitive behavioral model focuses on the influence of cognitions and cognitive processes on an individual's emotions and behavior (A. T. Beck, 1976; J. S. Beck, 1995). Cognitions occur at a number of levels, as articulated by J. S. Beck (1995). Core beliefs are developed from early child-hood experiences. They operate at a fundamental level, typically outside of awareness, and give rise to intermediate beliefs in the form of rules, attitudes, and assumptions (J. S. Beck, 1995; Ellis & Grieger, 1986). Some of these beliefs and assumptions are rigid, dysfunctional, and maladaptive, whereas others are flexible and adaptive. Of primary interest to cognitive behavioral therapists are the dysfunctional beliefs that contribute to the development of psychological disorders (J. S. Beck, 1995). These beliefs can skew information processing and contribute to a negative triad of distorted perceptions about oneself, the future, and the world (A. T. Beck, 1976). For example, a client who has internalized standards of beauty that are defined by the nondisabled world might believe that to be attractive, she must look as nondisabled as possible. In this case, having a disability that interferes with adherence to beauty norms (e.g., using assistive equipment such as a wheelchair, cane, or crutches) may significantly affect the way that the client thinks about herself. These thoughts may result in negative emotions such as sadness and anger and could lead to maladaptive behaviors such as social withdrawal (Galvin & Godfrey, 2001).

Physical barriers and the negative attitudes of others may interact with beliefs to increase the likelihood of developing cognitive distortions. For example, if this woman holds the culturally based belief that women should dress stylishly when leaving the house, she may feel the need to dress up and wear makeup to feel good about herself. However, in her attempt to do so, she may encounter physical barriers in transportation, retail stores, dressing rooms, display counters, and public restrooms. She may find herself being treated as if she is not worthy of respect by merchants, and she may be patronized regarding her efforts to dress well "despite" her disability. These kinds of experiences may feed into the types of distortions previously noted, in which negative experiences and invalidating feedback come to be viewed as universally prevalent, permanent, and accurate assessments of one's self-worth.

Radnitz and Tirch (1997) integrated many of the important factors to be considered in working with disabled people in a model that focuses on the interactional relationship among preexisting factors (e.g., cognitive and attributional style), environmental elements (e.g., physical barriers, social barriers, cultural milieu), and potential negative psychological consequences of living with a disability, (e.g., body image disturbance, lifestyle disruption, feelings of loss). Although this model is derived primarily from clinical experience with the SCI population, it may be helpful with people with varying types of acquired conditions. It is important to note that this model is not meant to capture all aspects of the disability experience but its interactional perspective provides a starting place for cognitive behavioral conceptualizations of clients adjusting to disability. Disability may not be central to the presenting problem for every disabled person who seeks therapy. At the same time, disability is part of the context in which the presenting problem occurs and in which treatment will take place (just as gender, ethnicity, and social class would be for both disabled and nondisabled clients).

Cognitions

Living with a disability affects the spectrum of interactions that a person has with her or his world (Tirch & Radnitz, 2000). The cognitive model holds that the situation itself does not directly determine how the individual feels; instead, emotional reactions are a function of perceptions of the situation (J. S. Beck, 1995). Although various authors have characterized cognitive distortions that are typical to people experiencing a range of psychological difficulties (e.g., A. T. Beck, Rush, Shaw, & Emery, 1979; J. S. Beck, 1995), there have also been efforts to describe cognitive distortions that may be uniquely shaped by the experience of disability (Needham, 1988; Radnitz & Tirch, 1997; Tirch & Radnitz, 2000).

Specifically, Radnitz and Tirch (1997) identified six categories of cognitive distortions relevant to people with disabilities: (a) an overly negative view of the world and others; (b) the belief that all people they encounter are insensitive, reducing the likelihood of positive social interactions; (c) the expectation and perception of rejection on the basis of disability

(Van Dorsten, 2000, added that these disability-based expectations would be likely to permeate initial interactions with the social environment, reducing the likelihood of disconfirming experiences); (d) hopelessness and the expectation of consistent failure, leading to depression, anxiety, and despair; (e) a sense of personal entitlement; and (f) feelings of vulnerability, potentially arising from the fact that people with disabilities are at increased risk for poverty and consequently may live in high-crime neighborhoods, thus increasing their vulnerability and potential for victimization.

In a similar vein, Needham (1988) and colleagues identified several cognitive distortions that may be experienced by visually impaired individuals in particular. The first type of distortion they posited is based on the person's appraisal of her or his own self-worth and value. The second type of distortion involves a feeling that people with visual impairments have a unique psychological constitution (e.g., that "only the blind can understand the blind"). The third type of distortion involves the idea that the visually impaired have a special relationship with other people and society in general (e.g., "blind people don't need to know how to cook or clean for themselves"), similar to Tirch and Radnitz's (2000) fifth category of entitlement. The fourth type of cognitive distortion suggested by Needham involves the idea that there are magical circumstances about visual impairment, such as the potential for improbable cures to be found.

Revisiting Cognitions Within a Disability Perspective

It is important to note that, in the preceding models of cognitive distortions, responsibility for the distorted thinking is being placed on the individual with the disability. This approach is derived from the medical model, in which disability is a defect of the individual and people with disabilities are believed to hold irrational beliefs—another defect of the individual—that need to be corrected by the cognitive behavioral therapist. In light of the social model, however, we believe that societal factors need to be considered: prejudice, oppression, marginalization, and, in particular, stigmatization. Reframing the aforementioned "distortions" from an interactionist perspective might be more culturally appropriate.

People with disabilities' experiences with marginalization and discrimination may contribute to their risk for cognitive patterns we label as distortions when they have generalized to other, less problematic, settings or have been internalized in ways that are harmful. This is difficult to avoid because of pervasive messages challenging the worth of diverse persons. In our culture of prizing perfection, bodies that are not "normal" are seen as less desirable than those that more closely fit societal ideals. Internalized stigma, most often studied in terms of mental illness, applies to some people with disabilities as well. However, we see the role of the cognitive behavioral therapist as helping the client to recognize and challenge these societally derived beliefs, while recognizing that these distortions are derived from problematic social conditions.

ASSESSMENT

The purpose of assessment in CBT is to understand the person and her presenting concerns with attention to the biopsychosocial factors most salient in the present moment. Through brief screens and a clinical interview, therapists should be prepared to engage the individual in the establishment of a collaborative treatment plan using cognitive behavioral approaches appropriately adapted to be delivered in a disability culture–congruent manner (Clemency Cordes et al., 2017).

As noted earlier, APA's (2012) 13th guideline for assessment of and intervention with persons with disabilities reads, "In assessing persons with disabilities, psychologists strive to consider disability as a dimension of diversity together with other individual and contextual dimensions" (p. 52). For psychologists working with disabled people, the assessment process should take into consideration factors including the unique and intersectional experiences that arise from being disabled within the context of other cultural identities, environmental barriers, experiences of marginalization, as well as the assessment of behavioral health concerns (Clemency Cordes, Mona, & Saxon, 2016; Olkin, 1999). People with disabilities experience the world as shaped by multiple intersecting identities, of which disability is just one. Mental health providers must evaluate the degree to which people with disabilities identify with disability as a key cultural or demographic marker and how salient their other identity dimensions are, as well as how much they interact (Clemency Cordes, Cameron, et al., 2016)

Brief, validated screening measures may assist clinicians in both identifying concerns and monitoring treatment effects over time; however, therapists must keep in mind that the majority of these screens have not been specifically validated for use with people with disabilities and should therefore be interpreted with caution (Clemency Cordes, Cameron, et al., 2016). For example, the somatic items on depression measures may artificially inflate scores for people with disabilities. In addition, it is important to keep in mind that abuse and violence occur at a higher rate to people with disabilities compared with nondisabled individuals (Nosek, Howland, Rintala, Young, & Chanpong, 2001). Thus, tools such as the Abuse Assessment

Screen—Disability may assist therapists in facilitating important conversations relevant to their presenting concerns.

Before beginning any assessment process with people with disabilities, assessment materials, processes, and directions may need to be modified to accommodate the functional abilities of the client. For example, most self-report measures are designed to be paper-and-pencil tasks, which may pose difficulties for some clients with visual or motor impairments. Therapists need to be prepared to offer alternative modalities, for example, via computer, large print, screen readers, interpreters, or assistance from another person to complete assessment tasks (Clemency Cordes, Mona, & Saxon, 2016). Telephone-based therapy, telemental health services, and other methods that reduce potential transportation-related barriers can further promote access to care and have been found effective for individuals with acquired disabilities (Dorstyn et al., 2010).

Comprehensive assessments may benefit from the inclusion of measures of well-being. Positive psychology brings a focus on strengths, values, and other positive aspects of personhood, rather than a singular focus on problems and psychopathology (Seligman & Csikszentmihalyi, 2000). Emotionally significant experiences may comprise both positive and negative dimensions. For example, the literature on posttraumatic growth and disability has shown that the majority of people studied have found disability to be both a source of positive growth, and at the same time, a significant challenge (Hayward, 2013).

INTERVENTION

Therapeutic Relationship

When working with persons with disabilities, it is important that therapists spend time and energy on building the therapeutic relationship and openly talking about the cultural differences between themselves and the client. Genuineness, warmth, empathy, and positive regard can facilitate the application and success of CBT (A. T. Beck, 1976). Therapists' ability to respectfully broach topics related to disability help to build trust.

It is essential that therapists identify and challenge their own implicit biases about disability. Toward this end, models of disability should be explored as a way of beginning self-assessment and taking a first step toward disability cultural competence. As a therapist, attention to one's ableist beliefs and attitudes may lead to more effective and efficient therapeutic encounters due to enhanced rapport and greater insight into a potential source of patients' stress, anger, or alienation (Clemency Cordes et al., 2017).

Behavioral Techniques

Cognitively oriented therapists use a variety of behavioral techniques to assist clients in regaining a sense of control and effectiveness in daily activities. These include activity scheduling, engaging in activities that provide feelings of pleasure and mastery, graded task assignments, cognitive rehearsal, and problem-solving. Behavioral strategies may also focus on enhancing interpersonal effectiveness (e.g., assertiveness training) or on improving physiological functioning (e.g., relaxation training; A. T. Beck, 1976; Young, Weinberger, & Beck, 2001).

When working with disabled people, it is important that the therapist validate clients' emotional experiences while still encouraging them to try new activities. Therapists should also recognize that clients might not enjoy or master all the activities that are attempted. Clients' trial-and-error process of identifying new pursuits or activities must be normalized. A graded task approach in which simpler tasks are assigned and mastered before undertaking more complex ones, and cognitive rehearsal in which clients mentally rehearse the steps required to achieve specific goals, can be particularly useful for clients with disabilities. These approaches help clients to realistically pace themselves and assist in the process of anticipating and addressing the physical, social, and cognitive roadblocks they may encounter. For clients to benefit from therapy, cognitive behavioral therapists encourage clients to practice the skills they are learning in therapy in their day-to-day surroundings (J. S. Beck, 1995). Practicing these skills first in the office can prepare clients for situations and individuals that may be rejecting and discriminatory. If negative situations do occur, therapy time can be used to process the experience and decrease the likelihood that it will be regarded as confirmatory evidence that activities that challenge the extent of one's abilities are not worth trying.

Cognitive Techniques

The thought record is a central tool for restructuring unhelpful automatic thoughts and eventually modifying intermediate and core beliefs (J. S. Beck, 1995). This multistep strategy helps clients to gain awareness of negative thoughts and their connection to negative mood states, then to develop proficiency in examining the validity of these negative thoughts and devising more adaptive responses (J. S. Beck, 1995; Greenberger & Padesky, 1995). Over time, clients learn to treat their thoughts as hypotheses rather than facts.

In considering the distortions that may occur at each level of cognition, it is important to recognize the objective aspects of situations that clients encounter. As Beck and colleagues have argued, the goal of CBT is to become more realistic, not simply more positive (A. T. Beck et al., 1979). Substituting realistic thinking for cognitive distortions allows for coping responses that are more likely to match the situation, yielding optimal outcomes. Thus, the client becomes more empowered and better able to accurately appraise stressors. People with disabilities have often experienced highly aversive interpersonal situations due to prejudice and discrimination. If the therapist's interventions appear to minimize these experiences, the client may feel misunderstood and marginalized.

In his work with people who have experienced a limb amputation, Van Dorsten (2000) highlighted the need to reframe negative cognitions and decatastrophize the impact of the disability. In addition, he held that it may be beneficial to help clients recognize the personal factors that have not been changed by the disability, thus challenging the distortion that "nothing will ever be the same" (Van Dorsten, 2000, p. 75). However, it is essential for the cognitive behavioral therapist to take a cross-cultural perspective in evaluating such beliefs and attend to the environmental context that gives rise to these beliefs rather than place emphasis entirely on the client's cognitions as the root of distress.

Strengths and Limitations of CBT for Clients With Disabilities

The strengths of using CBT with people with disabilities have been conceptualized clinically through the merits of assisting both clients' and therapists' ability to explore misconceptions about living with disability within assessment and clinical treatment strategies. Accordingly, limitations of using CBT with disabled clients can surface when there is a lack of awareness or an intentional choice not to include disability-affirmative practice as a context in which to use this evidence-based practice.

CASE EXAMPLES

The following examples[1] present clinical data from two individuals with disabilities who received CBT. These examples were chosen to illustrate the multiple layers of identity that are frequently relevant to clients with disabilities. Rather than provide a detailed account of the course of therapy, our goal is to highlight the ways that disability influences the focus and process of therapy.

---

[1]Case material in this chapter has been disguised to protect client confidentiality.

Frank

Frank, a 50-year-old divorced Latino man, was born in El Salvador and came to the United States at age 12. Frank was the youngest in a family of five children and the only son. He was diagnosed with cerebral palsy (CP) at birth. (CP is a term that describes a group of impairments that affect movement control.) In recent years, he has experienced greater difficulty walking, and his speech has become increasingly slurred.

Frank sought therapy because he was feeling "sad and anxious" that he was unemployed. Frank explained that he had worked as an accountant for the past 25 years but quit his job because he had been promoted to a senior position that required him to speak in public and entertain out-of-town guests for the company. He was so self-conscious about his slurred speech and his self-perceived "awkward" appearance that he started to have panic attacks at work, with symptoms that included hyperventilation. When Frank finally decided to quit, his coworkers did not seem upset, and therefore he concluded that they wanted him to leave.

During the first few sessions the therapist allowed Frank to tell her more about himself and his past. Frank shared that during his upbringing in El Salvador, his father was a successful businessman. However, because of political strife, Frank and his family were forced to flee their country and seek asylum in the United States. When asked how his family viewed his disability while growing up, Frank replied,

> It was rarely talked about. When I asked why I was different from the other children, I was told that when I was an infant, my mother had accidentally dropped me on a concrete floor, and this caused my CP. My parents were constantly telling me that I should not think of myself as disabled and I should try to achieve things that nondisabled people strive for. It was not until I was an adult that I learned what really caused this condition.

Frank described how his family's *creencias Latinos* (Latin beliefs) dictated certain expectations regarding his role within the family given that he was the youngest child and the only son. Frank stated,

> My family was proud to be in the United States, where there was more opportunity. They made it very clear to me when we arrived that I would be the one who everyone would work very hard for to send to college. During college, I had difficulty keeping up with the pace of work, and I knew it had to do with my disability. When I would explain to my parents why it was taking me longer to finish, they would say, "Don't worry about it, just finish."

At age 40, Frank fell in love with a woman who had recently immigrated to the United States from Peru, marrying her 6 months after they met.

Frank believes that the main reason she married him was because she wanted to be legalized in this country. He explained that during the first 2 months of their marriage, his wife avoided his attempts at sexual initiation. Frank became very self-conscious about his body, thinking that perhaps his wife was "repulsed when she looked at it." However, after several discussions, his wife admitted that she feared "becoming pregnant and giving birth to a child with his *enfermedad* [disease]." Frank understood her concerns and set up a medical appointment in which he had a physician explain to her the cause of CP and the fact that there was a low probability of their children inheriting this condition. After this occurred, Frank and his wife began to engage in sexual activity with one another; however, Frank continued to believe that there were parts of him that were unattractive to his wife. For example, he stated,

> I never felt that I could please her as a woman because I could not move my body during sex the same way that other men do. Most of the time, I would run out of breath and needed her to help me out to give her pleasure. I never felt like I could live up to that macho image we Latin men are given.

Despite these concerns, Frank and his wife conceived and give birth to three daughters.

Frank remained married for 8 years, after which his wife filed for divorce. Frank explained that the divorce was "very nasty" as his wife attempted to get full custody of their children, claiming that he was unfit to be a parent. Frank shared,

> I will never forget the day 1 asked my lawyer on what grounds she was accusing me of being a bad parent, and he told me that it was because of my CP. I fought this custody battle with everything I had, and fortunately the court granted me partial custody. But after this episode, I was changed. I began to have a hard time concentrating at work and started feeling like everyone was noticing things about my disability. It was then that I began to question what other ways my condition was affecting me.

Frank's primary focus in psychotherapy was to reduce anxiety to facilitate a return to the workforce. It was determined that CBT would be an effective approach for Frank because it would allow him to explore his thoughts and feelings related to his anxiety at work and also about his disability. The accumulation of negative life events, including the onset of his divorce, the custody battle, and the loss of his job, appeared to have triggered some of his negative core beliefs. Until this time, his compensatory strategies (i.e., working hard and not identifying himself as a disabled person) had helped to keep his negative core beliefs at bay. These core beliefs included "Being disabled means that I am not good enough" and "My disability makes me unattractive." Intermediate beliefs (which mediate between core beliefs and automatic thoughts) included "I must work very hard to show people that I am good enough" and "If I identify myself as a disabled man, I will be rejected."

Core cultural beliefs also were identified during therapy, such as "Being the only male in my family, I should be able to prosper and make my family feel proud of me" and "As a Latino male, I should be the one who has the most physical strength in the marriage to please my wife and make her feel safe." These beliefs are not inherently negative, particularly within the cultural context that gives rise to them; however, they became a source of vulnerability for Frank given his CP, his unemployment, and the breakup of his marriage. In Frank's case, when these beliefs were applied inflexibly, they led to shame and dysphoria. The goal in therapy was to expand these beliefs rather than to attempt to change Frank's identification with his Latin culture. For example, a more helpful version of these beliefs for Frank was, "I can make my family proud by having integrity and being a good father, not just by achieving financial success," and "As a male, I can respect and care for a woman in a way that makes her feel safe and protected." Thus, Frank's traditional views of his roles as son, husband, and father were made more flexible and concordant with his strengths as a disabled person.

Frank had initial concerns about completing thought records because his motor impairment meant that writing was extremely difficult. The therapist suggested completing thought records through dictation to his computer, and Frank subsequently sent the records through secure messaging to his therapist. A typical thought record dealt with Frank's anxiety facing a professional situation that involved mingling with a large group of people. Frank experienced a particularly distressing automatic thought: "These people are uncomfortable because I am not able to reach out and shake their hand the way normal people do." He also described emotions of nervousness, embarrassment, and shame. Frank weighed evidence supporting the thought ("I can tell that people's expressions and body gestures change when I come into the room or approach them" and "They seem to avoid making eye contact and they become stiffer when I get close to them"). He considered evidence contradicting the thought ("There are some people who will sometimes smile and come over to speak to me," "No one has actually ever said that I make them uncomfortable and walked away," and "Not everyone expects a handshake"). Ultimately, his conclusions were more balanced: "There are some people who may be uncomfortable being around me but they will still make an effort to acknowledge my existence and speak to me," "There are quite a few people who do seem to enjoy greeting me and asking me what I think about something," and "These people always smile at me and are not staring at my body."

By the time the therapy ended, Frank had a better understanding of what his disability meant to himself and others. After decades of experiencing his disability as a potential source of shame and inadequacy, something to be minimized as much as possible, he began to experience it both as a more central part of his identity and, at the same time, as a less dire and threatening reality. This gentler and more matter-of-fact approach suggested that he was beginning to adopt a belief system more characteristic of disability cultural values. In fact, Frank had been somewhat avoidant of befriending other people with disabilities because of his belief in the importance of presenting himself as a nondisabled person. Over the course of therapy, he found himself reaching out to a neighbor about 15 years older than himself. This man, also Salvadoran American, had lost his eyesight secondary to diabetes but was happily married and integrated into the Latin community. Although Frank and this neighbor did not speak directly about their experiences with disability, Frank found himself viewing this man as an older male role model.

Frank came to understand that his assumption that others would dislike him because of his disability also meant that he did not experience himself as likable. By examining the global nature of his assumption, he saw his situation with greater nuance. He recognized that although socially painful encounters were inevitable, he did not have to base his self-image on the insensitive behavior and comments of others. His self-esteem improved as he was able to devote more of his attention to the people in his life whose feelings toward him reflected a more complete picture of his personality and character. Through completing thought records, Frank realized that many people genuinely liked him, including family members, neighbors, and former coworkers. This support served as a buffer against some of the thoughtless remarks he received from others.

Frank also benefited from completing several home practice assignments that helped him to generate evidence challenging his beliefs. The homework assignments involved engaging in social activities to test whether people were really rejecting him. For example, he attended a parent–teacher conference at his daughters' school. He was very nervous about this event, but he forced himself to go and then felt proud about it afterward. Despite his divorce and the difficult custody battle, Frank's relationship with his children continued to provide him with a sense of himself as a family man, which was particularly important to him given his Latino upbringing that emphasized family roles. As he became less anxious and more self-confident, he began to realize that his experiences of social rejection and self-doubt made him particularly empathic to his daughters' trials and tribulations, and he relished their willingness to talk with him about their fears, anxieties, and triumphs.

Another homework assignment involved going to several job interviews for positions in which he had little interest. This activity gave him the opportunity to notice how new people actually did react to him. After several interviews, he started to feel more relaxed. He began to attend less to his own perceived inadequacies and more to whether the potential employers seemed aware of legal requirements regarding workplace accommodations for people with disabilities. Over time, Frank stopped waiting for the therapist to give him homework assignments and started taking risks on his own, signaling his readiness to terminate therapy.

Lisa

Lisa was a 55-year-old European American woman and a single parent of a 30-year-old son with Down syndrome. She grew up in a family with conservative Christian values. Both her parents were active participants in the church and expected Lisa and her older brother to follow their faith. At age 25, Lisa gave birth to her son without being in a relationship with a partner. Her family and friends expressed disappointment and warned her that it would be difficult to raise a disabled child as a single parent. Lisa was hurt by their lack of encouragement and thought, "I will show everyone that it is possible to care for my son with or without family assistance." For the next 30 years, Lisa devoted herself to working full time in retail jobs to provide for her son. She took pride in the fact that she was "always able to hold a job and simultaneously raise a child with a disability."

At the age of 54, Lisa had a stroke and began using a wheelchair. Her realization that she could no longer walk contributed to feelings of depression, and she decided to quit her job. She began to tell herself, "I am no longer the woman I used to be. I am of no use to anyone." In describing the feelings that led her to seek therapy, Lisa also reported experiencing guilt because she could no longer physically provide care for her son and was forced to make arrangements for him in a special assisted living facility. Thoughts that accompanied this decision included self-condemnation, such as "I am a horrible mother because I cannot take care of my son anymore."

Lisa's depression and anger began to take a toll on her friendships and eventually led her to seek therapy. She indicated that she was feeling "impatient and temperamental" with people around her. Her irritability led her to yell at people when they made mistakes or failed to show up on time. Lisa said that she recently spent a lot of time crying while viewing photographs of her life before the stroke. She reported a loss of interest in pleasurable activities and fears that she would be "unhappy and alone" for the remainder of her life. During the first session, she also briefly mentioned that although she found herself "a little attracted to women" most of her life, these feelings had become stronger, and she was feeling confused and ashamed because of her traditional religious beliefs. At the time that she entered therapy, Lisa was living in an apartment that was minimally wheelchair accessible, and she had volunteer personal assistance services to help her with activities of daily living (e.g., shopping, cooking, bathing).

Several core beliefs contributed to Lisa's depression and anxiety, including, "I am only worthwhile if I am self-sufficient," "I am a failure if I am not able to care for my son perfectly," and "Having a disability means others will not love me or find me attractive." Her intermediate beliefs included "If I do not care for my son, my family will be right about me," "I will never be the woman that I used to be," and "Being attracted to women is wrong."

Throughout Lisa's life, these intermediate and core beliefs about being a failure, a disappointment, and not good enough motivated her to work hard and to be an involved mother. Additionally, her success in maintaining an excellent work history, providing for her son's financial needs, and physically and emotionally caring for her son full time enabled her to feel good about herself despite holding some negative core beliefs. Her stroke and subsequent concerns about disappointing her son and family, distress about being unemployed, uncertainty about the future, difficulty coping with architectural barriers at her apartment, and confusion about being attracted to women undermined her ability to function in the way that she had previously and led to emotional distress.

The beginning of therapy focused on building rapport, discussing cultural differences related to her Christian upbringing that might affect therapy, and introducing the CBT model. Homework consisted of activity logging to better understand how Lisa was currently spending her time. Her completed activity log suggested that she spent much of her time at home alone, which contrasted greatly with a typical day before her stroke. As she explained, "Six months ago, my schedule was packed with work activities, appointments for my son, lunch dates with my girlfriends, and house chores. Now I cannot do any of that."

The therapist spent time exploring and validating Lisa's feelings about her inability to do some of the things that she previously enjoyed doing (e.g., jogging, physically caring for her son in her own home). The therapist recognized the importance of not only challenging the automatic thought but also identifying the grain of truth in the thought and addressing the subsequent reality-based feelings of loss. Together, Lisa and her therapist examined her negative automatic thought, "I cannot do the things that I used to enjoy doing." An automatic thought record was introduced, and evidence for and against the accuracy of this thought was examined. With help from her therapist, Lisa was able to challenge this thought and create the more balanced statement, "I can still do many of the things that I like to do while using a wheelchair." Over time, the therapist assisted Lisa to challenge and restructure her beliefs about being a bad mother because of her disability and a failure as a person because of her attraction to women.

Behavioral strategies were also implemented, beginning with activity scheduling. Lisa was asked to schedule two pleasurable activities into her day and rated the amount of mastery and pleasure that she anticipated she would feel before engaging in the activity. She was then asked to rerate her pleasure and mastery while doing the activity. As predicted, Lisa's anticipatory ratings for going out to lunch with her friends were significantly lower (*pleasure* = 3, *mastery* = 4) than her feelings while at lunch (*pleasure* = 8, *mastery* = 7).

Lisa was encouraged to schedule not only pleasant events but also tasks that would allow her to feel accomplished and worthy. For example, she took the initiative to make arrangements for public transportation to visit her son every other day. Being able to see her son and provide even a small amount of care for him had a dramatic effect on Lisa's mood. She reported that now that she was spending less time alone and getting more things done, her feelings of sadness and frustration lessened. These behavioral strategies were continued until Lisa was regularly engaging in pleasurable activities and her mood had improved.

Lisa was also taught problem-solving strategies aimed at facilitating adjustment to her disability. Assertiveness training was provided to help Lisa express herself in a more effective manner. Specifically, Lisa was asked to focus on the difficulties she was having in communicating with the people around her. When asked what interactions were particularly troubling, Lisa said, "I am mostly bothered when someone treats me like I'm some sort of alien." She provided an example of a waiter treating her differently by avoiding eye contact and using a different tone of voice than he used with her companion. She reported feeling very upset and complaining to the manager, whose response was invalidating and rejecting. She said she then yelled at the manager and left the restaurant feeling misunderstood, discriminated against, and ostracized.

The therapist validated Lisa's anger and provided the opportunity for Lisa to discuss her experience of discrimination and resulting feelings. She described a sense of helpless anger mixed with self-denigration. The therapist asked Lisa to consider whether she could have expressed her anger differently and discussed with her the difference between passive, assertive, and aggressive communication. Lisa was willing to role play and practice her new assertive style of communication with the therapist over several sessions. With practice, Lisa learned to express her thoughts and feelings without losing control of her temper.

Becoming more assertive did not always yield satisfactory outcomes in situations Lisa encountered, but overall it did work well. For example, when she finally moved to an apartment that was supposed to be wheelchair accessible, she found that the bathroom door was installed so that it opened into the bathroom, making it impossible for her to shut the door while inside. The apartment manager initially responded with indifference to the fact that she would be unable to have privacy, but Lisa was able to persist until he realized how unacceptable the situation was and arranged for the door to be installed appropriately. Throughout this experience, despite feeling intensely upset at times, Lisa was able to retain a sense of humor about the absurdity of the situation and the manager's oppressive response. She eventually concluded that she had had a deep positive influence on the manager by shaking up his assumptions and helping him to experience an empathic response.

CONCLUSION

CBT is an evidence-based intervention that is well-suited for use with clients with disabilities and can be leveraged to reduce distress and to promote well-being and empowerment. Therapists can begin to develop disability cultural competence through attention to frameworks for understanding disability that incorporate biopsychosocial, familial, and sociopolitical factors; by gaining self-awareness and challenging ableist attitudes; and by attending to the reality of minority experiences and oppressive contexts when working with clients to change behavior and challenge dysfunctional attitudes and cognitions. This chapter highlighted the complexity of disability by drawing attention to the socioenvironmental context of disability and the ways in which thoughts, feelings, and behaviors can be addressed in therapy without minimizing the real constraints that are imposed by environments that limit access. Although negative beliefs may be rooted in real-life oppressive and discriminatory situations, it is appropriate to challenge the interpretations of these negative experiences so that more adaptive functioning can be facilitated. Disability cultural values may provide an important foundation for therapists seeking to promote strength and resilience for clients with disabilities. It is our hope that the information presented in this chapter is a step toward the creation of a larger body of clinical work that more critically explores the CBT conceptualization, assessment, and treatment of people with disabilities from a cultural lens.

REFERENCES

American Psychological Association. (2002). Ethical principles of psychologists and code of conduct. *American Psychologist, 57,* 1060–1073. http://dx.doi.org/10.1037/0003-066X.57.12.1060

American Psychological Association. (2012). Guidelines for assessment of and intervention with persons with disabilities. *American Psychologist, 67,* 43–62. http://dx.doi.org/10.1037/a0025892

American Psychological Association. (2017). *Ethical principles of psychologists and code of conduct* (2002, Amended June 1, 2010 and January 1, 2017). Retrieved from http://www.apa.org/ethics/code/index.aspx

Andrykowski, M. A., & Hunt, J. W. (1993). Positive psychosocial adjustment in potential bone marrow transplant recipients: Cancer as a psychosocial transition. *Psycho-Oncology, 2,* 261–276. http://dx.doi.org/10.1002/pon.2960020406

Bandura, A. (1977). Self-efficacy: Toward a unifying theory of behavioral change. *Psychological Review, 84,* 191–215. http://dx.doi.org/10.1037/0033-295X.84.2.191

Banks, M. E., Brown, K. S., Mona, L. R., & Ackerman, R. J. (2014). Women with disabilities: Affirmative practice and assessment. In C. Z. Enns, J. K. Rice, & R. L. Nutt (Eds.), *Psychological practice with women: Guidelines, diversity, empowerment* (pp. 159–190). Washington, DC: American Psychological Association.

Beach, J. D., Robinet, J. M., & Hakim-Larson, J. (1995). Self-esteem and independent living skills of adults with visual impairments. *Journal of Visual Impairment & Blindness, 89,* 531–540.

Beck, A. T. (1976). *Cognitive therapy and the emotional disorders.* New York, NY: International University Press.

Beck, A. T., Rush, A. J., Shaw, B. F., & Emery, G. (1979). *Cognitive therapy of depression.* New York, NY: Guilford Press.

Beck, J. S. (1995). *Cognitive therapy: Basics and beyond.* New York, NY: Guilford Press.

Bonanno, G. A., Kennedy, P., Galatzer-Levy, I. R., Lude, P., & Elfström, M. L. (2012). Trajectories of resilience, depression, and anxiety following spinal cord injury. *Rehabilitation Psychology, 57,* 236–247. http://dx.doi.org/10.1037/a0029256

Chevalier, Z., Kennedy, P., & Sherlock, O. (2009). Spinal cord injury, coping and psychological adjustment: A literature review. *Spinal Cord, 47,* 778–782. http://dx.doi.org/10.1038/sc.2009.60

Clemency Cordes, C., Cameron, R. P., Eisen, E., Coble-Temple, A., & Mona, L. R. (2017). Leveraging integrated behavioral health services to promote mental health among women with disabilities. In K. Kendall-Tackett & L. R. Ruglass (Eds.), *Women's mental health across the lifespan: Challenges, vulnerabilities, and strengths* (pp. 119–140). New York, NY: Routledge.

Clemency Cordes, C., Cameron, R. P., Mona, L. R., Syme, M. L., & Coble-Temple, A. (2016). Perspectives on disability within integrated healthcare. In L. A. Suzuki, M. Casas, C. Alexander, & M. Jackson (Eds.), *Handbook of multicultural counseling* (4th ed., pp. 401–410). Thousand Oaks, CA: Sage.

Clemency Cordes, C., Mona, L. R., & Saxon, L. C. (2016). Integrated primary behavioral health care for women veterans with disabilities. In S. E. Miles-Cohen & C. Signore (Eds.), *Eliminating inequities for women with disabilities:*

An agenda for health and wellness (pp. 227–242). Washington, DC: American Psychological Association. http://dx.doi.org/10.1037/14943-012

Craig, A. R., Hancock, K., Chang, E., & Dickson, H. (1998). Immunizing against depression and anxiety after spinal cord injury. *Archives of Physical Medicine and Rehabilitation, 79,* 375–377. http://dx.doi.org/10.1016/S0003-9993(98)90136-8

Craig, A. R., Hancock, K. M., & Dickson, H. G. (1994). A longitudinal investigation into anxiety and depression in the first 2 years following a spinal cord injury. *Paraplegia, 32,* 675–679. http://dx.doi.org/10.1038/sc.1994.109

Dorstyn, D. S., Mathias, J. L., & Denson, L. A. (2010). Psychological intervention during spinal rehabilitation: A preliminary study. *Spinal Cord, 48,* 756–761. http://dx.doi.org/10.1038/sc.2009.161

Elliott, T. R., Godshall, F. J., Herrick, S. M., Witty, T. E., & Spruell, M. (1991). Problem solving appraisal and psychological adjustment following spinal cord injury. *Cognitive Therapy and Research, 15,* 387–398. http://dx.doi.org/10.1007/BF01173033

Ellis, A., & Grieger, R. (1986). *Handbook of rational-emotive therapy* (Vol. 2). New York, NY: Springer.

Ferguson, E., Matthews, G., & Cox, T. (1999). The Appraisal of Life Events (ALE) scale: Reliability and validity. *British Journal of Health Psychology, 4,* 97–116. http://dx.doi.org/10.1348/135910799168506

Fine, M., & Asch, A. (1988). *Women with disabilities: Essays in psychology, culture, and politics.* Philadelphia, PA: Temple University Press.

Fitzgerald, R. G. (1970). Reactions to blindness. An exploratory study of adults with recent loss of sight. *Archives of General Psychiatry, 22,* 370–379. http://dx.doi.org/10.1001/archpsyc.1970.01740280082015

Galvin, L. R., & Godfrey, H. P. D. (2001). The impact of coping on emotional adjustment to spinal cord injury (SCI): Review of the literature and application of a stress appraisal and coping formulation. *Spinal Cord, 39,* 615–627. http://dx.doi.org/10.1038/sj.sc.3101221

Gerry, L. & Crabtree, J. (2013). Cognitive behavioral therapy and the impact of internalized societal discourses in people with intellectual disabilities: a case example. *Advances in Mental Health and Intellectual Disabilities, 7,* 59–65. http://dx.doi.org/10.1108/20441281311294710

Gill, C. J. (1995, Fall). A psychological view of disability culture. *Disability Studies Quarterly.* Retrieved from http://www.independentliving.org/docs3/gill1995.html

Greenberger, D., & Padesky, C. A. (1995). *Mind over mood: Change how you feel by changing the way you think.* New York, NY: Guilford Press.

Guest, R., Craig, A., Nicholson Perry, K., Tran, Y., Ephraums, C., Hales, A., . . . Middleton, J. (2015). Resilience following spinal cord injury: A prospective controlled study investigating the influence of the provision of group cognitive behavior therapy during inpatient rehabilitation. *Rehabilitation Psychology, 60,* 311–321. http://dx.doi.org/10.1037/rep0000052

Harkins, S., Elliott, T., & Wan, T. (2006). Emotional distress and urinary incontinence among older women. *Rehabilitation Psychology, 51,* 346–355. http://dx.doi.org/10.1037/0090-5550.51.4.346

Harper, S. K., Webb, T. L., & Rayner, K. (2013). The effectiveness of mindfulness-based interventions for supporting people with intellectual disabilities: A narrative review. *Behavior Modification, 37,* 431–453. http://dx.doi.org/10.1177/0145445513476085

Hassiotis, A., Serfaty, M., Azam, K., Strydom, A., Blizard, R., Romeo, R., . . . King, M. (2013). Manualised individual cognitive behavioural therapy for mood disorders in people with mild to moderate intellectual disability: A feasibility randomised controlled trial. *Journal of Affective Disorders, 151,* 186–195. http://dx.doi.org/10.1016/j.jad.2013.05.076

Hayward, H. (2013). *Posttraumatic growth & disability: On happiness, positivity, & meaning* (Unpublished doctoral dissertation). Harvard University, Cambridge, MA.

Huurre, T. M., Komulainen, E. J., & Aro, H. M. (1999). Social support and self-esteem among adolescents with visual impairments. *Journal of Visual Impairment & Blindness, 93,* 26–37.

Kef, S. (2002). Psychosocial adjustment and the meaning of social support for visually impaired adolescents. *Journal of Visual Impairment & Blindness, 96,* 22–37.

Kemp, B. J., & Krause, J. S. (1999). Depression and life satisfaction among people ageing with post-polio and spinal cord injury. *Disability and Rehabilitation, 21,* 241–249. http://dx.doi.org/10.1080/096382899297666

Kennedy, P., Lude, P., Elfström, M. L., & Smithson, E. (2010). Cognitive appraisals, coping and quality of life outcomes: A multi-centre study of spinal cord injury rehabilitation. *Spinal Cord, 48,* 762–769. http://dx.doi.org/10.1038/sc.2010.20

Kennedy, P., Marsh, N., Lowe, R., Grey, N., Short, E., & Rogers, B. (2000). A longitudinal analysis of psychological impact and coping strategies following spinal cord injury. *British Journal of Health Psychology, 5,* 157–172. http://dx.doi.org/10.1348/135910700168838

Kennedy, P., & Rogers, B. A. (2000). Anxiety and depression after spinal cord injury: A longitudinal analysis. *Archives of Physical Medicine and Rehabilitation, 81,* 932–937. http://dx.doi.org/10.1053/apmr.2000.5580

Longmore, P. K., & Umansky, L. (Eds.). (2001). *The new disability history.* New York, NY: New York University Press.

Martz, E., Livneh, H., Priebe, M., Wuermser, L. A., & Ottomanelli, L. (2005). Predictors of psychosocial adaptation among people with spinal cord injury or disorder. *Archives of Physical Medicine and Rehabilitation, 86,* 1182–1192. http://dx.doi.org/10.1016/j.apmr.2004.11.036

Mehta, S., Orenczuk, S., Hansen, K. T., Aubut, J. A. L., Hitzig, S. L., Legassic, M., . . . the Spinal Cord Injury Rehabilitation Evidence Research Team. (2011). An evidence-based review of the effectiveness of cognitive behavioral therapy for psychosocial issues post-spinal cord injury. *Rehabilitation Psychology, 56,* 15–25. http://dx.doi.org/10.1037/a0022743

Mona, L. R., Cameron, R. P., & Clemency Cordes, C. (2017). Disability culturally competent sexual healthcare. *American Psychologist, 72,* 1000–1010. http://dx.doi.org/10.1037/amp0000283

Mona, L. R., Romesser-Scehnet, J. M., Cameron, R. P., & Cardenas, V. (2006). Cognitive behavior therapy with persons with disabilities. In P. A. Hays & G. Y. Iwamasa (Eds.), *Culturally responsive cognitive–behavioral therapy: Assessment, practice, and supervision* (pp. 199–222). Washington, DC: American Psychological Association. http://dx.doi.org/10.1037/11433-009

Needham, W. E. (1988). Cognitive distortions in acquired visual loss. *Journal of Vision Rehabilitation, 2,* 45–54.

Nosek, M. A., Howland, C., Rintala, D. H., Young, M. E., & Chanpong, G. F. (2001). National study of women with physical disabilities: Final report. *Sexuality and Disability, 19,* 5–40. http://dx.doi.org/10.1023/A:1010716820677

Olkin, R. (1999). *What psychotherapists should know about disability.* New York, NY: Guilford Press.

Olkin, R., & Pledger, C. (2003). Can disability studies and psychology join hands? *American Psychologist, 58,* 296–304. http://dx.doi.org/10.1037/0003-066X.58.4.296

Papadopoulos, K., Montgomery, A. J., & Chronopoulou, E. (2013). The impact of visual impairments in self-esteem and locus of control. *Research in Developmental Disabilities, 34,* 4565–4570. http://dx.doi.org/10.1016/j.ridd.2013.09.036

Papadopoulos, K., Paralikas, T., Barouti, M., & Chronopoulou, E. (2014). Self-esteem, locus of control and various aspects of psychopathology of adults with visual impairments. *International Journal of Disability, Development and Education, 61,* 403–415. http://dx.doi.org/10.1080/1034912X.2014.955785

Perry, A., & Weiss, J. (2007). Evidence-based practice in developmental disabilities: What is it and why does it matter? *Journal on Developmental Disabilities, 13,* 167–171.

Peter, C., Müller, R., Cieza, A., & Geyh, S. (2012). Psychological resources in spinal cord injury: A systematic literature review. *Spinal Cord, 50,* 188–201. http://dx.doi.org/10.1038/sc.2011.125

Peter, C., Müller, R., Post, M. W., van Leeuwen, C., Werner, C. S., & Geyh, S. (2015). Depression in spinal cord injury: Assessing the role of psychological resources. *Rehabilitation Psychology, 60,* 67–80.

Pinquart, M., & Pfeiffer, J. P. (2011). Psychological well-being in visually impaired and unimpaired individuals: A meta-analysis. *British Journal of Visual Impairment, 29,* 27–45. http://dx.doi.org/10.1177/0264619610389572

Quale, A. J., & Schanke, A. K. (2010). Resilience in the face of coping with a severe physical injury: A study of trajectories of adjustment in a rehabilitation setting. *Rehabilitation Psychology, 55*, 12–22. http://dx.doi.org/10.1037/a0018415

Radnitz, C. L., & Tirch, D. D. (1997). Physical disability. In R. L. Leahy (Ed.), *Practicing cognitive therapy: A guide to interventions* (pp. 373–389). Northvale, NJ: Jason Aronson.

Schulz, R., & Decker, S. (1985). Long-term adjustment to physical disability: The role of social support, perceived control, and self-blame. *Journal of Personality and Social Psychology, 48*, 1162–1172. http://dx.doi.org/10.1037/0022-3514.48.5.1162

Seligman, M. E., & Csikszentmihalyi, M. (2000). Positive psychology: An introduction. *American Psychologist, 55*, 5–14. http://dx.doi.org/10.1037/0003-066X.55.1.5

Shapiro, J. P. (1994). *No pity: People with disabilities forging a new civil rights movement* (pp. 16–18). New York, NY: Times Books.

Tirch, D. D., & Radnitz, C. L. (2000). Spinal cord injury. In C. L. Radnitz (Ed.), *Cognitive behavioral therapy for persons with disabilities* (pp. 183–204). Northvale, NJ: Aronson.

Tyc, V. L. (1992). Psychosocial adaptation of children and adolescents with limb deficiencies: A review. *Clinical Psychology Review, 12*, 275–291. http://dx.doi.org/10.1016/0272-7358(92)90138-X

Van Dorsten, B. (2000). Amputation. In C. L. Radnitz (Ed.), *Cognitive behavioral therapy for persons with disabilities* (pp. 59–76). Northvale, NJ: Aronson.

World Health Organization. (2011). *Sexual and reproductive health core competencies in primary care*. Geneva, Switzerland: Author.

Young, J. E., Weinberger, A., & Beck, A. T. (2001). Cognitive therapy for depression. In D. H. Barlow (Ed.), *Clinical handbook of psychological disorders: A step-by-step treatment manual* (3rd ed., pp. 264–308). New York, NY: Guilford Press.

11

AFFIRMATIVE COGNITIVE BEHAVIOR THERAPY WITH SEXUAL AND GENDER MINORITY PEOPLE

KIMBERLY F. BALSAM, CHRISTOPHER R. MARTELL,
KYLE P. JONES, AND STEVEN A. SAFREN

Cognitive behavior therapy (CBT) is the most widely studied evidence-based treatment for a wide range of mental health and interpersonal problems. Due to the stress of living as a member of a stigmatized group, there are elevated rates of mental health problems in sexual and gender minority individuals. Therefore, there is a great need for resources to provide evidence-based practice for sexual and gender minorities, although relatively few empirical studies address its use with this population. Although cognitive behavioral techniques are similar for clients of all sexual orientations and gender identities, cultural sensitivity and knowledge about working with the unique needs of this population will enhance the success of CBT practice and, if neglected, can hinder treatment. This chapter addresses the use of a culturally sensitive, affirmative CBT approach in treating diverse sexual and gender minority clients.

http://dx.doi.org/10.1037/0000119-012

Culturally Responsive Cognitive Behavior Therapy, Second Edition: Practice and Supervision, G. Y. Iwamasa and P. A. Hays (Editors)

TERMINOLOGY AND CONCEPTS

Because sexual and gender minority people are a stigmatized group, an awareness of terms and concepts can help promote an affirmative environment for therapeutic work. *Sexual minority* refers to individuals who are marginalized on the basis of their sexual identity or sexual behavior and is often used as an umbrella term to refer to lesbian, gay, and bisexual (LGB) people in general. *Gender minority* refers to individuals who are marginalized based on their gender identity or gender expression and is also used as an umbrella term to refer to transgender and gender nonconforming (TGNC) people. The acronym *SGM* (sexual and gender minorities; sometimes referred to as GSM) refers to gender and sexual minorities as a whole, similar to the common acronyms *LGBT* (lesbian, gay, bisexual, and transgender) and *LGBTQ* (lesbian, gay, bisexual, transgender, and queer).

Sexual orientation is an umbrella term that describes the gender or genders of a person's emotional and sexual attractions. Sexual orientation comprises three dimensions: identity, behavior, and attraction (Eliason, 2014). *Sexual identity* is a more specific term that refers to a person's self-identification, usually including recognition of one's sexual orientation and sexual behaviors and the meanings one places on them. Specific identity labels include (but are not limited to) *lesbian*, *gay*, *bisexual*, and *queer*. The term *queer*, once used pejoratively, has been reclaimed by some individuals and communities and is now often used as an affirmative self-identification, preferable to lesbian, gay, or bisexual as being less confined to binary conceptions of sexual identity. Additionally, an individual may adopt one or more sexual identity labels at any given time, and these labels may change over the course of the life span.

Separate but related to sexual identity is an individual's *sexual behavior*. A person may engage in same-sex sexual behavior without self-identifying as lesbian, gay, bisexual, or queer. Conversely, a person might identify as lesbian, gay, bisexual or queer without having any previous same-sex sexual experience. As with sexual behavior, sexual attraction may or may not be congruent with sexual identity at any given time point or over the course of one's life span. Indeed, in a population-based cross-sectional sample of urban women, Meyer, Rossano, Ellis, and Bradford (2002) found that only 33% of women with any same-sex orientation reported all of the following three components of sexual orientation: same-sex identity, same-sex behavior, and same-sex attractions. Additionally, in a Canadian study of adolescents with an LGB identity, only 68.8% reported same-sex attraction and 45.3% endorsed same-sex behavior (Igartua, Thombs, Burgos, & Montoro, 2009). Thus, considering all three of these components of sexual orientation is important in conceptualizing the identity or behavior of clients, and how this does or does not relate to their presenting problem(s).

Similarly, there are several concepts and terms that must be considered working with TGNC clients. *Gender identity* refers to someone's internal sense of their gender—for example, a person may have a deeply held sense of self as male, female, both, or another gender identity. *Gender expression* refers to how someone presents their gender identity, usually in the form of physical characteristics, clothing, and outward behaviors. Both of these are distinct from *sex assigned at birth*, which is the term used to refer to an individual's assignment as male, female, or intersex at birth.

Western societies typically view sex and gender as being binary (male–female) and congruent with one another. However, it is important to note that many indigenous cultures around the world have recognized gender as a separate construct and have even designated specific gender identities for individuals who are outside of the sex binary. Some examples include the Mahu of Hawaii, the Fa'afafine of Samoa, and the Muxes (pronounced "moo-shey") from the city Juchitán in Mexico (Link, 2004; Mirandé, 2014; Odo & Hawelu, 2001; Schmidt, 2016). All three groups represent a gender variant unique to their respective culture and are sometimes considered a third gender.

Transgender is a contemporary Western umbrella term that refers to people whose gender identity differs from their sex assigned at birth. More recently, the term *TGNC* has been used as a more inclusive umbrella term. Some individuals adopt a nonbinary gender identity, as both male and female, neither male nor female, or another gender altogether. Such individuals may use terms such as *nonbinary*, *genderqueer*, *genderfluid*, or *gender variant* to refer to their gender. Some TGNC people choose to *transition* and live as a gender other than their sex assigned at birth. This can involve gender-affirming medical procedures such as hormones and surgery, as well as social transitions such as change in name and style of dress. However, it is important to recognize that not all TGNC people want to transition fully or at all.

Terms related to sexual and gender identity do not universally apply to people of all cultural backgrounds, even within the United States. Many communities of color have specific terms that are more culturally relevant for individuals with these identities. For example, among Native American people who may have sexual or affectional attractions to people of the same gender, the term *two-spirit* or a specific tribal term is often used in place of LGBTQ. These terms may refer to the historical acceptance of sexual and gender diversity and the traditional social role for these individuals in some Native communities (Jacobs, Thomas, & Lang, 1997). Among African American women, the terms *stud*, *aggressive*, and *femme* have been used to refer to gender diversity within sexual minority women's communities, also referred to as *women-loving* women (Moore, 2011; Wilson, 2009). African American men, due to multiple social stigmas, may maintain a heterosexual identity and outward appearance yet engage in sexual behavior with men on the *down low* (Han, 2015). In some Latino cultures, specific sexual behavior is related to sexual identity. For example, a man may have sex with men but not consider himself to be gay if he is the active partner sexually (Reisen et al., 2010).

SOCIAL CONTEXT FOR SEXUAL AND GENDER MINORITIES

Although sexual and gender minority people are diverse in terms of social identities, demographics, and life experiences, there are some commonalities that stem from growing up and living in a society that assumes heterosexual and cisgender identities as the norm. The term *heterosexism* refers to an ideological system that denies, denigrates, and stigmatizes any nonheterosexual form of behavior, identity, relationship, or community (Herek, 1990). A similar but related term is *homophobia*, used to refer to irrational fear, hatred, and intolerance of homosexuality (Weinberg, 1972). Additionally, the phenomenon of *transphobia* is an emotional sensation of fear, disgust, and revulsion toward people who do not align with society's typical expectations of gender (i.e., masculine men and feminine women; Hill & Willoughby, 2005). A related term is *genderism*, which, like heterosexism, refers to the cultural and social belief systems that frame gender as binary and consistent with sex assigned at birth (Beemyn & Rankin, 2011). Bisexual people are also subject to *biphobia*, defined by Ochs (1996) as the "discrimination, hostility, and invalidation" experienced by bisexuals in both the lesbian/gay and heterosexual communities (p. 217). A related stigma is *monosexism*, which is defined as the belief that sexuality is essentially dualistic and that individuals can only be lesbian, gay, or heterosexual (Roberts, Horne, & Hoyt, 2015). In all of its forms, discrimination and stigma against SGM people have negative effects on the individual. For many SGM people, oppression based on their sexual orientation and gender identity intersects with other forms of oppression, such as racism, classism, and sexism; this may be relevant to culturally appropriate delivery of CBT.

Developmental Issues and Challenges

Unlike ethnic and cultural minority identities that are often shared with family members, sexual and gender minority identities are often experienced as difference from family of origin. Most SGM people grow up in a household that lacks SGM role models and in which traditional, binary gender norms for behavior are enforced. For young children who have, or who become aware of, same-sex attractions or gender identities (or both) that differ from sex assigned at birth, a great deal of confusion can result. From a cognitive–behavioral perspective, children and adolescents who display such behaviors typically experience punishments from their environment in the form of rejection, criticism, and even verbal and physical abuse (D'Augelli, 1998; Toomey, Ryan, Diaz, Card, & Russell, 2013). Conversely, children are rewarded through praise and social support for conforming to norms for heterosexual and cisgender behavior.

Negative societal messages about SGM identities and orientations affect the way SGM individuals think and feel about themselves. This is referred to as *internalized homophobia* or *internalized homonegativity* and has been linked empirically to psychological distress (Newcomb & Mustanski, 2010). Transgender individuals may also experience a similar construct, *internalized transphobia*, as a result of internalizing societal negative messages about "normative" gender identity. They may experience shame or self-hatred individually or prejudice toward other transgender people, as a result (Bockting, 2015). Internalized transphobia has specifically been linked to greater lifetime suicide attempts, suicidal ideation, and a negative impact on self-esteem and is associated with psychological distress in transgender and TGNC individuals (Austin & Goodman, 2017; Testa et al., 2017).

Another distinguishing feature of this group is that unlike more visible minority identities, some SGM people have the option of concealing or disclosing their stigmatized status. This is truer for those who are gender conforming; SGM people with visible gender expressions that differ from norms associated with their sex assigned at birth are typically more visible to others. For sexual minorities, the process of becoming aware of one's sexual orientation and disclosing this to others is referred to as *coming out*. It is important to understand that coming out is a continuous process over the life span, as sexual minority individuals negotiate their identities and decisions about disclosure on a day-to-day basis. Furthermore, this process varies across cultures (Aranda et al., 2015; A. Smith, 1997). For example, among some ethnic minority groups, family members may accept one's sexual orientation without ever having an explicit discussion about it. For European Americans, greater *outness* (self-disclosure to others), for example, is associated with lower psychological distress (Morris, Waldo, & Rothblum, 2001). However, it is important to look at the social context when considering the function of outness. For example, in some cultural communities or family situations, keeping sexual orientation private may be more adaptive and promoting of mental health if coming out would lead to increased rejection from family or society, or even increased risk for violence or abuse.

Understanding outness among transgender and gender nonconforming people requires a more complex and nuanced view. Physical changes, such as facial hair or changes in voice because of efforts to transition, cannot be easily concealed. This can result in increased isolation or negative social consequences for transgender individuals who have begun to transition but have not yet negotiated the coming-out process (Collazo, Austin, & Craig, 2013). However, efforts to transition in childhood and young adulthood have been linked to greater psychological function and well-being, in recent studies (de Vries et al., 2014; Olson, Durwood, DeMeules, & McLaughlin, 2016).

The impact of heterosexist and genderist oppression on an individual is best understood in a framework of intersectionality (Crenshaw, 1991) along with other important social identities such as race, ethnicity, immigration status, socioeconomic status, disability status, and age (Parent, DeBlaere, & Moradi, 2013). For example, A Chinese American cisgender lesbian woman working in a traditionally male-dominated field may feel physically threatened by her male coworkers and may fear reprisal if she comes out at work, yet she may feel intense pressure from her immigrant parents to succeed in her profession. A White cisgender bisexual woman who is visible and politically active in the LGBTQ community may be distressed by homophobic comments from her neighbors and online harassment that she receives on social media, while her more closeted bisexual friend who is married to a man may be distressed at her relative "invisibility" and by the assumption of heterosexuality that her marital status confers. A transgender biracial woman whose voice remains low and deep posttransition may be constantly mis-gendered (i.e., her gender assumed incorrectly) and referred to as "sir" when answering the phone.

Sexual and Gender Minority Individuals in CBT

Sexual minority adults are more likely to attend psychotherapy and take psychiatric medications than their heterosexual counterparts (Grella, Greenwell, Mays, & Cochran, 2009). This finding may be due to several factors, including cultural acceptance within LGBTQ communities of going to psychotherapy and the self-exploration and personal growth associated with the sexual and gender identity formation processes (Bradford, Ryan, & Rothblum, 1994). As with any client population, SGM clients may present with a wide range of concerns that may or may not be directly related to their sexual orientation or gender identity. Population-based studies of sexual minority adults conducted over the past 20 years have consistently found elevated rates of depressive and anxiety disorders, suicide attempts, and substance use disorders compared with heterosexual populations (Cochran, 2001; King et al., 2008). More recently, studies that have included transgender populations have found similar disparities and, in some cases, even higher risk for these disorders relative to LGB cisgender peers

(Burgess, Tran, Lee, & Van Ryn, 2007). SGM clients may also present for help with stressors related to their sexual orientation and gender identity, including discrimination, rejection by family members and friends, conflict between SGM identity and religious beliefs, and internalized homophobia (see Berg, Mimiaga, & Safren, 2004).

The impact of sexual orientation–based oppression on the individual LGB person has been referred to as *minority stress* and linked to mental health problems and disparities with heterosexual populations (Meyer, 2003). More recently, this model has been extended and adapted to address the impact on gender minorities (Hendricks & Testa, 2012; Testa, Habarth, Peta, Balsam, & Bockting, 2015) Mays and Cochran (2001) reported that LGB individuals surveyed reported greater lifetime and day-to-day experiences of discrimination. Additionally, a robust body of research has demonstrated that SGM people experience relatively high rates of interpersonal trauma over the life span including bias-related victimization (Herek, Gillis, Cogan, & Glunt, 1997) and other forms of victimization, such as childhood abuse (Friedman et al., 2011; Reisner, White, Bradford, & Mimiaga, 2014) and sexual assault in adulthood (Rothman, Exner, & Baughman, 2011). These experiences are associated with several psychological disorders and symptoms and may prompt contact with a mental health professional.

Strengths and Limitations of CBT With SGM Individuals

There are a number of advantages to using CBT with SGM clients. First, the history and development of cognitive and behavioral approaches to therapy is grounded in empirical findings, with strong support for treatment of many of the disorders (e.g., depression, anxiety) prevalent in SGM populations. Second, unlike therapeutic approaches that locate the source of psychopathology within the individual's psyche, contemporary CBT pays close attention to the environmental and social context of clients' lives. Third, in CBT, therapists take a collaborative, problem-solving approach, helping clients to develop and test hypotheses about problems and try out new behaviors in everyday life. Living in a society that assumes heterosexuality and cisgender identities, SGM clients frequently do not fit the dominant culture's expectations and may particularly benefit from an approach that allows them to voice their unique perspectives. Fourth, the skills-training focus can give clients concrete tools to cope with stressors related to sexual and gender minority status and gender dysphoria. Fifth, CBT does not conceptualize behavior as good or bad, but rather as functional or not functional. This nonjudgmental approach is especially appropriate with clients who experience judgment and stigma from their social environment. Sixth, cognitive–behavioral techniques are useful in countering the assumption that internalized stigma (homophobia, transphobia) beliefs represent "the truth" and in reconceptualizing these beliefs as thoughts that can be changed.

Although the benefits of using CBT with SGM clients are numerous, some limitations require mention. First, types of behavior therapy were historically used to assist some LGB clients to change their sexual orientation (Adams, Tollison, & Carson, 1981). These techniques are unethical, harmful to patients, and do not work (Haldeman, 1994). These types of treatments often result in serious psychological consequences for those who attempt them (Shidlo & Schroeder, 2002). Because of this history, some SGM clients, particularly those who came out in the pre-Stonewall era, may consequently approach behavior therapy with skepticism and mistrust. The American Psychiatric Association (2000), the National Association of Social Workers (1996), and the American Psychological Association (2012) directly oppose or strongly recommend against the use of these types of therapies. However, given this history, some SGM will need further explanation of how behavior therapy can be used in an affirmative way.

Another possible limitation is that while CBT approaches have robust empirical support for numerous mental health disorders, there are only a limited number of treatment studies that have assessed for sexual orientation and gender identity and thus have not included specific approaches for addressing the developmental and sociocultural concerns of diverse SGM clients. Combining an understanding of CBT and the SGM literature has allowed several writers to offer empirically grounded suggestions for working with this population (Austin, Craig, & Alessi, 2017; Martell, Safren, & Prince, 2004; Padesky, 1989; Purcell, Campos, & Perilla, 1996), but more research is needed in this area. Recently, a few published studies have begun to address this gap. For example, Pachankis, Hatzenbuehler, Rendina, Safren, and Parsons (2015) conducted a randomized trial of the ESTEEM (Effective Skills to Empower Effective Men) protocol, a 10-session intervention adapted from Barlow et al.'s (2010) Unified Protocol that focuses on addressing minority stress among gay and bisexual men. This protocol significantly reduced depression, alcohol use, and sexual risk behaviors compared with a waitlist control.

Several other nonrandomized pilot studies have been conducted with promising results. An intervention targeting depression in sexual minority youth was a single-arm pilot study done by Lucassen, Merry, Hatcher, and Frampton (2015). They examined the Rainbow SPARX program, a seven-module intervention in which participants interacted with a virtual world and worked with a virtual therapist. Depression symptoms decreased over time in this small sample ($n = 19$). Craig and Austin (2016) tested another group intervention with a sample of diverse sexual and gender minority youth. This eight-module cognitive behavioral skills group focused on traditional CBT techniques and resulted in reductions in depression and increases in reflective coping (i.e., thinking about effective coping strategies). Finally, N. G. Smith et al. (2017) tested an eight-session group intervention for young gay and bisexual men: Project PRIDE (Promoting Resilience in Discriminating Environments). Results indicated significant increases in self-esteem and small reductions in loneliness, alcohol use, and sexual risk behaviors.

Traditional Versus Third-Wave CBT

Traditional CBT typically involves examining ways in which psychological symptoms or distressing and interfering negative emotions emerge or are maintained by three interacting components: (a) the cognitive component, (b) the behavioral component, and (c) a physiological component. Generally speaking, the cognitive component involves thoughts that occur in response to a stimulus in the environment and underlying core beliefs that filter how one might interpret or think in these situations. The behavioral component involves what one actually does that might maintain or exacerbate the problem. The physiological component involves the physical symptoms that come along with distress. Typical CBT aims to directly change the cognitive and behavioral responses that maintain distress. There are newer treatments that have emerged, such as acceptance and commitment therapy, functional analytic psychotherapy, dialectical behavioral therapy, and mindfulness-based CBT, that are referred to as *third-wave* CBT (Hayes, Strosahl, & Wilson, 2012; Kohlenberg & Tsai, 1991; Linehan, 1993; Segal, Williams, & Teasdale, 2012). These treatments generally move away from the approach of directly trying to change distress and symptoms but instead focus on strategies such as acceptance, being mindful, and regulating one's emotions via focusing on activities surrounding personal meaning and value. These treatments can be ideally suited for working affirmatively across gender identity and sexual orientations.

Assessment and Case Conceptualization

Assessment and case conceptualization play an important role in CBT. As with any cognitive–behavioral approach, therapists working with SGM clients are advised to develop a problem list; gain an understanding of the environmental, historical, behavioral, cognitive, and physiological variables that may be influencing the client's problems; and work collaboratively with the client to develop a treatment plan that addresses the problems and fits with the client's goals. In addition, therapists working with SGM clients must consider the role of sexual orientation and gender identity and their intersection with other identities in the client's presenting problem and treatment.

For some clients, sexual orientation or gender identity (or both) may play a prominent role in the presenting problem and may be a central focus of treatment (Benson, 2013; Martell et al., 2004). For example, a 35-year-old Latina heterosexually married cisgender woman may present for treatment to understand her emerging same-sex attractions, address anxiety related to internalized homophobic and biphobic beliefs, and explore her options regarding relationships and identity within the context of her traditional Latin American cultural beliefs. On the other end of the spectrum, sexual orientation or gender identity may have little to do with the presenting problem. For example, a 45-year-old White gay man who has been out for 25 years may present with panic disorder, having nothing to do with his sexual orientation. In such cases, it is possible for the therapist to over-emphasize sexual orientation or gender identity, which can also be considered a form of bias (Garnets, Hancock, Cochran, Goodchilds, & Peplau, 1991). For many SGM clients, sexual orientation or gender identity has some significance to the presenting problem but does not play a central role.

Key to SGM-affirmative therapy is the assessment of the role of sexual orientation and gender identity in the presenting problem. The assessment should include questions about identity, behavior, and attractions, and the client's thoughts and feelings about any discrepancies between these dimensions of sexual orientation. It should also include gender identity, gender expression, gender transition experiences, and desires. Measurement instruments designed to assess SGM-specific concepts such as the Lesbian, Gay, Bisexual Identity Scale (Mohr & Kendra, 2011), the Outness Inventory (Mohr & Fassinger, 2000); the Daily Heterosexist Experiences Questionnaire (Balsam, Beadnell, & Molina, 2013); and the Gender Minority Stress and Resilience Scale (Testa et al., 2015) can be used to assess identity, stress, and resilience. Regarding historical factors, the therapist might inquire about the client's sexual and gender identity development, asking when and how the client became aware of his or her sexual orientation, how and when they disclosed to others, and what were the key events or turning points in this process. In assessing the role of the current environment, the therapist would determine the extent to which the client is out and feels accepted in various settings and by important people and cultural communities. The therapist should assess the degree to which these environmental factors, along with the client's own beliefs about being SGM, might be causing distress. This may include questions regarding possible discrimination, harassment, or victimization and the extent to which the client attributes these experiences to sexual orientation.

Some common outcome measures used in CBT are useful with all clients regardless of gender or sexual orientation, such as the first and second editions of the Beck Depression Inventory (Beck, Steer, & Brown, 1996), the Beck

Anxiety Inventory (Beck, Epstein, Brown, & Steer, 1988), the Addiction Severity Index (McLellan et al., 1992), and the Quality of Life Inventory (Frisch, 1994). These instruments are more appropriate because they do not ask questions specific to sexual orientation, and they are gender neutral.

Anxiety inventories that ask questions about social anxiety using phrases such as "discomfort with members of the opposite sex" make an implicit assumption that people who have anxiety about dating will be anxious interacting in mixed company. It is better to ask if there is discomfort "around a person to whom I was physically or emotionally attracted." Couple inventories frequently use forms for *husband* and *wife* that are inappropriate for same-sex couples. *Partner A* and *Partner B* differentiate the two people more inclusively (e.g., see the Frequency and Acceptability of Partner Behavior scale by Christensen & Jacobson, 1997, and the Dyadic Adjustment Scale by Spanier, 1976). Intake forms or scales for parents can be labeled *Parent 1*, and *Parent 2*, and not *mother* and *father*.

For all general psychological measures, it is important to consider the populations on which they were normed when using them with diverse SGM clients. Virtually no general psychological measures report information on the sexual orientation or gender identity of the standardization samples, although they are assumed to be heterosexual and cisgender, as well as White. Thus, norms for these measures are more likely to be useful when using them with SGM clients who approximate the standardization sample in other ways, such as in binary cisgender identity and/or race/ethnicity, education level, and so on. Keo-Meier and Fitzgerald (2017), in a review article, noted that assessment becomes particularly problematic for TGNC clients when measures have different norms for men and women along binary lines, as is common in neuropsychological, forensic, and other forms of assessment. At this time, little information exists to suggest which of these norms, or which new norms, may be most appropriate for transgender and gender nonbinary clients.

SEXUAL AND GENDER MINORITY–AFFIRMATIVE CBT

In conducting CBT with sexual and gender minority clients, it is recommended that therapists take a culturally informed approach similar to those recommended for other diverse populations (Boroughs, Bedoya, O'Cleirigh, & Safren, 2015). First and foremost, therapists must take a nonpathologizing and accepting therapeutic stance, recognizing that all sexual orientations and gender identities are valid (American Psychological Association, 2012, 2015). Cultural awareness is also indicated through use of language on forms and in the initial meeting. For example, clients' identities and preferred gender pronouns should be inquired about rather than assumed.

An affirmative CBT therapist will also stay informed about cultural norms for diverse SGM people. For example, among some SGM, particularly gay and bisexual men, consensual nonmonogamy is not uncommon and should not be assumed to be problematic for the client (Solomon, Rothblum, & Balsam, 2005). Another area in which cultural norms may play a role is in the client's definition of family. Because sexual and gender minority clients may have experienced rejection by or hostility from their families or cultural communities, friendship circles may be their family of choice (Galupo, 2009; Galupo et al., 2014).

Therapists doing affirmative work with sexual and gender minority clients need to be aware of the potential to make mistakes in therapy that clients may experience as microaggression and be willing to address and repair relationship ruptures (Spengler, Miller, & Spengler, 2016). Even culturally informed therapists may potentially mis-gender clients (i.e., assume the wrong gender without asking which pronouns they prefer) or say something that is inadvertently offensive, given a client's unique history. SGM clients may be particularly sensitive to such microaggressions in interpersonal relationships given their history of rejection and lack of visibility in the broader cultural context (Austin & Craig, 2015). Therapists should be willing to continually examine and address their own biases outside and in session regarding SGM people. Further, the collaborative nature of CBT can help to reduce the damage of therapeutic ruptures when therapists request feedback in each session as to what has helped or not helped, or what the client may wish to change. Spengler et al. (2016) also recommend that therapists ask directly whether clients have experienced anything in therapy that is similar to microaggressions they have experienced outside of therapy.

Another key element in culturally sensitive treatment with SGM clients involves attention to the social context of homophobia/heterosexism and transphobia and, when appropriate, helping clients to identify sources of oppression in their environment and link these to symptoms and other presenting problems (Austin & Craig, 2015). Explaining the minority stress model (Meyer, 2003; Testa et al., 2015) can be a useful tool in understanding these links. It is imperative that therapists listen carefully to clients and not jump too quickly to recommendations that could lead to harmful consequences—for example, encouraging a client to come out or to socially transition without a full understanding of the client's context and therapeutic goals. On the other hand, it is helpful to examine areas in which a client may be engaging in avoidant behavior related to sexual orientation or gender identity. For example, clients may avoid contact with colleagues or conversing with new neighbors for fear of exposure of their sexual orientation or gender identity. In such cases, clinicians may conduct a functional analysis of avoidant behaviors and help the client to develop alternative behavioral responses while realistically taking into account the social contexts and stigma in the client's life. Cognitive restructuring, a key intervention in CBT, can also be used to counter negative beliefs about self or the LGBTQ community that may be based on stereotypes or internalized homonegativity or internalized transphobia.

Another area of clinical focus with sexual and gender minority clients is social support, including the client's connection with a community. Social support has been linked cross-culturally to positive mental health among sexual and gender minority adults and youth (Grossman, D'Augelli, & Frank, 2011; Frost & Meyer, 2012). For some sexual and gender minority people, fear of living more openly as SGM may be linked to a fear of losing supportive relationships. Additionally, some relationships may be supportive in some domains yet unsupportive of the client's sexual orientation or gender identity. For SGM of color, these issues can be even more complicated because individuals may find it difficult to find people or communities that support and affirm all of their minority identities (e.g., Balsam, Molina, Beadnell, Simoni, & Walters, 2011). To assist clients in finding SGM-affirmative social supports that are also affirming of other identities, clinicians need to be knowledgeable about local community resources for diverse SGM and be willing to work with clients creatively to build an affirmative and culturally sensitive support system.

CASE EXAMPLE 1: ROBIN

Client Description and Presenting Problem

Robin[1] was a 26-year-old European American self-identified queer, gender-nonconforming woman of Scandinavian and German descent, who lived alone in an apartment near the university campus in a Northwestern city. When she presented for treatment, she was in graduate school studying for her PhD in history. She had been active in the LGBTQ rights movement for several years, volunteering for a national organization and publishing a local newsletter. Robin had been dating Jenna, a woman she met at school, for about 5 months. Her parents and younger brother all lived in the Midwest, in the town where she was born.

Robin initially found the therapist's phone number in a local LGBTQ business directory. Her initial complaints were of "sleep problems and stress." Upon assessment, she revealed that her sleep problems were largely due to nightmares and feelings of agitation at the slightest sound in her apartment.

---

[1]Case material in this chapter has been disguised to protect client confidentiality.

She was having difficulty concentrating on her schoolwork and had been spending less time socializing with Jenna and other friends. She had become increasingly irritable and reported tearfully that lately she was "snapping" at her girlfriend for no reason. Robin also reported symptoms consistent with a panic attack on at least two recent occasions.

Suspecting a diagnosis of posttraumatic stress disorder (PTSD), the therapist inquired about a history of trauma. Robin acknowledged that a male friend had sexually assaulted her at age 19 in her dorm room. This incident occurred after the two had been drinking together at a campus party. According to Robin, at the time, she was beginning to recognize her attraction to women and to openly express her masculine gender identity. Although she enjoyed the company of this man, she turned down his sexual advances after he walked her home. After attempting to verbally coerce her and calling her a "dyke," he used physical force to rape her. Although she had a great deal of psychological distress in the following months, Robin never disclosed this to anyone.

After the incident, staying at that school was difficult. She transferred to another college the following year. The development of her sexual orientation and gender identity became more and more salient to her, and she slowly chose to come out to her parents, her siblings, and her friends. In the ensuing years, she had intermittent nightmares but generally managed to "push away" thoughts and feelings about the rape during the day. She generally tried to avoid reading about or watching any accounts of rape on television because this would make the nightmares increase. She also rarely drank alcohol and avoided parties and other large gatherings where people were drinking. Periodically she experienced street harassment based on her gender nonconforming appearance, which triggered memories of the rapist's slurs.

According to Robin, 3 months before treatment, she walked into one of her classes and was shocked to discover that the professor bore a striking resemblance to the man who had raped her. Her symptoms immediately increased, and she began to have intrusive thoughts about the rape. She stated that she was beginning to feel pretty hopeless about her situation and referred to herself as "weak" for letting this incident bother her so much. Although Jenna suspected that something was wrong and had encouraged her to seek therapy, Robin feared that if she knew about the rape, Jenna would not respect her.

Case Formulation and Course of Treatment

The therapist diagnosed Robin as having PTSD secondary to the traumatic experience of rape. Compared with heterosexual and cisgender people, SGM people are at elevated risk for interpersonal trauma experiences such as rape, childhood abuse, and physical assault over the lifespan (Balsam, Rothblum, & Beauchaine, 2005). Thus, therapists working with SGM clients are likely to see clients for whom a traumatic event or events play a prominent role in their presenting concerns.

Sexual and gender minority clients who present for therapy with trauma-related problems may also experience additional symptoms related to thoughts and feelings about their sexual orientation and gender identity. For example, assaults that are perceived to be bias-related produce more stress than do other types of assaults (Herek, Gillis, & Cogan, 1999). Sexual and gender minority individuals also contend with pervasive cultural myths regarding the "cause" of minority sexual orientations (Balsam, 2003). For example, in one study, nearly half of LGB survivors of childhood sexual abuse reported that at one time they had questioned whether the abuse "made them" LGB (Balsam, 2002). Furthermore, PTSD and other trauma-related symptoms may be exacerbated by additional traumas. Although social support is an important factor in reducing symptoms after trauma, some sexual and gender minority people who are not out or who are isolated from their families or cultural communities may lack this support.

After learning Robin's history, the therapist asked her to complete the PTSD Checklist for *DSM–5* self-report measure (Blevins, Weathers, Davis, Witte, & Domino, 2015) and then followed up with a clinical interview to arrive at the diagnosis of PTSD.[2] The therapist looked for symptoms of depression, other anxiety disorders, and substance abuse and assessed changes in Robin's life after the event, including her beliefs about the rape and its role in her life. The therapist provided Robin with some handouts describing common reactions to rape; this gave Robin the feeling that she was "not alone" with her reactions and some hope that she could reduce her symptoms through treatment.

The therapist's approach to treatment with Robin was based on Foa and Rothbaum's (1998) prolonged exposure therapy, a specific type of CBT. This treatment has demonstrated empirical support with survivors of rape (Foa, Rothbaum, Riggs, & Murdock, 1991) as well as other traumatic events. Prolonged exposure therapy targets avoidance of trauma-related environmental cues and memories of the trauma using exposure-based techniques. The rationale for the treatment is that PTSD symptoms are reduced as the client habituates to the traumatic memories. Like many other clients, Robin was initially skeptical about this approach and reluctant to engage in treatment that would require her to relive the rape event. The therapist discussed

---

[2]Although case examples in this chapter describe the use of assessments for determining diagnoses according to *Diagnostic and Statistical Manual of Mental Disorders* (fifth ed.; *DSM–5*), all providers must now use *International Classification of Diseases* (10th revision) diagnostic codes for insurance reimbursement claims.

Robin's reluctance and provided her with information about the rationale and efficacy of exposure-based treatment.

Prolonged exposure therapy includes both imaginal and in vivo exposure. During imaginal exposure, Robin relived the rape during therapy sessions by describing aloud the details of the event in the present tense to the therapist. The therapist tape-recorded the description and Robin was instructed to listen to these tapes daily at home between sessions. The following is an excerpt from Robin's first in-session imaginal exposure exercise:

> *Robin:* Now we're in my dorm room. . . . I turn on the light and thank Joe for walking me home. . . . He doesn't leave . . . now he's coming toward me and he smells like beer . . . [pause] . . . He said that he knew I wanted to have sex with him . . . [pause]
>
> *Therapist:* He's *saying* that he *knows* I want to have sex with him . . .
>
> *Robin:* Right, present tense, okay, I . . . I tell him that I just want to be his friend . . . I don't know what to think . . . he's standing so close to me . . . he's rubbing my back . . . [starts to ring her hands]
>
> *Therapist:* You're doing just fine, Robin. Stay with this image.
>
> *Robin:* I tell him to stop. . . . He's squeezing my arm. . . . Now he's starting to . . . he's calling me names, he's saying "you f***ing dyke" . . . [breathing rapidly]
>
> *Therapist:* Okay, what is your anxiety level now on the 0-to-100 scale?
>
> *Robin:* It's . . . I think it's 90.
>
> *Therapist:* I know this is difficult. Keep going . . .

During this initial imaginal exposure exercise, the therapist's focus was on gently prompting Robin to stay in the present tense and keep the narrative going. During later sessions, the therapist used more prompts to help Robin activate feelings of distress and confront the aspects of the event that were most fear-producing for her. After several weeks of imaginal exposure exercises in session and at home, Robin's distress decreased, and she reported fewer intrusive thoughts and nightmares about the rape.

For in vivo exposure, Robin developed a hierarchy of feared and avoided situations and gave each situation a Subjective Units of Distress Rating. This is a scale that ranges from 1 to 100, with 1 being the least anxious and most relaxed one could feel and 100 being the most anxious that one could feel or imagine feeling. Robin's hierarchy included talking to friends about the first college she attended (with a rating of 50), going to class with the professor who resembled the perpetrator (60), reading a newspaper article about a rape

(70), talking to her girlfriend about the rape event (80), attending a social event where people are drinking alcohol (90), and going back to the campus where the rape occurred (90). The therapist and Robin worked together to plan exposures to these stimuli between sessions.

Robin's clinical presentation included feelings of guilt and shame accompanied by distorted cognitions such as "It was my fault that I was raped" and "A strong woman wouldn't feel scared." Foa and Rothbaum (1998) suggested adding a cognitive restructuring component to prolonged exposure treatment for clients with PTSD who have this clinical presentation. Robin's therapy included standard elements of cognitive restructuring, including identifying and challenging distorted beliefs about the rape, herself, and her relationships with others. The therapist addressed Robin's belief that others might attribute her sexual orientation and gender identity to the rape via cognitive restructuring techniques and by asking Robin to read written accounts of other queer and gender nonconforming women's accounts of sexual assault. Robin was eventually able to talk with Jenna about the experience. The support and empathy she received from Jenna upon disclosure was useful in challenging the belief that she was somehow at fault or that the rape showed that she was "weak."

The therapist also worked with Robin to develop a proactive coping response to situations in which she experienced homophobic harassment or slurs. Understanding the minority stress model (Meyer, 2003; Testa et al., 2015) helped Robin to contextualize these microaggressions based on her sexual and gender identities. Using the guided self-dialogue technique (Foa & Rothbaum, 1998), Robin learned to talk herself through potentially stressful situations, use coping self-statements (e.g., "I can handle this") and provide herself with reinforcement for successfully managing stressful situations.

By the end of treatment, Robin reported a dramatic reduction in PTSD symptoms and no longer met criteria for the disorder. She no longer avoided class and was better able to concentrate on her studies. Discussing the rape with Jenna increased her feelings of intimacy, and the two planned to move in together the following summer. She also felt empowered by her ability to reconcile her traumatic history with her self-image as a strong, gender-nonconforming woman and LGBTQ activist. At the time of her final session, she was investigating an opportunity to write for a national newsletter on violence against LGBTQ people.

CASE EXAMPLE 2: ED

Ed was a 39-year-old African American man who, at the time of his initial session, had been working in an administrative position at a legal office for more than a year. Ed reported that he had previously been unemployed for significant periods of time. He grew up in Virginia with his mother, grandmother, and aunt and described his upbringing as religious and strict. His family still lived in Virginia. He was currently living in a large Northeastern city.

On the telephone before the first session, Ed described his presenting problem as depression with some anxiety. Ed stated that his depression was affecting his ability to get to work on time and to complete projects he was assigned. He reported that he eventually wanted to return to college but that he felt too depressed to take any action. As a result of his depression, he also reported that he had been less involved with his 13-year-old son than he would like.

When Ed arrived for the first session, the therapist explained the process of the evaluation for CBT, which included a diagnostic interview followed by feedback, and then a discussion of what CBT might entail. The therapist used questions from the Structured Clinical Interview for DSM–5 (First, Williams, Karg, & Spitzer, 2015). Ed met criteria for a major depressive disorder, recurrent, of moderate severity and for a mild panic disorder (controlled with medications). While assessing Ed's depressive symptoms including his libido, a discussion about dating situations and romantic relationships emerged. Ed stated that he did not date often. He added that he avoided situations in which he would meet potential dates because he believed that many (White) men were either not interested in Black men or were interested only in sex.

Because this was a general outpatient clinic and Ed had not previously mentioned sexual orientation as an issue, it had not occurred to the therapist that Ed might be gay. As a result, up until this point, the therapist had conducted an assessment typical of many cognitive and behavioral intake assessments. However, after Ed made this comment, the therapist was able to go back and obtain additional information. This example illustrates why assessing sexual orientation should be a part of most general intake interviews.

The therapist subsequently learned from Ed that he had struggled with his sexuality throughout his life. Due to pressure from his family and community, he had dated women until he was in his late 20s. He was sexual with several women, and one of them became pregnant with his son. During the time he dated women socially and sexually, Ed was also sexual with men. These relationships were kept secret because neither he nor his partners were out. During this time, Ed struggled with alcohol abuse, which cost him several jobs.

A complete cognitive behavioral case formulation revealed that Ed's depression was exacerbated by social isolation; some significant social anxiety, particularly around meeting romantic partners; his desire for a meaningful relationship with another man; and negative core beliefs he had about himself related to his sexual orientation. Although he had previously struggled with both alcohol and finances, Ed had been alcohol-free for several years and had an income on which he could live. Ed still struggled to reconcile his religious beliefs and the messages he grew up with in a devout family with his current sexual identity and behaviors.

Because his panic disorder was under control with medication, and the alcohol problem was stable, cognitive–behavioral treatment focused on the depression and, as a secondary component of this, his social anxiety. This is because the underlying core beliefs and situational cognitions were similar in terms of causing him depression and social anxiety. One of the early interventions involved mood and activity monitoring. Investigation revealed that his mood was much better during the day when he was at work, where he would socialize with his coworkers. However, his mood dropped when he was at home without plans, and this was worst over the weekend. This led to a discussion about the need to find enjoyable non–work-related activities. Ed's main exposure to other gay men had been in bars and clubs, where he found it difficult to meet men who were not interested only in sex.

Over the course of several sessions, Ed agreed with some reluctance to consider alternative ways of meeting other gay men. Ed and the therapist came up with several suggestions, including a hiking club, a gay running club, and volunteering. Ed rejected the idea of a hiking club because he said he hated the outdoors, he thought the running club would be too difficult a place to start, but he thought he could probably volunteer at a local AIDS community center, although he expressed some anxiety about it. Ed had heard about volunteering there but had some ambivalence. The following discussion emerged as part of a cognitive restructuring intervention.

> *Therapist:* Let's try to figure out exactly what it is that is making you reluctant to try this out. Let me ask you to, for a minute, pretend that you have called and made an appointment with the volunteer coordinator.
>
> *Ed:* Okay.
>
> *Therapist:* You have an appointment to go next week and learn about the kinds of things they offer. Picture yourself going in to the appointment. What is going through your head?
>
> *Ed:* Oh my god, I can't believe I am doing this.
>
> *Therapist:* Okay, why, in your head, are you thinking that you can't believe you are doing this?
>
> *Ed:* This guy is not going to like me.
>
> *Therapist:* Okay, what else?

Ed:	If this guy is gay, he is going to wonder why the f*** I am there, since I am so different from other gay men.
Therapist:	What else is going through your head?
Ed:	Well, the other thing is that if he does like me, it will only be because he is interested in me sexually. And if I am too friendly, he is going to think that I am interested in him sexually or that I'm just there to meet men.
Therapist:	And why, in your head, would that be bad?
Ed:	Because only someone totally f***ed up would need to resort to going to a place like that to meet friends.

One of the first steps in cognitive restructuring procedures is to list the thoughts that make one feel depressed or anxious. This was done earlier, as noted. Additional steps include identifying distortions or errors in one's thinking and learning to use objective evidence to dispute the thoughts and come up with a rational response. Ed was able to recognize that he was using "all or nothing thinking" and "mind-reading" in making assumptions that volunteer coordinators would either dislike him or only accept him because they were sexually attracted to him (although he was not completely convinced that he was incorrect about this view). He also made some gains with respect to his mood, structuring his weekend and after-work activities (although not always social activities). Over time, he was able to use conversations like that just described to test his negative predictions about social situations. In turn, this led to decreased avoidance of social situations and increased satisfaction with these interactions.

Throughout the course of treatment, Ed gradually built on his early success with activity planning. He eventually began volunteering at a local organization for HIV, where he was well liked among the staff, and his negative predictions did not come true. This allowed him to become more open to other cognitive restructuring exercises aimed at increasing his social activities, including slowly meeting friends and maintaining friendships and dating relationships. By becoming more integrated into the LGBTQ community and feeling better about being gay, he also felt he could be more honest about who he was to his heterosexual friends and that these relationships could therefore grow.

CONCLUSION

Sexual and gender minority individuals face a variety of stressors related to their sexual orientation and gender identity and to their intersections with other identities. When presenting for mental health treatment, many SGM clients may also have difficulties similar to heterosexual and cisgender clients, including anxiety, depression, relationship problems, and coping with life stressors. Even when the presenting problem is not explicitly related to sexual or gender minority, however, it is important for clinicians to be aware of the myriad ways in which identity and social context may impact treatment for the client. Thus, while CBT can be applied to this population, an adequate knowledge base about sexual and gender minority issues is important to assist in formulating a functional analysis and case conceptualization. Sometimes stress related to one's sexual orientation and gender identity is the primary reason treatment is needed; at other times, it is a peripheral cause; and at yet other times, it has nothing to do with the presenting problem. It is important to note that much of the literature on CBT interventions does not report on sexual orientation, and it appears that it is not routinely assessed in these studies. Hence, the therapeutic techniques described in this chapter are based on the general CBT literature, case studies, and the clinical experience of the authors. It will be important for future research to investigate further the presenting concerns of sexual and gender minority clients and to develop and test approaches to address these concerns.

REFERENCES

Adams, H. E., Tollison, C. D., & Carson, T. P. (1981). Behavior therapy with sexual deviations. In S. M. Turner, K. S. Calhoun, & H. E. Adams (Eds.), *Handbook of clinical behavior therapy* (pp. 318–346). New York, NY: Wiley.

American Psychiatric Association. (2000). *American Psychiatric Association Commission on Psychotherapy by Psychiatrists position statement on therapies focused on attempts to change sexual orientation (reparative or conversion therapies)*. Washington, DC: Author.

American Psychological Association. (2012). Guidelines for psychological practice with lesbian, gay, and bisexual clients. *American Psychologist, 67,* 10–42. http://dx.doi.org/10.1037/a0024659

American Psychological Association. (2015). Guidelines for psychological practice with transgender and gender nonconforming people. *American Psychologist, 70,* 832–864. http://dx.doi.org/10.1037/a0039906

Aranda, F., Matthews, A. K., Hughes, T. L., Muramatsu, N., Wilsnack, S. C., Johnson, T. P., & Riley, B. B. (2015). Coming out in color: Racial/ethnic differences in the relationship between level of sexual identity disclosure and depression among lesbians. *Cultural Diversity and Ethnic Minority Psychology, 21,* 247–257. http://dx.doi.org/10.1037/a0037644

Austin, A., & Craig, S. L. (2015). Transgender affirmative cognitive behavioral therapy: Clinical considerations and applications. *Professional Psychology: Research and Practice, 46,* 21–29. http://dx.doi.org/10.1037/a0038642

Austin, A., Craig, S. L., & Alessi, E. J. (2017). Affirmative cognitive behavior therapy with transgender and gender nonconforming adults. *Psychiatric Clinics*, 40, 141–156. http://dx.doi.org/10.1016/j.psc.2016.10.003

Austin, A., & Goodman, R. (2017). The impact of social connectedness and internalized transphobic stigma on self-esteem among transgender and gender nonconforming adults. *Journal of Homosexuality*, 64, 825–841. http://dx.doi.org/10.1080/00918369.2016.1236587

Balsam, K. F. (2002). *Traumatic victimization: A comparison of lesbian, gay, and bisexual adults and their heterosexual siblings* (Unpublished doctoral dissertation). Burlington, University of Vermont.

Balsam, K. F. (2003). Traumatic victimization in the lives of lesbian and bisexual women. *Journal of Lesbian Studies*, 7, 1–14. http://dx.doi.org/10.1300/J155v07n01_01

Balsam, K. F., Beadnell, B., & Molina, Y. (2013). The Daily Heterosexist Experiences Questionnaire: Measuring minority stress among lesbian, gay, bisexual, and transgender adults. *Measurement and Evaluation in Counseling and Development*, 46, 3–25. http://dx.doi.org/10.1177/0748175612449743

Balsam, K. F., Molina, Y., Beadnell, B., Simoni, J., & Walters, K. (2011). Measuring multiple minority stress: The LGBT People of Color Microaggressions Scale. *Cultural Diversity and Ethnic Minority Psychology*, 17, 163–174. http://dx.doi.org/10.1037/a0023244

Balsam, K. F., Rothblum, E. D., & Beauchaine, T. P. (2005). Victimization over the life span: A comparison of lesbian, gay, bisexual, and heterosexual siblings. *Journal of Consulting and Clinical Psychology*, 73, 477–487. http://dx.doi.org/10.1037/0022-006X.73.3.477

Barlow, D. H., Farchione, T. J., Fairholme, C. P., Ellard, K. K., Boisseau, C. L., Allen, L. B., & Ehrenreich-May, J. T. (2010). *Unified protocol for transdiagnostic treatment of emotional disorders: Therapist guide.* New York, NY: Oxford University Press. http://dx.doi.org/10.1093/med:psych/9780199772667.001.0001

Beck, A. T., Epstein, N., Brown, G., & Steer, R. A. (1988). An inventory for measuring clinical anxiety: Psychometric properties. *Journal of Consulting and Clinical Psychology*, 56, 893–897. http://dx.doi.org/10.1037/0022-006X.56.6.893

Beck, A. T., Steer, R. A., & Brown, G. K. (1996). *Manual for the BDI–II.* San Antonio, TX: The Psychological Corporation.

Blevins, C. A., Weathers, F. W., Davis, M. T., Witte, T. K., & Domino, J. L. (2015). The posttraumatic stress disorder checklist for *DSM–5* (PCL–5): Development and initial psychometric evaluation. *Journal of Traumatic Stress*, 28, 489–498. http://dx.doi.org/10.1002/jts.22059

Beemyn, B. G., & Rankin, S. (2011). *The lives of transgender people.* New York, NY: Columbia University Press.

Benson, K. E. (2013). Seeking support: Transgender client experiences with mental health services. *Journal of Feminist Family Therapy*, 25, 17–40. http://dx.doi.org/10.1080/08952833.2013.755081

Berg, M. B., Mimiaga, M. J., & Safren, S. A. (2004). Mental health concerns of HIV-infected gay and bisexual men seeking mental health services: An observational study. *AIDS Patient Care and STDs, 18,* 635–643. http://dx.doi.org/10.1089/apc.2004.18.635

Bockting, W. (2015). Internalized transphobia. In W. Patricia & A. Bolin (Eds.), *The international encyclopedia of human sexuality* (pp. 583–625). Hoboken, NJ: Wiley. http://dx.doi.org/10.1002/9781118896877.wbiehs236

Boroughs, M. S., Bedoya, C. A., O'Cleirigh, C., & Safren, S. A. (2015). Toward defining, measuring, and evaluating LGBT cultural competence for psychologists. *Clinical Psychology: Science and Practice, 22,* 151–171. http://dx.doi.org/10.1111/cpsp.12098

Bradford, J., Ryan, C., & Rothblum, E. D. (1994). National Lesbian Health Care Survey: Implications for mental health care. *Journal of Consulting and Clinical Psychology, 62,* 228–242. http://dx.doi.org/10.1037/0022-006X.62.2.228

Burgess, D., Tran, A., Lee, R., & Van Ryn, M. (2007). Effects of perceived discrimination on mental health and mental health services utilization among gay, lesbian, bisexual and transgender persons. *Journal of LGBT Health Research, 3,* 1–14. http://dx.doi.org/10.1080/15574090802226626

Christensen, A., & Jacobson, N. S. (1997). *Frequency and Acceptability of Partner Behavior* (Unpublished questionnaire). (Available from Andrew Christensen, University of California, Department of Psychology, Los Angeles, CA 90095.)

Cochran, S. D. (2001). Emerging issues in research on lesbians' and gay men's mental health: Does sexual orientation really matter? *American Psychologist, 56,* 931–947. http://dx.doi.org/10.1037/0003-066X.56.11.931

Collazo, A., Austin, A., & Craig, S. L. (2013). Facilitating transition among transgender clients: Components of effective clinical practice. *Clinical Social Work Journal, 41,* 228–237. http://dx.doi.org/10.1007/s10615-013-0436-3

Craig, S. L., & Austin, A. (2016). The AFFIRM open pilot feasibility study: A brief affirmative cognitive behavioral coping skills group intervention for sexual and gender minority youth. *Children and Youth Services Review, 64,* 136–144. http://dx.doi.org/10.1016/j.childyouth.2016.02.022

Crenshaw, K. (1991). Mapping the margins: Identity politics, intersectionality, and violence against women. *Stanford Law Review, 43,* 1241–1299.

D'Augelli, A. R. (1998). Developmental implications of victimization of lesbian, gay, and bisexual youths. In G. M. Herek (Ed.), *Stigma and sexual orientation: Understanding prejudice against lesbians, gay men, and bisexuals* (pp. 187–210). Thousand Oaks, CA: Sage. http://dx.doi.org/10.4135/9781452243818.n9

de Vries, A. L., McGuire, J. K., Steensma, T. D., Wagenaar, E. C., Doreleijers, T. A., & Cohen-Kettenis, P. T. (2014). Young adult psychological outcome after puberty suppression and gender reassignment. *Pediatrics, 134,* 696–704. http://dx.doi.org/10.1542/peds.2013-2958

Eliason, M. J. (2014). An exploration of terminology related to sexuality and gender: Arguments for standardizing the language. *Social Work in Public Health, 29,* 162–175. http://dx.doi.org/10.1080/19371918.2013.775887

First, M. B., Williams, J. B. W., Karg, R. S., & Spitzer, R. L. (2015). *Structured clinical interview for DSM–5 disorders, clinician version (SCID–5–CV)*. Arlington, VA: American Psychiatric Association.

Foa, E. B., & Rothbaum, B. O. (1998). *Treating the trauma of rape: Cognitive-behavioral therapy for PTSD*. New York, NY: Guilford Press.

Foa, E. B., Rothbaum, B. O., Riggs, D. S., & Murdock, T. B. (1991). Treatment of posttraumatic stress disorder in rape victims: A comparison between cognitive-behavioral procedures and counseling. *Journal of Consulting and Clinical Psychology, 59*, 715–723. http://dx.doi.org/10.1037/0022-006X.59.5.715

Friedman, M. S., Marshal, M. P., Guadamuz, T. E., Wei, C., Wong, C. F., Saewyc, E., & Stall, R. (2011). A meta-analysis of disparities in childhood sexual abuse, parental physical abuse, and peer victimization among sexual minority and sexual nonminority individuals. *American Journal of Public Health, 101*, 1481–1494. http://dx.doi.org/10.2105/AJPH.2009.190009

Frisch, M. B. (1994). *The quality of life inventory: Manual and treatment guide*. Minneapolis, MN: National Computer Systems.

Frost, D. M., & Meyer, I. H. (2012). Measuring community connectedness among diverse sexual minority populations. *Journal of Sex Research, 49*, 36–49. http://dx.doi.org/10.1080/00224499.2011.565427

Galupo, M. P. (2009). Cross-category friendship patterns: Comparison of hetero-sexual and sexual minority adults. *Journal of Social and Personal Relationships, 26*, 811–831. http://dx.doi.org/10.1177/0265407509345651

Galupo, M. P., Bauerband, L. A., Gonzalez, K. A., Hagen, D. B., Hether, S. D., & Krum, T. E. (2014). Transgender friendship experiences: Benefits and barriers of friendships across gender identity and sexual orientation. *Feminism & Psychology, 24*, 193–215. http://dx.doi.org/10.1177/0959353514526218

Garnets, L., Hancock, K. A., Cochran, S. D., Goodchilds, J., & Peplau, L. A. (1991). Issues in psychotherapy with lesbians and gay men: A survey of psychologists. *American Psychologist, 46*, 964–972.

Grella, C. E., Greenwell, L., Mays, V. M., & Cochran, S. D. (2009). Influence of gender, sexual orientation, and need on treatment utilization for substance use and mental disorders: Findings from the California Quality of Life Survey. *BMC Psychiatry, 9*, 52. http://dx.doi.org/10.1186/1471-244X-9-52

Grossman, A. H., D'Augelli, A. R., & Frank, J. A. (2011). Aspects of psychological resilience among transgender youth. *Journal of LGBT Youth, 8*, 103–115. http://dx.doi.org/10.1080/19361653.2011.541347

Haldeman, D. C. (1994). The practice and ethics of sexual orientation conversion therapy. *Journal of Consulting and Clinical Psychology, 62*, 221–227. http://dx.doi.org/10.1037/0022-006X.62.2.221

Han, C. S. (2015). No brokeback for Black men: Pathologizing Black male (homo)sexuality through down low discourse. *Social Identities, 21*, 228–243. http://dx.doi.org/10.1080/13504630.2015.1041019

Hayes, S. C., Strosahl, K. D., & Wilson, K. G. (2012). *Acceptance and commitment therapy: An experiential approach to behavior change* (2nd ed.). New York, NY: Guilford Press.

Hendricks, M. L., & Testa, R. J. (2012). A conceptual framework for clinical work with transgender and gender nonconforming clients: An adaptation of the minority stress model. *Professional Psychology: Research and Practice, 43,* 460–467. http://dx.doi.org/10.1037/a0029597

Herek, G. M. (1990). The context of anti-gay violence: Notes on cultural and psychological heterosexism. *Journal of Interpersonal Violence, 5,* 316–333. http://dx.doi.org/10.1177/088626090005003006

Herek, G. M., Gillis, J. R., & Cogan, J. C. (1999). Psychological sequelae of hate-crime victimization among lesbian, gay, and bisexual adults. *Journal of Consulting and Clinical Psychology, 67,* 945–951. http://dx.doi.org/10.1037/0022-006X.67.6.945

Herek, G. M., Gillis, J. R., Cogan, J. C., & Glunt, E. K. (1997). Hate crime victimization among lesbian, gay, and bisexual adults. *Journal of Interpersonal Violence, 12,* 195–215. http://dx.doi.org/10.1177/088626097012002003

Hill, D. B., & Willoughby, B. L. (2005). The development and validation of the genderism and transphobia scale. *Sex Roles, 53,* 531–544. http://dx.doi.org/10.1007/s11199-005-7140-x

Igartua, K., Thombs, B. D., Burgos, G., & Montoro, R. (2009). Concordance and discrepancy in sexual identity, attraction, and behavior among adolescents. *Journal of Adolescent Health, 45,* 602–608. http://dx.doi.org/10.1016/j.jadohealth.2009.03.019

Jacobs, S., Thomas, W., & Lang, S. (1997). *Two-spirit people: Native American gender identity, sexuality, and spirituality.* Urbana, IL: University of Chicago Press.

Keo-Meier, C. L., & Fitzgerald, K. M. (2017). Affirmative psychological testing and neurocognitive assessment with transgender adults. *Psychiatric Clinics, 40,* 51–64. http://dx.doi.org/10.1016/j.psc.2016.10.011

King, M., Semlyen, J., Tai, S. S., Killaspy, H., Osborn, D., Popelyuk, D., & Nazareth, I. (2008). A systematic review of mental disorder, suicide, and deliberate self-harm in lesbian, gay and bisexual people. *BMC Psychiatry, 8,* 70. http://dx.doi.org/10.1186/1471-244X-8-70

Kohlenberg, R. J., & Tsai, M. (1991). *Functional analytic psychotherapy: Creating intense and curative therapeutic relationships.* New York, NY: Springer Science+Business Media.

Linehan, M. (1993). *Cognitive-behavioral treatment of borderline personality disorder.* New York, NY: Guilford Press.

Link, M. (2004). When Captain Cook met Kalanikoa. *The Gay & Lesbian Review Worldwide, 11,* 28–30. Retrieved from https://search.proquest.com/docview/198667195?accountid=14522

Lucassen, M. F., Merry, S. N., Hatcher, S., & Frampton, C. M. (2015). Rainbow SPARX: A novel approach to addressing depression in sexual minority youth. *Cognitive and Behavioral Practice, 22*, 203–216. http://dx.doi.org/10.1016/j.cbpra.2013.12.008

Martell, C. R., Safren, S. A., & Prince, S. E. (2004). *Cognitive-behavioral therapies with lesbian, gay and bisexual clients.* New York, NY: Guilford.

Mays, V. M., & Cochran, S. D. (2001). Mental health correlates of perceived discrimination among lesbian, gay, and bisexual adults in the United States. *American Journal of Public Health, 91*, 1869–1876. http://dx.doi.org/10.2105/AJPH.91.11.1869

McLellan, A. T., Kushner, H., Metzger, D., Peters, R., Smith, I., Grissom, G., . . . Argeriou, M. (1992). The fifth edition of the Addiction Severity Index. *Journal of Substance Abuse Treatment, 9*, 199–213.

Meyer, I. H. (2003). Prejudice, social stress, and mental health in lesbian, gay, and bisexual populations: Conceptual issues and research evidence. *Psychological Bulletin, 129*, 674–697. http://dx.doi.org/10.1037/0033-2909.129.5.674

Meyer, I. H., Rossano, L., Ellis, J. M., & Bradford, J. (2002). A brief telephone interview to identify lesbian and bisexual women in random digit dialing sampling. *Journal of Sex Research, 39*, 139–144. http://dx.doi.org/10.1080/00224490209552133

Mirandé, A. (2014). Transgender identity and acceptance in a global era: The Muxes of Juchitán. In J. Gelfer (Ed.), *Masculinities in a global era* (pp. 247–263). New York, NY: Springer. http://dx.doi.org/10.1007/978-1-4614-6931-5_14

Mohr, J., & Fassinger, R. (2000). Measuring dimensions of lesbian and gay male experience. *Measurement and Evaluation in Counseling and Development, 33*, 66–90.

Mohr, J. J., & Kendra, M. S. (2011). Revision and extension of a multidimensional measure of sexual minority identity: The Lesbian, Gay, and Bisexual Identity Scale. *Journal of Counseling Psychology, 58*, 234–245. http://dx.doi.org/10.1037/a0022858

Moore, M. R. (2011). Two sides of the same coin: Revising analyses of lesbian sexuality and family formation through the study of Black women. *Journal of Lesbian Studies, 15*, 58–68. http://dx.doi.org/10.1080/10894160.2010.508412

Morris, J. F., Waldo, C. R., & Rothblum, E. D. (2001). A model of predictors and outcomes of outness among lesbian and bisexual women. *American Journal of Orthopsychiatry, 71*, 61–71. http://dx.doi.org/10.1037/0002-9432.71.1.61

National Association of Social Workers. (1996). *Code of Ethics of the National Association of Social Workers.* Retrieved from https://www.socialworkers.org/About/Ethics/Code-of-Ethics

Newcomb, M. E., & Mustanski, B. (2010). Internalized homophobia and internalizing mental health problems: A meta-analytic review. *Clinical Psychology Review, 30*, 1019–1029. http://dx.doi.org/10.1016/j.cpr.2010.07.003

Ochs, R. (1996). Biphobia: It goes more than two ways. In B. A. Firestein (Ed.), *Bisexuality: The psychology and politics of an invisible minority* (pp. 217–239). Thousand Oaks, CA: Sage.

Odo, C., & Hawelu, A. (2001). Eo na Mahu o Hawai'i: The extraordinary health needs of Hawai'i's Mahu. *Pacific Health Dialog, 8,* 327–334.

Olson, K. R., Durwood, L., DeMeules, M., & McLaughlin, K. A. (2016). Mental health of transgender children who are supported in their identities. *Pediatrics, 137,* e20153223. Advance online publication. http://dx.doi.org/10.1542/peds.2015-3223

Pachankis, J. E., Hatzenbuehler, M. L., Rendina, H. J., Safren, S. A., & Parsons, J. T. (2015). LGB-affirmative cognitive-behavioral therapy for young adult gay and bisexual men: A randomized controlled trial of a transdiagnostic minority stress approach. *Journal of Consulting and Clinical Psychology, 83,* 875–889. http://dx.doi.org/10.1037/ccp0000037

Padesky, C. A. (1989). Attaining and maintaining a positive lesbian self-identity: A cognitive therapy approach. *Women & Therapy, 8,* 145–156.

Parent, M. C., DeBlaere, C., & Moradi, B. (2013). Approaches to research on intersectionality: Perspectives on gender, LGBT, and racial/ethnic identities. *Sex Roles, 68,* 639–645. http://dx.doi.org/10.1007/s11199-013-0283-2

Purcell, D. W., Campos, P. E., & Perilla, J. L. (1996). Therapy with lesbians and gay men: A cognitive behavioral perspective. *Cognitive and Behavioral Practice, 3,* 391–415. http://dx.doi.org/10.1016/S1077-7229(96)80025-3

Reisen, C. A., Zea, M. C., Bianchi, F. T., Poppen, P. J., Shedlin, M. G., & Penha, M. M. (2010). Latino gay and bisexual men's relationships with non-gay-identified men who have sex with men. *Journal of Homosexuality, 57,* 1004–1021. http://dx.doi.org/10.1080/00918369.2010.503510

Reisner, S. L., White, J. M., Bradford, J. B., & Mimiaga, M. J. (2014). Transgender health disparities: Comparing full cohort and nested matched-pair study designs in a community health center. *LGBT Health, 1,* 177–184. http://dx.doi.org/10.1089/lgbt.2014.0009

Roberts, T. S., Horne, S. G., & Hoyt, W. T. (2015). Between a gay and a straight place: Bisexual individuals' experiences with monosexism. *Journal of Bisexuality, 15,* 554–569. http://dx.doi.org/10.1080/15299716.2015.1111183

Rothman, E. F., Exner, D., & Baughman, A. L. (2011). The prevalence of sexual assault against people who identify as gay, lesbian, or bisexual in the United States: A systematic review. *Trauma, Violence, & Abuse, 12,* 55–66. http://dx.doi.org/10.1177/1524838010390707

Schmidt, J. (2016). *Migrating genders: Westernisation, migration, and Samoan fa'afafine.* New York, NY: Routledge.

Segal, Z. V., Williams, J. M. G., & Teasdale, J. D. (2012). *Mindfulness-based cognitive therapy for depression* (2nd ed.). New York, NY: Guilford Press.

Shidlo, A., & Schroeder, M. (2002). Changing sexual orientation: A consumer's report. *Professional Psychology: Research and Practice, 33,* 249–259. http://dx.doi.org/10.1037/0735-7028.33.3.249

Smith, A. (1997). Cultural diversity and the coming out process: Implications for clinical practice. In B. Greene (Ed.), *Ethnic and cultural diversity among lesbians and gay men* (pp. 279–300). Thousand Oaks, CA: Sage.

Smith, N. G., Hart, T. A., Kidwai, A., Vernon, J. R., Blais, M., & Adam, B. (2017). Results of a pilot study to ameliorate psychological and behavioral outcomes of minority stress among young gay and bisexual men. *Behavior Therapy, 48,* 664–677. http://dx.doi.org/10.1016/j.beth.2017.03.005

Solomon, S., Rothblum, E. D., & Balsam, K. F. (2005). Money, housework, sex, and conflict: Same-sex couples in civil unions, those not in civil unions, and heterosexual married siblings. *Sex Roles, 52,* 561–575. http://dx.doi.org/10.1007/s11199-005-3725-7

Spanier, G. B. (1976). Measuring dyadic adjustment. *Journal of Marriage and the Family, 38,* 15–28. http://dx.doi.org/10.2307/350547

Spengler, E. S., Miller, D. J., & Spengler, P. M. (2016). Microaggressions: Clinical errors with sexual minority clients. *Psychotherapy, 53,* 360–366. http://dx.doi.org/10.1037/pst0000073

Testa, R. J., Habarth, J., Peta, J., Balsam, K., & Bockting, W. (2015). Development of the Gender Minority Stress and Resilience Measure. *Psychology of Sexual Orientation and Gender Diversity, 2,* 65–77. http://dx.doi.org/10.1037/sgd0000081

Testa, R. J., Michaels, M. S., Bliss, W., Rogers, M. L., Balsam, K. F., & Joiner, T. (2017). Suicidal ideation in transgender people: Gender minority stress and interpersonal theory factors. *Journal of Abnormal Psychology, 126,* 125–136. http://dx.doi.org/10.1037/abn0000234

Toomey, R. B., Ryan, C., Diaz, R. M., Card, N. A., & Russell, S. T. (2013). Gender-nonconforming sexual and gender minority youth: School victimization and young adult psychosocial adjustment. *Psychology of Sexual Orientation and Gender Diversity, 1*(S), 71–80. http://dx.doi.org/10.1037/2329-0382.1.S.71

Weinberg, G. (1972). *Society and the healthy homosexual.* New York, NY: St. Martin's.

Wilson, B. D. (2009). Black lesbian gender and sexual culture: Celebration and resistance. *Culture, Health & Sexuality, 11,* 297–313. http://dx.doi.org/10.1080/13691050802676876

III

CULTURAL ISSUES IN CLINICAL SUPERVISION

12

CULTURALLY RESPONSIVE COGNITIVE BEHAVIOR THERAPY CLINICAL SUPERVISION

GAYLE Y. IWAMASA, SHILPA P. REGAN,
AND KRISTEN H. SOROCCO

In the first edition of this volume, we reported that there was a fairly substantial literature on multicultural supervision, and the literature that existed was mainly theoretical in nature, outlining models and components that should be addressed in teaching students about multicultural issues during clinical practicum (Iwamasa, Pai, & Sorocco, 2006). However, while training issues in cognitive therapy, behavior therapy, and cognitive behavior therapy (CBT) were mainly discussed in books and manuals, supervision issues were not widely studied or discussed in the CBT literature. Not surprisingly, the literature on supervision in general also appeared to mainly separate therapy approach (e.g., CBT) from cultural and diversity issues. For example, Watkins's (1997) *Handbook of Psychotherapy Supervision* contained chapters on supervision in behavioral, cognitive, and rational emotive behavior therapy (Fruzzetti, Waltz, & Linehan, 1997; Liese & Beck, 1997; Woods & Ellis, 1997, respectively). This same volume also contained one chapter devoted

http://dx.doi.org/10.1037/0000119-013
Culturally Responsive Cognitive Behavior Therapy, Second Edition: Practice and Supervision, G. Y. Iwamasa and P. A. Hays (Editors)

to cultural competence in supervision (López, 1997). In 2006, we found no books or articles specifically devoted to culturally diverse CBT supervision.

As we revised this chapter in 2018, we found that although still mostly separate, there is now increasing integration of these competencies in the supervision literature. Of particular note are two recent publications: *Multiculturalism and Diversity in Clinical Supervision: A Competency-Based Approach* (Falender, Shafranske, & Falicov, 2014) and *Guidelines for Clinical Supervision in Health Service Psychology* (American Psychological Association [APA], 2015), which not only focuses on general supervisor competency but also includes diversity as a major domain of supervision skills and also weaves issues of culture throughout the document.

CBT remains one of the most influential forms of psychotherapy in many countries. Recent studies have examined various adaptations to the traditional CBT model, including the integration of culturally relevant content and modification of interventions based on the cultural characteristics of clients. In addition to our book, the text *Transcultural Cognitive Behaviour Therapy for Anxiety and Depression* (Beck, 2016) summarizes research and provides case examples with culturally diverse populations. Further, in the first of its kind, Hwang et al. (2015) conducted a randomized clinical trial examining CBT and culturally adapted CBT for Chinese Americans.

Twelve years ago, we discussed the need for the field of CBT to keep up with the changing demographics of the United States (Iwamasa et al., 2006). This is especially important now given the current sociopolitical climate in the United States, where people of color are being specifically targeted for exclusion and the theme of American patriotism is equated with being of European heritage. On its website, SafeHome provides commentary regarding the role of hate on social media (SafeHome.org, n.d.). The decrease in respectful discourse and understanding at the highest levels of leadership in the United States indicates that the "golden rule" may no longer be a mainstream U.S. value.

During these tumultuous times, cognitive behavior (CB) therapists need to demonstrate that their professional knowledge and skills are beneficial for a wide variety of clients, including those in distress due to racism or discrimination. Fortunately, every chapter in this updated volume provides CB therapists with helpful tools and resources for their work with culturally diverse populations. This chapter complements those population-specific resources with information for supervisors of students learning CBT and supervisees who are learning to be effective CB therapists. For the purpose of this chapter, culturally responsive CBT supervision includes situations in which a CBT clinician under supervision works with a culturally different client and situations in which the supervision dyad or group comprises culturally different individuals.

In the previous edition of this chapter, we noted Yutrzenka and colleagues' assertion that ethnic and cultural diversity in the training of mental health professionals was imperative if the mental health field is to keep up with the changing demographics (Yutrzenka, 1995; Yutrzenka, Todd-Bazemore, & Caraway, 1999). Psychology as a profession recognized the importance of these issues, as demonstrated by the recent update of the *Multicultural Guidelines: An Ecological Approach to Context, Identity, and Intersectionality* (APA, 2017). Additionally, there has been interest in establishing multicultural clinical supervision benchmarks. In 2013, *The Counseling Psychologist* published a Major Contribution issue focusing on this topic (Falender, Burnes, & Ellis, 2013), with articles and responses from those involved with the development of professional psychology competencies. Some of these articles are summarized later in this chapter.

Since the first edition of this book, the literature on clinical supervision has seen significant growth and development. As Falender and Shafranske (2017) noted, much of this growth has occurred in an era of accountability where mental health professionals are expected to demonstrate competence in the provision of mental health services. Some health care systems assess competence in terms of outcomes, sometimes referred to as measurement-based care, such as client self-report ratings on symptom checklists and satisfaction with services reported in exit surveys. Given the increasingly diverse population of the United States and the current sociopolitical climate, the implementation of culturally responsive clinical supervision is even more important.

Falender and Shafranske (2017) noted that clinical supervision has

> multiple goals of monitoring the quality of services provided to clients; protecting the public and gatekeeping for the profession; and enhancing the professional competence and professionalism of the supervisee, including developing skill in the use of science-informed assessment procedures, empirically-supported treatments and evidence-based practices. (p. 4)

They also stated that, consistent with these goals, supervision should be conducted with sensitivity to individual differences and with recognition of its multicultural context. Consider the following supervision scenario:[1]

> Suzanne, a 34-year-old European American woman from an upper-middle-class background, was a staff psychologist at a small private university counseling center. She was excited about serving as supervisor for students in the master's program in psychology. In a supervision session with Diane, a third-generation Mexican American, Suzanne asked Diane to explain her treatment plan regarding Marco, an 18-year-old Puerto Rican man who was experiencing anxiety regarding his desire

---

[1]Case material in this chapter has been disguised to protect client confidentiality.

to tell his family that he was gay. Diane indicated that she was not familiar with sexual orientation issues among Latino men and asked Suzanne for some references. Suzanne was surprised, became defensive, and responded that, as a Latina, Diane should be the one to know about such issues, not Suzanne.

In this scenario the supervisor became defensive when asked for references by a supervisee. Why did the supervisor become defensive? Would she have reacted the same way if Diane had asked her for resources about working with single mothers? First-time college students? Widowers? The point of this case example is that culturally competent supervisors should be skilled, aware, and supportive of their supervisees in general. A defensive reaction to a request for support and information from a supervisee indicates that a supervisor does not possess the basic competence skills for providing supervision (APA, 2015). The supervisor in this case should review her own abilities and skill set and remediate those areas that are underdeveloped if she wishes to become a competent supervisor.

Psychologists continue to voice the need for improved ethnic and diversity education and training of mental health professionals (Soheilian, Inman, Klinger, Isenberg, & Kulp, 2014). Unfortunately, it is still mostly the case that students in training programs that emphasize specific models of therapy such as CBT, or that have a clinical science approach to training, continue mainly to learn about multicultural applications as the "special case," whereas those who attend training programs that emphasize diversity rarely receive training in specific therapies such as CBT. Interestingly, there appear to be differences in emphasis on diversity issues by type of training program. Rodriguez-Menendez, Dempsey, Albizu, Power, and Campbell Wilkerson (2017) found that students in PsyD programs reported more perceived training in multicultural issues including assessment and with evidence-based treatments compared with students in PhD programs. However, PhD students reported more experiential approaches used in their clinical supervision, such as observations or review of session videos. Included in their list of suggestions for psychology training programs, Rodriguez-Menendez et al. recommended that clinical faculty encourage clinical supervisors to raise issues of diversity in supervision and that they use guidelines and develop a network of subject matter experts who can discuss diversity issues with trainees when clinical supervisors lack that knowledge. We do note that there are some psychology graduate training programs that work to emphasize the importance of multiculturalism in their students' training. As one example, Bardone-Cone et al. (2016) summarized the process and content of how multicultural issues are addressed in the clinical psychology training program at the University of North Carolina, Chapel Hill.

In summary, there has been progress in acknowledging the need to incorporate diversity issues in the clinical supervision process. However, there still continues to be segregation of the CBT literature, the multicultural literature, and the supervision literature. The segregation of these three domains means that there is currently no CB approach to supervision that integrates cultural considerations. Toward the goal of developing such an integration, this chapter provides information regarding each area, beginning with an overview of the supervision research in CBT, followed by a summary of multicultural supervision research, and finally, several suggestions regarding the integration of these areas. Because this chapter focuses mainly on the training of novice therapists, we point those readers who are independent practitioners or are no longer in training to Comas-Díaz's (2012) book, *Multicultural Care: A Clinician's Guide to Cultural Competence*, which describes the application of cultural competence to different parts of one's clinical practice.

SUPERVISION OF COGNITIVE BEHAVIOR THERAPY

Newman and Kaplan's (2016) *Supervision Essentials for Cognitive Behavioral Therapy* provides an excellent melding of the CBT supervision literature with the practice of CBT and includes helpful case examples to illustrate their points. Cognitive behavior supervision (CBS), as defined by Newman and Kaplan, is consistent with the emphasis on competencies as well as measurement-based care. Key principles of CBS include an effective supervisory relationship with the goal of providing clients with good care where client progress and outcomes are measured. Additionally, CBS has the goal of advancing the professional development of supervisees using supportive and corrective feedback during actual clinical experience, the teaching of CBT methods, establishing expectations for supervision, and evaluating supervisees.

As in the practice of CBT, Newman and Kaplan (2016) indicated that individual supervision should be collaborative and individualized based on the supervisee's level of development. They suggested conducting a needs assessment to better understand the developmental level of the supervisee and also communicate that the supervisor is interested in the supervisee and in customizing supervision. Newman and Kaplan provided an excellent list of competencies to address in supervision, including discussion of cross-cultural issues. They also highlighted the utility of competency benchmarks in CBS, which can aid in goal-setting and assessment of the supervisee's progress throughout the year. The Revised Cognitive Therapy Scale by Blackburn et al. (2001) is a structured tool that can be helpful with this assessment.

In addition to weekly supervision meetings, Newman and Kaplan (2016) described methods of supervision such as live observation, audio- and videotape review, review of the supervisee's notes and differences between individual and group supervision. They also discussed importance of good documentation, as well as the use of instruction, modeling, and role playing.

Newman and Kaplan (2016) included a chapter on handling special issues such as dealing with defensiveness and ethical concerns. It is within this chapter that multicultural issues were more fully discussed and some suggestions provided for how supervisors can initiate discussion of the role of culture in therapy. They also provided helpful suggestions on supervisor development and self-care, including consultation and metasupervision (i.e., the supervision of supervision).

In a review of the CBT supervision literature, Reiser (2014) summarized "best practices" of CBT supervision. These include agenda-setting for supervision, use of observation (audio, video, or live), varied training techniques (e.g., experiential exercises or experiments), and providing feedback. Other potential best practices listed included modeling, demonstrating, using treatment manuals, and being interactive. In an effort to quantify CBT supervisory competence, Milne and Reiser (2014) developed a tool called SAGE (Supervision: Adherence and Guidance Evaluation). They provided some promising initial results with SAGE, but note that due to its method of live observation of supervision, directive feedback, and potential for emotional arousal, there are cross-cultural and professional barriers to using SAGE as a supervision competence assessment.

In their article focusing on supporting CBT supervisors, Corrie and Lane (2016) provided an excellent review of the professional development needs of CBT supervisors and a framework for professional development. Their model, called PURE (Prepare, Undertake, Refine, Enhance), may be used to assist supervisors with identifying skills in each of the four areas. They also provide practical suggestions for how CBT professionals can support and professional development.

Recent research has shown that supervision improves therapy skills and outcomes. For example, Weck, Kaufmann, and Höfling (2017) found that competence feedback provided to CB therapists in training before their next session resulted in higher levels of CBT competence. With trainees attending a CBT workshop, Bearman, Schneiderman, and Zoloth (2017) found that all students had improved their knowledge of CBT after supervision. Those supervisees who received performance feedback, modeling and role playing in addition to "usual" supervision activities such as agenda-setting, conceptualization discussions, and developing alliance, also demonstrated higher fidelity to the CBT model during training compared with trainees who did not. Similarly, O'Keeffe, Watson, and Linke (2016) found that with weekly supervision, inexperienced psychology trainees had 75% of their CBT clients improve anxiety symptoms at the end of therapy.

CULTURALLY COMPETENT SUPERVISION

Grace, a 37-year-old, third-generation Japanese American faculty member, supervised practicum students in a traditional scientist–practitioner PhD program that emphasized CBT. Amanda, a third-generation Swedish American student in her third year of practicum, summarized an intake session with Bin, a 25-year-old chemistry student from China. Following the intake session, Bin did not come to his next appointment, and Amanda was unable to contact him. Bin was experiencing anxiety and some depression related to how his lab partners were treating him. The students were asked by their graduate advisor to complete several experiments by a certain date. The group members met several times but were unable to successfully complete the experiments. Subsequently, Bin stayed up late several nights and was able to complete the experiments on his own. Although he informed the graduate advisor that the work was a result of the team's efforts, the other graduate students, all European American, were upset with Bin and accused him of trying to make himself look better than his team members. In group supervision, Grace asked Amanda to consider whether cultural factors might have influenced the situation, including Bin's behaviors, the other students' behaviors, and Bin's premature discontinuation of therapy. With the group's help, Amanda was able to recognize how the cultural perspective of Bin (which emphasized collectivism and self-sacrifice) contrasted with the cultural perspective of his lab partners (who valued individualism and competition) and how everyone's lack of understanding regarding these differences contributed to the conflict. Amanda also realized that her own European American perspective contributed to her unintentional reinforcement of the dominant cultural values.

The *Guidelines for Clinical Supervision in Health Service Psychology, Domain B: Diversity* (APA, 2015) indicates that diversity competence is an essential part of overall supervision competence and includes competence in working with diversity issues and with culturally diverse individuals, including those with a similar cultural background as the supervisor. Specifically, *culturally competent supervision* refers to

> working with others from backgrounds different than one's own but includes the complexity of understanding and factoring in the multiple identities of each individual: client(s), supervisee, supervisor and

differing worldviews. Competent supervision attends to a broad range of diversity dimensions (e.g., age, gender, gender identity, race, ethnicity, culture, national origin, religion, sexual orientation, disability, language, and socioeconomic status), and includes sensitivity to diversity of supervisees, clients/patients, and the supervisor. (APA, 2015, p. 36)

The five *Diversity* Guidelines are as follows (APA, 2015):

1. Supervisors strive to develop and maintain self-awareness regarding their diversity competence, which includes attitudes, knowledge, and skills.
2. Supervisors planfully strive to enhance their diversity competence to establish a respectful supervisory relationship and to facilitate the diversity competence of their supervisees.
3. Supervisors recognize the value of and pursue ongoing training in diversity competence as part of their professional development and lifelong learning.
4. Supervisors aim to be knowledgeable about the effects of bias, prejudice, and stereotyping. When possible, supervisors model client/patient advocacy and model promoting change in organizations and communities in the best interest of their clients/patients.
5. Supervisors aspire to be familiar with the scholarly literature concerning diversity competence in supervision and training. Supervisors strive to be familiar with promising practices for navigating conflicts among personal and professional values in the interest of protecting the public. (pp. 36–37)

In their chapter on multiculturalism and diversity, Falender and Shafranske (2017) took this one step further and indicated that it is an *ethical responsibility* to provide culturally competent supervision. They suggested using Falicov's (2014) multidimensional ecological comparative approach where the supervisor and supervisee take an approach based in curiosity about others and consider eco-systemic factors such as immigration and acculturation, context, and family organization and life. Within this frame, supervisors and supervisees can use their own multiple identities, sense of belonging, participation, and identification in supervision.

Tsui, O'Donoghue, and Ng (2014) summarized how various aspects of both supervisor and supervisee influence the multicultural supervision experience. In addition to the personal characteristics and cultural values of the supervisor and supervisee, they review how the political context, organizational context, and professional practices of both influence supervision.

Their review of these considerations on a larger societal context using specific international examples provides an excellent explanation for how supervisors and supervisees from differing cultural contexts must endeavor to genuinely be interested in learning about the cultural experiences and values of the other for effective multicultural supervision to occur.

Using a mixed-methods approach, Ladany, Mori, and Mehr (2013) conducted a study with trainees to identify "best" and "worst" supervisory characteristics and qualities. Characteristics shared across "best" supervisors include being able to develop a good relationship with the trainee, promoting autonomy and fostering openness, demonstration of clinical skill and knowledge (including supervisor self-disclosure), and provision of positive and challenging feedback. They also found that "worst" supervisors included those who did not attend to multicultural issues in supervision. Using their results, they describe an effective and highly competent supervisor as someone who is able to develop a strong alliance with the trainee by agreeing on the goals and process of supervision and who is able to demonstrate basic therapy skills such as listening and reflection. Effective supervisors are also described as attentive, collegial, and task-oriented and are noted to self-disclose when appropriate to foster development in clinical skills and knowledge. Evaluations of trainees would be based on review of stated goals of supervision.

Phillips, Parent, Dozier, and Jackson (2017) examined how the depth of examination of intersecting identities in supervision would affect the supervisory alliance and the trainee's self-efficacy related to diversity and general counseling skills. They found that supervisees reported that the more gender, ethnicity, and sexual orientation were discussed, the more supervisory working alliance and multicultural and general self-efficacy scores increased. An interesting finding was that students of color and sexual minority students reported that issues of ethnicity and sexual orientation were discussed more in depth in supervision compared with White students.

The failure to incorporate multicultural topics can contribute to a supervisee's frustration and, ultimately, lack of responsiveness to supervision. Supervisors who fail to attend to the cultural aspects of supervisees or clients often report that the supervisory relationship is negatively impacted (Falender, Burnes, & Ellis, 2013). Although either member of the supervisory dyad may introduce multicultural concerns, the power differential warrants initiation by the supervisor (Hird, Cavalieri, Dulko, Felice, & Ho, 2001). Newman (2010) also noted that the minimal step of initiating conversations about culture can affect the supervisory relationship and suggests it is a foundational skill of CBT supervisors. The supervisor's deliberate attention to culture helps create a climate of psychological safety and comfort within the supervisory relationship.

The lack of attention to diversity in supervision may result from the lack of multicultural training among supervisors (Ancis & Ladany, 2010). However, by being willing to reveal this as an area of weakness and discuss the steps one is taking to address it, the supervisor can further facilitate an accepting learning environment. Supervisors who examine their own knowledge, assumptions, attitudes, perceptions, and feelings are more able to assist the supervisee as he or she engages in a similar process (Falender et al., 2013). Even with a lack of knowledge, it is the openness and willingness to learn from the other person (trainee or client) that makes supervision and CBT more effective because rapport has been established. For example,

> David, a 42-year-old European American clinical psychologist, was supervising Kelly, a 22-year-old European American male practicum student. Kelly's new client was an 18-year-old single Laotian mother who was pregnant with her second child. David was fairly certain that Kelly, who was raised in an upper-middle-class suburb of Chicago, had little exposure to Laotian culture or single parenting. David also had little experience in these areas. Thus, he contacted several individuals, including a Chinese American classmate from graduate school, and conducted a PsycINFO search on Laotians and single parenting, to be prepared for his supervision session with Kelly.

Conversations about important issues to research for therapy help to establish rapport between the supervisor and supervisee, emphasize the significance of culture in supervision and therapy, and create a mutual language concerning cultural issues. One simple exercise to conduct at the start of supervision is to share training experiences in diversity and discuss how diversity is incorporated into case conceptualization. The supervisor can thus model for trainees how discussions involving cultural diversity are important in treatment even when they may initially be potentially uncomfortable.

Over the years, researchers have developed several measures to assess supervisees' cultural competence. Review of each of the tools is beyond the scope of this chapter, and we refer readers to Matsumoto and Hwang (2013) for a more thorough review of the psychometric properties of cross-cultural competence measures. Such tools may provide supervisors with a general baseline assessment of various skills and assist in tracking the supervisee's progress in developing multicultural awareness, knowledge, and skills. In an excellent effort to integrate assessment of general clinical competence and multicultural competence, Tsong and Goodyear (2014) developed the Supervision Outcome Scale. Their initial findings indicated that it may be a useful tool for assessing both supervisor and supervisee competence because it correlates strongly with the supervisory working alliance.

INTEGRATION OF CULTURE AND CBT IN SUPERVISION

How do CBT supervisors achieve the goal of being competent in both CBT and multicultural supervision? They must view both as integral to effective and competent supervision. As mentioned previously, supervisors must start with themselves. Given that cultural competency is an ongoing process, supervisors do not have to be "the expert" in multicultural therapy or diversity issues as long as they are willing to model the steps toward increasing one's level of multicultural competence. Indeed, we are always going to learn more about others and ourselves as long as we remain open to learning and observing. Included in the personal development work of a supervisor is an understanding of the role of one's own culture, values, and beliefs and their effects on communication with the supervisee.

Treating diversity issues as an integral component of the clinical experience enables the supervisor and supervisee to raise and discuss issues related to diversity in a more comfortable and integrated manner throughout the supervision process. As an example, in group supervision with mixed-level clinical psychology graduate program, the first author focused initially on development of case formulation skills using both CBT and multicultural frameworks. Wenzel, Dobson, and Hays's (2016) cognitive behavioral case conceptualization, Persons and Davidson's (2014) cognitive behavioral case formulation, and Tanaka-Matsumi, Seiden, and Lam's (1996) Culturally Informed Functional Assessment were reviewed and discussed in the group supervision meetings. Students were then required to use one of the approaches in presenting the case formulation of their client to the team, along with a discussion of cultural context and CBT interventions and strategies planned. Most students verbalized that this approach was helpful in their development of clinical knowledge, skills, and use of client information in a meaningful way. Group case formulation discussions could then be further reviewed in individual supervision, building on the knowledge and discussions from group supervision and allow supervisors and trainees to pursue multicultural discussions in more depth on an individual basis as needed or desired.

Establishing diversity issues initially as an integral aspect of clinical work also allows supervisors to use all the available resources and tools, both in the CBT literature and the multicultural therapy literature. Current events (e.g., the preponderance of sexual assault and sexual harassment claims described in mainstream and social media in the fall and winter of 2017) offer ongoing opportunities to discuss cultural influences in supervision.

Psychologists, whether new or seasoned, can benefit from learning both CBT supervision models and multicultural supervision guidelines such as those described in this chapter to develop or enhance their culturally responsive approach to supervision. Experienced supervisors who already work from a multicultural focus can integrate the CBT "best practice" components of supervision into their existing approach. Similarly, experienced CBT supervisors can integrate multicultural components described in this chapter into their current approach. For example,

Steve, a 42-year-old European American supervisor, realized that he did not have much experience supervising cases in which clients presented with issues related to sexual orientation and ethnic identity development. Anticipating that his supervisees would have increasingly culturally diverse clients, he decided to focus his group supervision on these topics. He structured group supervision so that the first hour would consist of student presentations on a specific topic followed by group discussion with questions and answers. At the first group supervision of the year, he presented the following topics for students to select from: cultural competence, the coming-out process, single parenting, ethnic identity, racial identity, biracial individuals, and disability issues. His students were excited because this was the first time a practicum supervisor had acknowledged that these issues were potentially important in the therapy process.

CONCLUSION

The CBT literature, the multicultural literature, and the supervision literature continue to be largely separate and lack meaningful integration. However, there is a growing research literature on supervision that emphasizes clear behavioral indicators of competent supervision. Existing literature also suggests that the integration of CBT and multicultural approaches in supervision provides practicing psychologists with the skills and resources they need to provide care in an increasingly diverse world. To provide culturally competent CBT supervision, supervisors must first be willing and able to examine their own values, beliefs, attitudes, and worldview. This foundation of self-awareness and the ongoing assessment it involves will increase the supervisor's comfort in raising and addressing cultural questions with supervisees. Integrating both a CBT and multicultural focus at the outset of supervision allows both supervisors and supervisees the ability to more fully explore diversity issues throughout the supervision process. Since the previous edition of this chapter, we have been impressed with the increased attention that CBT and multicultural influences are receiving from researchers and clinicians. We look forward to the continued efforts to empirically examine culturally competent CBT supervision.

REFERENCES

American Psychological Association. (2015). Guidelines for clinical supervision in health service psychology. *American Psychologist, 70*, 33–46. http://dx.doi.org/10.1037/a0038112

American Psychological Association. (2017). *Multicultural guidelines: An ecological approach to context, identity, and intersectionality.* Retrieved from http://www.apa.org/about/policy/multicultural-guidelines.pdf

Ancis, J., & Ladany, N. (2010). A multicultural framework for counselor supervision: Knowledge and skills. In N. Ladany & L. Bradley (Eds.), *Counselor supervision* (4th ed., pp. 53–95). New York, NY: Routledge.

Bardone-Cone, A. M., Calhoun, C. A., Fischer, M. S., Gaskin-Wasson, A. L., Jones, S. C. T., Schwartz, S. L., . . . Prinstein, M. J. (2016). Development and implementation of a diversity training sequence in a clinical psychology doctoral program. *Behavior Therapist, 39*, 65–75.

Bearman, S. K., Schneiderman, R. L., & Zoloth, E. (2017). Building an evidence base for effective supervision practices: An analogue experiment of supervision to increase EBT fidelity. *Administration and Policy in Mental Health and Mental Health Services Research, 44*, 293–307. http://dx.doi.org/10.1007/s10488-016-0723-8

Beck, A. (2016). *Transcultural cognitive behaviour therapy for anxiety and depression: A practical guide.* New York, NY: Routledge.

Blackburn, I. M., James, I. A., Milne, D. L., Baker, C., Standart, S., Garland, A., & Reichelt, K. (2001). The revised cognitive therapy scale (CTS–R): Psychometric properties. *Behavioural and Cognitive Psychotherapy, 29*, 431–446. http://dx.doi.org/10.1017/S1352465801004040

Comas-Díaz, L. (2012). *Multicultural care: A clinician's guide to cultural competence.* Washington, DC: American Psychological Association. http://dx.doi.org/10.1037/13491-000

Corrie, S., & Lane, D. A. (2016). Supporting the supervisor: Organizing professional development to enhance practice. *The Cognitive Behaviour Therapist, 9*, e23. http://dx.doi.org/10.1017/S1754470X1500046X

Falender, C. A., Burnes, T. R., & Ellis, M. (2013). Multicultural clinical supervision and benchmarks: Empirical support informing practice and supervisor training. *The Counseling Psychologist, 41*, 8–27. http://dx.doi.org/10.1177/0011000012438417

Falender, C. A., & Shafranske, E. P. (2017). *Supervision essentials for the practice of competency-based supervision.* Washington, DC: American Psychological Association. http://dx.doi.org/10.1037/15962-000

Falender, C. A., Shafranske, E. P., & Falicov, C. J. (Eds.). (2014). *Multiculturalism and diversity in clinical supervision: A competency-based approach.* Washington, DC: American Psychological Association. http://dx.doi.org/10.1037/14370-000

Falicov, C. J. (2014). Psychotherapy and supervision as cultural encounters: The multidimensional ecological comparative approach framework. In C. A.

Falender, E. P. Shafranske, & C. J. Falicov (Eds.), *Multiculturalism and diversity in clinical supervision: A competency-based approach* (pp. 29–58). Washington, DC: American Psychological Association. http://dx.doi.org/10.1037/14370-002

Fruzzetti, A. E., Waltz, J. A., & Linehan, M. M. (1997). Supervision in dialectical behavior therapy. In C. E. Watkins (Ed.), *Handbook of psychotherapy supervision* (pp. 84–100). New York, NY: Wiley.

Hird, J. S., Cavalieri, C. E., Dulko, J. P., Felice, A. A., & Ho, T. A. (2001). Visions and realities: Supervisee perspectives of multicultural supervision. *Journal of Multicultural Counseling and Development, 29,* 114–130. http://dx.doi.org/10.1002/j.2161-1912.2001.tb00509.x

Hwang, W.-C., Myers, H. F., Chiu, E., Mak, E., Butner, J. E., Fujimoto, K., . . . Miranda, J. (2015). Culturally adapted cognitive-behavioral therapy for Chinese Americans with depression: A randomized controlled trial. *Psychiatric Services, 66,* 1035–1042. http://dx.doi.org/10.1176/appi.ps.201400358

Iwamasa, G. Y., Pai, S. P., & Sorocco, K. H. (2006). Multicultural cognitive-behavioral therapy supervision. In P. A. Hays & G. Y. Iwamasa (Eds.), *Culturally responsive cognitive–behavioral therapy: Assessment, practice, and supervision* (pp. 267–281). Washington, DC: American Psychological Association. http://dx.doi.org/10.1037/11433-012

Ladany, N., Mori, Y., & Mehr, K. E. (2013). Effective and ineffective supervision. *The Counseling Psychologist, 41,* 28–47. http://dx.doi.org/10.1177/0011000012442648

Liese, B. S., & Beck, J. S. (1997). Cognitive therapy supervision. In C. E. Watkins (Ed.), *Handbook of psychotherapy supervision* (pp. 114–133). New York, NY: Wiley.

López, S. R. (1997). Cultural competence in psychotherapy: A guide for clinicians and their supervisors. In C. E. Watkins (Ed.), *Handbook of psychotherapy supervision* (pp. 570–588). New York, NY: Wiley.

Matsumoto, D., & Hwang, H. (2013). Assessing cross-cultural competence: A review of available tests. *Journal of Cross-Cultural Psychology, 44,* 849–873. http://dx.doi.org/10.1177/0022022113492891

Milne, D. L., & Reiser, R. P. (2014). SAGE: A scale for rating competence in CBT supervision. In C. E. Watkins & D. L. Milne (Eds.), *The Wiley international handbook of clinical supervision* (pp. 402–415). New York, NY: Wiley.

Newman, C. F. (2010). Competency in conducting cognitive–behavioral therapy: Foundational, functional, and supervisory aspects. *Psychotherapy: Theory, Research, & Practice, 47,* 12–19. http://dx.doi.org/10.1037/a0018849

Newman, C. F., & Kaplan, D. A. (2016). *Supervision essentials for cognitive–behavioral therapy.* Washington, DC: American Psychological Association. http://dx.doi.org/10.1037/14950-000

O'Keeffe, F., Watson, S., & Linke, S. (2016). Training novice clinical psychologist trainees to implement effective CBT for anxiety disorders: Training model and clinic outcomes. *The Cognitive Behaviour Therapist, 9,* e38. http://dx.doi.org/10.1017/S1754470X16000246

Persons, J. B., & Davidson, J. (2014). Cognitive-behavioral case formulation. In K. Dobson (Ed.), *Handbook of cognitive-behavioral therapies* (3rd ed., pp. 172–195). New York, NY: Guilford Press.

Phillips, J. C., Parent, M. C., Dozier, C., & Jackson, P. L. (2017). Depth of discussion of multicultural identities in supervision and supervisory outcomes. *Counselling Psychology Quarterly, 30,* 188–210. http://dx.doi.org/10.1080/09515070.2016.1169995

Reiser, R. P. (2014). Supervising cognitive and behavioral therapies. In C. E. Watkins & D. L. Milne (Eds.), *The Wiley international handbook of clinical supervision* (pp. 493–517). New York, NY: Wiley. http://dx.doi.org/10.1002/9781118846360.ch24

Rodriguez-Menendez, G., Dempsey, J. P., Albizu, T., Power, S., & Campbell Wilkerson, M. (2017). Faculty and student perceptions of clinical training experiences in professional psychology. *Training and Education in Professional Psychology, 11,* 1–9. http://dx.doi.org/10.1037/tep0000137

SafeHome.org. (n.d.). *Hate on social media.* Retrieved from https://www.safehome.org/resources/hate-on-social-media/

Soheilian, S. S., Inman, A. G., Klinger, R. S., Isenberg, D. S., & Kulp, L. E. (2014). Multicultural supervision: Supervisees' reflections on culturally competent supervision. *Counselling Psychology Quarterly, 27,* 379–392. http://dx.doi.org/10.1080/09515070.2014.961408

Tanaka-Matsumi, J., Seiden, D. Y., & Lam, K. N. (1996). Culturally Informed Functional Assessment (CIFA) Interview: A strategy for cross-cultural behavioral practice. *Cognitive and Behavioral Practice, 3,* 215–233. http://dx.doi.org/10.1016/S1077-7229(96)80015-0

Tsong, Y., & Goodyear, R. K. (2014). Assessing supervision's clinical and multicultural impacts: The Supervision Outcome Scale's psychometric properties. *Training and Education in Professional Psychology, 8,* 189–195. http://dx.doi.org/10.1037/tep0000049

Tsui, M., O'Donoghue, K., & Ng, A. K. T. (2014). Culturally competent and diversity-sensitive clinical supervision: An international perspective. In C. E. Watkins & D. L. Milne (Eds.), *The Wiley international handbook of clinical supervision* (pp. 238–254). New York, NY: Wiley.

Watkins, C. E. (1997). *Handbook of psychotherapy supervision.* New York, NY: Wiley.

Weck, F., Kaufmann, Y. M., & Höfling, V. (2017). Competence feedback improves CBT competence in trainee therapists: A randomized controlled pilot study. *Psychotherapy Research, 27,* 501–509. http://dx.doi.org/10.1080/10503307.2015.1132857

Wenzel, A., Dobson, K. S., & Hays, P. A. (2016). *Cognitive behavioral therapy techniques and strategies.* Washington, DC: American Psychological Association. http://dx.doi.org/10.1037/14936-000

Woods, P. J., & Ellis, A. (1997). Supervision in rational emotive behavior therapy. In C. E. Watkins (Ed.), *Handbook of psychotherapy supervision* (pp. 101–113). New York, NY: Wiley.

Yutrzenka, B. A. (1995). Making a case for training in ethnic and cultural diversity in increasing treatment efficacy. *Journal of Consulting and Clinical Psychology, 63,* 197–206. http://dx.doi.org/10.1037/0022-006X.63.2.197

Yutrzenka, B. A., Todd-Bazemore, E., & Caraway, S. J. (1999). Four winds: The evolution of culturally inclusive clinical psychology training for Native Americans. *International Review of Psychiatry, 11,* 129–135. http://dx.doi.org/10.1080/09540269974294

INDEX

Duncan, J. W., 89
Duran, B., 36
Duran, E., 36
Dwairy, M. A., 196
Dwight-Johnson, M., 85
Dynamic sizing, 119
Dysfunctions, behavioral, 215

EACI (European American Cultural Identification), 38
Eap, S., 141
Early Warning: Crisis and Response in the Climate-Changed North (Lord), 57–58
Ecological niches, 79
Educational therapy, for Latinx, 83
Effective Skills to Empower Effective Men (ESTEEM), 294
Elders, ethnic minority, 231–248
  adapting CBT interventions, 244
  African American, 121
  American Indian, 18, 28, 35, 42, 65, 66
  anxiety, 235
  Arab American, 194
  Asian American, 135, 139
  caregiver stress, 236
  case example of CBT with, 245–248
  and CBT, 241–244
  chronic medical conditions, 237
  cohort-specific problems, 239
  common presenting problems in, 234–240
  cultural concepts of distress, 239
  dementia/neurocognitive disorder, 235
  depression, 235
  discrimination against, 234
  end-of-life issues, 238
  explanatory models of illness, 233
  grief/bereavement, 236
  initial assessment, 241
  intergenerational issues, 237
  mental disorders, 238
  Mexican and Latinx, 96
  Orthodox Jewish, 217
  population, 231
  South Asian Americans, 168, 172
  strengths/limitations of CBT with, 240–241

treatment issues with, 233–234
variability in, 232
Elfström, M. L., 264
Ellis, J. M., 288
Emotions, 11, 18
Empathy, 93
Enculturation, of Asian Americans, 136–137
End-of-life issues, 238–239
End sessions, with Asian Americans, 147–148
English, as second language, 147
Environment, 11
  conditions of, 16
  constructed conditions in, 16
  negative aspects of, 15–16
  positive aspects of, 16
  problems in, 15–17
Environmental interventions, 200–201
Erickson, C. D., 189
Eska-Aleutian language, 58–59
"Eskimo" culture, 58–59
Essence reflection, 144
ESTEEM (Effective Skills to Empower Effective Men), 294
Ethical Principles of Psychologists and Code of Conduct, 257
Ethical responsibility, 324
Ethnic identity, 109, 136–137, 191
Ethnicity (ADDRESSING acronym), 63
Eurocentrism, 115–116
European American Cultural Identification (EACI), 38
European Renaissance, 185
Europeans, 28–29, 55
Evidence-based practice, 6–8
  intervention, 8
Explanatory models of illness, 233
Extended family, in African American culture, 108–109

Facial expressions, 66
Falender, C. A., 319, 324
Falicov, Celia, 79, 324
Families, 16, 18
  African American, 107, 108, 109, 116, 118, 120, 121
  Alaska Native, 54, 62, 68
  American Indian, 38, 42, 43

ABOUT THE EDITORS

Gayle Y. Iwamasa, PhD, received her doctorate in clinical psychology from Purdue University. She completed her predoctoral internship and a clinical research fellowship at the University of California, San Francisco. Dr. Iwamasa currently serves as National Mental Health Technical Assistance Specialist and National Inpatient Mental Health Services Coordinator for the Department of Veterans Affairs (VA). In these roles she provides technical assistance and consultation across the VA system regarding implementation of evidence-based treatments and required mental health services, and serves as subject matter expert regarding inpatient mental health care. She is also a trained facilitator and leads workshops and trainings both internal and external to the VA. Prior to her current position she spent 16 years in academia educating and training clinical, community, and counseling psychology graduate students. She has served in several leadership roles in several professional psychological organizations, including president of the Asian American Psychological Association. Dr. Iwamasa has numerous publications in peer-reviewed journals, chapters, and coedited books. She has presented on cultural diversity issues in psychology nationally and internationally and has also been featured in several psychotherapy videos.

Pamela A. Hays, PhD, received a doctorate in clinical psychology from the University of Hawaii and served as a National Institute of Mental Health postdoctoral fellow at the University of Rochester School of Medicine, followed by 11 years on the graduate faculty of Antioch University Seattle. Her research has focused on multicultural practice, including work with Muslim women in North Africa, and Vietnamese, Lao, and Cambodian people in the United States. In 2000, Dr. Hays returned to her hometown on the Kenai Peninsula of Alaska, where she has worked with the community health center, for the Kenaitze Tribe's Dena'ina Wellness Center, and where she is in private practice. She is the author of several books on multicultural practice, including *Addressing Cultural Complexities in Practice: Assessment, Diagnosis, and Therapy; Connecting Across Cultures: The Helper's Toolkit;* and *Creating Well-Being: Four Steps to a Happier, Healthier Life.* The American Psychological Association has produced numerous videos of her work as a therapist demonstrating cognitive behavior therapy and culturally responsive practice. For more information on her clinical practice, publications, videos, and workshops, visit her website (http://www.drpamelahays.com).